THE AMERICAN WEST

THE AMERICAN WEST

AN INTERPRETIVE HISTORY
Second Edition

Robert V. Hine

University of California, Riverside

Scott, Foresman and Company
Glenview, Illinois   London, England

Library of Congress Cataloging in Publication Data

Hine, Robert V., 1921–
    The American West.

    Bibliography: p. 379
    1. West (U.S.) — History.   I. Title.
F591.H663   1984   978   84-962

ISBN 0-673-39341-0

45678910-MVN-95949392919089

Picture Credits

Page 6 — California Museum of Photography, University of California, Riverside. 11 — Historical Pictures Service, Chicago. 15 — Historical Pictures Service, Chicago. 17 — The Bancroft Library, Berkeley, CA. 20 — Courtesy of California Historical Society, San Francisco/Los Angeles. 21 — Reproduced from the collections of the Library of Congress. 22 — Historical Pictures Service, Chicago. 23 — Reproduced from the collections of the Library of Congress. 27 — Historical Pictures Service, Chicago. 28 — Nelda C. and H. J. Lutcher Stark Foundation. 29 — Historical Pictures Service, Chicago. 33 — Reproduced from the collections of the Library of Congress. 34 — Rare Book and Manuscript Library, Columbia University. 36 — Historical Pictures Service, Chicago. 39 — Reproduced from the collections of the Library of Congress. 43 — The National Gallery of Canada, Ottawa. 51 — Reproduced from the collections of the Library of Congress. 54 — Missouri Historical Society. 56 — Reproduced from the collections of the Library of Congress. 60 — William H. Emory, *Report of the United States and Mexican Boundary Survey* (Washington, D.C., 1857) I, ff. p. 68. 62 — Academy of Natural Sciences, Philadelphia. 65 — Reproduced from the collections of the

(Continued on page 393)

To my brother and sister,
Richard and Katherine,
for whom, as once with many frontiersmen,
old ties remain strong.

Preface

Once upon a time there was an American West. It was part economic and social fact, part myth; while the facts changed the myth survived. Its history, even up to the present, has always been revised by dream. The first scene of the western drama was set on the Atlantic beaches. Thereafter the tale unfolded rapidly, and the trans-Mississippi region set the stage for a climax in the nineteenth century; the denouement came in the adaptation of the old facts to new conditions. First in order of appearance were the native races, followed by a motley cast — transient adventurers and land-craving settlers — spilling over from European cultures and helping to begin a fresh history. The plot, written by historians, repetitiously dwelt on the individual — a modern version of an unrestrained, unfettered Prometheus proclaiming his freedom.

The story attracted America's foremost historical theorist, Frederick Jackson Turner. As a young college professor, he noticed that in 1890 the U.S. Census Bureau had declared that it could no longer distinguish clearly between regions with populations greater than two persons per square mile or less. Until that time the frontier had absorbed the American expansionist and imperialist drives, filling in the vast spaces acquired through clever diplomacy and aggression. Turner prophesied that the nation with no more frontier would turn to overseas adventures. Within a decade, he was proved right in Cuba, the Philippines, Puerto Rico, and Guam. It was a grand outcome for the frontier ideology based so squarely on the presumed power of the individual.

In the twentieth century, however, the individualistic western myth grew increasingly unacceptable. Previously ignored elements crept in, and the tale began to seem too full of racial prejudice, violence, frenzied speculation, and recklessness toward nature. Conflicts were found to be deeper. Individuals shunned responsibility for themselves and for their communities, and began roaming, restless and unfulfilled. In accordance with the myth, their deepest ethical and religious instincts corroded and they became corrupted with storied riches. Self-righteousness and the arrogance of power came to permeate the new American myth.

Yet some happy western characteristics in the tale endured. Alongside the land speculators and the greedy stood honest people respectful of the soil — strong-willed men like Jules Sandoz, coaxing his orchards, and Hopi Indians, resisting intrusions into their wind-scoured mesas. For Germans, Frenchmen, and blacks, the frontier was an escape from unhappiness, an avenue leading away from old alienations. The West, particularly during the early stages of development, was a more promising land than many of the places from which its new settlers had come.

This retelling of the western story makes no pretense at objectivity or comprehensiveness. It is an interpretive account, and the selection of theories ultimately is the result of presupposition. But good, bad, indifferent, and preconceived, "the West has been the great word of our history. The Westerner has been the type and master of our American life." So wrote Woodrow Wilson, and he was neither the first nor the last to grandly interpret the American West.

Those who have helped in the interpretation that follows, those to whom I owe so much, include, first, James T. Brown, Clyde Duncum, Linda Fischer, Christina Nunez, Jack Goldwasser, and Allison Hine. My colleagues on the Riverside campus of the University of California who have critiqued portions of the manuscript are Carlos E. Cortés, Edwin Scott Gaustad, and Irving G. Hendrick.

In the wider historical world my gratitude goes to John Faragher, former student, now friend and invaluable critic; Edwin R. Bingham, whose earlier collaboration with me in editing a selection of documents on the American West remains the happiest of memories; Howard Lamar of Yale University; Rodman Paul of the California Institute of Technology; Ruth Sutter of San Francisco; Wilcomb Washburn of the Smithsonian Institution; the late Mitchell Wilder and the Trustees of the Amon Carter Museum of Western Art; Robert Berkhofer of the University of Michigan; and Earl Pomeroy

of the University of California, San Diego, whose detailed criticism
has left me immeasurably in his debt. I am also grateful to my editors
Bradford Gray and Lauren Green.

Is it possible adequately to thank Shirley when she has done so
much?

Contents

Contents

Maps

THE AMERICAN WEST

1

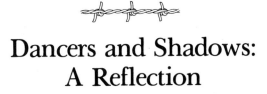

Dancers and Shadows:
A Reflection

In a woods near Plymouth in 1630 stood a maypole around which young Massachusetts Indian men and women danced, intertwining their flowers and ribbons with those of Thomas Morton and a few Pilgrim friends. On learning what was happening here at Merry Mount, the colonial militia gathered, hacked down the pole, quashed the sensuous, heathenish festivities, and (as the poet said) "the woods threw forth a more sombre shadow."[1] Two hundred sixty-five years later — not long after the 1890 massacre of Indians at Wounded Knee — an Oglala Sioux and the men of his tribe performed the Sun Dance. On the final day of the tribal rite, with skewers in the flesh of his back, the man dangled helplessly from the center pole. The ritual affirmed the insignificance of the individual before the community, but to the white frontiersmen the ceremony was fiendishly pagan, an act to be outlawed. For that Sioux dancer, Plenty Horses, it was also a catalytic experience; shortly afterwards, he walked up to a young white army officer and shot him dead. Sixty-five years into the following century, on a vacant lot overlooking the bars and brothels of Los Angeles, a mixed band of southwestern Indians danced at dawn. Voluntarily displaced from the reservation, seeking work in the white society, these young men from the Drum and Feather Club had moved from the shadows of pool tables, bars, and jail cells to the cover of the night. Without drums or flowers or maypoles or guns, still they danced.

For centuries these dancers of the woods and plains and city dawn had proved an obstruction to the European usurpers of their continent. In the pages that follow, that strong Indian spirit should never be forgotten even when it goes unmentioned. But the Indian should be considered a maker of history, not simply a backdrop against which the European or American narrative is told. The native welcomed the white man, helped him to succeed, then blocked his way, and eventually fought him with vigor. The effects of these encounters, as from a whirling double-edged sword, were deep on both sides. For the Indian they nearly spelled cultural death; for the white man, fear and guilt.

The Indian stood for what the white man had so long tried to prune out of his own culture — worshipful reverence for nature, acceptance of the body and the sensual appetites, and a subjugation of the individual for the good of the group. Thus between the two lay chasms of cultural difference. These threats to the underpinnings of Judeo-Christian ways sent the governor to Merry Mount in 1630, caused Washington to outlaw the Sun Dance in 1904, and brought police to round up the Navajos on the vacant lots of Los Angeles in 1965. The cultural gulf made the misunderstandings over treaties and the ultimate battles over land harder for the Indian because he lost so much, and easier for the white man because they justified his winning.

But all this is to know the end of the story before the beginning has been told. Around the eleventh century A.D., native Americans, whose ancestors had tramped southward across North America at least twenty thousand years earlier, met the first Europeans on the foggy north Atlantic seaboard. The Norsemen called the Americans *skraelings* (little people) and admitted their initial friendliness. Once, however, according to the sagas, the skraelings fearfully hid beneath their canoes, and the Norsemen killed eight of them like wild game.

Four hundred years later Christopher Columbus, redheaded, strong-willed man of Christ and son of the Renaissance, considered it unquestionably appropriate that he should capture twelve natives to exhibit in Spain. Columbus found the naked, guileless men he first met on San Salvador to be unexpectedly kind and "of subtle wit."

Those who came after Columbus assumed that all the natives of the New World were one people, but in fact there was no such thing as an Indian. The term was a white construct for the dwellers of three continents, none of which had anything to do with India. From the native American standpoint there were more than two hundred separate peoples living north of Mexico in 1492 — peoples of different physical makeups, different languages, different cultural traditions. The term *Indian* ridiculously lumped together Aztec imperialists, Hopi

2

communalists, and Narraganset farmers. At first, Europeans had no concept of this diversity. As their expansion along the seaboard brought Indian cultural differences to light, the conclusion was drawn that Indian behavior was unpredictable and inscrutable. Unless his character was constant, the native could not be controlled.[2] That, of course, has been the goal of any missionization from New Spain to Vietnam: to bring the pagan or foreigner into the realm of predictable behavior, to restrain passions, to inject reason, to redeem.

On the other hand, because these varying peoples of North America — whether hunter-gatherers or farmers — were tribal, they shared certain premises. Except for the native Mexican imperialists, the tribes lived in small communities where social relations were personal and face-to-face, where everybody knew everybody else and shared common values. Cultural tendencies, though not universal, were often widespread enough in North America to stand generalization.

The Indian respect for nature was more than joy in its mere existence. For good and for bad, human beings shared a kinship with all living things. A pantheon of supernatural forces linked mankind with the natural world. If that chain was broken, the great cycles were damaged, and illness and disorder ensued.

The spirits dwelt within the valleys, the plants, and the animals. Therefore, the Indian honored animal intelligence and power. If he failed as the spiritual warden of the natural world, he and his people would suffer. Perhaps this anxiety explains a Micmac practice that arose after the tribe was engaged in the heavy slaughter of the fur trade. The Indian took to gouging out the eyes of his trapped beaver lest the animal's spirit see its hunter.[3]

Such an attitude toward life spilled over into human relations, even in the most extreme of contacts: warfare. In general, the Indian did not retain standing armies and, before the European involvement, seldom engaged in protracted wars or seiges. If battles were costing dearly in casualties, the tendency was to quit and withdraw. In a few cases, such as in California with its dense Indian population, warfare was almost unknown.

The mother of all life was the land, the solid earth, and it followed that the Indians resisted a system that withdrew land from the community and placed it in private hands. A few New England tribes did allocate specific areas for planting and hunting, but even here ownership rested with large kinship groups. However land was held, the fewer traces man left on it, the better. Disturbance of the earth, its plants, or its animals broke that sense of place, of belonging to a region.[4]

Indian life was one of seasons and cycles, a mythic rising from the earth and returning to its warm body. Time was like that, too: full of returning and rebirthing, with no clearer beginning or end than could be found in a circle of dancers. There was little room for progress here, little linear history moving inexorably toward a better day. Utopia resided in the past with the fathers of the people. Myth was far more important than history; it was one more aspect of nature and its frightening, comforting, creative spirits.

Across the cultural gulf lay the premises of the European. How could he doubt his own superiority? After all, he — not the Indian — had sailed the unknown seas, had shaken his fists at the storms, and had found a new world. The Indian view of nature was all very good, but in the person of Saint Francis, the European tradition had also communed with its brother the sun and talked with the feathered and furry creation. Still the Christian God had revealed himself as a man, not a coyote or a whale. Christians were indeed wardens of the game, yet their mission was to assert the divine will over all life. They held no injunction to destroy nature but to "replenish the earth and subdue it, and have dominion over every living thing that moveth upon the earth." Man should make nature fruitful that he and it might multiply.

In the eyes of Christians, the best way to make the soil fertile was to own it as private property. If man scarred the land, that was no more than a mark of Cain, an affirmation of his additional right to wander, to escape the fetters of nature, to love a newfound place no less than the old, to inherit proudly Adam's curse to labor in the sweat of his brow, and thus to remain unique in the eyes of the Creator. Private ownership and land tenure were other ways of rooting a person to a place. One might even be suspicious of an Indian culture that avoided individual responsibility by denying private ownership of the land.

European man happily declared his role in history and never doubted that time led ultimately to the fulfillment of God's will. Admittedly that divine will was mysterious; God was above both nature and man. Divinity could hardly be known through myths, though these might provide glimpses. Even the sacred word of God in the scriptures was an incomplete insight into the historic linear drama — the creation, the fall of man, the flood, the prophets in the wilderness, the glorious redemption, and the final judgment. On that line of cosmic progress Europeans moved from the old world to the new.

Fishermen and explorers were supplanted in this New World by traders and colonists, and with new and sustained interaction came disease. Europeans carried back alien forms of syphilis which flared through Italy and France, and later Spain. But because of their long expansion that began with Marco Polo, Europeans had acquired immunity to most other communicable viruses. In contrast, the antibodies in the Indian bloodstream were helpless. Waves of smallpox, measles, typhoid, tuberculosis, and dysentery, not to mention alcoholism, were to devastate the Indian inhabitants.

Indeed, epidemics were the chief cause of rapid population decline. Demographers now estimate that there were as many as twelve million Indians north of Mexico at the time of Columbus's arrival. In the following centuries the number fell by some 90 percent.[5] This tragic decimation reinforced the European feeling of superiority and granted both military and psychological advantages.

For the Indian there were other, more subtle, effects. Native rituals and medicine men, unable to redress the waves of death, undoubtedly suffered loss of prestige, a cultural deficit that may have given the missionary an unexpected edge.

The European advantage, once again, cut deep. Few aspects of culture went untouched. The trader, for example, had offered knives, kettles, and guns to the Indian. Though primitive tools often were equally effective for his needs, still the native admired the new technology. Unwittingly he became a consumer dependent on a market that originated in boardrooms in London, Paris, and Madrid. As with any consumer, desire led to vulnerability. The Indian consequently was required to overstep his own morality, engaging, for instance, in the killing of beaver far beyond the limits of his own needs. The spiral of cultural change, economic demands, desires for technological things, and the watering down of belief had begun.[6]

With time and changing circumstances natives' and Europeans' ideas about one another shifted in both directions. Though historical sources on the Indians are more difficult to come by, it seems likely that they at first ranked Europeans as physically and mentally inferior to themselves. How else could they explain starving times among early settlers in a land which they knew to be abundant? In many other ways the Indian might have looked down on the white settler. When the European was frustrated he spoke out, while the Indian instinctively, and to his mind correctly, remained silent. Anthony Wallace, student of culture and personality, in an analysis of Iroquois dreams, has concluded that the males of that tribe were repressing deep desires for passivity. If Wallace's finding is valid, then to these people white culture must have appeared frantic, madly energetic, and even arrogant; such traits probably reflected the white man's failure to incorporate religion, with its calming attributes, into daily life and politics.[7]

The economic role of the Indian in the fur trade: Plains Indian women curing hides, c. 1875.

The spectrum of Europeans' ideas on Indians is better known. In the seventeenth century, philosophers such as Montaigne and Locke used the society of the noble savage to expose the faults in their own social structures. To Montaigne even New World cannibals, unlike Frenchmen, had an innate sense of equality, evidenced in the absence of poverty. Europe was still considered the center of the world and the pinnacle of civilization, but its aristocracy could be seen as corrupt and decadent. For the philosophers the sun-browned muscle and the cooperative tribe were models on which improved life-styles and revolutions could be based.[8]

When the Indian became a potential convert or neighbor, the European tended to decry his lack of discipline and his ignorance of manners. Martin Frobisher, an English explorer, likened Indian habits to those of animals. The natives did not use tablecloths or utensils, he said, and ate grass from the field and meat from the bone "like brute beasts devouring the same."[9] One cause of such deportment was thought to be Indian child-rearing practices, allowing the wild freedom and nudity of children. Ultimately, it was thought, these practices induced social disorder and taught little respect for authority.

There was, of course, no universal agreement on such cultural interpretations. Even such emotional and derogatory words as *savage* came and went and were used differently by Spaniards, Frenchmen, and Englishmen.[10] Changing attitudes toward Indian women illustrate how these swings have been influenced by shifts in white society. For centuries the Indian wife was described as a browbeaten drudge, a workhorse, a squaw dominated mercilessly by the male. Since the 1960s the changing role of modern women has led to a different interpretation. The Indian woman is now seen as an efficient provider of as much as 90 percent of the food in her household. Even in hunting situations the man brought in the skins, but the woman prepared the finished product, and in some mid-Atlantic tribes she was responsible for the trade of that product outside the tribe. Instead of being a drudge, then, she began to assume qualities of a businesswoman.[11]

Some beliefs have, however, remained stable. The white world has consistently refused to conceive of the Indian as a person. Only on occasion have figures in the past found the Indian capable of being both a saint and a scoundrel, both a shining idealist and a grubby materialist, both a lover of his enemies and a hater of his friends.[12] Whenever there grows a dichotomy between "us" and "them," the tendency is to see those "others" as all the same, in one unrealistic lump. The Indians all danced the same dance, and who could tell one dancer from the other? This viewpoint was unfortunate but not unusual; it ultimately assumed tragic proportions when, as we shall frequently trace, one group developed the tools and resources to destroy the "others." Then the pathos of a Hopi query stood stark: "Why do you punish us for being what we are?"[13]

> We danced, O Brave, we danced beyond their farms,
> In cobalt desert closures made our vows. . . .
> Now is the strong prayer folded in thine arms,
> The serpent with the eagle in the boughs.[14]

7

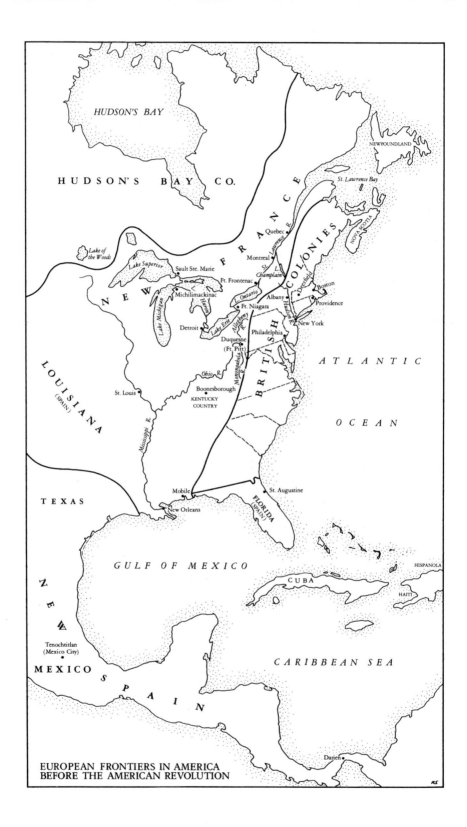

HUDSON'S BAY

HUDSON'S   BAY   CO.

NEWFOUNDLAND

St. Lawrence Bay

Lake of
the Woods

Lake Superior

Sault Ste. Marie

Quebec

Montreal

NOVA SCOTIA

Lawrence R.

N   E   W   F   R   A   N   C   E

Ft. Frontenac

St. L.
Champlain

Michilimackinac

Lake Michigan

Lake Huron

Ontario

Deerfield

Albany

Boston

Ft. Niagara

Providence

B   R   I   T   I   S   H

C   O   L   O   N   I   E   S

Detroit

Lake Erie

Allegheny R.

New York

Duquesne
(Ft. Pitt)

Philadelphia

A   T   L   A   N   T   I   C

St. Louis

Ohio R.

Monongahela R.

Boonesborough

KENTUCKY
COUNTRY

O   C   E   A   N

L   O   U   I   S   I   A   N   A

(SPAIN)

Mississippi R.

Mobile

St. Augustine

T   E   X   A   S

FLORIDA
(SPAIN)

New Orleans

N
E
W

GULF   OF   MEXICO

HISPANOLA

CUBA

HAITI

Tenochtitlan
(Mexico City)

S
P
A
I
N

CARIBBEAN   SEA

M   E   X   I   C   O

Darien

EUROPEAN FRONTIERS IN AMERICA
BEFORE THE AMERICAN REVOLUTION

RS

2

The Great Encounter: Native American and European

NEW SPAIN

The Indians whom Columbus first met were Tainos, an Arawak people. They cultivated corn and yams, made brown pottery and cotton thread, and fashioned darts from fish teeth and wood. They had used these weapons to drive off previous inhabitants and to protect themselves against the aggressive Caribs. Columbus thought the Tainos had no weapons. His conclusion was based on a curious test: he handed them swords and observed that they grasped the blades and cut their fingers. Steel had come to a people who previously had worked only with bone and stone.

Columbus assumed Europeans were superior to these people and believed he could read their minds. When they lifted their hands to the sky, Columbus thought the Indians were implying that the Spaniards were children of heaven. The explanation was at best only one of several possibilities. The Indians may have been referring to birds or perhaps exclaiming, "Great God, what now!"

We can be a bit more sure of what lay in the minds of the Europeans. Just after describing the Indians' loving, cooperative, peaceful, unarmed state, Columbus wrote, "with fifty men they could all be subjected and made to do all that one wished."[1] If these people were inferior and could not defend themselves, why should they not be slaves?

Columbus was, of course, Italian, but the Spanish conquistadors who followed him into the New World — men such as Balboa, Ponce de León, and Cortes — were equally sure of their culture, their God, their church, and their superiority. The attitude of the conquistadors was further colored by a long history of fighting infidels in their homeland, the Iberian peninsula. Sons of Allah from Africa had flooded western Europe to a high-water mark in the eighth century and had thereafter been pushed southward through Spain. These wars had absorbed the energies and directed the crusading propensities of generation after generation of young Spaniards. In 1492, marvelous year, Granada, the last Moorish stronghold in Spain, fell to the warriors of the Catholic kings. As a result, Spain could turn its attention to exploration in the New World.

Vasco Núñez de Balboa was seventeen when Granada fell. He sailed for the New World in 1501 and farmed unsuccessfully for a time on Hispaniola, in the West Indies, but his thoughts began to roam toward the mainland to the west. He stowed away on a vessel bound for Darien on the Isthmus of Panama (now in Panama), where in 1510 a small settlement had begun its struggle against yellow fever.

In swashbuckling fashion, Balboa established his leadership, eliminated his enemies, organized systems of Indian labor, and secured an appointment as governor in 1513. He led a small band across the isthmus and shared with the coastal natives the sight of the Pacific. He sufficiently understood the importance of his discovery to begin building ships on the Pacific coast, an appropriate task for the holder of the new title "Adelantado of the South Sea." For a few years he crested the conqueror's wave, profited from Indian labor, collected revenues, and then fell into disfavor. Six years after his discovery of the Pacific, he was beheaded by his enemies. So rose and fell the first great conquistador of the mainland of the New World.

The archetypal conquistador, however, and the man who did most to develop the institutions of New Spain, was Hernando Cortes. Bernal Diaz, who knew Cortes well during the conquest of Mexico, described him as physically strong, with a broad chest and shoulders, a good horseman, sexually attractive, slow to anger but sometimes aroused to speechless fury, at which time the veins in his neck and forehead would swell. He knew Latin and wrote poetry. When he led men, he demanded the toughest of discipline. Around his neck he wore a golden chain bearing "the image of Our Lady the Virgin Saint Mary with her precious son in her arms."[2]

This was the man who in 1519 commanded eleven ships sailing from Cuba to conquer the mainland of Mexico with four hundred men. Díaz later described Cortes as fond of gambling at cards and dice.

Protestant interpretation of the Spanish conquest: sixteenth-century engraving by Teodoro De Bry.

He now gambled for the highest stakes in the New World. Shortly after his arrival, on the coast of Mexico, he ordered the ships dismantled. The game was winner take all, and the Virgin Mary was on his side.

The people of Mexico, whom Cortes must now defeat, differed vastly from the gentle Tainos who greeted Columbus. The Aztecs numbered somewhere between eleven and twenty million, compared with Spain's population at that time of under five million. Included in the Aztec empire were a number of allies loosely subject to the emperor Montezuma.

This ninth Aztec ruler lived in the princely city Tenochtitlán (Mexico City), which was resplendent with stepped pyramids, stone temples, feathered ceremonies, golden vessels, and causeways with cleverly engineered dams and irrigation canals. Montezuma was well aware of the presence of the Spaniards on the Caribbean islands. He may have sensed that two worlds were on a collision course when he learned that these bearded newcomers had landed on his own shores. For years there had been omens — comets, heavenly lights, monstrous two-headed births, foaming lake waters, an insane woman wailing through the night, "My children, where shall I take you?"[3] We know of these details through extraordinary efforts of a Spanish friar, Bernardino de Sahagún, who learned the Nahuatl language and with the help of the native informants recorded the Aztec view of Cortes's conquest.

Montezuma's power was based largely on religion. Very much like Europe's kings, he held his office in trust for a god (Quetzalcoatl) who had left the earth but would someday return in wrath. From all reports the newly arrived Spaniards had frightening attributes that suggested the approach of Quetzalcoatl and his retinue: they rode on creatures larger than deer from whom flecks of foam fell like soapsuds. The bodies and heads of the men were covered with iron, and they shot guns, which killed. "Come forward, my Jaguar Knights," called the emperor, "come forward. It is said that our lord has returned to this land. Go to meet him. Go to hear him. Listen well to what he tells you; listen and remember."

Montezuma sent gifts of gold and feathered treasure, "divine adornments," and his messengers trembled and kissed the earth before Cortes. Taking special notice of the gold, the Spaniard asked, "And is this all?" The answer was yes, at least for the moment. The Spaniards began to march toward Tenochtitlán.

How the "invincible four hundred" conquered an empire that could at any time raise thousands of well-trained fighting men is not easy to explain. Certainly there is more to the question than a religious illusion among the conquered. Malcontents and factions plagued the empire, and Cortes had an unerring sense of how to play upon internal hatreds. He himself, of course, was ignorant of the language and of the subtleties of Aztec history, and he could not have directed such diplomacy without native help. That assistance came to him in the form of one of the cleverest young ladies of history, his mistress, Malinal or Malinche, baptized and called by the friars the Lady Marina. In acceptable Indian style she had been given to Cortes by the natives shortly after his arrival on the coast; it became tradition for an Indian to be baptized before such a union with a conquistador. Eventually she bore him a son, one of five children Cortes had by his various mistresses. Marina remained with Cortes during the conquest, translated for him, and advised him skillfully. William Prescott, writing in the comfortable superiority of nineteenth-century Boston, said of Lady Marina:

She had her errors . . . but they should be rather charged to the defects of her early education, and to the evil influence of him to whom in the darkness of her spirit she looked with simple confidence for the light to guide her. All agree that she was full of excellent qualities, and the important services which she rendered the Spaniards have made her memory deservedly dear to them; while the name of Malinche — the name by which she is still known in Mexico — was pronounced with kindness by the conquered races, with whose misfortunes she showed an invariable sympathy.[4]

A yawning gap of interpretation is exposed when we notice that to the modern Mexican nationalist the word *malinche* is synonymous with the worst traitor.

Montezuma vacillated and agonized: "My heart burns and suffers, as if it were drowned in spices!"[5] One after another of his allies fell before Cortes, yet when the Spaniards came to Tenochtitlán, he officially welcomed them. Within months he was dead, and when his body was thrown from the city walls, no one mourned. His people burned the remains without ceremony, and the chroniclers unfeelingly described the cremated body: "It sizzled and smelled bad."

The fighting continued. In 1520, in spite of Spanish reinforcements that had been arriving for eight months, the Mexicans rose up and expelled the Spaniards from the city. In that *noche triste* eight hundred of fourteen hundred fleeing Spaniards were killed, and the canals were so full of bodies that the last retreaters could march over them as if they were bridges.

In the second coming of the Spaniards to the city, during the fall of 1521, Cortes claimed that one hundred seventeen thousand Indian fighting men were killed.[6] The Aztec chronicle described the general scene: "The people were tormented by hunger and many starved to death. There was no fresh water to drink, only stagnant water and the brine of the lake, and many died of dysentery. The only food was lizards, swallows, corncobs and the salt grasses of the lake."

The European conquest took its toll not only of the Indian but also of the land. A modern historian has described the mark the Spaniards unintentionally left on the environment of the great valley of Mexico:

The equilibrium of resources and population changed abruptly. The conquerors cut down huge quantities of timber for building material and fuel. Their plows cut more deeply into the earth than had the Indian digging sticks, and their cattle and sheep cropped the land bare. New irrigation systems and grist mills concentrated or redistributed the water flows. No one of the new developments was disastrous in itself, but the combined effect over the years was an accelerated depletion of agricultural land. In the rainy season, top soil was washed to the valley bottom. Erosion produced gulleys, and slopes that had once been capable of cultivation became barren.[7]

With the accounts of blood and misfortune before us, it seems at first incomprehensible that Lewis Hanke can write that the conquest was "one of the greatest attempts the world has ever seen to make Christian precepts prevail in the relations between peoples."[8] But Hanke is pointing to the uniqueness of the zeal with which some Spaniards worked to obtain justice for the natives. Bartolomé de Las Casas is the best example of this drive.

As a boy on the streets of Seville, Las Casas had watched the parade of Indians Columbus had brought back in 1493. Thinking little of the event at the time, he went on to the university and then sailed for the New World in 1502 with fortune, not philosophy, on his mind. He became a priest, but he also acquired a large estate in Cuba, where, as a gentleman-ecclesiastic, he held Indian slaves and worked them hard on the fields and mines. Then in 1514 at the age of forty, Las Casas experienced a change that would dominate the remaining fifty years of his long life. He became tenacious in the fight to secure humane and just treatment for the Indians. On the mainland he experimented with new colonies where soldiers were excluded, where only the kindliest farmers were allowed, and where the most highly motivated priests worked without guns for support. The colonies were not failures, but in time their ideals were broken by the intrusion of colonizers who held other ideas. As with Cortes, who once said, "I came to get gold, not to till the soil like a peasant,"[9] dreams of riches corroded ideals.

Las Casas, however, never ceased his work. When, late in his life, he wrote his monumental *Historia de las Indias*, he epitomized the feelings of the group of his countrymen who loved and helped the natives, denounced those who placed gold above humanity, and added one of the great statements to the world's literature on human justice.

The two poles of exploitation and humanity in New Spain were supported by at least three institutional frameworks — the encomienda, the mission, and the vast network of political control. The encomienda was a solution to two almost contradictory problems: how to impart the ideals of European civilization to the native and how to obtain a labor supply for the conquerors. The Spaniards assumed, as did all sixteenth-century colonizing peoples, that the new lands belonged to the Crown of the discoverer. The Catholic Church had ratified this idea by approving the Treaty of Tordesillas in 1494, dividing the New World between Spain and Portugal.

Bartolomé de Las Casas (1474-1566), by Tomas Lopez, 1791.

The Castilian Crown thus held the right to grant land to men such as the young Las Casas, who sought wealth overseas. The distribution of such land was always a touchstone of colonial development. The encomienda gave to the grantee the labor of the natives living on the land, provided the grantee agreed to educate and Christianize them. In the words of one such deed, the king assigned the natives:

> . . . so that you may use and profit by them in your estates and commerce, provided that you indoctrinate them and teach them in the things of our Holy Catholic Faith, and treat them according to the Royal Ordinances which have been issued or may be issued, for the good and increase of the said Indians.[10]

Theoretically, on the assumption that the Europeans were superior and that natives were depraved pagans, the system had merit. At least it assumed that the Indian was worth saving, that he was a human being and potentially equal to the European. By no means did all Europeans feel this way. The encomienda was partly responsible for the fact that four million Indians were baptized by the Spanish in the first fifteen years of their presence.[11]

In practice the encomienda tended more toward exploitation than toward education. Las Casas inveighed strongly against it as "a horrible iniquity damaging to the bodies and the souls of the Indians," which ought to be "terminated and destroyed as a mortal pestilence."[12] Las Casas was responsible for a temporary cessation of the encomienda system, but as the Indian population decreased, largely from disease (in the valley of Mexico by 1600 numbers had dropped by 80 percent),[13] and the demands for labor increased, an outright allocation of Indian labor supplanted the more idealistic encomienda. The encomienda was not actually abolished, however, until the eighteenth century.

The labor supply had from the beginning been tied to another kind of slavery as well — the importation of black people. Within ten years of Columbus's first landing, partly because of Indian decimation, a load of black slaves had been shipped from Africa to the Caribbean, ostensibly to reduce dependence on Indian labor. On San Salvador, where Columbus found the Tainos, blacks outnumbered whites fifteen to thirteen by 1560, and the Tainos were virtually extinct because of harsh treatment and disease. By the end of the sixteenth century Negro slaves in the Spanish colonies were estimated at forty thousand, vastly outnumbering the white population on many of the Caribbean islands.

On the mainland, New Spain edged northward, carrying with it a pervasive frontier institution, the Spanish mission. In the late seventeenth century, missions were introduced into the remotest areas, such as Texas and California. Twentieth-century tourists visit pocked adobe mission walls and cracked tiles, quaint and lovely, but they seldom perceive the institution described by Herbert E. Bolton: a tough, pioneering agency that served as church, home, fortress, town, farm, and imperial consulate. This corporate body made it possible for two missionaries with three or four soldiers to create an orderly town out of several thousand Indians, often from diverse and mutually hostile clans.[14] Indeed, the hostility of the natives in the north made difficult the expansion of the encomienda, thriving as it did on the docility of native labor.

The primary aim of the mission was to Christianize people who had not yet heard the true Word of God. It shared other aims of the encomienda — though not in the same order of priority — such as economic development and social discipline. The mission, an arm of the state, also worked as a defensive fortress before the presidios were manned. Priests sent reports and observations to Mexico City to be studied by generals and civil administrators. In some years the funds for missions and war were kept in the same account. Such a practice was sensible because, where few Spaniards were available,

California mission Indians playing games, 1822, by Ludovik Choris.

Indians conceivably could be transformed into citizens. These Indian colonials would be unified through education and language. The Indians learned Spanish readily, and unification through a common tongue was not a farfetched idea; it worked well enough a century or so later for the British in India. The mission served, too, as protection against the disruptions of land speculators and unscrupulous boomers. It introduced breeds of cattle and agricultural products such as grapes and citrus, laying deep economic foundations that are still apparent. In an unexpected way, the padres promoted their provinces in letters and reports, extolling the beauties and values of their new homes, rather like modern-day chambers of commerce, though hardly as effective. After an examination of the functions served by the missions beneath the carved altars and the pepper trees, it is not surprising that colonial administrators were willing to support their activities from the royal treasuries, though in fulfilling their principal purpose, the conversion and reeducation of Indians, the missions were only partly successful.

More than twenty thousand natives were housed at one time in the Alta California missions alone, but their mortality rate was high. The Indians died of dysentery, fevers, and venereal disease, as well as from changes in diet and confinement indoors. Visitors such as Frenchman Jean François de Lapérouse charged that the Indians were being transformed not into new men but into slaves. Lapérouse compared the missions to plantations in the Caribbean. He wrote that the missionaries were convinced "either by prejudice or by their own experience that reason is almost never developed in these people, which to them is sufficient motive for treating them as children."

Looking backward from the twentieth century, hostile commentators such as Carey McWilliams have called the missions charnel houses and have compared them with Nazi concentration camps. Almost as misleading because of the disregard for different motives and contexts are those who consider Indians silly sheep and the padres gentle but effective shepherds. Perhaps the modern anthropologist Alfred L. Kroeber came closest to proper balance when he wrote, "It must have caused many of the fathers a severe pang to realize, as they could not but do daily, that they were saving souls only at the inevitable cost of lives."[15]

Spanish America was divided into two parts, New Castile and New Spain. The latter stretched from the Isthmus of Panama in the south to California in the north, from the Caribbean islands in the east to the Philippines in the west. At its heart was Mexico City, an imperial seat with shady parks, well-dressed people parading in coaches, splendid churches towering over the sites of Montezuma's temples, a university (founded in 1553), a government mint, hospitals, monasteries, and wealthy homes. Below the glittering surface lay the sufferings of peon and slave, both Indian and black.

New Spain at its zenith in the sixteenth century presented a brilliant political network. At its head was the new Montezuma, the viceroy, regent of the Spanish king, and in the New World as powerful as the king himself. There were sixty-one viceroys during the nearly three hundred years until independence. Beneath them, effective bureaucratic control reached down through provinces and finally to the local magistrate, the alcalde, who administered justice, executed imperial policies, and collected taxes in more than two hundred cities and towns.

Spreading fanlike from the center of this imperial domain emerged the northern borderlands of New Spain, the southern region of what is now the United States. This frontier swept like a great vague compass arc from Florida on the Atlantic along the Gulf coast, to Texas, New Mexico, and California. Colonizing efforts like those of Ponce de León in 1512 were valiantly but futilely aimed at securing this frontier.

In 1528 an attempt to settle the Florida peninsula was dispatched from Spain under the leadership of Pánfilo de Narváez, but storms wrecked the ships on the Florida coast, and within a year only a handful of men were left. The subsequent seven years of their lives were typical of the history of those border regions. Their leader, Alvar Núñez Cabeza de Vaca, became the first overland westerner by contending that in marching toward the sunset he would find what he desired. On their long westward trek they survived partly because they treated the Indians well, curing them of disease and refusing excessive gifts. In 1536 Cabeza de Vaca and his one surviving companion, a black slave, Estevan, chanced upon a Spanish expedition seeking Indian slaves in the far northern Mexican province of Sonora.

Although Cabeza de Vaca's trek is one of the astounding feats of survival in all history, its main significance lay in its reports of lands to the north. In these accounts were the roots of legends that impelled men for generations — the Seven Golden Cities of Cíbola, and Quivira, where the king took his siesta under a tree of golden bells. These heady myths, based on nothing firmer than the adobe pueblos of New Mexico, sent Coronado as far north as modern Kansas, and set Cabrillo sailing for the first time along the coast of modern California.

Behind these explorers the permanent settlement of New Spain slowly advanced. Cattle had been transported from herds on the Caribbean islands to Mexico almost before Cortes was settled in the capital. "The hardy and tough-sinewed Spanish cattle," writes Tom Lea, "tinged with the savage blood of the fighting bulls of the plazas, seemed exactly fitted to thrive in the new continent's wilderness."[16] And thrive they did in the sixteenth century. By the end of the century in regions around Jalisco and Durango herds numbered up to seventy thousand, and one owner branded thirty thousand calves in one spring.[17] With them came miners. The new conquerors opened mines around Mexico City, and mining settlements developed at Toluca and Taxco. The northern areas were sparked in 1546 when a small Indian silver-mining effort at Zacatecas was expanded into a major operation. The mines were manned by slaves, usually Indians brought from the south. About the middle of the century a technological breakthrough, the use of mercury in the extraction of silver, injected new strength into the industry. During the second half of the sixteenth century, gold production in Mexico doubled, and silver production increased twenty-seven times.[18] Both industries — cattle and mining — nurtured in their infancies by the economic and political structures of New Spain, would in later centuries have an immense impact on the Anglo-American push to the West.

New Spain's history discloses problems common to all American frontiers — especially in the relations between native races and invading Europeans and, consequently, in the balance between them and

"Recollections of life on a Mexican rancho in the 1840s"
by James Walker (1818-1889).

the environment in which they moved. The Spaniard was one of the earliest European immigrants and one of the earliest pioneer types. He carried across the Atlantic the intellectual baggage of medieval knight and crusader. He brought militant Christianity, hierarchical government, and a desire for personal gain. His dreams of gold, however, were more than Spanish; they were European, "a kind of illness,"[19] in Eric Wolf's words. But far more important in the long run were changes in the Spaniard's ideas and the way this pioneer man exploited the land and its people for his personal ends. The Spaniard was a new breed, a capitalist, representing the commerce and technology that were shattering the medieval patterns of Europe. As capitalist, his stance toward the native varied greatly from his stance as Christian missionary. The Indian was either an impediment to the acquisition of new land or a potential labor supply.

NEW FRANCE

As the Spaniard wrestled with these questions, similar desires impelled another European people into a far different environment. In 1534, while Cabeza de Vaca ministered to the tribes along the Gulf of Mexico, the St. Lawrence Indians marveled at two ships larger

Jacques Cartier ascending the St. Lawrence River, lithograph, 1893.

than any they had seen sailed by fishermen. The vessels were mastered by Jacques Cartier, whose king, Francis I of France, was ready to compete with imperial Spain. Cartier had come to seek the Northwest Passage to India and to establish French claims to lands "where it is said that he should find great quantities of gold."[20] On Cartier's second trip he brought colonists. The Indians were remarkably helpful. They suggested, for example, a potion of boiled bark that cured almost magically an epidemic of scurvy threatening to wipe out the company. The bitter cold, however, was beyond relief. Mountainous snowdrifts lay against the ships in the harbor, and "masts, spars, and cordage were thick with glittering incrustations and sparkling rows of icicles; a frosty armor four inches thick encased the bulwarks."[21] By May 1536 the entire colony was on its way home. Despite further attempts by Cartier, it was not until the dawn of the seventeenth century that the French permanently colonized Montreal and Quebec, their first major settlements in the New World.

Samuel de Champlain, as a result of his travels to the West Indies and to Mexico City between 1599 and 1601, envied Spanish success

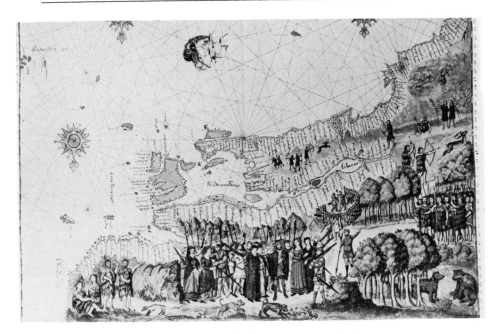

Landing of Cartier and colonists, from 1546 map.

in the New World. His interest, backed both by the King and by merchants, led to the command of a colonizing expedition that arrived in New France in 1603. Five years later he planted the first permanent French settlement on the bluffs at Quebec. As a vigorous governor for twenty-five years, until he died on Christmas day in 1635, Champlain always sensed the importance of good relations with the Indians.

The fur trade was emerging in New France as an industry to compare in magnitude with mining and cattle raising in New Spain. As the mines and ranches of Mexico depended on native labor, so was the trapping of beaver and otter in New France based on the work of the Indians. Champlain understood this simple necessity and therefore moved out very early in canoes to talk and negotiate with them. The seeking out of the Indian in his own village came to differentiate the approach of the French from that of the Spanish and English. Economics motivated the French, for the Indians had the peltry that the white men needed, but Champlain also had religious aspirations: he wished to see the Indians converted to the Christian faith.

The natives of the northern forests, latter-day skraelings, were unlike any the Spaniards knew. Living in the midst of crystal lakes and spruce woods, the Algonquians and Iroquois sent their men into the

Champlain exploring the Canadian wilderness, lithograph, 1893.

woods as hunters. Their women sometimes raised maize, beans, squash, and tobacco. These tribes tended to live in towns and to form diplomatic confederacies. The chief of these, the five-nation League of the Iroquois (comprised of the Mohawk, Oneida, Onondaga, Cayuga, and Seneca tribes), had united during the sixteenth century, though their legends push the founding back another century to the time of the saintly Hiawatha. Other confederacies — the Delaware and the Powhatan, for example — were large but organizationally less impressive than the Iroquois League.

The northeastern woodland Indians, such as the Mohawks, are often considered to have been more warlike than tribes in other areas. The distinction is dubious. Though the Iroquois often decimated their enemies, they also adopted entire tribes, such as the Tuscaroras, and treated them as their own. A large part of their belligerence resulted from their use by the French and British as ploys in imperial designs. Champlain, as early as 1609, the year after he founded Quebec, allied the French with the Algonquians. The significance of this alliance became apparent later in the century when the British joined with the Algonquians' enemies, the Iroquis. The conflict between leagues would scar the continent until climaxing in the French and Indian War.

Meanwhile, remnants of feudalism were installed along the rivers of New France in the seventeenth century. Cardinal Richelieu devised a scheme and persuaded his king, Louis XIII, to proclaim it in 1628. The Company of One Hundred Associates — young nobles, army officers, and merchants — was granted immense privileges from Florida to the Arctic Circle in exchange for supervision of the religious and economic development of the area. The company had to transport to the New World at least four thousand settlers and an appropriate number of priests and support them all for three years. Christian Indians were to be considered French citizens. The company held permanent monopoly over the fur trade and over commercial activities, except fishing and mining, for fifteen years. It could grant land, which it did in large swaths along the waters of the St. Lawrence River. Because rivers were everywhere in New France, and made convenient highways, estates extended like ribbons from river frontages. Usually less than eight hundred feet wide, they would run back ten times that length. The seigneur, or lord, of each manor divided his land among men who then owed him homage and dues (such as one fish out of every eleven). These obligations, though pittances, were seldom paid, and the seigneurs, in desperation, often drifted off to make their fortunes illegally, as unlicensed fur traders. The company had trouble attracting its quota of colonists and in 1663 surrendered its charter to the king, Louis XIV, suggesting that he find other means to care for his New World empire. Other companies had failed, too, and stimulating growth was thus left up to the Crown.

A spurt of activity came in the late 1660s under the leadership of Jean Talon. New prosperity was injected into the fishing and trapping industries and into supporting agriculture, which had heretofore languished. The French population of New France doubled under Talon.

Governor Louis de Frontenac, Talon's successor in spirit though not in actual position, quickened the French impulse to plunge deeper into the continent. More than a century after Coronado had marched northward into the Mississippi basin, the French tested the limits of their imperial drive in roughly the same region. They followed the natural arc of waterways that began with the St. Lawrence River, swept southwest across the Great Lakes, and then ran down the brown Mississippi to the Gulf of Mexico. In 1673 Jacques Marquette, a Jesuit priest, and Louis Jolliet traveled two-thirds of the way down the Mississippi to the Arkansas River. In 1682 Robert Cavelier de La Salle, leading a bickering but courageous expedition, traveled all the way to the mouth of the Mississippi. There in the swampy delta he planted a cross, turned a spade of earth, and claimed all land drained by those waters for King Louis XIV. In Francis Parkman's classic words:

> On that day, the realm of France received on parchment a stupendous accession. The fertile plains of Texas; the vast basin of the Mississippi, from its frozen northern springs to the sultry borders of the Gulf; from the woody ridges of the Alleghenies to the bare peaks of the Rocky Mountains — a region of savannahs and forests, sun-cracked deserts, and grassy prairies, watered by a thousand rivers, ranged by a thousand war-like tribes, passed beneath the scepter of the Sultan of Versailles; and all by virtue of a feeble human voice, inaudible at half a mile.[22]

The Spanish empire had fleshed out its basic form in the seventeenth century, the French in the early eighteenth. New France became a giant triangle — the interior heartland of North America embracing the two immense river systems of the St. Lawrence and the Mississippi joined by the five Great Lakes. Its dimensions were nearly as breath-taking as the sweep of New Spain, whose northeastern borders it touched. The boundaries of the two empires, vague as they were, actually overlapped. The French, too, had settlements along the Gulf of Mexico — at Biloxi (established in 1699, seventeen years after La Salle stood at the mouth of the Mississippi) and at New Orleans (after 1718). Except for these ports, however, French eyes turned inward to the land of Louis XIV, called Louisiana. The eyes were usually those of Jesuit missionaries and trappers, not of settlers, and thus the typical settlements of New France along its forested waters were temporary missions and fur-traders' posts. These symbols and instruments of the French empire retained their significance long after New France was only a memory.

In 1611, three years after Champlain founded Quebec, the first Jesuit missionaries arrived in New France, bearing from the king an exclusive jurisdiction to convert the Indians. Among the priests was Isaac Jogues, who would eventually be declared a saint. His story can be seen as a study in the way these Frenchmen faced the wilderness and its native population.

Jogues was born of French nobility, a timid and gentle boy, slight of build. His thin body helped make him a swift runner, and his meekness quickly turned to vigor whenever his faith was challenged. He was trained and ordained by the Jesuits in France and was sent to the New World in 1636. Almost immediately he found himself in what was virtually a French missionary's home, a birch canoe, on a long journey by water to the far Great Lakes, carrying the word of Christ to the Hurons. He fell ill on the way and had to rest, but spent the time perfecting his knowledge of Indian languages. Once recuperated, he moved from tribe to tribe for the next three years, preaching and baptizing. In 1642 he was captured by the Iroquois, who by virtue of their alliances, were enemies of the French. His nearly two years as prisoner and slave of the Iroquois, which he described ruefully as the "path of Paradise," were often times of torture — skin was cut in small strips from his back, fingernails torn, a thumb cut off slowly with clam shells, his body cudgeled and speared in a long gauntlet. Through it all Jogues continued to baptize, secretly if necessary, on one occasion with his lacerated and bleeding hands, on another using for water the few raindrops clinging to a green ear of corn thrown to him for food.

In time he was rescued by the Dutch and sent back to France where his wounds healed, as much as his deformities would allow. In 1644 he was back in New France, where he received orders from his superior to return to the Iroquois, his former captors, as a missionary. His first reaction, he later admitted, was to recoil at the thought. (As a disciplined Jesuit, soldier of Christ, this admission was cloaked in shame.)

The Mohawk segment of the Iroquois, among whom Jogues was working in 1646, was suffering bad times. A plague of caterpillars had destroyed their corn, and the diseases of the white man raged among them. In such circumstances most human societies seek scapegoats. The Mohawks came to regard Jogues, who carried a small black box of personal and religious belongings, as a sorceror. In 1646 he was attacked by an Indian warrior, tomahawked, and beheaded. His skull was placed on a pole facing the route from which he had come. One of his fellow Jesuits called the murder "the death of a martyr before the angels."[23]

Jogues was a saint, and so he is hardly typical of Frenchmen in the New World. But his experience does illustrate the religious thrust of France's activity on the frontier. Jesuits, individually or in small groups, sought the Indian in his own habitat, learned his language, lived with him, and tried mightily to win his pagan soul for the true God. Indeed, though they worked through different frontier institutions, Isaac Jogues and Bartolomé de Las Casas differed not a whit in their desire to convert the Indians.

Just as the Spanish priest had to contend against the secular economic pressures of the encomienda and the search for precious metals, so did the French missionary face the fur trader. By the early eighteenth century the terminology of the trapper, used wherever he trod the continent, was eloquent proof of the importance of the French in the development of trade — *coureur de bois* (runner of the woods, or trapper), *engagé* (hired trapper), *voyageur* (trapper who traveled primarily by canoe), *bourgeois* or *partisan* (officers of fur companies

Hudson's Bay Company trader, by Frederic Remington, 1892.

at central posts). Even Britain's Hudson's Bay Company was founded by two disgruntled French voyageurs. Although Hudson's Bay Company would add the culture of London to the fur trade, and John Jacob Astor would contribute the flavor of New York, they would not destroy the fur trade's French foundations.

The French trapper lived in the wilderness, like the missionary, but he hardly shared the Jesuit's ethics. In Bernard De Voto's words, the *coureurs de bois* "fought, murdered, drank, whored, and wived as they pleased. Their morals were nothing the settlements could approve."[24] Liquor was a source of contention. It was good business for the trapper to trade whisky for furs. In the missionaries' eyes, the human consequences of liquor made the trade abominable and, like Las Casas, they did their best to keep the Indians uncontaminated. One of Jogues's Jesuit contemporaries wrote:

> Our French cannot refrain from selling, nor the Savages from buying it [liquor], whenever an opportunity presents itself — especially the young men who are guilty of a thousand acts of insolence when drunk. . . . The Savages have told me many a time that they did not buy our liquors on account of any pleasant taste that they found in them, or because they had any need of them, but simply to become intoxicated — imagining, in their drunkenness, that they become persons of importance![25]

François Lucie, Cree half-breed guide, by Paul Kane, c. 1847.

It is easy to assume, but hard to prove, that the Spanish and the French brought different qualities to their territory in the New World. Salvador de Madariaga, a Spanish scholar teaching at Oxford, once summed up the differences with the words *el honor* (meaning the Spanish soul and passion) and *le droit* (the French intellect and reason).[26] Whether the different psychological states implied by these words can be identified in specific historical events is doubtful. It is easier to attribute qualitative differences between Spanish and French settlements to the geography faced by the French and the Spanish — the lakes and waterways of the north versus the deserts and tropics of the south. The pursuit of gold, too, must elicit human qualities different from those called up by the search for fish and furs.

These contrasts may be mirrored in at least one specific relationship — varying attitudes toward the Indians. The Spanish tended to lead the Indians to the missions or encomiendas. The French at times simply enslaved the Indians, as in the lower Mississippi valley; but as a rule, French trappers and missionaries found it more profitable to live and work as equals with the natives. The French *coureur de bois* may well have been the best example of European man accepting the Indian as an equal and judging him on his individual merits. Both the

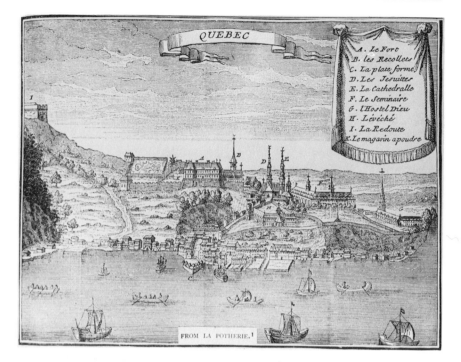

Eighteenth-century view of Quebec.

French and Spanish exploited the Indian for commercial profit, but the Spanish were more easily tempted by such unique opportunities as the encomienda system, which gathered large numbers of pliable natives. From a religious standpoint, however, both groups considered the Indian a human being with a soul worth saving. By no means would all subsequent inheritors of the North American continent agree.

THE ENGLISH COLONIAL FRONTIER

The peoples who settled the lands between sprawling New Spain and water-laced New France seldom attained the same level of relationship with the Indians. The English tended to be farmers and would have wondered at Cortes's comment that he had not come to till the soil like a peasant. Of course, they too, had their dreams of riches, but perforce their avenue emphasized agriculture and commerce. They were also liberally interspersed with such other farming nationalities as the Scotch-Irish, Dutch, Germans, and Swedes.

Although latecomers to the New World, the English planted Jamestown in 1607, the year before Champlain established Quebec. Jamestown, however, was not the first place in the New World over which the flag of England flew. In 1497 John Cabot had discovered Newfoundland and Nova Scotia, and in 1576 Martin Frobisher had found Baffin Island in the north Atlantic. Sir Humphrey Gilbert, however, was the first to consider America a place for Englishmen to live. Gilbert and his expedition arrived in Newfoundland in 1583. Though few people stayed and two ships — including the one carrying Gilbert — were lost, the enterprise stirred the imagination of other Englishmen. Most interested was Gilbert's half brother, Sir Walter Raleigh, whose near-legendary colony on Roanoke Island began its brief existence in 1585. The mysterious disappearance of the Roanoke colonists, who left behind only the word *Croatoan* crudely carved on a post, instilled in the English a fearful attitude toward Indians.

Yet the Indians, in fact, were partly responsible for the English presence. The farmer came for land, others for trade and fishing, but they all shared the hope of converting the heathen soul. To the English, the Indian was a worshiper of sun, moon, and stars, an idolater innocent of the word of Christ. Saint Paul had first posed the question that Englishmen in the sixteenth century were asking: How can a man believe in Christ if he has never heard of him? Catholics from Spain and France had taken the Gospel to the New World, and it was high time for the Protestants to do the same. Waiting there was an area between the French and the Spanish. What an opportunity for Protestants to move in and permanently separate the Catholics!

The most wholesome way to illuminate the Christian virtues was to involve entire families — men, women, and children. In colonial settlements the family unit would make full testimonial to the beauties of Christian life, and conversions would follow like miracles in contrast to the results obtained by celibate priests in black robes. The transplanting of households became typical English procedure, and, in the words of Edwin Scott Gaustad, "This basic position shaped all British policy and changed all American history."[27]

Because the English came in family groups, it was understandable that Queen Elizabeth I was concerned about their full protection. The colonies backed by Raleigh were to be considered permanent settlements. In the charter that she had granted Raleigh, the queen decreed that the colonists "may have all the privileges of free Denizens, and persons native of England." Here, as in virtually all the subsequent English charters, the common law and liberties of England were transferred intact to the New World. No such provisions were applied in

New Spain and New France. By this time, however, Spain was stipulating protection of the Indian in its land grants. The civil rights of the natives were seldom mentioned by the English. In William Brandon's words, "The governor and council (corresponding to president and board of directors) of the parent joint stock company were answerable to no one for any action against Indians, up to and including enslavement or annihilation."[28]

Funds for the English colonial effort often came from a joint-stock company, which became an important institution in the English colonies. The company sold shares of stock in various quantities. The money raised in this manner was sufficient to meet initial costs without help from the monarch, who granted a charter for the colony to the company. The investor was liable only for the amount he invested, and if the venture failed he could not be sued for his remaining resources. Raleigh, one of the few who did not work through a company, lost £40,000 in the Roanoke disaster, and discovered how much failure could cost the single capitalist. A company would have distributed the loss among many small investors.

By 1600, the year the great East India Company was founded, the pattern of the English joint-stock company was already set. The Virginia Company, the Massachusetts Bay Company, and the Hudson's Bay Company became examples of the institution. Not all English colonies were initiated by corporations; proprietary colonies like Pennsylvania and Maryland were run by individuals, not companies. But these distinctions were relatively unimportant on the frontier.

Nevertheless, the first English settlers in the Virginia and Plymouth colonies were well received and assisted by the natives. Squanto, for example, showed the New Englanders how to fertilize cornhills with fish. But as the populations became better established and less in need of native help, sorry relations developed and old ideas reasserted themselves. John Smith of Virginia always considered the Indians barbarous and savage, though his life had been saved by Pocahontas and he had presented the Indian girl to Queen Elizabeth in London. Smith regarded the Indians as unregenerate, crafty, covetous, and malicious.

Some later English views of the Indian were only slightly more elevated. Mary Rowlandson, captured by the Indians in the seventeenth century and later returned to the English settlements, described her captors as brutish, atheistic, and diabolical. The Indian was not an animal, but one could readily observe from his way of life that he was not civilized or Christian. He lay in bondage to Satan because he had not embraced Christ. Christians are engaged in eternal war against Satan, and, when placed in the wilderness facing the Devil's children, their response could be only to destroy or be destroyed.

These attitudes help to explain the Pequot War, which broke out in Massachusetts in 1636. Through a system of alliances, the Pequot tribe had become powerful enough to alarm the colonists. Although in 1632 the Indians had murdered a few whites, there had been no recent provocations for the action taken by the colonists. They gathered, armed, and attacked the Pequot villages. On a foray led by Captain John Mason, the English wiped out a settlement of more than five hundred men, women, and children. Captives of the war were either enslaved in New England or sold into the West Indies slave trade. The Pequots' lands were quickly absorbed by colonial expansion.

One participant in the Pequot War emerged from it as a man of peace. "Rhode Island was purchased by love," said its founder Roger Williams, implying, quite correctly, that he had shaped a very special relationship with the Narraganset Indians. He had come to Massachusetts in 1631 overflowing with zeal to bring Christ to the Indians. Soon after, he occasionally went to live with the natives in their "filthy, smoky holes," struggling to learn their language. The contacts proved fortunate, for Williams held political and religious ideas that went beyond the limits of acceptability, and he was banished from Massachusetts. During the desperate winter of 1635 he lived with the Narragansets, and in the spring founded a new colony, which would become Rhode Island. The Pequot War severely tested his friendship with the tribes. He negotiated skillfully and kept the Narragansets at peace. They trusted him because he maintained that Europeans had no right to grant or buy land except with prior Indian agreement and that purchase might not transfer sovereignty. Williams assumed that Englishmen should remain subjects of local sachems unless their colonies had, like his, been "purchased by love," through honest understanding. Beyond these doctrines, so curious to English practice, Williams had few illusions about the Indians. In the final analysis few of them would be converted, he believed, at least until the Apocalypse. He allowed that they were children of Adam with full consciences, and that peace and gentle relations should be the rightful order between white and red man. But if the Indian assumed the role of aggressor, then war should follow. As Edmund S. Morgan has summarized, "He despised their religion and found many of their customs barbarous, but he was ready to live with them and deal with them on equal terms."[29]

Efforts to convert the Indians were institutionalized in New England

John Eliot preaching to the Indians.

as early as 1643 by the establishment of the Society for the Propagation of the Gospel. While Roger Williams built Rhode Island, another clergyman, John Eliot, was working for the Society in Massachusetts. In the 1640s he learned Indian languages, translated the Bible into Algonquian, and, recognizing the tribal distaste for living near the white man, brought together fourteen villages of "praying Indians" with more than a thousand converts. These self-governing communes were the closest the English ever came to the Spanish missions, but they lasted only until King Philip's War in 1675.

Philip Metacomet was a Wampanoag chief who forged an alliance of retaliation against land encroachment by the white man. Once again, inspired by fear, the colonists regarded all Indians as children of Satan. Eliot worked hard to protect his converts from the settlers, but to little avail. Their villages were attacked and the inhabitants dispersed by King Philip's warriors and by white militiamen. Eliot's work collapsed. Even Roger Williams, lame and in his seventies, after finding his own house and 80 percent of the other houses of Providence in smoking ruin, led Rhode Island troops against his former friends the Narragansets.

Eliot's Indian Bible (Matthew I), 1661.

The victory of the English over King Philip's confederation was hardly surprising. It is true that the Indians were well armed as a result of the illegal trade in firearms kept alive by trappers, Frenchmen, and profiteers. Their total population in the region, however, had slipped far below that of the colonists; estimates range from ten to twenty thousand natives in comparison with fifty to seventy-five thousand whites. The number of Indians was further reduced by the wars.[30] Hundreds of Indians were taken as slaves, including the wife and child of King Philip. More important, from this time on the Englishmen (with the exceptions of such figures as Jonathan Edwards in Massachusetts, David Brainerd in Connecticut, and Eleazar Wheelock at Dartmouth) seemed to see only two alternatives for dealing with the Indian — removal or extermination.

The policy was basically the same in England's southern colonies. After 1622, the year of the first great fight between Indians and Virginians, a state of war had existed between the natives and the tough frontier farmers, who increasingly moved westward because of exhausted tobacco lands. Aware that they were losing ground to the white man, the Indians regarded the establishment of all new settlements as provocation. When the Indians attacked, the white man felt fear, the most powerful emotion, rather than his usual feeling of contempt.

Nathaniel Bacon mirrored these feelings. Farming far up on the James River, he and his neighbors were exposed to attack. By 1676 the price of tobacco had fallen to a new low. For this economic distress it was easier to blame the colonial government in Virginia than the English Acts of Trade. When trouble with the Indians broke out on the frontier, petitions to the governor for troops were as successful as efforts to raise the price of tobacco. Consequently, Bacon and his friends took the law into their own hands, a typical reaction on the frontier. They watched as the friendly Occaneechees fought the Susquehannas and were pleased when thirty of the latter were killed. Bacon turned his rebel group on the Occaneechees. Then the armed farmers found another friendly tribe, the Pamunkeys, and killed eight of them. Bacon took forty-five captives and much plunder and called it "a mighty conquest."[31] Such provocation of the natives prompted the governor to order the regular army against Bacon. The frontiersmen charged the governor's men, defeated them, and marched victoriously into the capital of Jamestown, with Nathaniel Bacon leading six hundred rebels. At this point in the drama, Bacon suddenly died. Leaderless, his followers were rounded up and six of them were executed. In describing Bacon's death, Governor Berkeley seriously commented that "God had so infected his blood that it bred lice in an incredible number."[32] One is tempted to think the governor was also speaking metaphorically.

Bacon's Rebellion of 1676 was the first expression of frontier agrarian dissent in American history. It nearly coincided with King Philip's War in New England, and the two events were indicators of the pressures building along the colonial frontier. Western farmers were testing the limits of Indian endurance and the strength of eastern seaboard controls. These issues were not yet widespread, but they would become so in the years ahead.

Generalizations rest most comfortably in the presence of their exceptions, and no account of frontier relations with Indians should omit William Penn. Arriving in America in 1682, Penn flourished almost a generation after John Eliot and Roger Williams, but he towers above them as a symbol of generous understanding with the native peoples. Benjamin West's painting of Penn under a spreading elm, presenting the feathered tribes with a treaty of friendship, has done much to color our opinion, but there can be no doubt that

Penn's treaty with the Indians, by Benjamin West, c. 1771.

Penn treated the natives as human beings with rights and feelings. He negotiated for needed lands and kept the treaties inviolate. He did his best to protect the Indians from the liquor traffic and from fur traders. The Indians responded with loyalty, and there was no frontier warfare in Pennsylvania while Penn lived.

During the eighteenth century some new peoples moved to the fringes of English settlement — the Germans and the Scotch-Irish. Their impact on the American frontier would be immense. Germans by the thousands poured out of the Rhineland beginning around 1713 as the result of depressed farm conditions, wars in which they did not believe, and New World advertisements. They were Pietists, pacifists, and above all, good farmers. They sought fertile land in the interior, first along the Mohawk valley in New York, where they had trouble with speculators, and then southward down the Susquehanna and the Shenandoah all the way to the Carolinas. Some of them, such as the Mennonites and Amish, came to be termed, improperly, Pennsylvania Dutch. Wherever they went they were a sober, pious people willing to endure hardships, sometimes starvation, if the future promised harvests and well-filled barns.

The Scotch-Irish, who began pouring into western areas about 1717, colored the frontier far more than did the German Pietists. The Germans sank deep roots and tended to remain in one place; the Scotch-Irish pushed constantly on. They were the fighters, the hunters, the marksmen, and they bred Andrew Jackson, John C. Calhoun, and Sam Houston. They had been transplanted from Scotland to northern Ireland around Ulster, a hard land that encouraged aggressive qualities. Certainly they learned there to hate and fight Englishmen, and it is not surprising that in America they immediately got as far away from the English on the seaboard as they possibly could. By 1776, three hundred thousand of them (among a total of 2.5 million in the English colonies) had squatted on the western fringes from Massachusetts to Georgia.

Passionate Presbyterians, they were viewed thus by such eastern traditionalists as the Anglican minister Charles Woodmason: "If they cannot cheat, rob, defraud, or injure You in your Goods — they will belye, defame, lessen, blacken, disparage the most valuable Person breathing, not of their Communion in his Character, Good Name, or Reputation and Credit."[33] Like many Puritans, whom they mightily resembled, they were certain that the Indian was a savage servant of Satan, and allowed their long rifles to kill with the sweet savor of holiness.

The English colonial governments might agree with the Scotch-Irish in principle, but their policies included the use of the Indian for larger political purposes: the red man could fight white men's battles. Three wars — King William's War (1689-1697), Queen Anne's War (1702-1713), and King George's War (1745-1748) — mirrored in America antagonisms among England, France, and Spain. The American Indian was forced to play a role in each. Ancient hostilities between Iroquois and Algonquian were fanned by old hostilities between Europes. The British were trying to drive a diplomatic wedge between Bourbon France and Hapsburg Spain. In the New World, however, the wedge was geographically more literal. There, by the eighteenth century, Spain was a subsidiary problem. The Spanish were doing their best to shore up the defenses along the vague endless northern borders of New Spain, and the English establishment of Georgia was partly an effort to keep the Spanish in their place. The most dramatic conflict came to the north and northwest of the English settlements. Sporadically during the eighteenth century, wherever New France touched the British colonies, the gargantuan struggle between France and England for North America mounted toward its stirring climax in the French and Indian War.

One point of the English wedge was westward across the Appalachians where the Monongahela and Allegheny rivers create the Ohio River. There, to incorporate the Ohio in their waterway system, the French had built Fort Duquesne. In 1755 General Edward Braddock, a Scottish Coldstream Guard, led more than two thousand Englishmen and fifty Indian scouts from Virginia toward the fort. Among them was a young lieutenant, George Washington, who knew that wilderness reasonably well. The army was ambushed by the French and their Indian allies, and Braddock lost his life. His body was buried in the trail, and the entire English detachment was marched over it to destroy the traces. Braddock's defeat was part of a long series of setbacks for the British, though Fort Duquesne eventually was taken (and renamed Fort Pitt).

The decisive British victory came in 1759. The English commander was Lord Jeffrey Amherst, a vigorous hater of Indians who later proposed the distribution of small-pox-infected blankets to exterminate the red-skinned vermin. He sought a final showdown with the French, then commanded by the Marquis de Montcalm. The British planned a pincers attack on Quebec, the heart of New France. Amherst would march north along the traditional water route once taken in reverse by Father Jogues on his way to martyrdom — Lake George, Lake Champlain, the Richelieu River, to the St. Lawrence River — and would attack Quebec from the west. Meanwhile, thirty-two-year-old General James Wolfe, redheaded and romantic (he once said he would rather have written Gray's "Elegy" than take Quebec), would sail from Cape Breton Island, across the Gulf of St. Lawrence, and up the St. Lawrence River to attack Quebec from the east. Amherst was delayed, and Wolfe, waiting on the river, decided to go it alone. Twice his men made frontal assaults on Quebec from the river, failing both times. He then devised a scheme worthy of a wilderness scout — a night maneuver up a cleft in the bluffs two miles behind the city. At dawn on September 13, 1759, the French on the Plains of Abraham behind Quebec faced a British force of forty-five hundred men, as large as their own. In a day's hard fight, Montcalm was killed and Wolfe was shot three times. Before Wolfe died, he knew the battle was won. In effect, at that moment England supplanted France in North America. At approximately the same time England acquired India as well and became thereby the greatest imperial power the world had yet known.

The bells were loud in London and silent in Paris. New France was no more. In *Candide* Voltaire could describe Canada as a few acres of worthless snow. England could afford a smile for an answer, as British firms took over the fur trade. West of the Mississippi, France had surreptitiously ceded Louisiana to Spain, but aside from New Orleans,

Death of Montcalm, Battle of Quebec, 1759; aquatint, 1789.

all territory east of the great river was English — a thousand green valleys and fair forests for those who bore the Kentucky rifles and carried speculator's maps.

The new British west had various exploiters, not all of whom were compatible. English fur traders, for example, building on French models, wanted the Indians kept and protected for purely economic reasons; land speculators and settlers wanted the Indians cleared out.

A decision on a policy for the western lands was not helped by the renewal of war in the region. This time it was Indians alone against the British, but it included a confederacy of major proportions under the proud Ottawa chief Pontiac, who was thoroughly incensed with Amherst's hateful policies toward the Indian. For some months in 1763 the English were pushed back steadily, and Pontiac and his allies held dominion over the Ohio valley. Given their display of strength, they were completely mystified that their former friends, the French, would not now join them simply because other Frenchmen were signing papers in a far-off land. The English made concessions, including an agreement to restrain settlement in the Ohio valley, and when the regular British army was finally dispatched, the Pontiac alliance broke.

With trappers and Indians and settlers to contend with, London tried to clarify its western policy in the Royal Proclamation of 1763. Some areas would be opened for settlement, but these would be at the geographical extremes of North America — Quebec in the north and the Floridas in the south. The region between, beyond the ridge of the Appalachians, would be closed to settlement, and none of the land could be purchased from the Indians or from anyone else. In western Pennsylvania and Virginia, farmers were already beyond the Appalachian divide, but His Majesty's secretaries in London seem not to have known that fact. At any rate they were listening more to the Indians and trappers than to land speculators.

Dissatisfaction with British land policies was one factor — and an important one — leading to the American Revolution. But western grievances were often directed at the eastern establishment. The westerner wanted to do as he pleased, assuming he knew the best way to get ahead, to cut timber, trap for furs, speculate in land, build a farm on rich soil. He supported whoever stood to help him. He fought against restrictions such as the Proclamation Line, but not because he wanted the government to get out. He petitioned strenuously for government assistance against the Indians; if the colonial governments refused it, he became furious, as Nathaniel Bacon had, and took the law into his own hands. He was conservative, Tory, Whig, liberal, democrat, republican, radical, rebel — whatever he had to be to protect his own interests.

Far on the western fringes of Quaker Pennsylvania, in a log-cabin cluster called Paxton on the smooth waters of the Susquehanna, the frontier farmers viewed the colonial government in Philadelphia as if through the wrong end of a telescope, and felt themselves only weakly represented there. The Paxton community, largely Presbyterian, looked askance at the Quakers who controlled Pennsylvania. How could those sons of William Penn, effete Philadelphia pacifists and notorious coddlers of savages, know the needs of God-fearing Presbyterians in the west? Thirty miles from Paxton lay a village of Conestoga Indians — poor, peaceful descendants of a tribe that had once fought proudly but had long lived in submission. There were rumors, though, that the Conestogas were spying on Paxton. Red-blooded whites could hardly allow that, and in December 1763 a small band of men from Paxton descended on the Conestogas, killing three men, two women, and a child. Fourteen Conestogas sought asylum, and the government housed them in the jail at Lancaster. The residents of Paxton were furious and, after a short delay for Christmas, stormed the Lancaster jail, massacring all the Indians in it. Other Indians became frightened enough to seek protection, and consequently more than a hundred of them were lodged in Philadelphia. The Paxton Boys were so incensed that they marched on the capital itself. Philadelphia officials, genuinely alarmed, sent out an army, including a troop of artillerymen, and dispatched negotiators led by Benjamin Franklin. Franklin had already written an essay expressing his sympathy with the Indians and calling the Paxton Boys "Christian white savages." But he satisfied the frontiersmen that their cause would be heard by the colonial assembly and the governor; so, leaving a long written remonstrance, the farmers marched home to Paxton.

In the petition the Paxton Boys agreed that their conduct bore "an appearance of flying in the face of Authority" (a lovely euphemism for an armed rebellion). But, they argued, their grievances were great, chiefly because the government showed a "manifest Partiality for Indians." The Conestogas had been "cherished and caressed as dearest friends" by the politicians. The public had thereby been made "tributaries to savages," and the poor frontier farmers had been forced to fend for themselves. As the remonstrance continued, deeper frictions surfaced. The frontiersmen wanted more effective political representation and the abolition of property qualifications for voting. Further in the background lay the economic indebtedness of western farmers to eastern financiers. Altogether the uprising in Pennsylvania was an agrarian revolt not unlike that of Nathaniel Bacon, and it had mounted to the point of threatening the colonial establishment.

In 1767 in the backwoods of South Carolina murders, thefts, and anarchy reached a peak; it was a "disaster area."[34] Even members of a new religious sect, the Weberites, turned homicidal and murdered their "holy ghost" (a Negro) and their "holy son" (a white man). Miscreants were often captured and, when tried in Charleston, almost as often pardoned. The established law thus seemed to be in the wrong place producing the wrong results. Consequently, men on the frontier began to take the law into their own hands. When they were able to identify an outlaw group, a small band of farmers would descend on the hideout and scatter the outlaws. The governor was upset and called the farmers licentious spirits, but the settlers banded together and called themselves Regulators. One thousand of them signed an agreement to protect one another until the crime wave was stopped. Occasionally designated Rangers, especially when mounted, they roamed the backcountry, pursuing suspected criminals as far as necessary, whipping some, hanging others, but usually bringing them in to be tried in the proper manner.

Often their violent and bloody methods were as notorious as those of their quarry. Their historian, Richard Maxwell Brown, asserted, "The cruelty of outlaws who burned and tortured their victims was matched by the sadism of honest and respectable Regulators who shredded the flesh of miscreants at orgiastic flogging sessions while fiddles played."[35] The jungle morality on both sides was undoubtedly the consequence of barbarities still fresh in these men's minds from the Cherokee War of 1760 to 1761. Like the Paxton Boys, the back-country Regulators clothed their criminal savagery in the cloak of political legitimacy. They wanted better representation in the colonial legislature, better courts in the frontier areas, more schools and jails, more regulation of taverns and public houses, more restrictions on hunters and lawyers (both of whom were offensive), and even distri-bution of Bibles at public expense. A remonstrance covering most of these points was signed by four thousand men. Nevertheless, by March 1768 sentiment was rising against the Regulators' illegal actions. They themselves could argue, however, that their work was done, the crime wave over, and their remonstrances made.

The South Carolina Regulator movement is sometimes paired with the actions of the Paxton Boys as an example of a frontier rebellion. In some ways they were radically different. The Pennsylvanians chal-lenged the authority of the government. The Regulators were con-cerned more with ridding their local areas of crime, and although they acted unlawfully, like the Paxton Boys, their goals were different. Both groups were agrarian dissenters. The men from Paxton, however, functioned like a lynch mob, attacking a minority and then using the occasion to carry their grievances further. The Regulators were early practitioners of vigilantism — action taken by allegedly responsible members of society to clean up local corruption. Both lynch mobs and vigilantes would appear and reappear in only slightly varied guises on every successive frontier. The terms *regulator* and *regulation* were first used in the backcountry of South Carolina, but were picked up in North Carolina and became standard until events in San Francisco in 1851 shifted popular usage to *vigilance* and *vigilante committee*.

The Paxton Boys and the Regulators were rebels, men willing to raise arms against established authority to further their independent goals. The importance of their actions as a model for seaboard colonists in their fight for independence from England will probably never be known. If events in the West had any great significance for the Amer-ican Revolution, it would be as a psychological softening operation: a series of small, riotous vigilante actions made it easier for others to consider violent rebellion.

Militarily the West helped the revolutionary cause very little. In the first place, support for revolution was not unified. How could the Paxton Boys and the South Carolina Regulators rally behind the colonial governments they had so recently defied? Some westerners remained Tories, loyal to the Crown, though surprisingly at least half

Joseph Brant, by George Romney (1734-1802).

of the Regulators did become revolutionary Whigs. It seems, then, that the West was not acting as a separate section. In western Pennsylvania, claims historian David Hawke, settlers tended to follow not their region, but their religious, social, and economic counterparts in the East.[36]

Though not unified on the politics of revolution, the westerners could always agree on the menace of Indians. The British had an essential advantage because they kept the tribal allies they had won in their long fight against the French. The revolutionary frontiersmen subverted only a few Indians, such as the Shawnees and the Delawares, and then for limited periods. Consistently arrayed against them year after year were the Iroquois and a brilliant Mohawk soldier, Joseph Brant. After he led the Indian victories at Oriskany (1777) and Cherry Valley (1778), Brant's name summoned more fear to western hearts than any Indian since Pontiac. Brant, a true Iroquois ally of the British, had fought against Pontiac. Remaining consistently English in his orientation, Brant was even converted to the Anglican church. In the early years of the American Revolution he had been entertained in England, seeing London in the company of no less a Londoner than James Boswell and sitting for his portrait in oils by no less a painter than George Romney.

The only western soldier who could match the fighting skill of Brant was George Rogers Clark who, between 1778 and 1780, managed to turn the war in the West in favor of the Americans. Clark, a six-foot, redheaded Virginian who knew well the lands along the Ohio River in Kentucky, held as a truism that if land was worth claiming (something he had already done), it was worth protecting (something he was about to do). His first victory against the British, at Kaskaskia in 1778, was followed by successes at Cahokia and Vincennes and earned for him the accolade of having won the West for the new nation. Teddy Roosevelt referred to him as "a tower of strength" for harassed Kentucky.[37]

Between 1780 and 1782 Joseph Brant mounted offensives that cast shadows on the successes of George Rogers Clark. Unless they were directly hit, however, the majority of the westerners seemed little concerned. Much of the time they were more intent on engrossing the best lands in preparation for the postwar years than they were on fighting. The city of Nashville was settled in 1780. In Kentucky, Boonesborough was established in 1775 and had its first spurt of development in the years of the Revolution. In spite of Clark's victories, the old West was not won by frontiersmen on the battlefield.

Why, then, did the British at the 1783 peace table in Paris give to the upstart rebels the land between the Appalachians and the Mississippi River? The answer suggests the vagaries of history. The English minister, Lord Shelburne, shrewdly assessed the situation and foresaw the impossibility of limiting Americans like Boone and the men of Nashville behind an artificial political boundary. Such containment policy would be no more successful than the Proclamation Line of 1763, which had failed to keep frontiersmen east of the Appalachians; it would simply lay seeds of serious trouble. By various diplomatic maneuvers, John Jay, Benjamin Franklin, and John Adams, the American negotiators, were thus able to draw the western boundaries of the new United States roughly along the Great Lakes, the Mississippi River, and the northern line of the Floridas, providing a huge and momentous buffer for expansion.

The English had inserted a Protestant wedge between New Spain and New France. British policy encouraged permanent settlement, and as the population increased, the economic drive for land grew with it. War with the natives replaced early friendly contacts, and dedicated missionary work was often swept aside. To the English the

Indian was not economically vital, as he was for the fur-trading French. The Indian was useful in war, however, and so he played a role in the French and Indian War — the mighty struggle that left the northern parts of the continent under the English Crown. By the time the thirteen colonies revolted from that sovereignty, the American push to the West had begun, and a brawling breed of frontier types, especially the Scotch-Irish, were leading the pack. The Appalachians were breached, and only the Mississippi River barred the way.

3

The Land and Its Markers

When the thirteen colonies achieved their independence, they took from under the British Crown 3 million white people plus uncounted Indians living on 541 million acres, an area roughly seventeen times the size of England. The western lands, those beyond the generally accepted boundaries of the new states, covered about 230 million acres, nearly half of the new country. This territory raised serious questions: Did the lands belong to the Indians, to the respective states, or to the central government (embodied in the Continental Congress)? How should the lands be distributed? When stated in the abstract, these questions may seem insignificant. But they are abstractions wrung from human dreams — the simple hope of owning a little land and prospering from laboring upon it. In a rural economy such dreams are important enough to cause the rise and fall of whole political systems.

The Declaration of Independence gave no clue as to who should take the unassigned acres from the Crown. The king, through his charters, had given the land to the colonies, so it might have followed that the states, counterparts of the colonies, would take possession of it. Such states as Virginia and New York, which in their charters had received large grants, were quick to take that stand. States such as Maryland, sensing a decline in their power, were less certain. Whenever men wished to strengthen the central government under the Articles of Confederation, they called for the states to surrender any rights they presumed over the public domain. Finally, the Confederation government won control of the public lands. Most of the states had decided to knuckle under by 1784, though Georgia did not finally cede its last portion until 1802.

Almost as important as the matter of who would have jurisdiction over the land was the problem of how to distribute it. Should the government sell the land and bring in revenue? If so, should it be sold in small portions for the poor or in large ones for the wealthy? Should it be given away, as the British government had considered doing as early as 1754, when it planned to allot to each frontier settler one thousand acres? Should some of the land be withheld for such government purposes as roads (and eventually railroad routes), bounties for soldiers, and schools? Should the government hold out for high prices as settlement advanced? Should planning be so orderly that adjacent areas might open one after another? Should mineral rights be separated from landownership, as was the case under the crowns of Europe? It is tempting to imagine what the consequences might be had the government decided very early to preserve large tracts simply for their aesthetic and spiritual values as wilderness.

When the Congress of the Confederation faced some of these questions about its greatest asset, the western lands, it did not start from scratch. The colonies had developed systems of land distribution that intriguingly wove geographical factors such as the composition of soil and the location of river systems with philosophical ideas such as the importance of the congregational community. Between the flinty hills of New England, for example, land tended to be granted by the colonial government to groups of people or to congregations moving with their minister into new regions close to the established settlements. These grants were relatively small and already surveyed. The congregation would analyze the configurations of their grant, designating the best place for the town center, or common, with its church, roads, pasturage, and most fertile farming fields. Within the area thus surveyed, each family would receive a town lot around the common and a farm plot farther out, assuming rights on both the common and the general pasture lands. There were wide variations within this pattern, and by the end of the seventeenth century, as the churches lost their central position, the system broke down. Nevertheless, elements of the New England system became fundamental to the disposition of the public domain, and were replicated wherever New Englanders relocated.

In the South, land and climate had made possible a single-crop agriculture (tobacco or cotton) and, consequently, larger farms than in the North. The southern individual typically sought out a large tract that he found appealing, even if it was relatively far from the nearest settlement, and requested ownership from the colonial government. When he received his grant, he thus assumed obligations for an independent development, unlike the New Englander, who could expect help from the community. Here again, approaches varied, but after the Revolution, the Continental Congress had at least these two models to use in fashioning a policy.

The Land Ordinance of 1785 pragmatically drew from both. From New England it took the idea of prior survey and orderly contiguous development. From the South it incorporated allocation directly to the individual. The ordinance provided that government surveyors would march first across the West and mark out the land in great grids. Prime meridians and base lines would be run north and south, east and west, chain by chain, transit by transit, no matter where the rivers ran or the ridges intervened. From the intersections of these large meridians and base lines additional lines would be set down to designate ranges of townships. Each township was six miles square, containing thirty-six one-mile square chunks called sections. These were the neat, rational building blocks, 640 acres apiece, which underlay the settlement of the West.

The surveyed land was to be sold at auction to the highest bidder, providing the bids were no less than one dollar per acre. Some of the land would be saved for the good of the nation at large. Section 16 in each township was set aside for schools, and sections 8, 11, 26, and 29 were reserved for future government purposes. A section had originally been intended for the support of religion, but that provision was stricken before passage of the ordinance.

The policy had all the advantages and disadvantages, clarity and distortions, of any rational approach to human affairs. The survey assured clear boundaries and firm titles, highly important in wild new lands. However, it pressed upon the land a uniformity that took no account of different valleys, different climates, or different men who might wish for other arrangements of acre and contour. An immense amount of the history of the settlement of the West would be no more than a working out of values and misfortunes stemming from the Land Ordinance of 1785.

The thinking behind the ordinance stressed orderly, compact population movement. Though this was traditionally a New England model, southerners such as Thomas Jefferson and George Washington strongly favored it over dispersed development, which could foster factionalism and lawlessness. Washington worried about that "parcel of banditti"[1] who roamed with speculative eyes over the West. These speculators had no love for the land ordinance, and they and their cohorts in the East (among whom must be numbered George Wash-

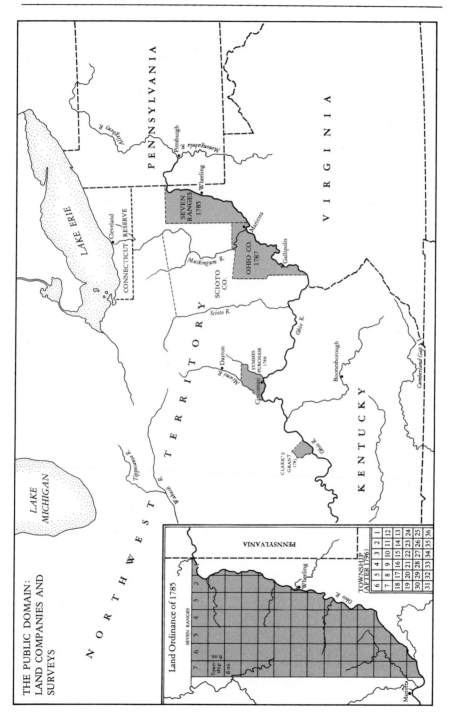

THE PUBLIC DOMAIN:
LAND COMPANIES AND
SURVEYS

LAKE MICHIGAN

LAKE ERIE

Allegheny R.

PENNSYLVANIA

Pittsburgh

Monongahela R.

Wheeling

SEVEN RANGES 1785

CONNECTICUT RESERVE

Cleveland

VIRGINIA

Marietta

OHIO CO. 1787

Gallipolis

Muskingum R.

SCIOTO CO.

Scioto R.

Ohio R.

N O R T H W E S T   T E R R I T O R Y

Tippecanoe R.

Wabash R.

Dayton

Miami R.

SYMMES PURCHASE 1788

Cincinnati

Boonsborough

KENTUCKY

Cumberland Gap

CLARK'S GRANT 1784

Ohio R.

Land Ordinance of 1785

SEVEN RANGES

PENNSYLVANIA

Wheeling

Ohio R.

Township 6 mi.

E-W 9

Marietta

TOWNSHIP (AFTER 1796)

6	5	4	3	2	1
7	8	9	10	11	12
18	17	16	15	14	13
19	20	21	22	23	24
30	29	28	27	26	25
31	32	33	34	35	36

ington, incidentally) made the land policy very different from that established in theory and by law.

The land ordinance prohibited the granting of any land until the surveyors completed seven ranges. Nevertheless, before that work was done, the Congress was undermining its own law. The Congress was worried about its future, and in the summer of 1787 the constitutional convention was drafting a proposal for a new frame of government. Army officers were disgruntled at being paid in heavily discounted continental currency. At the same time the Congress was not happy with the way certain frontiersmen had been acting. Still fresh in memory was the rebellion of Daniel Shays, a poor farmer and Revolutionary War hero from western Massachusetts, who in the tradition of the Regulators had protested against monetary policies and farm foreclosures. In 1786 Shays led to Springfield a mob that prevented courts from sitting, and troops were needed to quell the riot. Furthermore, in the fall of 1787 the system of selling land at auction had proved less than wildly successful. It had netted the government only $117,000, and not a single township in block form had been sold. For frontiersmen it was proving far easier simply to squat on land in the Ohio valley. Partly to quiet the Indians, the Congress had even sent troops to sweep some areas clean of squatters. The situation discouraged sympathies with the small farmer and encouraged large business interests to stand between the government and the individual settler.

One such business group was lead by the restless energy of a Yale divine with a parish in Massachusetts and an eye roving often from heaven to a quick business dollar. Manasseh Cutler was one of those unquenchable spirits who combined a multitude of lives into one life. He studied and practiced law, then turned to the church. Thereafter, through a great variety of activities, he always led his parish, but in addition he learned medicine, astronomy, botany, and electricity. In his household he taught as many as twenty boys at once. Somewhere in his already full life, he found time to organize a group of army veterans into one of the largest business deals of his day.

Cutler and his friends, including Rufus Putnam of Boston, incorporated the Ohio Company of Associates and petitioned the Congress for a grant of one and a half million acres of lush green hills and valleys. Because of the large amount, the price per acre would have to be small, but Cutler had a convenient dodge for the conscience of the Congress. If the company could pay in depreciated currency, against the stipulation in the land ordinance, the books could still say that the price had been a dollar per acre (though in fact the cost was between eight and nine cents an acre). Geoge Washington approved the

Kansas land office, 1874.

plan (inconsistent with his land-ordinance ideas) because it would assuage the discontent of at least one group of his former officers. Congressmen who balked at upsetting the ordinance before it had even been implemented were brought around by threats: if the Congress refused to sell, the Ohio Company would buy from individual states, presumably those that had not yet ceded their western lands, thus costing Congress a tidy sum of which it was desperately in need. As a final coup Cutler proposed another scheme, the Scioto Company, in which recalcitrant congressmen could themselves profit from a similar venture upon the public domain. The Scioto Company was to receive five million acres along the Ohio River. The speculator had clearly won out over the settler, and the wealthy people of the society, including men in high office, would profit from the disposition of the public lands.

The Scioto scheme included one sideline drama that was humorous, tragic, and illustrative of speculative mania. It concerned Joel Barlow, whose energies matched those of Manasseh Cutler. A buoyant poet,

Barlow worked away from the time he was an undergraduate at Yale on his great American epic poem the *Columbiad*. Poetry was not earning him much income, however; nor was law, which he studied and practiced. So he applied to the Ohio Company as an agent, and during four months of traipsing around Connecticut he sold more than one hundred of its shares. Thereupon he set off for London and Paris and remained in Europe for the next seventeen years, becoming friendly with Thomas Paine and even being made an honorary citizen by the revolutionary government of France.

The Scioto speculators were a bit uneasy at the prospect of selling their shares in the United States, inasmuch as the Congress had not yet granted them land. They therefore looked to Europe as a source for capital. Manasseh Cutler, remembering Barlow's successes in Connecticut with the Ohio shares, proposed that he be the agent for Scioto. Barlow agreed, imagining riches pouring in, and set about to sell what he seemed always to believe were plots of land rather than shares in a company that could give its shareholders only preemption rights, or the first right to buy at whatever price was later determined. Barlow, along with a Britisher named William Playfair, went so far as to organize a whole shipload of eager French men and women to emigrate in a body to the green Ohio valley, where they dreamed of building a city to be called Gallipolis. The Scioto associates were appalled when they heard that colonists were on their way to land that the company did not yet even own. Barlow wrote enthusiastically, "I consider them as the fathers and founders of a nation."[2] Six hundred of them finally arrived in Ohio, where amid arm-waving and downcast hearts the émigrés discovered they had been defrauded by a company composed of the nation's leaders and a poet who was still writing the epic of his land:

> Ages unborn shall bless the happy day,
> That saw thy streamers shape the trackless way,
> While through the growing realms thy sons shall tread,
> And following millions trace the path you led.[3]

The French at Gallipolis drifted away, however, and by 1796 a visitor would have found fewer than one hundred of the unfortunates remaining.

Although the Ohio Company wrested from the government a principality in exchange for a pittance, it nevertheless was a responsible corporation that offered its land purchasers more than just the title to land. The company provided roads, mills to grind wheat, cities, churches, and schools. Marietta, an Ohio town planned on the New England model, was the particular pride of Cutler. Yet the area still lacked a scheme of political relationship to the established states. Since independence, and particularly since 1784 when Jefferson and other congressmen had drafted an early version of such a plan, it was widely assumed that the western lands would move, rather as the colonies themselves had done, toward full, independent statehood within the union. A contrary assumption, as widely held, called for a period of tutelage within which westerners could learn responsibility and prove their stable character.[4] By 1787 these ideas finally jelled in one of the most significant acts of the new nation, the Northwest Ordinance. In its final form it called for the division of the old Northwest into districts, not more than five nor less than three. A governor, secretary, and three judges would be appointed by the Congress to govern each district until it had five thousand male settlers, at which time they could elect an assembly. But the assembly could do no more than nominate ten men from whom the Congress would select five for the legislative council, which functioned as an upper house. The governor had an absolute veto and could select from the laws of the thirteen states those he wished to incorporate into the code of his district. When any district had sixty thousand residents, it could be admitted to the Union on equal terms with the existing states.

The Northwest Ordinance has been called, rather extravagantly, one of America's greatest contributions to political theory. Such praise may be justifiably aimed at the final stage of the plan, namely, the complete equality of the admitted state. With the exception of Texas and California (and Nevada, for which the minimum population regulation was overlooked), all the western states were admitted to the Union in accordance with this ordinance. The policy succeeded because it provided for an orderly abolition of the territorial or colonial status. The ordinance assumed that the best approach to such dependency, as with slavery, was to abolish it.

The law was not, however, a triumph of democracy and self-government. In the Northwest Ordinance's distrust of western self-government and in the undermining of the land ordinance through company grants, the negative attitude of the East toward the West may be discerned. The East seemed to demand that the West mature, throw off its frontier ways, and become heavily populated with easterners before accepting it into eastern society. Some congressmen felt that the only effective way to handle frontier bandits and squatters was to impose strong military control. But Manasseh Cutler believed that such an approach would handicap settlement, so he sought freer, civilian forms. But the Congress would not go too far along the self-government road. In the territorial phase the plan finally adopted was autocratic, reflecting eastern fears of violent mobs and frontier

Daniel Boone, after Chester Harding, 1819.

roughnecks that had been aroused by the Regulators, the Paxton Boys, and Daniel Shays.

The easterner never fully understood the westerner and always held ambiguous attitudes toward him, especially when the westerner was of a different religion or race. Mexican Catholics and Indians were beyond the pale, but sometimes antipathies extended further than these obvious minorities. Any westerner could be the low-down, shiftless, lazy riffraff whom William Byrd described sleeping till noon in a cabin on the fringes of North Carolina, or he could be a magnificent, self-reliant hunter roaming the untrod forest wilderness. The speculator in western lands could be seen as the midwife of civilization, helping growth by providing land and improvements, or he could be considered a rapacious scoundrel making a fast dollar by fleecing the poor farmer. Some of these ambiguities are apparent in the life and legend of Daniel Boone.

Boone was born on the Pennsylvania frontier and consequently had no schooling. He was illiterate and perhaps uncouth. During the

French and Indian War he had hired on as a teamster with Braddock's army, and on campaigns beyond the Appalachians he heard tales of the beautiful bluegrass valleys of Kentucky. When he returned to his farm, he fell in with a land speculator, Judge Richard Henderson. During the winter months, when farming ceased, Boone hired out for the judge to find and claim good western lands while trapping furs for himself. This was more or less his pattern during the winters of 1767 through 1771. Henderson organized the Transylvania Company, which signed on Daniel Boone as its field agent. In 1775 Boone crossed the Appalachians with his own family and other settlers, surveyed land, and established Boonesborough. In the next year the area became a county of Virginia, and Boone became a militia captain. It was wartime, but he was probably far more concerned with protecting his land and settlers from Indians than with fighting the British. He was twice a captive of the Indians and in 1778 displayed his frontier skills in a harrowing escape from the Shawnees. In addition to his work for the Transylvania Company, Boone had staked out claims for some ten thousand acres of land. Such desires to engross land were not atypical. Simon Kenton, one of Boone's contemporaries in Kentucky, wounded nearly to death from Indian torture, returned almost immediately to begin plans for claiming new lands. Boone's titles, however, proved defective, and by 1798 he was sufficiently unhappy to move on, first to West Virginia country and then to the Missouri region. Already a legend, he lived the rest of his life at St. Charles along the Mississippi, died in 1820, somewhat a father image for all frontiersmen.

Boone was many things to many men. On one hand he was a courageous hunter and trapper when not tilling his acres; he was also a shiftless farmer who turned to hunting because it was easier than farming, and whose relentless shooting of game helped shape the myth of American superabundance. He was the bearer of civilization to the undisciplined, pagan wilderness; he was a refugee from corrupt and effete society finding strength and truth in close harmony with nature. He was an illiterate backwoods oaf; he was the dispenser of the true wisdom that flows from natural virtue. A Kentucky hunter, hearing a strange noise in the woods, once cautiously moved up to find "a man bare-headed, stretched flat upon his back on a deerskin, singing at the top of his voice"[5]: it was Boone. He was a lazy drifter, and he was also a free man.

Close to nature, alone, and independent, the free man tended to be a romantic literary and philosophical creation; politically and economically, his situation was not so positive. Perhaps the land, the basic soil, reconciled the disparity. Whether profiting from it or

Boone rescuing his daughter Jemima in 1776, by G. W. Fasel, 1851.

emigrating to it, the easterner became the westerner by virtue of the land. Nothing would be more important than the frequent acquisition of fresh large chunks of land that periodically favored the new nation for three quarters of its first century — the western lands granted in the treaty of 1783, the Louisiana Purchase, Florida, Texas, the Oregon territory, the southwest conquered in the Mexican War, and the Gadsden Purchase. Vine De Loria, the Indian historian, points out that these were not so much transfers of land as of the right to extinguish Indian titles.

Whatever form the land acquisitions took — purchase or Indian dispossession — they have led such historians as Henry Adams and Bernard De Voto to contend that the Louisiana Purchase was "one of the most important events in world history."[6] That diplomatic coup irrevocably turned the nation's eyes westward, held the nation together, brought it incalculable natural wealth, and made possible the emergence of the United States as a world power.

Thomas Jefferson, the key American involved in the purchase, did not foresee its importance. Indeed, he expressed the opinion in 1801, in his first inaugural address, that the nation was already "possessing a chosen country, with room enough for our descendants to the thousandth and thousandth generation."[7] Yet Jefferson's interest in the West was deep and long-standing. In 1793 he had contributed funds to the American botanical explorations of André Michaux. In Europe, he had twice talked to John Ledyard, a young dreamer-explorer, and listened sympathetically to his proposals for western expeditions. One month before his inauguration, he hired Meriwether Lewis to prepare for a major western exploration.

Jefferson probably realized that the settlement and acquisition of Louisiana were likely. Diplomatically his concern was with New Orleans, the outlet for the agricultural produce of the interior. "The day that France takes possession of New Orleans," he wrote in 1802, "seals the union of two nations who, on conjunction, can maintain exclusive possession of the ocean. From that moment we must marry ourselves to the British fleet and nation."[8]

Starting from New Orleans, the boundaries of Louisiana were rough but generally understood to be the Mississippi on the east, the Great Lakes or the Lake of the Woods on the north, the Rocky Mountains on the west, and the northern border of the Spanish province of Texas on the south. In 1762 Louisiana had been transferred by France to Spain as indemnity for Spanish losses of the Floridas to England. Spain's weakness reduced its threat to the United States, unless the Spanish refused to let shipping pass through New Orleans up and down the great river. But Jefferson's worry about France was not unfounded. France had lost interest in the New World after the defeat of 1763, but in the late 1790s the generation under Napoleon began anew to dream imperial dreams. The remaining French islands, such as Haiti in the Caribbean, might be united effectively with the mainland, just as the Spaniards had done under Cortes. When Napoleon invaded Spain, the French dictated the Treaty of San Ildefonso in 1800, which transferred Louisiana back to France. But the treaty was secret, and the Americans knew of it only by rumor.

Napoleon's designs were thwarted by one of the great black soldiers of all time, François Dominique Toussaint L'Ouverture. Toussaint, a plantation slave on Haiti, was educated enough to read Caesar and revolutionary writings. During a slave insurrection in 1790, he applied what he had learned about tactics, quickly rose to leadership, and took the name L'Ouverture (The Opener). By 1798 blacks controlled Haiti. They installed Toussaint as governor for life, and a chill went over parts of the white world. The Haitian revolution was particularly disturbing to Napoleon, and he sent General Charles Leclerc to the island with twenty thousand troops. The largest army Toussaint could raise numbered eight thousand men, but by means of guerrilla war and slogans such as "This gun is your liberty," as well as an outbreak of yellow fever, Toussaint and his people decimated the French troops. There were temporary black surrenders, and Toussaint himself was captured and sent to a French prison where he died in 1803. The rebellion, nevertheless, led to independence for Haiti in 1804 and caused Napoleon to reconsider his plans for the New World. Besides, his attention had begun to center on Europe, and even for Napoleon one continent at a time was enough.

As president, Jefferson had sent three ministers (Livingston, Monroe, and Pinckney) to France to buy New Orleans and thus obviate the problem of Mississippi shipping. When Talleyrand, Napoleon's foreign minister, offered to sell them the whole of Louisiana for $15 million, little more than they had expected to pay for New Orleans, one of the most important comedies in all history ensued. The American ministers cautiously asked Talleyrand precisely what he meant by Louisiana, what its borders might be. His response was, in effect, "whatever it was we took from Spain." Beyond that he prophetically concluded, "You have made a noble bargain for yourselves, and I suppose you will make the most of it."[9]

Jefferson's earlier interest in far western exploration assumed new meaning and even urgency. The planned expedition commanded by Meriwether Lewis and William Clark left its rendezvous camp in the spring of 1804 and became the most illustrious exploring party in American history. Jefferson's stated aims were pragmatic and commercial, though it should be remembered that the Congress, under the Constitution, would make such purposes the basis for appropriating funds. If the expedition could find an easy route across the continent, even though some of it would cross foreign soil, the old hope of a Northwest Passage to India might be resurrected. Such a route would redirect some of the lucrative Canadian fur trade into American channels. More effective ways to exploit the sea otter trade of the northwest coast, and through it the commerce with China, might become corollary gains. The friendship of the Indians, and of England as well, would be essential. Scientific intentions — the investigation of the botany, zoology, and geology of the unknown regions — though they could not appear too prominent in the published listing of the expedition's purposes, were clearly important to both Jefferson and Lewis.

The main body of the forty men toiled up the Missouri and Jefferson rivers to the continental watershed ("the distant fountain of the waters"). On the western slope of the Rockies they followed the

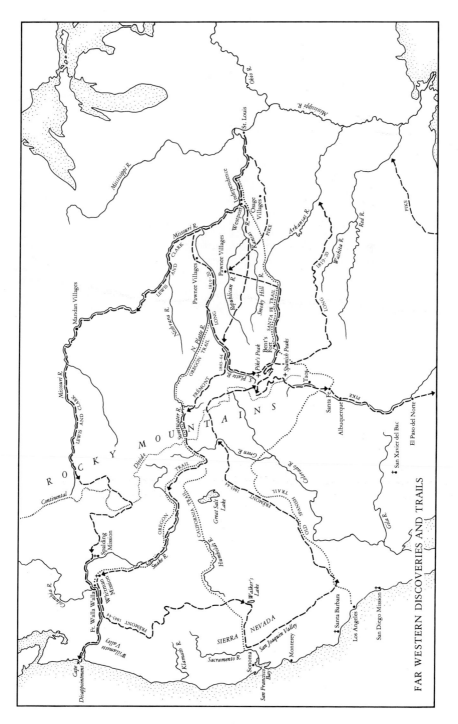

FAR WESTERN DISCOVERIES AND TRAILS

Surveyors in Texas, by John Weyss (1820-1903).

Snake River down to its junction with the Columbia. In the rainy November of 1805 they stood, like latter-day Balboas, on the shores of the Pacific. The return route was almost a reversal of the outgoing, and the hardened band stepped back into civilization in September 1806, twenty-eight months after it had left.

No one could question their bravery, intelligence, frontier skill, planning and foresight, diplomatic finesse, or scientific observation. Modern skeptics, however, point out that the job was not terribly difficult in comparison with other explorations — surveys of the Australian outback, for example, where nature provided little water, food, fuel, or protection from extremes of weather and hostile natives. But the captious commentators cannot obscure for Americans the drama of the Lewis and Clark Expedition, revealed in the eight volumes of their journals: Lewis's long-winded philosophizing on the future route of empire; his diplomacy with the Indians, who on several occasions might have wiped the expedition from the record; Clark, the century's worst speller, providing frontier know-how, as his brother George Rogers Clark had during the Revolution; the unexpected unity in spite of divided leadership; the Shoshone interpreter Sacagawea's endurance bearing her newborn son, and Clark's subsequent adoption of the boy; snowblindness, snakebite, venereal disease, and the one death that occurred (from a burst appendix, which would have been fatal anywhere).

Given the drama, was the trip worthwhile? The commerical purposes were at best only partly realized. A trade route was mapped, but it was not over navigable waterways, and some of it was hard going over the Rockies. The most immediate consequence was the opening of the fur trade in the Far West. In the long view, Lewis and Clark locked Louisiana securely into the minds and plans of the nation and associated the Oregon country with the Louisiana Territory so that Americans thereafter assumed Oregon was their natural preserve. Although it would be another generation before settlement would pour into the Northwest, popular interest was aroused, and men like John Jacob Astor began to incorporate Oregon into their schemes. No other exploration was "so excellent or so influential," wrote Bernard De Voto. "It satisfied desire and it created desire: the desire of a westering nation."[10]

The Lewis and Clark Expedition was the first exploration the young nation mounted and pursued with government encouragement and financial support. It set a pattern, establishing a precedent for a strong government role in the development of the West. The Congress appropriated $2,500 for the task. Historians, in their rush to develop the myth of the self-reliant western pioneer, have tended to overlook the basic preparations for westward expansion undertaken by the government — surveying the land, marking the routes, building the wagon roads, clearing the rivers for navigation, dredging the harbors along the coasts, planning and digging canals, subsidizing railroads, suppressing the protests of Indians, and in general standing close beside the pioneer as he elbowed his way to the Pacific. It should be noted, too, that the explorer seldom ventured into the wilderness without Indian guides.

Before Lewis and Clark returned, the army had other expeditions in the field. Zebulon Pike, for example, was ordered in 1805 to seek the sources of the Mississippi. He was largely unsuccessful. In the following year he set out for the headwaters of the Arkansas, which he failed to reach, and was supposed to return along the Red River, which he missed, following the Canadian River instead. He found Pike's Peak but did not manage to scale it. Needless to say, Pike's importance to history should not be sought in his skill as an explorer. Rather he is remembered for a climactic mishap — his capture by New Spain on the 1806 expedition. Knowing full well that as Pike moved southward in the Louisiana Territory he would approach the vague boundary with New Spain, the army had instructed him to

Oto Indians in council with the Stephen Long Expedition,
by Samuel Seymour, 1819.

move "with great circumspection." It was indeed a tricky area, fraught with international intrigue. Pike has been charged with involvement in the conspiracy of Aaron Burr and General James Wilkinson to promote a secession of the Louisiana Territory from the United States.

We may never know whether Pike's capture by the Spanish in the upper valley of the Rio Grande resulted from ignorance of geography or from deliberate spying on a neighboring state. At any rate, he was taken to Santa Fe and then to Chihuahua, in northern Mexico, as a political prisoner. His papers were confiscated, and he was carefully questioned before release. When he returned to the settlements, his tales about the two cities he had seen set commercial minds spinning. Without trade from the sea, both Santa Fe and Chihuahua needed all kinds of manufactured articles, blankets, knives, whisky, and kettles, and for exchange they had furs and precious metals. Pike set in motion ideas that would finally crystallize as the Santa Fe trade.

Meanwhile in the Ohio valley westerners had once more set their seal on expansion, this time in the form of war against England. The so-called war hawks of 1812 boldly called for the United States to face the fact that its conflict with the British at sea had its counterpart on land. Why not defeat the redcoats so soundly that all of Canada would be joined to the young United States? The drive, of course, was thwarted, and the imperialist destiny postponed.

The next significant explorer of the West was Stephen Long, a Phi Beta Kappa from Dartmouth, who had joined the Topographical Corps of the army after teaching mathematics at West Point. The corps sent him to the upper Mississippi in 1817 (he called it "a vogage in a six-oared skiff") and then to the Rocky Mountains in 1819. In the report of the latter survey he likened the Great Plains — now Kansas, Nebraska, Oklahoma, and eastern Colorado — to African deserts; pathless, barren, glaring, and inhospitable land whose sole monarch was the prickly pear, and chief inhabitant the horned toad. The region was, in short, the great American desert. If there was any value to the plains, it would be negative — as a buffer against foreign invasion and "a barrier to prevent too great extension of our population westward."[11] Long did not originate the idea; Pike had written much the same a dozen years before, but Long made it stick for at least a generation.

The desert myth that settled over the Great Plains contained elements of truth, for given the existing level of agricultural technology, the area would not be productive except for mining or grazing. Not until the last third of the nineteenth century did men devise means to break the sod, bring up water, and build transport to make life there bearable; still, attempting to cultivate that soil may have been faulty, for it led to the tragedy of the Dust Bowl in the 1930s. Modern conservationists tend to give Long credit for understanding the use and potential misuse of that land.

In the early nineteenth century the government increasingly became involved in the emergent West. One sign of its interest was the growing autonomy of the Topographical Corps, which by act of Congress in 1838 began reporting directly to the secretary of war. The scientific orientation of the corps was clear; its officers frequently represented the scientific community in organizations such as the American Philosophical Society, where Jefferson and Lewis had worked. The fraternization of science and government was encouraged by the founding of the Smithsonian Institution in Washington, D.C., in 1846. The Topographical Corps cooperated closely with these and other eastern scientific groups to plan observations and collections in the West. Printed reports of the corp's expeditions typically included expensive illustrations and appendixes detailing the botany, zoology, geology, meteorology, ethnology, and cartography of the new land. Scientists were still engaged in identifying and classifying, still trying to complete the great catalogue of the earth's plants and animals.

The interior of North America, like its shrouded counterparts in Asia and Africa, bore the answers to questions about the relations between species and the development of life on the planet.

John Charles Frémont became, if not the most typical, at least the most controversial product of the bond between science and government. An illegitimate child, Frémont had an eye for opportunity that may have been related to the insecurity of his birth. He took advantage of one friendship to get a naval appointment, which enabled him to master mathematics and engineering. With these scientific tools at his command, he caught his next golden ring in the courtship and marriage of Jessie Benton, daughter of Thomas Hart Benton, senator from Missouri and a powerful voice in Washington. Benton's contacts were strung along all the lines of command, and he cried out for attention to the needs of the West — greater support for explorations and surveys, land developers, and railroads. Jessie had inherited her father's outlook, energy, and iron will. When he opposed her marriage to the young, little-known Frémont, Jessie defied him and eloped.

Frémont's first assignment with the Topographical Corps was in 1842. He led a small surveying party up the Platte River to an easy route, the South Pass and the Wind River Mountains. His second expedition, in 1843 to 1844, spread Frémont's reputation nationwide. Carefully planned with Benton, the secretary of war, and even President Tyler himself, it surveyed what would be known as the Oregon Trail — up the Platte, through the South Pass in the Rockies, along the Snake, and down the Columbia. Through Frémont's report and the help it would give to migrants, they hoped to reinforce the American claim to Oregon. Fearing trouble with the British, Frémont's men pulled a howitzer the whole way. Washington ordered him back upon learning of the cannon, but Jessie stubbornly withheld the orders until her husband had gotten beyond reach.

The diplomats wished the expedition to appear strictly scientific, and science did remain its primary, though not sole, motivation. Frémont and his party brought the best European equipment — barometers, field telescopes, chronometers, and all the rest — taking special pains that they not be jostled or cracked. They calculated innumerable latitudes, longitudes, and elevations and observed such phenomena as the emergence of the first satellite of Jupiter. They collected fossils from the rocks, new plants (such as *Fremontia*), and hundreds of birds, fish, and mammals.

Frémont always loved the feeling of being first on the scene, and as he looked over the alkaline waters of the Great Salt Lake, he knew how Balboa must have felt. He thrilled to the fact that the voices of his party were the first human voices to drift over its sterile waters.

*John C. Frémont on "highest" peak of Rocky Mountains,
lithograph, 1856.*

(He ignored the Indians, equating "human" with "white man.") His greatest scientific contribution on this expedition was mapping the land he covered after leaving the Columbia — around Mt. Hood, down the Des Chutes River to the Great Basin, west across the Sierra Nevada through snowdrifts, south of Carson Pass into the Sacramento valley, and eventually home by the southern route. Jessie helped him polish his report, and it became a best-seller, exciting talk in thousands of eastern drawing rooms.

The style and presentation of the report indicated that it was more than a scientific treatise. Attention to availability of water and fuel, grass for pasturage, the ease of the grade — all spoke to immigrants. Frémont emphatically dispelled the idea of a great American desert. Unlike the useless region Long described, he found that "the soil of all this country is excellent, admirably adapted to agricultural purposes, and would support a large agricultural and pastoral population."[12] He gave the impression that immigration had begun. Domesticated cows released from wagon trains had been spotted among buffalo herds, and crude graves of travelers suggested that not all had survived the trip. Armchair readers who might consider going west because of the fur trade rather than the soil might have noticed that

Frémont's guides — Kit Carson, Thomas Fitzpatrick, and Lucien Maxwell — were unemployed trappers. Throughout the report the message was clear: the Far West was open for farmers, and the diplomats would have to recognize that in the press for settlement would be lodged the seeds of sovereignty. Frémont was so right that in his next expedition he threw off completely the garb of botanist and mathematician and assumed the cape of conqueror. The force of men who wanted land involved both science and the government in a drive called Manifest Destiny.

4

The Fur Trade and Freedom

In 1806 when Meriwether Lewis returned to the settlements from the Pacific with William Clark, he described the region of the upper Missouri River as "richer in beaver and otter than any country on earth."[1] The beaver was native to almost all North America. Sea otters, fur seals, sables, and martens flourished on the coasts; panthers, deer, and buffalo knew more restricted habitats in mountain and basin. The pelts of these creatures varied in value, and the profitability of the fur trade fluctuated according to far-distant demands.

To anyone, furs were warm and beautiful. In the Middle Ages only nobles and clergymen had the right to wear particular furs, such as ermine and sable. Supplies of furs from Russia and Scandinavia were seriously declining at about the time the New World was opening for Europe. In the eighteenth century the frantic pursuit of sea otters — leading nearly to their extinction — was stimulated by the mandarin courts of China. The beaver trade of North America reached major proportions when European men fancied tall, broad-brimmed, stove-pipe hats of slick beaver fur. Handsome headgear, its beauty played a part in fashioning the whole frontier of North America.

In New France and New England the fur trade grew quickly into one of the first large-scale corporate businesses on the continent. A board of directors sitting in London, Paris, New York, Montreal, or St. Louis coordinated a far-flung net of field workers; supplied them with traps, horses, food, boats, whisky, and trinkets for Indians; indicated the best routes for the largest returns; and prepared, collected, warehoused, and distributed the pelts.

Setting traps for beaver, by Alfred Jacob Miller, 1837.

The Muscovy Company trading out of London in the sixteenth century had dealt in furs, and there were many French companies, often sheltered by royal grants of privilege, the most famous of which was the Company of the Hundred Associates. But the prototype for the New World was chartered in 1670 under the name of the Governor and Company of Adventurers of England Trading into Hudson's Bay, rendered simply as Hudson's Bay Company. Its charter gave it a monopoly over the vast icy regions lying to the north of New France. The rich fur harvests along the fringe of New France and New England would produce commercial competition mirrored in an almost constant state of war between the two nations. The conflict continued until the French lost political control, at least symbolically, on the Plains of Abraham in the French and Indian War. After the peace treaty in 1763, the Hudson's Bay Company was not the only contender for the French trade, but its power and prestige were so great that its enemies soon used its initials to stand for "Here Before Christ." It became the Rolls Royce Corporation of its day — conservative and orthodox in business methods and very British in attitude.

The years after the French and Indian War unbridled a cutthroat competition between companies for the fur trade. The French, under the influence of their Jesuit missionaries, had officially outlawed the giving of liquor to the Indian. Now such restrictions were lifted, and whisky became an article of trade in an explosively competitive situation. Scotsmen, Englishmen, and French Canadians all vied for the best routes and for tribal advantages, and the Indians, as usual, suffered mightily. A group of traders, hoping to bring profit out of commercial confusion, worked out a partnership, the North West Company, chartered with a geographical monopoly in 1784. For a time it rivaled even the Hudson's Bay Company. The Nor'Westers, as the new men were called, had a special spirit and manner about them. They seemed more boisterous than the Hudson's Bay men; many were French Canadians and even more were Highland Scots. The company's rosters were sprinkled with McDougalls, MacDonalds, MacTavishes, and Stuarts. Its distant posts came to be fraternal centers, and Washington Irving described the Nor'Westers as feudal "lords of the lakes and forests," "hyperborean nabobs" engaged in "baronial wassailing."

The North West Company with all its color and flair was as natural a magnet for restless energies as the life of a cowboy would later be. One young spirit, John McLoughlin, as a boy in Quebec had watched Nor'Westers swagger through the streets. Sent to Scotland to become a medical doctor, he dutifully finished his training, but when he returned to New France in 1804, barely out of his teens, he abandoned Hippocrates and apprenticed himself to the North West Company. At the beginning of the nineteenth century there was another hectic period of rampant competition. Partnerships came and went; relations with the Indians were subverted with empty promises and whisky; the lure of high profit was coupled with a rising demand and no control over the unscrupulous. The two great firms were not immune from fraud and sharp practice, and the British government in desperation forced them to combine in an effort to curb the excesses. Thus in 1821 the North West Company was absorbed into its predecessor. McLoughlin weathered the period, and a few years later he reached a sufficient level of importance in the Hudson's Bay Company to be placed in charge of its operations in the Far West. He had become a partner in the firm, an exalted position that had come because of his good judgment and devotion. Whether his prematurely white hair, a distinguishing characteristic, resulted from the strain of ambition no one can say; his dignified appearance certainly did not hurt his rise to executive status. Ensconced on the Columbia River in the Oregon country, McLaughlin came to symbolize probity and Britain. The natives loved him and may have given him the title White-headed

Eagle. But whether the term was used or not, he was as proud and regal as the cloud-crested bird, and from 1824 to 1845 he majestically dominated the Northwest.

One of the first fortunes amassed in the United States was built on furs. John Jacob Astor was a stout, arrogant man who never lost the accent of his native Germany. He had left home early, joining his brother in a small musical instrument shop in London. Waiting until the American Revolution was over, he emigrated to the new land, taking with him his worldly capital — seven flutes. On the advice of a fellow German traveler, he transferred his interests from flutes to furs and thereby laid the foundation for a fortune that would let him die with assets of around $20 million, the richest man in America.[2]

Lewis and Clark returned in 1806 with their accounts of the land the United States had just acquired from France. In 1808 Astor, already a millionaire, was quick to form the American Fur Company to exploit the Louisiana Purchase. He dreamed of a financial empire controlled from a post at the mouth of the Columbia River on the Pacific coast, where furs from the interior would be shipped to the Orient. Astor knew that the British claimed the area and that the North West Company, for one, would fight hard to keep him out. In 1811 Astor sent a ship, the *Tonquin*, which mounted twelve guns and was laden with thirty-three young Scots and Canadian voyageurs and enough supplies (including molasses and gin) to build a fortified post, to be called Astoria, near the mouth of the Columbia. Jonathan Thorn, its master, turned out to be a murderous, if not mad, captain. He was on leave from the Navy, a veteran of the war with the Tripolitanian pirates, and a kind of Captain Bligh with his men. He was quick-tempered, haughty, and cruel; and, because he hated the sound of both a Scottish burr and a French accent, he was hardly the man to be involved with a trade so heavily loaded with Scotsmen and Frenchmen. The voyage was colored from the start with quarrels, suspicions of mutiny, and harsh disciplinary acts. There were also serious accidents, such as the loss of eight men who drowned searching for the channel at the mouth of the Columbia. Once the ship reached shore, the back-breaking work of construction got under way. The *Tonquin* sailed north to Vancouver Island for some trading. In the haggling, Captain Thorn, true to his character, provoked the Indians, whom he also hated, into a surprise attack on the ship. In the consequent melee the captain and so many of the crew were killed that the ship became helpless. In a vicious final bloody scene, a single remaining white man waited until the largest possible number of Indians were aboard or nearby and then blew up the ship, killing himself and at least a hundred natives.

Tales around the campfire, by Alfred Jacob Miller, 1837.

Astor had not placed all his hope in the *Tonquin*; he had also planned an overland expedition to establish Astoria. Wilson Price Hunt, its leader and a partner of the company, was less experienced with western overland travel than Thorn had been with the sea, and, like Thorn, encountered mountainous difficulties reaching the site of Astoria. Hunt left the Missouri settlements in April 1811, with a small group of company partners and some fifty voyageurs. Through the summer and fall and into the early winter they carried Astor's hopes into the face of almost every obstacle the wilderness could raise. Voyageurs plotted and deserted, Indians grew hostile, horses ran off, men were lost (necessitating long digressive search parties), boats were built for river transport and then were wrecked and discarded. At times hunger, thirst, cold, sickness, and death rode with the men; toward the end they splintered into isolated, struggling groups. Hunt himself reached Astoria in the cold February of 1812, ten months after leaving the Missouri settlements.

By 1813 Astor calculated that his investment at Astoria had been in the neighborhood of $200,000.[3] The amount would not have been excessive if the grand scheme had eventually come to pass. However,

Jonathan Thorn and Wilson Price Hunt had turned Astor's dream into a minor nightmare. Another blow to the venture was the War of 1812, which placed the business rivalry of the American Fur Company in a much more serious context. Before the war, Astor had been free to hire former Nor'Westers as executives and voyageurs. When two nations are at war, such transfer of allegiance ceases to be easy. At any rate, in October 1813, Indian summer along the Columbia, one of Astor's field partners signed the deed of Astoria over to the North West Company for $58,000. The Nor'Westers, true to form, jubilantly raised the British flag, broke a bottle of wine, and renamed Astoria Fort George, while the local Indians looked on in bewilderment, expecting the Americans to become slaves. Even under the new name the settlement was abandoned shortly thereafter for a better location farther up the river, Fort Vancouver. The North West Company became part of the Hudson's Bay Company in 1821, so when John McLoughlin arrived in the Oregon country the area was wholly British. A later generation of Americans, in the 1840s, would lay new claims to the Oregon country, which would be based not upon furs but upon farms.

The American Fur Company was based in the East, and it was logical that another center of trade would grow up in St. Louis. The Missouri and Mississippi rivers converged near that point, and frontiersmen from the young nation were ready to strike out for the upper Missouri where waited, as one of them said, "a wealth of furs not surpassed by the mines of Peru."[4] That expanding interest was seen in John Colter's experiences between 1806 and 1808. Colter had been a scout on the Lewis and Clark Expedition. As the Lewis and Clark party moved in 1806 down the Missouri on the last lap of its long trip, two Illinois hunters met them in camp near the Mandan Indian villages. Already on their way to trap along the upper Missouri, these men offered John Colter a share in their enterprise if he would guide them. Colter, accepting the offer, turned around and went back to the mountains for the winter. In the next spring, at the mouth of the Platte, he met another trapping party on its way up the Missouri. It was led by Manuel Lisa who persuaded Colter to turn around and go once more into the mountains. On this expedition Colter discovered and explored the Yellowstone country.

Manuel Lisa, in 1807, was just beginning his major schemes in the fur trade. Half French, half Spanish, half fox, half grinning alligator, Lisa had moved up the river from New Orleans as a boy of eighteen looking for his big chance. When Lewis and Clark returned, he was thirty-four, a ripe age for the frontier, and he immediately set into motion plans to organize and exploit the newly mapped lands. After

"Trapper's Last Shot," after William Ranney (1813-1857).

some lesser ventures like that with Colter, in 1808 he formed the Missouri Fur Company which, after his death in 1820, grew into the first large St. Louis–based outfit. In one happy business season Lisa made $35,000.

The fur market had its ups and downs. In a long period of depression during and after the War of 1812, international trade patterns caused serious economic dislocation. But in the 1820s prosperity for the fur trade returned. Men like William Ashley, respected citizen of St. Louis, brigadier-general of the militia, and lieutenant governor of Missouri, moved to invest in it. With a jutting chin that matched the strength and confidence he conveyed to others, Ashley motivated a series of partnerships that merged and failed and reorganized one into the other.

At about this time, a clean-cut, serious, straitlaced, blue-eyed boy, who did not, and never would, swear or smoke, appeared in St. Louis and was hired by Ashley for one of the general's first trapping ventures in the mountains. Jedediah Strong Smith, later to become one of Ashley's partners, spent only a decade in the West, but he firmly left his stamp upon it. He discovered the great South Pass through the Rockies (near the eventual construction site of the Union Pacific Railroad) and was the first white man to enter California over the Sierra Nevada. His physical endurance allowed him to cover the West like Paul Bunyan, with steps too large to be believed. As Dale Lowell Morgan has said, "he saw and was familiar with [the land] from the Missouri River to the Pacific, from Mexico to Canada."[5]

In 1823 on one of his first trips deep into the Rockies, Smith had occasion to demonstrate his physical makeup. He was faced suddenly with the fear and terror of all mountainmen — a grizzly bear, huge, menacing, and on the attack. He was mauled nearly to death. Some of his ribs were broken, one ear was hanging loose, and his scalp was exposed to the bone. Still conscious, Smith instructed his friends to take out needle and thread and sew up the skin of his head and ear, which they fearfully did. He drank some cold water. Though shaken, he mounted his horse and rode to camp.

Endurance, however, was not an uncommon ingredient in such men. What set Smith apart was his moralistic righteousness based on a religious quest. He bore a heavy weight of guilt. "O, the perverseness of my wicked heart," he wrote. "I entangle myself altogether too much in the things of time." Instead of tramping the wilderness, he felt he should be helping the poor, "those who stand in need," wherever they were.[6] But the wilderness, giving him few opportunities to help the poor, tended to turn him in on himself and intensify his feelings of guilt. The sense of guilt coupled with a vague search for personal fulfillment is an interesting phenomenon, and it may have appeared often enough on the frontier to explain some of the restlessness. At any rate, Smith probably never resolved his frustrations. He died thirsty and alone, his mouth undoubtedly still unprofaned, but his body shot through with Comanche lances.

In 1830, the year before he died, Smith had sold out to a new partnership, the Rocky Mountain Fur Company. Most of the men on its roster were what modern historian Don Berry called "a majority of scoundrels," but some of these scoundrels have attained in the American mind the stature of legends — Jim Bridger, Mike Fink, and Hugh Glass.[7]

Bridger was a tall, intelligent man who, like John McLoughlin, had been drawn to the fur trade as a boy. He came to know the northern Rockies better than any other white man, and, though he remained illiterate, his mind was an atlas of the peaks, passes, and meadows. He took three successive Indian wives — a Flathead, a Snake, and a Ute — and had four children. He got into trouble with the Mormons, but all others seemed to respect Jim Bridger as a man who shared abundantly the "land wisdom" of the Indians.

Mike Fink was riding high. As the "Snapping Turtle" of the Ohio River, he had begun to attract the legend-makers. A daring, courageous sharpshooter, "a figure cast in a mould that added much of the symmetry of an Apollo to the limbs of a Hercules,"[8] he could maneuver the heaviest keelboat through the murkiest water. That was the way folk tradition would recall him. At this time he was a brash young man, wandering west, and answering Ashley's call for mountain men. In view of Fink's experience on the Ohio and the Mississippi, Ashley must have hired him to help with the boats going up the Missouri. Upon his arrival in beaver country, Fink was sent off on a side excursion with two other men. Once, after fighting and ostensibly making up, Fink and his reconciled friends agreed to play the old William Tell game — to shoot a cup of whisky off each other's heads from a distance of sixty yards. Fink, however, shot the bearer of the cup through the head. The third man, realizing the shot could hardly have been an accident, Fink being the marksman he was, eventually found an occasion to shoot Fink. Thus died the man who became the legendary heir to Hercules and Apollo.

The character of Hugh Glass may not have been strikingly better than that of Fink, but it illustrates courage and stamina similar to that of Jedediah Smith. In an attack by a mother grizzly with cubs, Glass's throat was torn open and his body covered with bleeding lacerations. Abandoned by his friends as dead, he eventually pulled himself to a spring, ate berries and carcasses left by wolves, inched across present-day South Dakota, surprised his trapping fraternity, and a few weeks after his ordeal set out on another expedition.

In spite of (or maybe because of) its striking personnel, the Rocky Mountain Fur Company lasted only four years and was sold in 1834, nearly bankrupt. Small companies suffered increasingly from competition, and the Rocky Mountain had had a particular setback from a robbery. As usual, the big enterprises profited from the losses of the small: the Rocky Mountain's collapse benefited the American Fur Company, and Astor's fortune must have grown a little larger.

The French brought to the fur trade the idea of going out and living with the Indian; the British added posts of lordly "baronial wassailing." The Americans contributed the rendezvous, which produced the heyday of the free trapper. Few other assemblies, except perhaps medieval tournaments or New Orleans Mardi Gras celebrations, have matched the color of the American fur rendezvous. It was conceived by the sedate General Ashley as a device for saving the

Indian encampment near Green River rendezvous,
by Alfred Jacob Miller, 1837.

expense of establishing posts scattered around the country. The trading companies would determine a location a year in advance, any one of a thousand green meadows with streams and timber — in the Wind River Mountains, along the banks of the Bear or the Green, in Jackson's Hole or Pierre's Hole. There for a week in July or August, the poorest season for trapping, the mountain men would straggle in, their mules top-heavy with the season's harvest of skins. The eastern companies' caravans converged with those of merchants drawn like bears to the honey of profit, which was often several hundred percent. Indians would come, sometimes whole tribes, to barter furs or just to watch. And there was plenty to see.

As if they were sailors home from a long vogage, the trappers were ready for a wild debauch. Whisky from St. Louis and *aguardiente* (alcohol with red peppers) from Taos were drunk by the barrel. Glass trinkets went to Indian girls, compliant in the soft grasses. There were fights among drunken men, duels among the sober, gambling everywhere — on horse and footraces, at cards and dice. The lilt of a French-Canadian song ("A la Claire Fontaine") might melt into a Highland fling or the male half of a Mexican fandango. Black slaves might sing of home. A big rendezvous would attract more than a thousand trappers and traders. Imagine such a setting — sundown behind the Teton ridges, hundreds of tepees and tents, the smoke of woodfires rising above the cedars, the sounds and smells!

In the flush years of the late 1820s, traders, if not trappers, made handsome returns at the rendezvous. In 1825 Ashley took home furs worth nearly $50,000; in 1826 he made enough to retire with a fortune. Even in 1832, when competition was getting stiffer, the Rocky Mountain Fur Company took back furs worth $85,000.

Ashley had conceived of the rendezvous as a benefit to the companies. He did not foresee that it would also make the companies less stable by providing an ideal outlet for the free trapper, who worked for himself alone and sold his season's catch to the highest bidder. In the 1820s and '30s the free trapper became the backbone of the American trade. A beautiful example was old Bill Williams, the man whom Ralph Gabriel used in his book *The Course of American Democratic Thought* as an opening symbol for the extreme individualism of the nineteenth century.

William Sherley Williams was more religious in early life than was Jedediah Smith. He was only sixteen when he got the call in 1803 and started preaching as a hell-storming itinerant Baptist in Missouri. That was the year of the Louisiana Purchase, which turned his, like his country's, eyes west. A few years later he was taking the Word to the Osage Indians. Conversion followed: the Osages converted Williams. He settled down with them, took an Osage wife, and had two daughters. For the rest of his life he seemed to be deepening his Indian religious beliefs; he embraced the transmigration of souls, for example, and through revelations projected his own reincarnation as an unusually marked elk. His friends were warned that when, after his death, they saw his antlered head raised in the meadows, they were not to shoot; Old Bill would indeed still be roaming his wilderness.

The man thus stood between two cultures yet was an intimate part of neither. He became the lonely trapper, working when he wished and in the service of none. When his Osage wife died, he guided a party southwest to New Mexico. He tried once to open a little general store in Taos, but sitting behind the counter so irked him that he threw the bolts of cloth down the streets like rolls of confetti, laughed at the squaws and señoritas fighting over the pieces, and took off for his only true home, the mountains. He grew close to the Ute Indians who, like the Osages, adopted him, and he took a Ute wife.

Even in his own day he was the subject of tall tales among the trappers. Over six feet tall, redheaded, his pants smelly and shiny with grease, he was called Old Solitaire as well as Old Bill. He lived, still active, into his sixties (though for trappers the title "old" was more an honor than a description). He remained a loner, keeping his

Joseph Walker and his Indian wife, by Alfred Jacob Miller, 1837.

favorite trapping grounds secret and never working with more than a few others at a time. Though a "squaw man," he left his Indian wives at home. He was the patriarch of the mountains but ruled over none but his lone, free self. If freedom is defined as the absence of external restraint, then a mountain man like old Bill Williams may well be a supreme example of a free man, and in American thought and legend he has often been so considered. In such an evaluation, the engagé in a company's complex organization is overlooked in favor of the free trapper. He achieved, in William Brandon's words, "a high point of freedom in the career of humankind."[9] The idea is based on the nine-teenth-century belief in nature as a source of virtue. If, however, freedom is more of an internal state of mind and is founded on the self-confidence that comes from accepting perfect law, then we need to know more about the mountain man, chiefly whether he was psychologically content. It is arguable, though not provable, that he was frustrated and even maladjusted, that his apparent aversion to society was based on a restless pursuit of something he could neither find nor define. Jedediah Smith, once hallucinating from thirst and hunger, said he dreamed not of gold and honor but of family, friends, and home. A quest for freedom that becomes a relentless prod to move on into widening circles of loneliness, even selfishness, is a shallow purpose at best. It personifies the insight of William Goetzmann, who has described the mountain man as the prototype of Jacksonian individualism, the private-profit entrepreneur.[10]

Whatever his philosophy, the mountain man notched the wilderness at will. His main contribution to history was as explorer. He was unscientific and did not know his latitude from his longitude. But those who did, the later cartographers, the Frémonts and the Pikes, would have been helpless without the mountain man as scout and guide. When the heyday of the fur trade was over in the 1840s, the mountain man, trapped by history into becoming a tamed employee, led the immigrants across the plains and through the passes.

De Voto imagined that the trapper serenely pulled the wilderness round him "like a robe."[11] If so, the robe was of Indian design. This "white Indian" worked and lived intimately with the red Indians. He traded with them and picked their brains; he fought with and against them in battle and appreciated their courage. He recognized their savagery. (What went on in Jedediah Smith's pious mind as he watched his Sioux comrades in battle dismembering their enemy dead and dragging the pieces over the ground in glee?) To the mountain man the Indian was friend and enemy, tender wife or temporary whore. He knew the Indian naked or resplendent in dress; at times he esteemed him less than he did the beaver, at others, more highly than he did the wind spirits on the peaks. In short, he knew the Indian too well to generalize. The Indian woman had been vital to the economy of her tribe, and when she became the wife of a white trapper, her role in the trade was equally important. Work and home were one to her. The trapper, in turn, knew that she could increase his opportunities through tribe and kin. If we can generalize from Sylvia Van Kirk's study of such unions in western Canada, the marriages were seldom casual and illicit but were far deeper, developing into close-knit family units.[12]

The trapper's attitude toward the Indian was humane, automatically accounting for the range of individual differences within a racial group. Whether the same could be said for his approach to such minority groups as the blacks and the Mexicans is difficult to say. Some trappers owned black slaves; Jedediah Smith, for example, bought two slaves as an investment. At the lowest, "proletarian" level of the fur trade, there was so much mixed blood, especially French and

*Persistence of the fur trade: Indians trading skins in North Dakota
in the late nineteenth century.*

Indian, that it is doubtful whether the Mexican would have been much noticed. Farther up the social ladder in the hierarchy of the companies, however, the half-breed was increasingly the outcast.

Economics certainly affected racial attitudes: Indians who fit well into the fur trade were considered good; those who did not were bad. Thus natives along the California coast who were no help at all with furs came off rather poorly, while such tribes as the Nez Percé and the Flatheads, industrious trappers and cooperative traders, emerged virtuous. Sometimes attitudes toward a tribe would shift. For instance, George Simpson of the Hudson's Bay Company described Chippewa men as cunning, cowardly, and disgraceful to human nature, when they were independent and obstreperous; but seven years later, after the same Indians had submitted to the orderly dictates of the company, Simpson found them provident, sober, and admirable.[13] When the illustrious Ashley wrote a generous character reference of the Flatheads, attempting to correct a cruelty charge against them, his humanitarianism may have been colored by his company's good business relations with the tribe. But here, as always, the wellsprings of men's attitudes are hard to identify.

The trapper did his job so well that there was some danger that his target, the beaver, would become extinct. When he was superintendent of Indian affairs at St. Louis in 1830, William Clark talked about "a very perceptible decrease of the furred animals; this is attributed in part to the circumstance of their being hunted and trapp'd by the Whites as well as Indians."[14] By the 1840s whole valleys were trapped out. Lewis and Clark had heard the constant slapping of beaver tails. When Prince Maximilian, a German potentate-traveler-scientist, came through the same area during the same season thirty years later, he rarely heard the sound at all. Between Lewis and Clark and Maximilian the trappers had intervened. James Ohio Pattie once witnessed the destructive tactics of the mountain man. He was following a party of trappers down the Gila River. The group in the lead had so scoured the valley that Pattie could locate not a single animal, but when he ranged ahead of the others, he took thirty-seven beaver on the first night. Such intensive trapping, with no thought for the following season, was typical. In 1834 men of the Rocky Mountain Fur Company, experts all, announced one of their chief reasons for quitting: the supply of beaver had simply slipped too low.

We can only guess at the total number of beaver killed. In 1800 more than two hundred forty-five thousand beaver skins were exported from eastern ports alone. A little later one English ship carried more than twenty-one thousand pelts to Canton. Extrapolating from such shreds of evidence, and assuming a continuous rate of destruction, we must conclude that the beaver might not have held out. What saved the beaver was a decline in the market for its pelt: fashions changed. Silk hats became the mode, and the price of pelts slumped. The last real rendezvous was in 1840; in the following year only a few wagons met a handful of dispirited trappers. The trade continued, focusing on other kinds of fur, with less frantic activity and greater control by large companies. By the 1850s, once more large numbers of beaver tails slapped the waters of the upper Missouri country, but few free trappers heard them.

5

The Settlement of
Texas and Oregon

Settlement was the key to America's conquest of the continent. Common men, unmoneyed farmers and artisans, craved a piece of land, and such people were more powerful than soldiers in establishing sovereignty over the West. The Spaniards, the Mexicans, the French, and later the English all lost territory because American settlers shoved into their dominions. Other empires did not feel the internal dynamics of such a population surge. The governments of Spain and Mexico prodded and subsidized to get farmers to move into the northern borderlands of Texas and California. The results were lukewarm. The English, late in the eighteenth and early in the nineteenth centuries, succeeded only in establishing fur posts flung like distant stars across the map of the Far West, with few settlers between them. But, beginning in the 1820s and climaxing in the 1840s, Americans pushed and tugged their wagons and cattle west. In "Western Star" the American poet Stephen Vincent Benét pondered the force: "I think it must be something in the blood. Perhaps it's only something in the air."

The settlers did not go unaided. The federal government surveyed and explored for these men. The land itself, which Frederick Jackson Turner called "nature's richest gift," lay cheap, or so men expected. Other resources, such as timber and gold, were sometimes promised. Speculators advertised frantically to whip up desire and, belatedly, the government sent armies for protection. Yet none of these measures would have mattered without the settlers' readiness to take the soil. They were the catalyst and recipient, the cause and the reward. The push of people into Texas and Oregon may be viewed as case studies of the phenomenal impact of settlement.

Spain and Mexico successively understood the need for larger populations along their vulnerable northern frontier. In the eighteenth century New Spain hoped to inject vitality into the area by creating more effective administrative units, and formation of the province of Texas was one effort to encourage development. Texas was a sprawling country, with a spirit as wide as its prairie and as contradictory as its winds. In the north and west it stretched into dry sandy plains; in the south, it rolled in thick savannahs of knee-deep grass; in the northeast, it rose in woods and hillsides. Before 1762, while France remained in the picture, the northern boundary of Texas was claimed by the French to be as far south as the Rio Grande, though Spanish settlements were already on the Red River, more than four hundred miles to the northeast. The boundaries were made no clearer in subsequent transactions; in fact, sometimes the diplomatic ambiguities were deliberate. Not until 1819, in the treaty which ceded Florida to the United States from Spain, was the northern boundary of Texas fixed at the Sabine–32nd parallel–Red River line. Thus the eastern and some of the northern boundary was firmly established. The rest would be determined by war.

Whatever the political boundaries of the land, there were men from the United States, if not from Mexico, who were ready to profit from its untapped resources. One speculator was a Connecticut Yankee by the name of Moses Austin. With restless energy, Austin moved to St. Louis in 1797, where as an upright man he took an oath of allegiance to his new country, Spain. He applied his skills to lead mining in the region south of St. Louis. Lead, of course, was an important frontier commodity, chiefly for ammunition, and Austin prospered. The Louisiana Purchase in 1803 transferred his enterprise to American sovereignty. With humorless perseverance, he rose in the society, and founded the Bank of St. Louis. Following reverses in the panic of 1819, Austin's eyes roved southward to Texas on the fringe of New Spain. He traveled there, was convinced of its prosperous future, and planned for a grant of land and colonization.

New Spain, the government with which he had to deal, had developed serious internal fractures leading to a generation of political discord. In 1810 Father Miguel Hidalgo had cried aloud from the village of Dolores for reforms and independence from Spain. An outbreak occurred in 1813 led by José María Morelos. It was quelled, but a coup in 1821 placed Augustín de Iturbide at the head of the move-

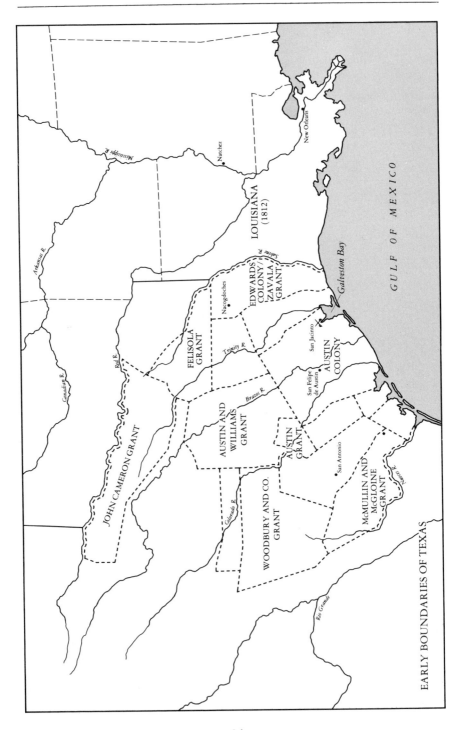

EARLY BOUNDARIES OF TEXAS

ment for independence. Iturbide was deposed in 1823, and the subsequent Republic of Mexico under its Constitution of 1824 severed forever the political cords with Spain.

Austin's application for land was eventually granted by the Spanish government — two hundred thousand acres of rich soil along the Colorado River — but in June 1821, before he could lead his colonists to the new Canaan, he was fatally stricken with pneumonia. Normally death would have conquered the dream, but Austin had a son who received his father's dying injunction to carry on the Texas enterprise. Young Stephen Austin had been schooled at a private academy in Connecticut. His father had suggested to the teachers that Greek and Hebrew be minimized in his son's education. These subjects were not relevant to business; it was more important, he contended, that his boy learn to think clearly and to write effectively in English. Austin, in his practicality so like a frontiersman, may have been somewhat dismayed when Stephen returned from school with a decided bent for music and dancing.

Young Austin was twenty-seven years old when his father died. His best dancing days were over, and he had already made a dignified mark on his community as a representative to the territorial legislature of Missouri from 1814 to 1820 and as a circuit judge in 1820. He was a bachelor and would remain one, later claiming to have married not a woman but the land of Texas. What William Penn was to Pennsylvania and Brigham Young would later be to Utah, Stephen Austin was to the Lone Star State. But Penn and Young were men of religion, and Austin was a man of opportunity. He hoped to make money but was only moderately successful.

In the fall of 1821 the first of the 297 initial colonists (whom Texans like to call the Old Three Hundred) had begun to arrive. Stephen Austin claimed that he could have enlisted hundreds more but that he had deliberately been selective; no one of low character and particularly none of those restless frontier hunters were allowed. If a settler was just going to farm, he would receive 177 acres; if his intention was to raise stock, his grant would be 4,428 acres. The differential reflected Spain's sound recognition that varying uses dictate differing policies of land distribution, a fact not fully realized in the United States for another half-century. Most of the Texas settlers decided that they would raise cattle and that farming would be a subsidiary interest. The grants of the Austin colony stretched along the rich bottomlands of the Colorado and the Brazos rivers, rolling gently down to the Gulf of Mexico. This was among the richest alluvial land in all the West. The cattle that fattened over its ranges and the cotton that flourished in its soil were soon major exports, almost all

Stephen Austin responding to news of an Indian raid, by Harry McArdle.

of which went to the United States. Trade with central Mexico was light and consisted mostly of horses.

Austin's settlers were overwhelmingly from the American South — Louisiana, Alabama, and Arkansas — and they brought slaves with them. By 1825 there were 443 Negro slaves and 1,347 whites in the colony. Mexico had abolished slavery in its Constitution of 1824. In Texas, however, a paper fiction called "contract labor" enabled slavery to remain an economic reality, though politically it was dead. This system was an uneasy solution to a sensitive issue.

An equally sensitive matter was religion. For Spaniards, Catholicism was a prerequisite to political activity and even to landholding, but Austin had initially worked out an arrangement whereby his colonists would not be required to attend mass. No churches or even priests were close at hand, as in most frontier areas, so such requirements were unenforceable, and no more than 10 percent of the Austin colonists became practicing Catholics. Following the independence of Mexico, secularization movements tended to relieve pressures over religious issues.

Austin's usual selling price for the land granted him — twelve and a half cents an acre — seems low enough, but some of the colonists came to believe that the Mexican government had intended for Austin to pass the land along to the settlers free of charge. Though Austin had a right to charge, his colonists' grumblings bothered him. He wrote letter after letter describing his labors over proper land titles, the improvements he had made, and his paternalistic love for his colonial "family":

> I have a better opportunity of knowing what will be advantageous to them as regards their conduct and intercourse with the Government than any of them could have had, and I feel almost the same interest for their prosperity that I do for my own family — in fact I look upon them as one great family who are under my care.[1]

Stephen Austin was what the Spaniards called an empresario, a contractor who received large tracts of land from the government in order to dispense them to settlers. As far as the government was concerned he encouraged settlement. He made possible for the settlers the purchase of small farms, but took on the aura of a land speculator. Indeed, a group of empresarios developed in Texas during the 1820s. In 1825 Green DeWitt from Missouri set out a colony just south of Austin's. Slightly earlier, along the Guadalupe River, Martin DeLeon attracted mostly Europeans and Mexicans to a similar enterprise. Some failed, among them Haden Edwards who, unable to fulfill the stipulation regarding settlers, lost his grant. By 1836, settlers in Texas probably numbered about forty thousand.[2]

In the Constitution of 1824 the Mexicans rather arbitrarily combined Texas with the state of Coahuila, thus making the Anglo-Americans in Texas a minority in the State of Texas-Coahuila. From the Mexican standpoint the move was justified by a deepening feeling that the United States would use the Texas settlers as an excuse for taking the territory away from Mexico — a feeling that subsequent history would hardly call illusory. American attempts to purchase Texas in 1825 and 1829 gave credence to the fear. But Texas settlers, more or less ignorant of Washington's intentions, believed Mexico was indifferent to their right of local self-determination.

The Indians, as usual, provided an excuse for local alarm. Many of the tribes along the Gulf coast, though missionized by the Spaniards, were given to pilfering supplies on their way from the coast to the settlers. Inland Indians such as the Wacos considered the Texans a threat and therefore burned their crops and stole their cattle. Austin

City of Austin, 1840.

declared the natives "universal enemies to man" and believed "there will be no way of subduing them but extermination."[3] One of his earliest acts, in 1826, was to appoint a band of rangers, and he later led a group of sixty-two settlers in battle against the natives.

By the mid 1820s, however, the colony was established; and under the new republican constitution, which so resembled that of the United States, the settlers could be optimistic. They could grumble at Austin and he would chide them like children, but the cotton acreage was expanding and the herds increasing. They wanted to avoid Catholicism, and Mexico made the avoidance easy. Their slaves, now under a different name, seemed secure. The Indians may not have been eliminated, but Austin felt that they were showing "respect" for the white man.

A traveling widow, Mary Holley, wrote the first book in English about Texas. The death of her husband had left this New England woman stranded as a governess on a sugar plantation near New Orleans. Worried about the future of her sickly son, she contacted her uncle, Stephen Austin. He reserved for her a tract on Galveston Bay. Her eastern friends thought her going to Texas in 1831 was only "a little less marvelous than the wandering of Dante on the other side of the Styx." But in her account she rhapsodized over the profound stillness and the soft air, which "filled the heart with religious emotions."[4] The people she described were bound happily together in a common interest, neither rich nor poor, and everywhere opening their houses to travelers. She had hoped to make money on the Galveston Bay land, but her speculation was cut short by her death from yellow fever in 1846. Meanwhile, however, her book of Texas travels, because of its feminine viewpoint, encouraged the more stable families to migrate.

In the ten years between 1826 and 1836, schools and roads, products of local government in the Anglo political tradition, went unbuilt. The issue of self-government aggravated such quiescent issues as religion and economic attachments. Widespread fear in Mexico City of encroachment from the "Rome of the North" did not help satisfy Texans' requests for more independence within Mexico. By 1836 Texas was ready to seek independence not within, but from, Mexico.

Even though the empresarios generally tried to screen their colonists, as their land grants required, many settlers drifted across the border and occupied the best land they saw. These people extended the brawling, bragging, violent society that the lower reaches of the Mississippi River seemed to generate. Unpredictable as the flooded delta channels of the Mississippi and as irksome as its bars and snags, these Crocketts and Houstons were the frontier hunters whom Austin had carefully excluded from his "family." In this itinerant region, Haden Edwards, now on a different grant, was given land for eight hundred families; but when the boundaries fell into dispute, the government revoked his grant and ordered him to leave. Instead he and two hundred followers in 1827 declared the independent Republic of Fredonia. They held out for a month before troops, including men from Austin's colony, forced a retreat to the United States.

Armed uprising, border disputes, even support for particular factions within Mexico — all fit neatly into the general Mexican view that the United States was intent on acquiring Texas one way or another, by fair means or foul. In 1830 the Mexican congress took forthright action to protect its border province and passed the Colonization Act of 1830. The border was closed to settlers from the United States. Energetic efforts were begun under federal rather than state control to attract more Mexican and European settlers to counterbalance the Americans, and troops were sent to enforce the provisions and to discourage argument.

Forced to cross the boundary illegally, the type of person who emigrated to Texas from the United States may have changed, but statistically the law had little effect. In the decade of the 1820s the number of Anglo-Americans in Texas grew to at least twenty thousand;

in the next five years it increased to approximately thirty thousand (plus four thousand Mexicans).[5]

The Colonization Act ushered in a five-year period in which the Mexican government's fear of aggression by the United States was increasingly confirmed. The Texas settlers grew aware that either they had to achieve a large measure of local determination, including separate statehood in Mexico for Texas, or they had to seek independence from Mexico. William B. Travis, an ambitious young lawyer, became a rallying point for civil rights against military oppression and found himself frequently in jail. Santa Anna, president of Mexico, was crushing other rebellious states in his drive to strengthen federal authority. Austin worked hard to keep his colonists loyal to Mexico, but events such as the imprisonment of Travis weakened his position. In 1834 and 1835 Travis was suspected of treason and was jailed in Mexico City for eighteen months, much of the time incommunicado, in a windowless, thirteen-by-sixteen-foot cell. The episode illustrated the strain in Mexican tempers. Austin's loyalty to Mexico was finally shaken, and his thoughts increasingly turned toward independence.[6]

Austin died late in 1836, and by then a more volatile breed of Texan was in the saddle, a type well exemplified by Samuel Houston. He was a giant of a man, at least six feet two inches tall (though most men thought he was six feet six), weighing 240 pounds; his Scotch-Irish temperament and his flair for capes and oratory contributed to his charisma. Unlike Stephen Austin, Sam Houston lacked a formal education. As it had been for his Scotch-Irish progenitors, Tennessee turned out to be more congenial for his energies than Virginia, his birthplace. Even in Tennessee he learned early that he could not stand storekeeping and moved off to live with the Cherokees nearby. Early in his life he seems to have crossed many symbolic rivers, leaving behind the old and established for the new and rebellious. After he had risen politically through two terms in Congress, he began a promising stint as governor of Tennessee. But when his young wife left him, he gave up politics and escaped to the life of an Indian trader. He had fought under Andrew Jackson against the Creeks in the War of 1812 but came to champion the Indian cause against bureaucrats and traders. Indian problems took him to Texas on two occasions after 1832, and by 1835 he was with the Lone Star to stay, just in time for the revolution.

As late as November 3, 1835, worried Texans at a meeting in San Felipe declared that they had the right to independence but would "continue faithful to the Mexican government so long as that nation is governed by the constitution and laws."[7] They still sought reform rather than revolution, a position reminiscent of the one taken by the New England colonists in the first days of the rebellion against England. In the fall of 1835 little provocation was needed, however, to transform a reformist rebellion into a revolution for independence.

Fighting broke out late in 1835, and Texan troops were placed under the command of Sam Houston; deserters and retreaters (absquatulators, as one Texan called them) were notable. In February 1836, 187 fighting men were trapped by Santa Anna in the Alamo, a small mission in San Antonio. Travis was there, now called "Buck" by his men, and with him were Jim Bowie and Davy Crockett, already the stuff of legend. Bowie, a tall, redheaded killer from Louisiana, best known for the shape and effectiveness of the knife in his belt, might have contended for leadership, but he fell sick with pneumonia. Travis, at twenty-seven years of age, took command. Santa Anna's troops were well trained and effective, but Travis and his men could have retreated. Instead Travis issued a "liberty or death" proclamation and swore not to give an inch. Travis was firm willed, and the men with him were full of frontier, ripsnorting bravado. When Davy Crockett had left Tennessee, he had told his former constituents: "You can go to hell; I'm going to Texas." The men at the Alamo in effect told Santa Anna that he could go to hell and the Texans would stay where they were. A ten-day siege was broken on March 6, 1836, after five hours of assault against what Santa Anna called "the lawless foreigners." Few, if any, of the *diablos Tejanos* within the Alamo survived, but a reliable body count showed they had killed sixteen hundred of the assault troops. The Alamo became for the Texans an emotional fulcrum that helped keep doubters in the camp of independence and potential deserters in the ranks. It was a lost battle that led to the winning of the war. For the Texans, military victory came at San Jacinto, where on April 21, 1836, Sam Houston and 918 Texans met Santa Anna and as many as twelve hundred Mexicans. Santa Anna was captured, the Mexican army surrendered, and Texas was independent.

Ten months later, on March 3, 1837, the United States recognized the independent Republic of Texas. Mexican cynics must have been surprised that annexation to the United States did not follow close upon recognition. At least a modicum of diplomatic decency was displayed by both Texans and Americans in holding off for nearly ten years.

Annexation in 1845 came because the United States feared Texas might fall into other foreign orbits and, of course, because an expansionist president had just been elected. Nevertheless, the Anglo-American settlement must be seen as the primary determinant of the annexation of Texas. Anglos quickly comprised a majority of the

First executive mansion of Texas:
Sam Houston's residence, 1837.

population, but for a time both they and the Mexican government had reason to believe they would become and remain good citizens of Mexico. However, between 1830 and 1835 discontent surrounding Roman Catholicism, slavery, and statehood generated the trend toward incorporation into the United States. Mexico, understandably, interpreted the movement as a pattern of infiltration and subversion rather than real discontent. In the United States the North perceived a southern plot "to cram more pens with slaves" or at least to extend the political power of the South. The South discerned a natural human progression toward self-government. One thing is certain, however: the story of the annexation of Texas is not complete in itself. A knowledge of simultaneous events in the Oregon country is essential to an understanding of what happened in Texas.

The story of the settlement of Oregon begins with easterners who, not unlike Moses Austin, combined a bit of idealism with heavy doses of speculative expectations. Hall Jackson Kelley, a Boston schoolteacher, talked of a new Massachusetts Bay Colony, another "city on a hill" throwing light into the wilderness. Nathaniel Wyeth, a Cambridge businessman who had represented New England companies at fur-trade rendezvous in the early 1830s, planned more concrete ventures, even inventing for his journey a combination boat-wagon for two colonizing experiments in 1832 and 1834.

New Englanders had long been aware of the Oregon country. As boys, Wyeth and Kelley could have watched the return to Boston harbor of great sailing ships smelling of tea and spice. Their holds spilled out rich profit from a trade that began on the northwest coast with barter among the Indians for sea otter furs, which were carried to China where they were traded for prized oriental goods. With such commerce in mind, the American government claimed sovereignty over the Oregon region. On May 11, 1792, Robert Gray entered Oregon's great river and left his ship's name, the *Columbia*, upon its waters. Likewise Lewis and Clark traversed the region by land and claimed it for the United States. Spain, in the Adams-Onis Treaty of 1819, surrendered to the United States all claims, such as they were, to lands north of the California border.

No American diplomat, however, was dull enough to lose sight of the strength of England's claim to the Oregon country. James Cook and George Vancouver had landed on its coast by sea in 1778 and 1792 respectively. Alexander Mackenzie had approached Oregon from overland long before Lewis and Clark. And the Hudson's Bay Company owned permanent posts in the area. The American could point only to Astoria, which after a short life of two years had been sold, alas, to the British. But England was not in a mood to press its claim, and America was thus happy to get an agreement in 1818 for joint occupancy which was to last for ten years and be renegotiated thereafter on an annual basis. It was evident that both nations were buying time.

Time for the Americans meant settlement. Congressmen such as John Floyd of Virginia spoke eloquently of Oregon, though he had never been there. Kelley described Oregon to Congress in 1829 as "the most valuable of all the unoccupied parts of the earth." Thus Hall Kelley and Nathaniel Wyeth answered the call to profit.

Religion helped enlarge the scant settlement. In 1831 four Nez Percé and Flathead Indians were welcomed in St. Louis by Governor William Clark, who heard them request the "book" and the "black robes" for their people. These natives may have been speaking of the Holy Bible and the Jesuits, but it is equally possible that they sought explanations for the white man's power as seen in his printing and in his religion. As news of the Indian's request flew from pulpit to pulpit, most Protestants interpreted the episode to mean that the Indians of the Northwest were meekly seeking the word of Christ and that they had been misled to think that Christ was synonymous with Roman Catholicism. The Methodists responded by sending the Reverend Jason Lee on the trail to Oregon. He traveled with Wyeth's expedition of 1834. Once in Oregon, he decided he was needed most by the colonists, and he located in the Willamette valley, thereafter giving little attention to the Indians. Indeed, it became ironic that many of the Protestant missionaries in Oregon served the settlers better than they did the Indians.

The Chinooks, however, along the Columbia River were not devoid of white influence. John McLoughlin of the Hudson's Bay Company, presiding royally over Fort Vancouver across the Columbia from the mouth of the Willamette, had persuaded the natives to abandon slavery and had even influenced their burial practices. They apparently respected him, and he in turn dealt fairly and honestly with them. Conceivably he was a better influence than were the missionaries; certainly the great troubles in Oregon between Indians and whites came only after McLoughlin lost his position of influence.

The colonial enterprisers and Lee himself, through letters and trips back East, continued to publicize the glories of Oregon. In 1839 with the joint occupation still in effect, Lee described "the germ of a great state,"[8] predicting more clearly than did Texans at a comparable time. In that year, however, no more than ninety-six American families lived south of the Columbia along the Willamette.

Marcus Whitman, a young medical doctor in western New York, yearned to combine his new medical skills with his religious zeal to influence the heathen in Oregon. He applied for assignment to the American Board of Commissioners of Foreign Missions, an ecumenical coordinator for Congregationalists and Presbyterians, among others. The board frowned on bachelors; and in overcoming that disapproval, Marcus met another zealous applicant, Narcissa Prentiss. The two were fond enough of one another to marry and thus in one leap surmounted two hurdles. In 1836 the newlyweds joined another young missionary couple, the Reverend Henry and Eliza Spalding, on the way to Oregon. Eliza Spalding probably expressed the feelings of the group when she wrote in her journal that she was "anxious to spend and be spent in laboring to promote my Master's cause among the benighted Indians."[9]

The wives quarreled and the men disagreed. When they reached Oregon, they set up mission stations a hundred or so miles apart, the Whitmans at Waiilatpu near the future Walla Walla, and the Spaldings at Lapwai, near modern-day Lewiston, Idaho. Their strong faith persisted, but it was challenged by mounting difficulties. The wives were unhappy with their burdens. Two-year-old Alice Whitman drowned in a small stream. Although the Spaldings, working with the Nez Percé, converted several chiefs (such as the elder Chief Joseph) and claimed

Emigrants crossing the plains, after F. O. C. Darley (1822-1888).

public confessions of as many as two thousand in one week, their actual baptized converts in the first ten years numbered no more than twenty. Their eastern patrons, the American Board, were not impressed and wrote that they should abandon the missions and return home.

The character of Marcus Whitman included a stubbornness (or courage, if you will) not unlike that of Buck Travis. Late in October 1842 Whitman set out on horseback with one companion for his famous winter ride to save Oregon. The winter proved to be monstrous, snowstorm after snowstorm blocking pass after pass. He was forced to swing far south to Santa Fe, but traveling even on the Sabbath, he covered four thousand miles in six months and reached the East in March. His appearance before the board in Boston induced it to rescind the order to return, and Whitman spent the early spring preaching up and down the Atlantic seaboard, eulogizing Oregon, drumming up interest and support. The great migration over the Oregon Trail in the summer of 1843 was well under way. Whitman's work certainly did not hurt it, and he joined the advance party in a triumphal return to the Columbia.

The push continued during the summers of 1844 and 1845. It was called Oregon Fever, but it was little different from the land mania and speculative hopes behind the settlement of Texas. Oregon was farther away than Texas, but its prospects were painted in brighter colors. Publicity about green meadows and rich forests was confirmed by the scientific explorations of John Charles Frémont in 1843. Thus both religion and science pointed the way to new sources of profit. And for any who might be tempted to Texas but for the issue of slavery, Oregon was a good alternative. By early 1846 as many as ten thousand Americans helped deepen the ruts on the trail to Oregon.

The British across the Columbia always had an easier time of it than did the Americans because the Hudson's Bay Company provided a framework of authority. In criminal cases, for example, the English directive was clear: the accused must be transported, at all costs, to the nearest permanent settlement for trial in regular courts. During the whole period of joint occupancy, the United States government had been so cautious about forcing the issue of sovereignty that American men in Oregon had to devise law where none existed. Unlike Texas, with its strong reaction against a prevailing Mexican system, Oregon might be a study in the origins of a social compact. Rousseau or Locke would have found the situation reminiscent of that hypothetical moment when humankind drew together and embraced the first society.

The first government in Oregon grew over a period of three years from a series of meetings devoted to various problems. For example, in 1841 Ewing Young, a trapper and cattleman who had amassed a substantial estate in the Willamette valley, died without leaving a will. No court existed for probate. A committee of American settlers appointed a judge who took care of the Young estate and then relinquished his position. Another meeting involved protection of livestock from predatory animals such as wolves, and from the meeting evolved rudimentary forms of taxation (collections), disbursement (bounties), and executive power (standing committees). Meanwhile, at other meetings there was talk of drafting more comprehensive laws and a constitution.

The first framework for a complete government was drawn by the Americans in May 1843. To social-compact theorists, the process would have been more interesting had these men had no preconceived ideas. In reality they worked from the one law book in the province, *Organic Laws of the State of Iowa.* Like the Articles of Confederation of the United States after 1783, the new constitution of Oregon provided for an executive committee of three men rather than a president, and it stipulated voluntary instead of compulsory taxation. The next summer, after the arrival of a new wave of settlers, the constitution was revised. The committee became a single executive, and taxes were made compulsory. Alcoholic drink was prohibited, and blacks were to be excluded. Negroes in the area were to be whipped at intervals of six months until they left; though this law was little enforced, it was on and off the books in Oregon until the 1920s.

Without the support of the Hudson's Bay Company, any government in the area was likely to founder. Thus Jesse Applegate, a member of the 1843 migration who had become a political leader in Oregon, negotiated with McLoughlin an oath of allegiance to the provisional constitution to be sworn to by Britisher and American alike, "consistent with my duties as a citizen of the United States, or a subject of Great Britain."[10]

The growing number of settlers south of the Columbia presented problems for the Hudson's Bay Company. Its post was harassed with the political problems of the colonists; the fur trade along the river was dwindling, and the company feared that in spite of its interests, the international boundary would ultimately be drawn further north. Consequently, the London directors decided to move the post north, to the southern point of Vancouver Island (present-day Victoria, British Columbia). McLoughlin quarreled with the company and resigned. He stayed on the Columbia, but his influence was largely gone.

Almost thirty years after their agreement on joint sovereignty, the United States and Great Britain in June 1846 concluded a treaty giving the Oregon country to the United States and drawing the northern boundary at the 49th parallel. When the line reached the sea, it dipped south through the Juan de Fuca Straits so that the Hudson's Bay Company post on the southern tip of Vancouver Island would remain in British hands. Ownership of the company's lands south of the 49th parallel was secured in the treaty; however, these guarantees were not fully observed, and the company sold its holdings south of the line in 1861.

The treaty of 1846 may be viewed from two directions — as a failure of the United States to press for its full demands or as a failure of England to claim its full rights. The United States could have fought for 54°40′; it was willing to fight for similarly excessive territorial demands against Mexico in 1846. The issues of the Mexican Southwest and the British Northwest were clearly linked, and the United States, if not President Polk himself, avoided simultaneous involvement in the two questions. The region between 49° and 54°40′ in the Oregon country was a sacrifice to the greater prize gained from Mexico.

On the other hand, England's claims to the region southward to the Columbia River were perfectly logical. In that whole area there

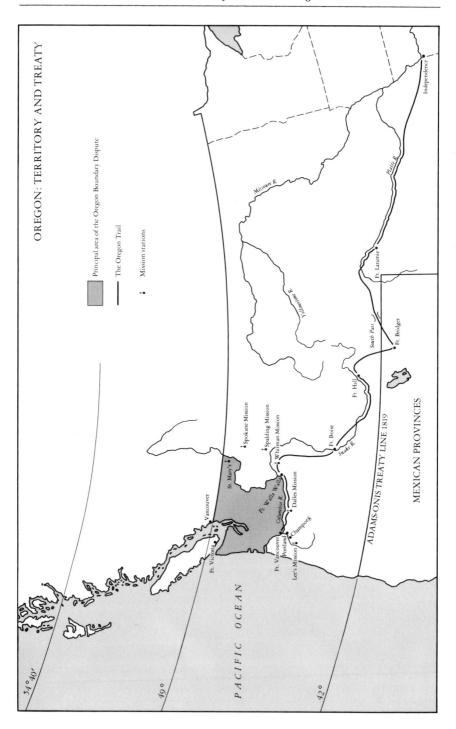

OREGON: TERRITORY AND TREATY

Principal area of the Oregon Boundary Dispute

The Oregon Trail

Mission stations

Oregon City, 1848, by Henry Warre.

were practically no Americans, and the Hudson's Bay Company had occupied many of the strategic points and fur-bearing waters. Had the Hudson's Bay Company not moved its headquarters from the banks of the Columbia in 1845, the international boundary might have looked very different indeed. England, however, was not yet inclined to press its claims. Robert Peel, the prime minister, was faced with serious problems at home, chiefly the potato famine in Ireland. Furthermore, his eyes were on domestic reforms. In the same year as the Oregon Treaty, for example, he pushed through Parliament the repeal of the Corn Laws, a landmark bill that placed England on the side of free trade. In such a political climate, to seek extensions of colonial influence would have been illogical. Fixing the northern boundary of Oregon was one of those happy situations where neither nation could afford to be aggressive or belligerent, and thus a reasonable compromise followed.

Meanwhile, the Protestant missionaries continued their battle for the souls of Cayuse and Chinook. The Whitmans knew moderate successes in the mid-1840s, but the rush of settlement that Whitman had helped prime would indirectly bring a grim conclusion to his life's work. The colonists who marched down the Blue Mountains through the Grand Ronde and the stark hills of the upper Columbia carried

Massacre of the Whitmans, 1847.

diseases such as measles, deadly to people without immunity. The Cayuse was one of the tribes nearly decimated by a measles epidemic in 1847, and survivors turned their grief to lashing hatred. John McLoughlin was no longer there to counsel moderation. The Protestants blamed the "black robes," though certainly unjustly, for looking the other way. In the cold morning of November 28, 1847, with ghosts of dead children behind them, Cayuse men broke into the Whitman mission and murdered Marcus, Narcissa, and ten other whites. Two children with measles, whom the Whitmans had nursed all through the previous night, died from inattention. Forty-eight men, women, and children were captured.

Numerically the Whitman massacre was insignificant in the total roster of violent deaths in the West, but coming so soon after the treaty, it caused easterners to remember that little had been done to bring order to the Oregon country. Before the treaty with England, justifying official neglect of Oregon by the United States was easy. But one year after the treaty, nothing had yet been done in Washington to make Oregon a territory. Citizens began meeting again along the Willamette to draft a petition to the Congress, pointedly remarking that neglect could be more intolerable than tyranny and that serious problems existed because of the ambiguity of their provisional government. An interim independent republic such as that in Texas was preferable to the uncertainties they were experiencing. The petition was given to Joe Meek, mountain man fresh from the wilderness, who crossed the continent posthaste in early 1848 and, coonskin cap in hand, presented the anxious views from Oregon to the national Congress.

The remonstrance worked. In August 1848 the Congress acted, and in March 1849 the newly appointed governor, Joseph Lane, declared, with fanfare, the existence of Oregon Territory. An army detachment arrived, and the United States mail service commenced.

The Oregon country had never been unified. From the days when John McLoughlin directed the American settlers south of the Columbia, reserving the north for his trappers, the two regions claimed differences, real or imaginary. By 1852, settlement north of the river had doubled, and industries other than trapping, such as lumbering around Puget Sound, were developing. In the winter of 1852, the Congress was persuaded to separate the two areas and create Washington Territory. Its new governor, Colonel Isaac I. Stevens, reflected some of the impatience of his new constituency. Rather than travel directly to the territory, he was commissioned to survey en route for a northern transcontinental railroad. When the railroad was completed, armies of settlers would come steaming along; for this boom, Governor Stevens, dogmatic and impetuous, was to prepare the way. The Indians, of course, would have to go, or at least be contained. In a series of treaties made between 1854 and 1855 the natives found themselves minus some sixty thousand square miles for which they received, in money or assorted benefits, about ten cents an acre. It was assumed that henceforth they would stay peacefully on reservations.

One of the treaty signers, a proud Nez Percé, the elder Chief Joseph, had been converted to Christianity by Henry Spalding and trusted the white man to mean what he said. Other Indians were more suspicious and uneasy over Stevens's "hurry-up" treaties. Gold rushes into the territories hardly calmed their fears. Small strikes along the Rogue River in southern Oregon were overshadowed in 1854 and 1855 by large booms along the upper Columbia at Colville. In the fall of 1855 the Indians' worries flared into a general multitribal uprising. For more than twenty years, until the last tragic stand of the young Chief Joseph in 1877, the Northwest was torn by increasingly restrictive policies of containment, and by skeptical and rebellious natives.

Meanwhile Oregon, with a population much larger than Washington's, suffered additional problems, many of which stemmed from a sizable group of small farmers from the American South. They tended to be antiblack and proslavery and at one point proposed that the entire West be formed into a large slave republic. They even flirted for a time with know-nothingism, the nativist political movement, but on the whole they stood so strongly for states' rights that other ideas could be submerged convincingly enough for the Congress to accept their free-state constitution. Oregon was admitted to the Union in February 1859. Washington Territory, in spite of its initial boost under Governor Stevens, waited a good deal longer. When the Northern Pacific Railroad was completed in 1883, settlement of the dark woods and rolling grasslands finally began to pick up. In 1889, along with Montana and the Dakotas, Washington became a state of the Union.

Washington's admission came forty-four years after that of Texas, a long time indeed on the American frontier. International rivalries among England, Mexico, and the United States; the national politics of slavery; local economic developments such as mining booms and changing markets — all played a role in the delay. Yet none assumed a part so vital as that of the settler-farmer, stubbornly claiming land, arrogantly dismissing the native, and lobbying his government. He even formed his own government if local conditions permitted. Settlement is indeed the seedbed from which the United States plucked at least two major segments of the West.

6

Two Wars and One Destiny

The fundamental realities behind the Mexican War were America's aggressive outlook and Mexico's suspicion, plus the resulting hostilities and fears. American filibusterers had sought to subvert New Spain, or Mexico, at least since 1805, when Aaron Burr conspired with General James Wilkinson. American offers to purchase California and Texas in the 1830s and 1840s were considered by Mexico to be thinly disguised imperialism (much as the United States might today view an offer from the Soviet Union to purchase Alaska). After 1821, the revolutionary situation in Mexico gave Americans an excuse to label Mexicans inherently unstable, in need of Yankee guidance. In California, in a call to revolution, Commodore John D. Sloat bluntly promised that Mexicans would notice an increase in real estate values if they revolted and joined their American neighbor. Mexico's Constitution of 1824 was modeled on that of the United States, but the political instability that followed its adoption seemed to indicate the superiority of the United States and the inability of Mexicans to cope with freedom. In 1836 Texans decided to revolt, an event that encouraged Mexico in the belief that Washington eventually would take the sizable chunk of Mexican soil. In 1845 when Texas was annexed to the United States, Mexicans nodded grimly. The revolution in Texas produced new cycles of hatred, and Texans longed for revenge against Mexico at the mere mention of the Alamo.

During the early 1840s intelligent observers in Washington were virtually certain of war between the United States and Mexico. The army and navy worked out contingency plans for the hostilities.

Sometimes the plans went embarrassingly awry. In 1842, Commodore Thomas ap Catesby Jones, believing war had begun, sailed the *United States,* flagship of the Pacific squadron, to Monterey, the capital of California. He sent his men ashore, took the fort, and raised the American flag. At the time twenty-nine regular troops and twenty-five raw recruits were manning the Mexican presidio; Jones commanded five hundred. When Jones learned that war had not been declared, he withdrew his men and the flag to the ship. The *United States* did not leave the harbor, however, until thirty-two days after the incident.[1] During that time, his firepower, three times that of the Mexicans, remained trained on the fort, ostensibly to protect Americans in Monterey from reprisals. The government in Washington eventually apologized to Mexico, but Jones was not punished, and Mexico understood only too well the thrust of American military orders.

Before the war the United States had some seven thousand men under arms (though the regular army was doubled in 1846). Mexico had an army of more than ten thousand men, better trained than the Americans and supported by what was believed to be highly superior artillery. Mexico considered itself the victim of aggression and therefore expected that when war came, the full power of morality would be on its side, within its borders as well as behind the American lines. Mexico expected to be supported by European allies, and because it had abolished slavery, a black uprising north of the border seemed a reasonable hope. America, of course, had industrial superiority, money, and western frontiersmen accustomed to fighting, shooting, and taking what they wanted.

By 1846 Mexico had installed as president Mariano Paredes, who was intensely hostile toward the United States. In 1845 America had elected by a narrow margin a determined expansionist, James K. Polk. A simple boundary dispute, which in another context would have had little bearing, brought their countries to war. The region in question lay between the Nueces River and the Rio Grande, a lush grassland that would subsequently support prosperous big cattle operations such as the King Ranch. It was not an insignificant strip. The mouths of the rivers were more than one hundred miles apart. The region in dispute was considered to extend as far north as the headwaters of the Rio Grande, into the southern part of present-day Colorado. The United States, in annexing Texas in 1845, agreed with the Texan interpretation of the boundary. Texas claimed the Rio Grande because General Santa Anna had agreed to it, while he was a prisoner of war, after the Texas revolution. This argument was weak in comparison with Mexico's contention that the belt as far north as the Nueces was settled only by Mexicans over whom Texas had never exercised jurisdiction. President Polk forced the issue by ordering General Zachary Taylor to protect the north bank of the Rio Grande. When the Mexicans crossed the river to contest Taylor's presence there, Polk confidently stated to the Congress in his call for a declaration of war that the United States had been forced into war "by act of Mexico." Polk, piously wrestling with his conscience, considered it America's duty to protect that region of Texas because, as he said, it was already drawn into congressional districts and was included in the revenue system of the nation. Congress, agreeing that "the cup of forbearance had been exhausted,"[2] declared war on Mexico on May 13, 1846, and, believing that victory would not take long, appropriated $10 million to get the job done.

Taylor had waited neither for the declaration nor for the appropriation. In the first weeks of May serious fighting had begun as Taylor engaged the Mexicans in two battles north of the Rio Grande, at Palo Alto and Resaca de la Palma. Those victories laid the groundwork for the active invasion that occurred when he finally had word of the congressional action.

The Mexican War ostensibly began as a limited war for limited objectives. In view of the events pointing toward relieving Mexico of its northern borderlands, it is not surprising that the war escalated dramatically, involving finally four major foreign invasions – from the north under General Taylor, over sea and land to Mexico City under General Winfield Scott, and in isolated campaigns in New Mexico and California – plus a total cost of more than thirteen thousand American dead and some $57 million in additional War Department appropriations alone. It was far easier to get into the war than to get out. Negotiations dragged on with hostilities, sometimes breaking off, then resuming. Mexican reactions on the battlefield, even in defeat, often were strong enough to result in guerrilla warfare.

American military leadership was an important factor in the war. Four men – Zachary Taylor, Winfield Scott, Stephen Watts Kearny, and John Charles Frémont – dominated the four theaters of action. They all had grown out of frontier conditions. Taylor had begun his military career fighting Indians under William Henry Harrison, Old Tippecanoe himself. He fought thereafter along all the frontiers from Wisconsin to Louisiana, including battles against the Sauks and the Seminoles. In 1845 he was a colonel, and at the annexation of Texas he was ordered to Corpus Christi to defend the border against Mexico.

Winfield Scott was more of a scholar than the others, writing books on tactics, but he came from a frontier Scotch family in Virginia. Like Taylor he had fought against the Seminoles. In addition

American atrocities in the Mexican War, 1847,
by Samuel Chamberlain.

Scott was involved in the tragic removal of the Cherokees from Georgia across the Trail of Tears to Oklahoma country. Early in the Mexican War General Scott openly criticized the ineffectiveness of Taylor's northern campaign. He called for a more daring invasion of the Mexican heartland, and was supported by hawkish men such as Thomas Hart Benton.

Stephen Watts Kearny had served almost continuously on the frontier. In St. Louis he married the stepdaughter of William Clark, thereby placing himself firmly in the frontier tradition. When the Mexican War began, he commanded the Army of the West.

John Charles Frémont was the youngest and most tempestuous of the four. We have already seen Frémont as a junior officer in the Topographical Corps eloping with Jessie Benton and coupling the cause of science with the expansionist drives of his government in a series of western expeditions. In 1845 he left Missouri with instruments and forty carefully selected men, on another expedition with scientific collections in mind. But undoubtedly the young captain of the Topographical Corps also carried the kind of instructions that Thomas ap Catesby Jones knew well: Keep your eyes open in California and when word of war comes, act decisively to secure that province for the United States. With no preliminary digressions to Oregon this time, Frémont's band of frontiersmen and scientists

Washing day in camp: Journal of Private William Richardson, 1848.

headed straight for California. In Monterey Frémont courteously requested of the Mexican military governor, José Castro, that he and his men be allowed to make scientific observations. The governor granted permission, and Frémont set up camp inland from the capital. In March 1846, three months after Taylor was ordered to the Rio Grande, Castro reconsidered his permission. By then Frémont had built a log fort on a peak overlooking the Salinas valley, a strategic point leading to the capital, and had raised an American flag. Castro was not amused by this "scientific" activity, and made it known. Frémont, like Commodore Jones three years before, took down the flag; he grudgingly moved northward through the Sacramento valley. With possible hostilities in mind he burned some Indian villages because they might be dangerous in case of war. A young marine from Washington overtook Frémont on the border of Oregon, and the party turned around and marched back down the Sacramento valley in defiance of the military governor's request for them to leave. Frémont camped with his forty marksmen near Sutter's Fort and tried not to appear directly involved in the provincial revolution that immediately ensued.

On June 6 a small group of farmers led by William B. Ide and Ezekial Merritt ineptly surrounded the house of General Mariano

"Texas Rangers" by Frederic Remington (1861–1909).

Vallejo in the village of Sonoma and received his sword in surrender. They raised a flag that bore the words "California Republic," the figure of a brown bear stalking, and a lone star, implying that California was embarking on the road Texas had taken years before.

The Bear Flag Republic, however, lasted not nine years but only one month. It could probably have succeeded longer because it would have been supported by a good number of Mexican Californios, including General Vallejo himself, who agreed with the American settlers that California should break with Mexico. But military events moved faster than they had for Texas. News of the declaration of war reached San Francisco Bay through Commodore John Sloat in early July. Commodore Robert Stockton took over from the aging Sloat and set to organizing the conquest. Frémont, his scientific sharpshooters, and the Bear Flaggers were all commissioned as a new fighting unit, the California Battalion. They, along with marines from Stockton's Pacific squadron, fought southward in a series of small encounters. By August, American troops were in control of Los Angeles, and it looked as though California had been taken.

Also in August General Stephen Kearny and his Army of the West reached Santa Fe, the two-century-old adobe capital of the New Mexico region between California and Texas. Kearny's sixteen hundred men entered without firing a shot. It is surmised that Governor Manuel Armijo capitulated so readily because of the offer of a satchel of gold coins, a bribe made by the United States government through James Magoffin, an American trader in the city. Kearny was charged with securing the interior and then proceeding to California to help in its conquest. His trip west had just begun when he learned that California, too, had been subdued. He thus left most of his men in Santa Fe. The Mexicans there were not happy with the transfer, and their uprisings necessitated vicious means of repression from Colonel Sterling Price.

In September, unknown to Kearny, Mexicans in California revolted against their American conquerors. General Andres Pico raised enough soldiers to rout the Americans from Los Angeles and return most of southern California to Mexican hands. When Kearny arrived from Santa Fe in December, he was met at San Pasqual in a pass through the coastal mountains by a Mexican force equal in numbers to his own. His troops were soundly and embarrassingly defeated and suffered heavy casualties. Only because Stockton was able to rush emergency forces from San Diego did Kearny escape at all.

In the first month of the new year, 1847, Kearny and Stockton recaptured Los Angeles, and Frémont belatedly moved down from the north. In spite of the presence of a general and a commodore, Frémont loftily accepted the surrender of the city. The anomalous situation foreshadowed conflicts among the three men in the future military government of the conquered province. With egotistical bravado, Frémont, an army captain, refused orders from General Kearny and reported instead to Commodore Stockton. The stand was characteristic and led to Frémont's court-martial.

Meanwhile, in September 1846, Taylor had moved south and taken the lovely town of Monterrey, in Mexico, parading in the plaza before its grand cathedral. Then in January he fought his climactic battle in northern Mexico, at Buena Vista. This fight in a rainstorm against General Santa Anna's superior numbers was the high-water mark of Taylor's career. From there, for Old Zach, the road to the presidency was direct and short. But Buena Vista was less than one-third the distance to Mexico City, and Santa Anna refused to negotiate peace while American troops remained on Mexican soil.

In spite of the American victories, there was still no evidence that Mexico would give up. Winfield Scott's contention that effective prosecution of the war required the capture of the capital city took on cogency. Conceivably the United States could retain its new territory by right of conquest but, in sensitive minds, the thought of raw aggression did not sit well. Certainly a treaty duly ratified by

General Scott's entrance into Mexico City, lithograph, 1851.

both governments would be preferable. Scott was placed in command of a naval invasion to land at Vera Cruz, more than five hundred miles down the Mexican coast from the Rio Grande. From Vera Cruz he could emulate Cortes marching to the halls of Montezuma.

Overcoming disease and supply problems, Scott moved inland in April 1847 and claimed his first major victory at Cerro Gordo. Through the spring and summer he engaged the Mexican army in a long series of major battles, climaxing in August at Contreras and Churubusco and in September at Chapultepec. Often Mexican losses would be followed by guerrilla actions, harassing American supply lines and indicating the mounting hatred for the invader. In September 1847, Mexicans sullenly watched the supreme ignominy of foreign troops — and American troops at that — marching into the capital.

As the war dragged on into its second year, American public opinion polarized. The majority of people, as usual, cared little or supported the president's policy in what they believed was a moderate position. They assumed that Polk's rhetoric about the duty of the nation to protect the cause of liberty had meaning and that he was struggling to extricate the country from a difficult situation. The Mexicans, so the argument ran, were backward economically, their political institutions were chaotic, and consequently they deserved to lose jurisdiction over regions that the Americans could so much more efficiently develop.

Out of these arguments grew the all-Mexico movement whose supporters contended that the American mission to regenerate Mexico could best be accomplished by complete annexation. The president had affirmed early in the war that the United States would never fight for conquest and that forced annexation was unthinkable. But he soon began to hedge under the guise of seeking repayment for the escalating costs of the war. The preferred reparation was California, including the peninsula of Baja California. Logic demanded that the territorial gap between Texas and California be included in the package. The region was worthless to Mexico, the argument ran, but was strategically, if not inherently, valuable to the United States, especially for a transcontinental railroad around the Rocky Mountains. Grander dreams were abroad, and Thucydides' ancient law that empires must expand or die seemed to be working. Why not take all of Mexico?

While Polk was talking of honor and duty, his secretary of the Treasury, Robert J. Walker, was sympathetically asking for a study of the fiscal implications of total annexation. His secretary of state, James Buchanan, reported that Mexicans dreaded the day when American troops would withdraw from Mexico City, so great were the benefits of American occupation. The vice-president of the United States, George M. Dallas, and Senators Lewis Cass of Michigan and Sidney Breese of Illinois all talked in this vein. The north Atlantic seaboard, judging from the large number of newspaper editorials, was the center of the all-Mexico movement. Much of the attack on the all-Mexico position was based on racist fears that American institutions would be contaminated by "the colored and mixed-breed" population of Mexico.

A third body of opinion not only opposed the all-Mexico movement but considered the entire war immoral and unworthy of the nation. The abolitionists, especially in New England, mounted this attack. They charged (with little proof) that the South had fomented the war to extend slavery and that any territory taken would be another area in which to cram slaves. Henry Thoreau considered the war so wrong that he refused to pay his taxes and went to jail. Ralph Waldo Emerson wrote sorrowfully in his journal, "The United States will conquer Mexico, but it will be as the man swallows the arsenic, which brings him down in turn. Mexico will poison us."[3] The Massa-

Franklin Pierce campaign poster of 1852 depicting Winfield Scott.

chusetts legislature condemned the war as unconstitutional and unsupportable by honest men. Josiah Royce, the philosopher, meditating on the Mexican War a few decades later, summarized the antiwar position: "Our mission in the cause of liberty is to be accomplished through a steadfast devotion to the cultivation of our own inner life, and not by going abroad as missionaries, as conquerors, or as marauders, among weaker peoples."[4]

One wonders how much respect even these men really had for the bravery and achievements of the Mexicans. Who gave credit to the men at San Pasqual, an extraordinary fighting force, given the numerical strength of the population from which it was drawn? Who understood the feelings of the guerrillas on the road to Mexico City defending their homeland or the quiet devotion of Catholic people in the face of Protestant bombast and egotism? The extremes of American opinion went far, but not far enough to include genuine respect.

President Polk had hoped for a short war, and he sent a peace emissary, Nicholas Trist, to march with Scott and seek negotiations at any opportunity. Trist's instructions were to acquire both Baja and upper California, New Mexico, and the Rio Grande boundary and to offer the Mexicans in exchange $30 million. Mexico's first negotiating position was to cede only Texas — or to admit officially that the United States had a right to claim Texas — and to discuss a buffer, a kind of demilitarized zone, between the Nueces and the Rio Grande. To the American belligerents Mexico sounded as if it were winning rather than losing the war.

Feeling the pressures of the all-Mexico extremists, President Polk recalled Trist for new instructions, presumably demands on Mexico for even more territory. Trist stubbornly ignored his new orders, and when he returned to Washington he had in his pocket a treaty based on the earlier aims. The accomplished fact undercut the extremists, and the Congress ratified the agreement in March 1848. The Treaty of Guadalupe Hidalgo confirmed the annexation of Texas to the United States and set the Rio Grande as its southern boundary. As reparations for the cost of the war, Mexico gave to the United States upper California (but not Baja California) and the province of New Mexico (covering the present-day states of New Mexico, Arizona, Utah, and Nevada). Quite illogically, unless it was "conscience money," the United States paid Mexico $15 million and reimbursed American citizens for claims they held against Mexico amounting to $3,750,000. A joint United States–Mexico commission was established with power to draw an exact boundary from Texas westward.

The American half of the commission had the impossible task of separating a surveying problem from sectional politics. When a New Englander, John Russell Bartlett, allowed the boundary to be the most northerly line of several possibilities, southerners howled. The resulting Gadsden Purchase of 1853, in which the United States acquired for $10 million the land south of the Gila River in present-day New Mexico and Arizona, was thus an extension of the Treaty of Guadalupe Hidalgo.

The total Mexican loss including Texas came to 602 million acres. Jefferson had thought Louisiana, at 529 million acres, would provide the nation with enough room for hundreds of generations, but an even larger territory had been added within forty-five years. Somehow the new lands seemed more extensive than statistics indicated because they were so varied — wind-blasted deserts, arid plateaus cut by chasms such as Zion Canyon and the Grand Canyon of the Colorado, the Rocky Mountains and the Great Salt Lake, the Sierra Nevada, the rich central valley of California still hiding its gold, and the magnificent harbors of San Francisco and San Diego.

Harder to assimilate than the terrain was the new Mexican minority, distrusted and misunderstood. The treaty had stipulated that Mexicans in the transferred territory could remain Mexicans or become full-fledged United States citizens, that their land claims should re-

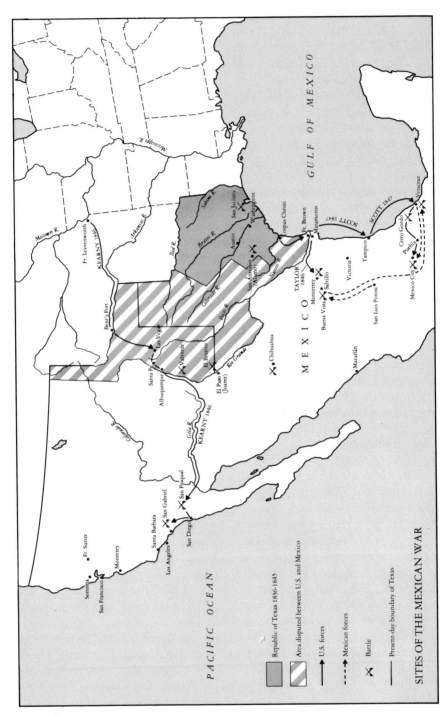

SITES OF THE MEXICAN WAR

main inviolate, and that their Roman Catholic faith should never be interfered with. None of these stipulations was fully realized: Mexican citizens were denied civil rights in mining camps; their land was not always protected; and traditional obligations of the Church in education were soon violated. It was not easy for Americans to understand a people who sent four Roman Catholic priests to their territorial legislature and addressed their leading citizens by the title Don. In Mexico, then, the war left a bitterness that receded slowly. In America those who had opposed the war thought of it with shame and guilt; the majority, however, saw it as a triumph of Manifest Destiny.

The doctrine of Manifest Destiny implied that America's superior morality had produced a superior Constitution, a superior form of capitalism, and a superior technology. The nation therefore held unique rights, even obligations, to disseminate its superior culture, to infiltrate and regenerate other peoples. Inevitably such notions both rationalized and encouraged continental expansion. Beyond that, who could tell where the spirit would lead?

Following the Mexican War, however, the possibility of land annexation overseas was a long way off; more immediate problems were at hand. If the nation's destiny was to be fully realized, then America had to remain united. If divisions and splinterings were tolerated, superiority might be questioned and efforts to regenerate would be weakened. The new western lands raised tensions that threatened to rip the seams apart. In which of the new regions should slavery be allowed? How would the new economies relate to the industrial North and to the agricultural South? Could such vast areas with undependable transportation and slow mail delivery be effectively governed? Would the assimilation of new peoples like the Mexican-Americans undermine the dominant culture? Could Indian tribes continue to be concentrated in what once had been a useless buffer area that was emerging as the heartland of the continent? The potential rifts were evident. The Civil War tested how far they would be allowed to widen.

All rifts, however, were diminished by the disagreement over slavery which, by 1850, was an overriding issue. The ramifications became less involved, though, the further west one went. In Texas, slavery was a going economic system; in some other areas, such as Kansas, it loomed as a dark question. Further west there was little serious expectation that slavery could be introduced successfully. Yet the legal stipulations over slavery in the new lands taken from Mexico and acquired through the Oregon settlement had to be determined. Should the magic line prohibiting slavery in the Louisiana Purchase north of 36°30′, drawn in the Missouri Compromise of 1820, be extended indefinitely westward? To do so would render California south of Monterey or Tulare, as well as the future states of Arizona and New Mexico, areas that protected slavery. California waited for two years under military government, and Oregon continued for almost as long under the provisional constitution, while the Congress stewed over solutions. In a series of bills during 1850 the Great Compromise was patched together. California instantly became a state, never passing through the territorial interlude, and it was free of slavery. The whole of the New Mexico province and Utah could enter the Union when ready, with or without slavery.

The peace of 1850 was broken in 1854 when the Little Giant, Stephen A. Douglas, chairman of the Senate Committee on Territories, pushed the Kansas-Nebraska Bill through Congress. Kansas and Nebraska were to make their own decision about slavery even though they were north of the 36°30′ line. Another comfortable certainty was thus lost. Kansas became the bleeding ground where men took sides and fought for their beliefs. Violence, shooting, and destruction were intensified by the frontier character of the territory; men knew the effectiveness of guns and the ineffectiveness of the established law.

The frontiersmen, especially in romantic literary descriptions, always prided themselves on serving a higher code of personal honor and on appealing to the eternal laws of right and wrong that the honest, independent man would find if he looked deeply within himself. John Brown of Kansas was this sort of frontiersman. "No man sent me here," he once said. "It was my own prompting and that of my Maker — or that of the Devil — whichever you please to ascribe it to. I acknowledge no master in human form."[5] An abolitionist avenging wrongs, he enacted the traditional role of western vigilantes when he and his four sons, all dedicated to freedom and righteousness, killed five men at Pottawatomie, Kansas, in the spring of 1856.

At about the time of John Brown's violent response to the violence of slavery, Oregon was wrestling anew with the problem, this time as part of its transition from territory to state. After 1844, when Oregon excluded slavery, general sentiment seemed far more antiblack than antislavery. Prohibiting slavery was one way to keep out blacks. These feelings were hardly unique. Californians at their constitutional convention in 1849 excluded slavery, and prejudice against blacks was strong. Both areas had to keep an eye on the Congress, however, knowing the politics of slavery. In its proposed constitution of 1857 Oregon decided to say not one word about slavery, the safest possible position.

Traditionally historians have interpreted the period between the Mexican War and the Civil War as a time of sectional tension, with North and South vying for the stakes of the West. As early as 1824 and 1825, a hotly contested election resulted in a westerner, Henry Clay, throwing his critical support to a northerner, John Quincy Adams. After the 1820s, especially following the completion of the Erie Canal in 1825, the volume of wheat and pork that moved southward along the Mississippi was dramatically overshadowed by fourfold and sixfold increases of trade with the Northeast. The West began to vote for protective tariffs to help northern industry, and the North began to vote for internal improvements and cheap public land to help the West. Gradually the bargain became clearer, reaching its climax in the birth of the Republican Party and the election in 1860 of Abraham Lincoln, which sealed the sectional contract. The South with its staple crop and "peculiar institution" was gradually excluded. When, in desperation, the South rebelled, the other two sections joined forces against her. The West-North bargain became particularly glaring in 1862 when, almost immediately after the Confederate states had left the Congress, the federal government granted the West two of its most cherished desires — cheap public lands in accordance with the Homestead Act and the Pacific Railroad to sew together the distant allies with steel.

Such an interpretation requires conceiving of the West as a section. Frederick Jackson Turner thought it was. He defined a section as a "faint image of a European nation,"[6] a region sufficiently unified to sense its own ideals and customs and so be conscious of its distinctiveness from other sections. The north Atlantic and the south Atlantic regions had undoubtedly developed such a sense of distinction. Did the West?

In reality, there were many Wests, not one. The Old Northwest, clustered along the Ohio and among the Great Lakes, had little in common with the Old Southwest, ranging along the lower reaches of the Mississippi. The prairies and plains were another West. The Mexican War added mountains and basins and seacoasts to confound any sense of geographical unity.

If we label the region west of the Mississippi as the Far West and examine it as of 1850, we find there were only five organized states (Texas, Missouri, Arkansas, Iowa, and Louisiana), which together accounted for 90 percent of the population of the whole region. California was still under military occupation, its population overwhelmingly male, and more than 50 percent transient miners. Territorial government was loosely imposed on areas such as Oregon and Utah. A good deal of the region was vaguely called the Indian Territory. The total United States population in 1850 was 23 million. No more than 2 million people lived west of the Mississippi. Although there were eight thousand miles of railroad in the Northeast, there was not a single mile of track in the West. Unconnected islands of settlement represented unrelated economic pursuits — mining, stock growing, agriculture, trapping — with trade moving along a few main arteries like the Santa Fe and Oregon trails.

The Far West thus hardly seems to have been a section by Turner's definition. What there was of unity was partly a dream out of romantic literature (no less important, of course, but for other reasons) and partly a booster's vision of the future. Instead of a section, the West in 1850 might be considered an underdeveloped region. There, isolated, rural, and unexploited areas were about to be impinged on by a profit-seeking, industrialized society. The West of 1850 was like parts of Africa and Latin America in the twentieth century.

The victory of the North in the Civil War confirmed what the Far West had already decided — that the nation should be a single, united continental power. Thus the Mexican War and the Civil War were two parts of one destiny. Thereafter the East could settle down in earnest to the job of exploiting its underdeveloped region, the Far West.

7

Mining: The Restless Frontier

A RECURRENT PATTERN

Some wit once imagined a special Providence for drunkards, fools, and the United States of America. The closest verification of such luck for the latter was the discovery of gold in California immediately following the conquest of the area. In America the political uses of the discovery were legion, including a justification for the costs of the war as a kind of divine reparation. Who could deny that Providence had waited to reveal her greatest riches until the chosen people had arrived? Those avaricious Catholic Spaniards seeking gold wherever they went had been miraculously blinded in California. Now it was the Protestants' day to reap the riches. As one minister preached: "God kept that coast for a people of the Pilgrim blood; He would not permit any other to be fully developed there. The Spaniard came thither a hundred years before our fathers landed at Plymouth; but though he came for treasure, his eyes were holden that he should not find it."[1]

True, the Spaniards had always been interested in New World mining. Silver and tin mines in northern Mexico had been worked since the middle of the sixteenth century and were as important in the northward expansion as the dreams of Cíbola. The Spanish economy in California did not create conditions conducive to the discovery of gold. Settlements there clustered around harbors or spread over the coastal valleys as cattle ranges. Stock raising does not involve disturbing the earth, so minerals were unlikely to be revealed even

Miner prospecting, after Charles Nahl (1818–1878).

accidentally. Adobe construction did require digging, but for clay rather than for quartz rock. However, the wooden houses desired by the Anglo-American farmers in the Sacramento valley meant that sawmills had to be set up in the foothills among the large pines. Saw-mills require waterpower and the diversion of water from stream to spillway. At such a spillway James Marshall discovered gold early in 1848. It was a demand for wooden houses, not Providence, that gave gold to the Americans.

It is not true, however, that the Spaniards were totally ignorant of the gold in California. Insignificant finds had been made here and there, but the mission fathers, putting first things first, knew how gold rushes could destroy missionary labors and certainly had no de-sire to pursue the metal. They might have been even more fearful had they known how an influx of gold seekers in the 1830s had pushed the Cherokees off their land in Georgia and had impeded Christianization.

But however it came, after the Mexican War mining provided a smashing impetus for the exploitation of the underdeveloped West. The first lodestone was California. By 1860 there were substantial strikes or rushes at Virginia City and the Washoe country in Nevada, in the Colorado mountains west of Denver, along the Gila River, in northeastern Washington, and along the Fraser River north of the Canadian border. In the 1860s Montana and Wyoming were added to the list; in the 1870s the Black Hills in South Dakota; in the 1880s the Coeur d'Alene region of Idaho; in the last decade of the century the cold Yukon; and later Alaska. In practically every region emerged the kaleidoscope of lonely prospector with mule and pan, jerry-built stores along a muddy street, a mirrored saloon, a silent poker game, dancing girls, outlaws, claim jumpers, the vigilance committee — all supplanted finally by the smelter and the mill, the slag heap, underground burrows, labor unions and Pinkerton detectives, the company town, and at last a strike with a fist instead of a shovel. Clearly, mining added a significant dimension to the social, economic, and imaginative development of the West.

The national production of gold rose from ten million to eighty-one million ounces between 1849 and 1852. Between 1860 and 1863 silver production shot from fewer than two hundred thousand to six and a half million ounces. Nearly all this increase was in the Far West. In California alone in the early 1850s, 45 percent of the world's annual gold supply was being extracted.

The economic effects of this bonanza were enormous, but economists do not agree on details. The nation's gold coinage, measured in dollars, increased twentyfold between 1848 and 1851. Between 1848 and 1854 the wholesale commodity price index (using a 1913 base of 100) rose from 84.7 to 102.5, and the general price level rose from 65.2 to 76.5. Foreign capital flowed into the country. Estimates of British investment in western mines between 1860 and 1901 go as high as £50 million, and by 1857 Englishmen held £80 million in American railroad stock, an investment closely related to mining.[2] These funds were inflationary, and the presence of the vast new supply of specie made it possible for the United States, through international price adjustments and through exporting gold, to finance a large import surplus such as steel for railroads. In all, the gold encouraged an international expansion of credit and emphasized the growing interdependence of the world's economies.

California stamped a pattern on practically every subsequent gold and silver frontier. By the summer of 1848 the word of gold had spread through the territory, still unsettled after its conquest. Men poured into the foothills with picks, shovels, and pans. Fanning outward, they learned that the mother lode lay some five hundred miles along the Sierra Nevada. The icy streams of the higher range cut the rock and washed out gold-bearing ores. A man needed little knowledge, minimal skill, and less capital to swish the sands in a flat pan with enough water to wash away the lightest ores, leaving the heavier gold grains in the bottom. The summer of 1848 was an "honest picnic." Plenty of streams held an abundance of sand for all who came, and the lore of the lode grew heavy with tales of men at Dry Diggings (Auburn) who panned from $800 to $15,000 worth of gold a day and of two men at Hangtown (Placerville) who made $17,000 a week. An estimated $10 million in gold was taken out of the California streams in 1848.

No more than those tales would have been needed to start the gold rush of 1849. But additional factors turned the rush into a frenzy. It was a time when young men might well be on the move. The Mexican War, like all wars, left its share of dislocated and unsettled veterans. Europe was recovering from revolutions that, in every major capital, had pushed a fearful establishment into severely repressive measures. After 1847 Irishmen began fleeing a long famine resulting from a blight on potatoes, the vegetable the Old World had so happily received from the New World more than two hundred years earlier. By 1860, Irish immigrants accounted for 15 percent of the population of California. Stories from California were told in every language — tales of the man who washed $16 in gold dust from his beard, of a windstorm that netted another $10 when the curtains were washed, of the sick miner who recovered only when he sweated out $49.50 worth of dust in a Turkish bath. By square-rigged ship from Hawaii and Australia and China, by slim clippers around the Horn, by both water and land across the Isthmus of Panama, by land alone across the plains and mountains, Sweet Betsy from Pike and more than fifty thousand Ikes jostled into California.

Two things happened in the few years following the rush. First, the take per miner was drastically reduced as the easily obtained surface supply of ore was exhausted. Even if the miner found his pile, he discovered that prices for tools, food, and clothes had skyrocketed, so that most of what he made ended up quickly in the pockets of merchants. The shrewd money-makers of the gold rush, men such as Mark Hopkins and Collis P. Huntington, wasted little time in the stream beds before they realized that fortune would come from selling shovels, canvas, food, and shirts.

Second, as the surface ore diminished, large corporate investments became desirable. By 1852 mills and smelters were rising to crush the ores that time and the river had not reached. If machinery could crush, it could also erode, and hydraulic mining — the use of high-pressured jets of water to scoop out the rocks — was devised. Placer mining became quartz mining, and there were 108 crushing mills in

Group enterprise (and male predominance) in the California mines:
Marysville, 1850.

California by 1852. These operations were most effectively organized around sources of large capital aggregated into corporations. The corporations required a labor force, so the lonely prospector and the disillusioned Ikes who had rushed across the continent to get rich quick took jobs with the company.

Labor organization began among the miners in the Comstock Lode of Washoe County, Nevada, where a successful strike over wages pulled the workers together as early as 1864. There, the Miners' Protective Association set a pattern that was followed in the western mines for decades: a deep sense of idealistic brotherhood combined with such immediate practical goals as wages and hours. In 1892, miners at Coeur d'Alene, Idaho, struck for union recognition. They were overpowered by troops, and seven miners died in the confrontation. The struggle in Idaho continued sporadically throughout the decade. Out of such conflict grew further organization, initially in the form of the Western Federation of Miners which, between 1893 and 1903, expanded to fifty thousand members. One of WFM's planks called for a prohibition of armed force against labor, a direct reference to the wounds of Coeur d'Alene. WFM leader Bill Haywood was instrumental in forming a larger union in 1905, the Industrial Workers of the World, of which the Western Federation became part.

Some miners refused to become either employees or unionists. Those who had been bitten by the bug of independence turned "rainbow chaser" and listened for tales of richer diggings over the hill. Mary Austin, in her delightful *Land of Little Rain*, described a lonely prospector, the "pocket hunter," whom she ran into from time to time. Threading the windy passes or by the water holes in the desert hills, "he traveled far and took a long time to it."[3] He once found an abandoned shaft that netted him $10,000, on which he traveled to London for a year — no more — and then returned to his burro in the dry camps and ravines.

Though $80 million in gold was taken out of California earth in 1852, it ceased to go into the hands of the independent prospector. The social ramifications of gold rushes spread widely. Storekeepers had to be supplied with goods, of course. Urban centers, freighting, shipbuilding, and the merchant marine felt the boom. The most dramatic effect was seen in the form of the clipper ship, designed to bring cargoes as quickly as possible from the East to San Francisco. In their high noon, about 1853, the ships placed America in the forefront of the world's maritime powers. In California fortunes were made by men who could corner markets in crucial items. Collis Huntington would row out in a dinghy to meet incoming ships with so many gold bags around his belt that capsizing would have sent him straight to the bottom. With gold on the barrel head he would buy every shovel aboard.

Booms in food supplies were to be expected. Here the results were not simply in trading and transportation but in local farming as well. Former Mexican cattle ranches in southern California expanded enormously in the decades after the gold rush, as Yankees such as the elder James Irvine bought up vast acreage. "Cattle on a thousand hills" is the phrase historian Robert Glass Cleland used to describe southern California at this time.[4] In the San Joaquin valley the increase in wheat farming was even more dramatic. According to John W. Caughey, production there in the decade after 1850 bulged annually from seventeen thousand bushels to nearly six million.[5] The initial expansion often was underwritten by eastern capital.

Though they fattened on one another's presence, mining and agriculture were not always congenial mates. Miners in their frenzy had turned over mountains of earth and disturbed the plant life and ground cover of whole watersheds. Even minor rainfalls became floods below — floods of mud, not just water. Hydraulic mining kept streams turgid, whether rains were heavy or not. Farmers with clogged irrigation systems and inundated crops fought bitter legislative battles before elementary regulations were introduced.

Expanding wealth may not improve the quality of life, but it does influence the quantity of culture. When John W. Caughey titled his book *Gold Is the Cornerstone*, he was referring to the fundamental influence of the gold rush on society, education, the theater, opera, literature, and journalism. Probably more Shakespeare was performed during the early days of the mining camps than has ever been staged in a single period since. On makeshift platforms, Jenny Lind sang to miners who might never even have considered buying tickets to hear her at home. H. A. W. Tabor used some of his mining money to build opera houses in Leadville and Denver. Mark Twain will forever be associated with Virginia City's *Territorial Enterprise*. San Francisco in the 1850s and 60s harbored a whole school of authors — Bret Harte, Joaquin Miller, Ambrose Bierce, and Ina Coolbrith. The titles of their new literary journals, *Golden Era* (1852-1893), *Pioneer* (1854-1856), and *Overland Monthly* (1868-1883), suggest their frontier status and the heights their authors felt they had achieved.

The first miners, those who came to the "honest picnic" and reveled in the rugged independence before the big companies came, were seldom the men who stayed around to read *Golden Era*. After 1854 they were off to British Columbia. Rumors from men who had been there along the Fraser River reported the daily average take per man was six ounces of gold. The Fraser's nearest harbor, on the Puget Sound, protected the ships whose crews had deserted for the gold fields. In 1858 some thirty thousand men left the California mines for the Fraser.

In the following year another choice was offered by strikes on the great Comstock Lode. A series of independent finds were made by such prospectors as James "Old Virginny" Fenimore and Henry "Old Pancake" Comstock before the magnitude of the vein was realized. Comstock himself was insignificant in the developing story. He talked a lot, calling the whole region "my mine" and "Comstock's Lode"; he sold one claim early, however, for $11,000, and another for two mules. In its heyday more than $300 million was taken from the Comstock, but it fed the fortunes of later comers like George Hearst and Adolph Sutro. The Consolidated Virginia Mining Company was bringing out ores worth $50,000 a day in 1876, and it paid dividends of $74,250,000 between 1874 and 1881.[6] Meanwhile, Henry Comstock had roamed on to Oregon, Idaho, and Montana.

The rush in Colorado followed close on the heels of the one in Nevada. Rumors of an 1858 boom along Cherry Creek on the eastern

Life in the mines: Pinon, Colorado, 1897, by Thomas McKee.

slopes of the Colorado Rockies were largely groundless, though local promoters built them into mountainous proportions. Fortunately for those who began tramping into Cherry Creek and Clear Creek in 1859, the boomers had guessed better than they had a right to. Gold Hill was opened next, and soon it became evident that a broad belt of gold-bearing ores nearly two hundred miles long waited to be removed. The take during the initial decade suffered by comparison with California's, with only about $25 million worth of gold extracted. In that period an estimated 60 percent of Colorado's miners left disillusioned. Nevertheless, the industry remained regionally important, and the 1870s saw a new rush, first for silver and later for lead, around the higher valleys at Leadville. The 1890s brought a second gold boom and the opening of copper and zinc deposits.

Henry Comstock's rambling was typical. Another miner, Granville Stuart, recounted an experience that might well have involved Comstock himself in Montana. Late one wintry evening the rumor of a new strike made the rounds: thirty miles away, the gravels were so rich you could shovel out pans of gold worth one hundred dollars each. Within hours the town was deserted as men streaked off without provisions despite the January weather. The ore was fool's gold, but the frame of men's minds was unchanged. Such rushing between dozens of gold and silver regions in the course of a half-century instilled the mining frontier with restlessness. Ralph Mann has carefully studied Grass Valley and Nevada City in California, and has found that of every hundred persons there in 1850, only five remained in 1856.

To call the prospectors drifters means little. They preferred a lonely life to working for a company, and independence was often as important as getting rich quickly. They must have sensed the fact that they would never be wealthy, or that, if they made a sudden pile as did Mary Austin's pocket hunter, they would blow it all in one grand spree and then return to their mule and pan. The phrase "gold is where you find it" often became "gold is where I ain't," a pessimism suggesting that gold may have been less important than the search for it.

So it was that the mining frontier began with an individual and a discovery, ran through a frantic rush, and then settled down to corporate domination, while the whole process resulted in rapid physical, social, and cultural transformation of the surrounding region. For more than a half-century this pattern was repeated in different parts of the Far West. It was a striking example of one aspect of Turner's description of the frontier — the constant return to primitive social conditions. Here groups of men had to redefine for themselves the social contract, as the farmers of Oregon had been forced to draft laws and constitutions. Of course, the immediate problems facing miners were much different from those facing farmers.

The makeup of the society in mining camps was unusual. In examining the demographics of 1850 Ralph Mann has found that males between twenty and forty years of age made up 90 percent of the population of Nevada City and Grass Valley, and that by 1860 one-half of the workers were foreign-born. Mining-camp society was the most polyglot collection of nationalities since Babel. Mrs. Louisa Amelia Knapp Clappe, who wrote literate and observant letters to newspapers under the pseudonym Dame Shirley, walked through the camp at Indian Bar and heard English, French, Spanish, German, Italian, and Kanaka (Hawaiian), as well as various eastern Indian and American Indian languages. She called the camp "a perambulating picture gallery, illustrative of national variety." One recent historian has wondered, "where else in all the world could Irish (33,000 in 1860) and Chinese (35,000) have competed for jobs?"[7]

The Americans, it should be remembered, except for the lapse of a few years, would have been the foreigners. But in the mining regions

Cosmopolitan saloon in the California mines, c. 1850, by Frank Marryat.

there was no previously settled Mexican population, and therefore the Americans could immediately become the majority group. Mexicans were not far behind, however, especially large contingents of families coming from the northern state of Sonora. Many of the first Mexican arrivals had experience in mines and were in great demand as technical advisers.

As it became evident that not everyone was going to get rich in the gold fields, the tight jaw of prejudice set in. Mexicans were driven out, and when physical assaults failed, legal assaults followed. A tax on foreign miners imposed monthly assessments of $16 and later $20. Some Mexicans were foreign immigrants, but many were native Californians or New Mexicans who had been guaranteed full rights of American citizenship by the Treaty of Guadalupe Hidalgo. We have no evidence, however, that any collector or law officer in the mines ever bothered to distinguish between Mexican-American citizens and Mexicans. The wartime residue of bitterness between the two peoples was not diluted in the mines.

Blacks comprised some one percent of the mining population, and only a small minority were brought as slaves. Free blacks came with the same ambitions and optimism as whites; the free plank in the California Constitution of 1849 gave them additional hope of avoid-

Double-duty saloon in Leadville, Colorado, c. 1879.

ing prejudice. But first, they expected economic freedom, as exemplified by the black man in San Francisco who spurned a request to carry luggage by instead holding high his own bag of gold dust. That story probably attracted Mifflin Gibbs to California, fresh from a lecture tour with Frederick Douglass. Gibbs, like Huntington and Stanford, was smart enough to enter business rather than the mines; his boot shop thrived in the 1850s. Gibbs helped establish an athenaeum in the city where blacks could meet, talk, and drink together. In the mines their fellows often yielded to the stony white directive to "keep moving." But even among the random sites that remained, they made good strikes. A mythology arose about the proverbial lucky black. There were examples of healthy black-white collaboration, but far more prevalent were the cases of harrassment and of southern hooligans driving blacks from good claims.

The Chinese came into the region a bit later, notably after the Taiping Rebellion had upset China in 1851. Within a year some 25,000 had come, amounting to 10 percent of California's population. The Chinese usually stayed together as a group, working in labor companies under contracts arranged in China. Thus in the eyes of Americans, who thought of themselves as rugged individualists, they were even more suspect than the Mexicans. Douglas Hill, historian of Canada, has examined the prejudice against blacks and Chinese in the mining camps of British Columbia. Blacks, dispersed throughout the community, suffered some overt oppression at the hands of the whites, but the Chinese, living together, were more often victims of threats and all manner of violence.[8]

In California, in addition to the tax on foreign miners, another discriminatory move was made against the Chinese. According to California law, the evidence of blacks and Indians was inadmissible in court. The judges put on the robes of anthropologists and declared that because the American Indian had migrated to North American eons ago from Asia, the Chinese in California must be considered Indians and so be denied the right to testify against a white man. No "melting pot" seemed to be in operation, no amalgamation of various groups and nationalities into a new America. Rather the prevailing Anglo-American culture excluded those who varied from the norm.

As for the predominance of males, it should still be remembered that women were there, often carrying the burden. Anne Ellis, for example, was the cook and "good angel" of a Colorado mining camp. She had arrived when Bonanza counted its population as thirty-six saloons and seven dance halls rather than by human inhabitants. Slender, blue eyed, and alert, she read a great deal — *Hamlet*, Plutarch's *Lives, Camille*. Her father had dragged the family from Missouri to Colorado, saying "We will go west where there are chances for a man." But he was a drifter, and Anne was reared on the trail as her father chased booms.

In order to protect the prevailing society, rules and regulations for the mining camp were needed. The social compact had to be drawn anew. Practical questions arose immediately. Who owned what? How could a man stake out land on which to dig or pan for gold? How much could he claim — a mountain ridge or a whole valley? Where would the deed be recorded? Could a man own land and leave it to be worked later? Who would protect the weak from the strong, the unarmed from the armed?

When Francis Parkman left the Missouri settlements in 1846, he bid "a long adieu to bed and board and the principles of Blackstone's Commentaries."[9] It was not merely English and American common law that the miners would reconstruct with difficulty; they had to create a corpus of mining law, for which they brought almost no usable precedent. Regulations for the English tin mines and for silver mines in New Spain were either unknown or reflected such different societies that they were meaningless in America.

In California the typical procedure was for a group of miners to come together in a kind of mass meeting, elect officers, and draft a few rules. This process happened at least five hundred times in mines there. No one has estimated how often it occurred throughout the West. Similarities emerged, partly because the problems were predictable and partly because of the movement of men from one place to another. Models worked out in California were often adopted elsewhere.

In general the laws allowed a man to stake out any "reasonable" amount of land, by which was meant an amount he could work in a season. He had to mark it clearly and file with the local recorder. Most important, he had to work the land. If he left it, he lost his claim. There would be no absentee owners in the mines. The Spanish-Mexican influence was evident in the attachment of water rights to all land. Thus, even if a man claimed a parcel far back from the banks of a stream, he still had the right to divert a reasonable amount of water to wash his dry gravels.

Political organizations varied, of course. The general meeting usually elected permanent officers — a recorder, a chairman, sometimes an alcalde (the Spanish term for local magistrate). Conflicting claims were arbitrated by committees, panels, juries, or sometimes by entire town meetings.

In some respects the mining codes appear highly idealistic. They seem to have been weighted in favor of the small miner. Some issues, however, were never raised. Indian rights went unrecognized. Gold-bearing streams occasionally ran through Indian hunting grounds or near Indian villages, but there is no record of any miners buying land, or seeking permission to mine, from Indians. Furthermore, some unusual provisions — restrictions on the size of the claim and the requirement for continued use — applied only to initial claims; anyone could buy from the first claimant as much land as he wanted and could choose not to work it. Large companies amassing extensive holdings found the early miners' codes quaint and irrelevant. The companies needed more uniformity between various districts, at least uniformity within a state. Statewide codes were devised only after the passing of the early years of individualism. By then the first comers, like Henry Comstock, were long gone.

A group of miners sitting together, applying common sense to their immediate problems, and coming up with workable mining codes, deserve respect and admiration. An observer might praise their directness and lack of humbug or legal complexities. In transactions involving property, this trait may indeed have been praiseworthy. On the other hand, when life and civil liberties are challenged, the lack of humbug, or disregard for due process, is considerably more serious,

Corporate mining: Virginia City, Nevada, c. 1885.

for such legal complexity protects a man from harm until he is proved guilty. Miners were quick to resort to lynchings and vigilante action, with or without the approval of courts and legal systems. Generations of historians have depicted good citizens aroused by injustice reluctantly banding together in vigilance committees and dispensing swift justice. Motives of economic gain or social prejudice have been ignored. Unfortunately, this type of activity was not confined to mining camps. We have seen it as the Regulator movement in South Carolina and among the Paxton Boys on the Pennsylvania frontier. In the Far West it would emerge again, most notably in relations between ranchers and cattle thieves, farmers and stock growers, growers and migrant laborers.

Activity on the mining frontier consisted of much more than digging gold and silver. The extraction of other minerals — copper, lead, coal, and oil — produced a resource base of enormous significance. Gold and silver, however, grasped the imagination so firmly and represented such a stroke of national good luck that they reveal a substantial part of the larger picture. The precious metals were a gigantic stimulus to economic development in many ways — adding an inflationary spiral to the economy; creating a balance of international trade favorable for imports; promoting growth in agriculture, transportation, and commerce. In its impact on the national character, however, the mining frontier may not have been so glowing. The opening of one mining region after another in the course of a half-century produced a drifting, restless population. The frenzy of gold rushes infected the national psyche with a "get rich quick" attitude. The mining camps became a curious amalgam of rapidly growing, predominately male, polyglot populations. Out of the jumble of racial and national groups came the worst kind of racial prejudice. Because the men in these camps had written their own codes, they frequently took the law into their own hands, giving their prejudices unusual power. This is not to say that the miners did not draft effective social compacts, including such ideas as the disallowance of absentee ownership and community control of the water supply. But such advantages tended to be lost as the individualism was supplanted by large corporate structures. In fact, the small miner was quickly submerged in the rapid rush of economic growth. The American people, however, persisted in believing that the mining frontier, like so much of the West, was characterized by individual initiative. Instead of smoking smelters and corporate boards of directors, they preferred to remember the lonely, restless prospector with his pan and mule beside a mountain stream.

THE LEGACY OF VIGILANTISM

In San Francisco during the gold rush, a displaced Mormon elder and imperious boomer named Sam Brannan rose to wealth and power as a printer, journalist, and storekeeper. In February 1851 he became incensed at the news that a fellow merchant, C. J. Jansen, had been robbed and beaten in his own dry-goods store on Montgomery Street. A hysterical mob, believing that the police would not act, located two Australians who Jansen thought were his assailants. Australians were logical suspects; as immigrants they congregated in an urban ghetto, and their label, "Sydney Ducks," automatically came to denote criminals. Brannan and the other good citizens made preparations for a hanging. William Coleman, another well-placed young man in the community, prevailed on the gathering to set up a court and thus give at least the impression of legality. So doing, the jury brought in an indecisive verdict, and the Sydney Ducks were put in jail instead of into the noose. The two men later were proved innocent.

In May a series of fires terrified the city and rumors pointed to criminals. Brannan assembled a few businessmen in his office, and they adopted a constitution for a committee of vigilance to clean up San Francisco. The next night, one John Jenkins was caught stealing

Vigilance court in session, 1874.

a safe small enough to carry under one arm. He was brought before the committee, sentenced, and in June was hanged by moonlight.

The good people of the committee moved earnestly to further purge their streets of riffraff. They arrested and tried eighty-nine people: four were hanged, one was publicly whipped, twenty-eight were banished, fifteen were handed back to the police, and forty-one were released. The committee smugly declared San Francisco clean, and in mid-September adjourned, receiving plaudits from all over the state.

By 1856, San Francisco was once more a city of unusual tension as typical urban problems were surfacing. Working-class alignments were being made among immigrant groups; political machines had begun to work with and for them, as Tammany Hall had been doing in New York. The mayoralty was in their hands, taxes were rising, and the businessmen of the city were distinctly unhappy.

In May of that year a murder crystallized some of these feelings. The victim was a newspaper editor, James King, whose journal had been denouncing the Democratic political machine of David Broderick. King had exposed the prison record of James Casey, one of

Broderick's political workers. Casey, a volatile New York Irishman, furiously sought out King and shot him.

As a result of this and other incidents, a vastly expanded vigilance committee was called to action. William Coleman, who in the intervening five years had risen to a prominent position in the mercantile world, was placed in command. More than six thousand citizens, mostly middle- and upper-class businessmen, volunteered for service. These vigilantes had already proved irresponsible by failing to vote and to volunteer under established law. A smaller law-and-order faction, mostly lawyers and intellectuals, protested the formation of the vigilance committee but were little heeded. The committee proceeded first to the jail, where Casey and another murderer were taken into custody with no resistance from 150 of the sheriff's men. In a barricaded building, a trial for the two men ended with their sentencing on May 22.

While most of the opposition attended King's funeral, Casey and the other murderer were hanged from a makeshift platform before a small crowd. Casey died after an emotional outpouring in which he protested that he had done only what he had always been taught to do — fight back against wrong. Casey's funeral procession numbered eighty-four carriages, eighty horsemen, and four hundred followers on foot, an indication that he did indeed represent a sizable portion of San Francisco's population. During the trial the vigilantes had refused to honor legally issued writs of habeas corpus, justifying their actions on the grounds of popular sovereignty. The voice of the people, they reasoned, was heard in the crowds that cheered the execution. Such justification overlooked the other crowd, walking silently behind Casey's coffin.

The governor declared San Francisco in a state of insurrection. William T. Sherman, major general of the California militia, should have suppressed the committee but found reasons not to march, one of which — too few arms — was legitimate. Cynics claimed that Sherman's real reason, however, was related to his extensive stock in a San Francisco bank. The bank was heavily indebted to members of the committee, and if Sherman moved against them, he might have feared that they would withdraw their deposits. Sherman resigned and shortly after wrote to his brother, "Being in a business where large interests are at stake, I cannot act with that decision that would otherwise suit me."[10]

Throughout the summer the committee worked, hearing witnesses, seeking suspects, holding trials, reaching verdicts, and executing its own sentences. Four men were hanged, and one committed suicide while still in jail. Thirty were deported, though hundreds of people

Hanging Tree, Helena, Montana, 1870.

left the city in fear. On August 18 the Committee held a jubilant parade and disbanded. San Francisco had been saved. But from what? Practically every person deported was an Irishman. One might conclude that San Francisco had been protected from Irish urban Democrats.

During its activities, the committee had organized a political party of its own, the People's Party, which proceeded to sweep the city elections in the fall. One result of the election was vastly reduced taxes for businessmen. Broderick's expensive programs were scrapped, and the new government so cut the budget that some schools were forced to close. With this in mind, Josiah Royce in 1886 called the whole affair a "businessman's revolution."

In Montana Territory, where the Bitterroot Mountains meet the plains, the early 1860s saw the birth of two mining towns, Virginia City and Bannock. In 1863 they were probably no further along in social organization than San Francisco had been in 1851. Sheriff Henry Plummer, for example, turned out to be the leader of a gang of outlaws who had reportedly commited a hundred murders. When Plummer's gang killed a local businessman, however, irate Montanans took a leaf from the San Francisco book and organized a vigilance committee. Thomas Dimsdale, a contemporary witness, claimed that before they were through recruiting, their ranks numbered nearly all of the good men of the territory. Dimsdale was the teacher of a singing school and a former Oxford student. He gloried in the exploits of the vigilantes and documented their history into what eventually became a kind of vigilante bible. He maintained the necessity and equity of such "mountain law" and was certain that the victims were all miscreants meeting a "dog's doom." He numbered the hangings at twenty-four, though later scholars have raised the figure to thirty. In any case, with Plummer and his gang decimated, "the face of society," said Dimsdale, "was changed as if by magic."[11]

Vigilante action, such as in these examples from the mining frontier, infected every region of the West. Sometimes it assumed the guise of popular sovereignty and fitted with decentralized, local responsibility. More often, however, and especially after 1856, it was characterized by class interest and appeared as part of the everlasting tension between the rich and the poor, the elite and the outcast, the established and the disinherited.

8

Cattle and the
Cult of Masculinity

The cult of the West is built firmly on the cattle kingdom. Nostalgia for the American past beats strongest when the cowboy is its focus. When "the Old West lives again," the resurrection involves steers and cows and ponies and Stetsons at the rodeo. Children on city streets play "cowboys and Indians," not "miners and trappers." A widespread adult organization calling itself The Westerners divides into "corrals" and "posses" and publishes "Brand Books." No region has become so "American" as the open range.

The first cattle came with the Spaniards, who also brought the horse, the essential adjunct, and the sheep. Coronado drove a herd of cattle into the Great Plains for food purposes, but after he left, they seem to have vanished like his own dreams of golden cities. Fifty years later, however, as part of his effort at settlement, Juan de Oñate ran more than a thousand cattle and four thousand sheep into the northern borderlands. Descendants of those cows still run in the Southwest, and since the days of Oñate, the industry of raising cattle for meat, hides, and tallow has never ceased. Just as fishing off the Northeast influenced the surrounding society, so did raising stock shape the culture of the Southwest.

Mission fathers in California in the late eighteenth century were responsible for building large herds, and to a lesser extent this was true in Texas. By 1835 more than three million head of stock, including horses and sheep, grazed between the Nueces River and the

Rio Grande. Anglo-Americans filtering into northern Mexico readily took to ranch life. In California Abel Stearns and Hugo Reid, for example, developed immense herds on their boundless leagues of land. Their counterparts in Texas, such as the Austin colonists, let little if anything supersede their interest in cattle. On the Texas range, cattle often escaped and ran wild, hiding in thickets or running in herds like buffalo across plains at night. The mix of their blood with other strains eventually produced the Texas longhorn, with horns up to six feet wide, a wild glint in its eye, and a racy flavor to its meat.

The cattle industry boomed in the southern counties of the new state of California when hungry miners rushed to the north. But the heartland of the cattle kingdom became south Texas, where the Nueces and the Rio Grande framed a lush land of streams and savannahs. This nursery stocked the expansion northward across the plains. The story of the King Ranch will illustrate those beginnings.

Richard King, as a boy of eleven, fled a Boston jeweler to whom he was apprenticed when the master had the poor judgment to make the boy tend his baby. A few years later he was running boats up the rivers from the Gulf of Mexico and did especially well on the Rio Grande during the Mexican War. He and a strong-willed Quaker, Mifflin Kenedy, became partners, and in 1853 the two men bought 15,500 acres of land in the Nueces–Rio Grande belt for $300. (Eventually the King Ranch spread over nearly a million acres.) During the Civil War cotton fields added another dimension to the enterprise. On occasion Richard King would run the Union blockade with his cotton by flying the Mexican colors, the same flag that once flew over his land before the Americans conquered it.

In only two decades, from 1865 to 1885, the cattle kingdom expanded until it stretched wide and open from Texas to Wyoming. Cattle were driven up and across the public lands. The stock fed freely on the nutritious plant life, the blue grass and the buffalo grass. From the southern to the northern borders there were few obstacles, and the government charged no fees and asked no questions. Buffalo herds and Indians added a little zest to the life of the cowboy. Railroad tracks and settlers breaking the sod and building fences posed minor threats on the horizon, but early in the period they were very far away. The nation generously provided the range and so encouraged the profits. There was certainly no dearth of grass.

The purpose of the great cattle trails was to transport the animals on the Texas ranges, where they had been born and bred, to railheads from which they could be shipped to market. As the railroads were built out onto the plains, so expanded the trails, keeping the intervening distance as short as possible. The average herd was two

Cattle drive, 1905.

thousand head of cattle, and fewer than a dozen mounted men were needed to drive it the eight hundred miles from, say, the King Ranch to Abilene, Kansas. Teddy Blue Abbott described the sun flashing on thousands of horns as the animals snaked out for a full mile along the trail. He also talked of dust like fur on the eyebrows of the drag men and black phlegm from their lungs. There was high drama, at least seen from afar: stampedes of hundreds of animals, dry runs with steers bellowing from thirst, blinding thunderstorms, the muddle of mingled herds, and fear of Indian attack. On most days men would describe themselves as wet, muddy, aching tired, and hungry, or even, in Charlie Duffield's words, "gloomy" and "heartsick."

The Chisholm Trail, named for a half-breed trader, handled one and a half million head of cattle on the way to the railroad yards at Abilene between 1868 and 1871. The Goodnight-Loving Trail, named for Charles Goodnight, a gruff rancher, and his partner Oliver Loving, ran to Denver and Cheyenne. The Western and Cimarron trails ended at Dodge City; the Sedalia Trail went to Missouri. The trails all streamed northward out of the Texas heartland. (See map, p. 154.)

At the end of the trails were the cattle towns, in the 1870s and '80s the most brawling, hard-fisted meccas of brutality and unshirted aggressiveness the West ever knew. However, Robert R. Dykstra, in a detailed study of five cattle towns (Abilene, Dodge City, Ellsworth,

Wichita, and Caldwell), found that excessive violence was limited to the earliest years of each community's life. Thereafter, the number of homicides dropped dramatically, amounting to no more than one or two a year per town.[1] The change came when economic functions became differentiated and entrepreneurial motives came to the fore. City councils may have enacted laws against prostitution and gambling, but officials usually considered these ordinances more sources of revenue than extensions of morality. Business continued as usual, and consciences were clear. On rare occasions when a police officer acted with too heavy a hand, the city council decisively removed him. Because only 20 percent of the population — and these mostly officeholders — owned 75 percent of the property, wealth had become rather unevenly divided, and power concentrated. Thus it was easy to effect leniency when economically desirable. Laxness with prostitution and gambling even spilled over into leniency with homicide, especially for defendants who were young, white, and from good families.

In 1880 the cattle industry began its great five-year boom. Profits were high and well publicized. In 1881 James Brisbin's *Beef Bonanza, or How to Get Rich on the Plains* carried the message widely. It unfolded a simple story as dazzling as a gold strike. A newborn calf could be bought in Texas for $5. Fattening for three or four years was free on the public domain, and the overhead to round up the cattle and drive them to market was no more than $5 a steer (including supplies and horses, salaries of about $300 a year, and food at eleven cents a day per cowboy). At Omaha, the animals could bring $45 a head. With an initial investment of $5,000, one could expect a profit of from 25 to 40 percent a year. Investments poured in from London and Edinburgh. From Britain alone in the 1880s came $45 million, and in roughly the same period some thirty-three companies were registered in Britain to engage in ranching. A Scottish firm, The Espuela Cattle Company, fenced a half-million acres in Texas and called itself the Spur Ranch. As a result of such investments the borders of the open range were pushed rapidly northward. In 1880, buffalo in Montana far outnumbered the two hundred fifty thousand cattle. Three years later, the range stock had increased to six hundred thousand, and the buffalo had all but disappeared. At the same time twenty domestic cattle companies were chartered in Wyoming alone, each capitalized from $20,000 to $3 million.

The cattlemen were not the first to attack the buffalo. Plains Indians had always hunted them, stalking on foot with bow and arrow or driving herds of animals to their deaths over bluffs. When tribes took to the Spanish horse and the efficiency of their hunting increased, the buffalo became central to the Indians' culture. Food, housing, clothing, rituals — all depended on the bison. Of all the sustainers of life for the Indian, only the sun was as important as the buffalo.

As early as 1846 a Cheyenne chief, Yellow Wolf, predicted the end of the buffalo at the hands of the white man.[2] The fur trader preceded the cattlemen, but the great day of the buffalo-hide hunter lay ahead. In the 1880s, pursuing profits from meats and hides, hordes of these hunters, along with sportsmen, descended on the plains and effectively wiped out the bison. In 1882 one St. Paul dealer alone bought between forty-five and fifty thousand hides. With them went the cheers of cattlemen, farmers, army men, and railroaders, who all considered the animals in their wild state an infernal and expensive nuisance. The cattle range, of course, expanded as the buffalo range shrank. To most white plainsmen, the disastrous effect on the Indians of the buffalo's demise was a happy result and a prime justification for the animals' slaughter. Missionaries and other humanitarians who wished to salve their consciences would argue that the Indians should settle on reservations, cease their nomadic hunting, become farmers and Christians, and learn to like the white man's beef. This may have been good Christian business ethics, but it overlooked the fact that the Indians had no money and the government would have to subsidize the purchase of beef from the cattlemen. The cattlemen hardly objected. They could get good prices from the government and then send to the reservations the worst of their animals. Who would care?

The transition from buffalo to cattle had an unfortunate ecological effect that was not immediately apparent. In the natural cycle the buffalo ate the grasses, produced manure for new plant life, and in death returned nutrients to the earth. Because the Indian remained in the same general region, his inclusion in the cycle did not seriously disturb it. The cattle, however, after fattening on the plants of the plains, were transported long distances for slaughter at maturity. Their blood and unused remains were dumped in rivers, and their flesh went even farther afield. The natural cycle of life on the plains was thus broken.

The buffalo's disappearance helped the boom of the cattle industry, but even without the wild animals, bust would follow the boom. The ranges became overstocked, and both speculation and absentee ownership were excessive. As early as the winter of 1882 to 1883 prices began to sag. But the glut was considered temporary, and besides, there were ways to handle the market. Producers, seldom favoring competition when it threatens them, began to combine into

The blizzards of 1886: "Waiting for a Chinook" by Charles Russell (1864-1926).

large livestock associations, which could hold out for higher prices, control wages, and protect themselves.

One thing they could not control, however, was the weather. A series of natural disasters hit the cattle kingdom between 1885 and 1887: in succession two of the coldest winters on record were interspersed with droughts. Cattle tend to drift slowly along in the cold winds, and in those intense northers some herds drifted for eighty miles, starving and collapsing on the way. In the winter of 1886 to 1887 there were losses of 90 percent over wide regions. A cattleman's journal commented ruefully: "An overstocked range must bleed when the blizzards sit in judgment."[3] "A whole generation of cowmen," said J. Frank Dobie, "were dead broke."[4]

The disastrous winters between 1885 and 1887 pushed cattlemen into changes that had been long in the wind. Consumers began to demand more tender beef, not the flesh of half-wild creatures that had run on the open plains. More careful breeding was undertaken.

Melancholy introspection: "Cowboy Singing" by Thomas Eakins,
1888.

Increased investment in breeding necessitated fencing to prevent
contamination of the breed as well as to keep fat on the animals'
bones. Fencing implied land ownership and purchase, which had
been pointless earlier except to control water holes and streams.
With less natural roaming on the range, the animals required feed
during the winter months. Ranchers had to buy land to raise hay.
Change moved in the direction, in Lewis Atherton's words, "of
making ranching a science rather than a gamble."[5] The old days of
rule of thumb were over, reported the Wyoming Stockgrowers
Association. One could no longer count cows by notching a shingle.

The cowboy, like the prospector before him, became a wage
earner in a large corporate, even oligopolistic, enterprise. The myth
of his free, individualistic life, however, would not only refuse to die
but would have an even more vigorous life in literature and general
opinion in the years ahead. Thomas Eakins, perhaps America's
greatest nineteenth-century painter, placed his version of the cowboy
on canvas in 1888 — a lone man seated before a camp fire, singing,

his broad-brimmed hat pushed back from his face. He played a banjo, and the songs he sang spoke of loneliness ("I'm a poor lonesome cowboy and a long way from home"), of lost love ("Spanish is a lovin' tongue"), of death ("I saw a cowpuncher all wrapped in white linen, cold as the clay"; "Bury me not on the lone prairie"), of sensitive or sentimental melancholy ("When the curtains of night are pinned back by the stars"). He was like the medieval troubadour at the court of love, elevating his woman on a pedestal from which she could be worshiped but not touched. The most independent man on earth, he was proud and highly sensitive to criticism. He was reticent and soft-spoken, self-confident, and sometimes contemptuous of others, though loyal to his outfit. The cowboy was the knight, the cavalier, the natural aristocrat, the southern gentleman wearing the banner of a white hat. Boys looked up to him from the dust below as young Joey looked up to Shane in the movie. Boys like Joey came west in droves to become cowboys, and because they knew how the part was played, they acted it skillfully.

The cowboy stereotype concealed some realities; it was a white man's image. The role of blacks was simply ignored. Because Texas, a slave state, was the heart of the cattle kingdom, black men — especially freedmen after the Civil War — were involved in the industry. A major source of labor was blacks. Until the work of Philip Durham, Everett Jones, and Kenneth Porter on the black cowboys, historians and western writers simply disregarded this fact. Durham and Jones, however, pointed out that probably as many as one third of the men who drove the cattle north were black and Mexican, and one fourth were black.[6] Many blacks, such as Deadwood Dick, emerged from the shadowy recesses of legend as white men.

Then, at times, instead of behaving as knights fighting for the truth, cowboys with their colts assumed that might makes right. A French traveler in the cattle country, Baron Edmond de Mandat-Grancey, overheard cowboys weighing the value of friends and principles and concluding, "[Give me] a big revolver and self-reliance!"[7]

The cowboy stereotype also concealed brutality and violence. The work itself was anything but pretty. Existence was hard for the men, but it was worse for the animals. It involved roping and branding (searing flesh with red-hot irons), castration of bulls, and driving animals over dry trails to the limits of their endurance. These were the brutal aspects of the job; the fact that they were necessary for the industry to profit does not make them any more humane.

How much of this kind of brutality spilled over into relations between human beings is not easy to determine, but one cowboy-author, Larry McMurtry, thought it had a good deal to do with the

The inherent violence of the profession: castrating a steer,
by A. A. Forbes (1862–1921).

traditional Texas treatment of Mexicans: "The way to handle Mexicans is to kick 'em in the ribs." This was how McMurtry phrased the attitude that classified Mexicans as animals. He added that he never knew a cowboy who was truly gentle. Such a statement hardly coincides with the soft-spoken essentially peaceful hero one usually meets in fiction.

Another way of understanding the myth of the cowboy is to compare him with his arch-rival, the settler. The cowboy called the farmer a nester, and his lip curled a bit when he said it. The mounted knight has always looked down on the pedestrian peasant grubbing in the soil. Perhaps it all started with the conflict between Cain, the tiller of the earth, and Abel, the keeper of the animals. Throughout history, farmers and herders have felt disdain for each other. On the plains of America the antithetical occupations fought for supremacy. The cowhand was easygoing and generous with his money; the farmer was hardheaded and thrifty. The cowboy was half wild, living in a saddle or out of a chuckwagon on wheels; the nester was rooted to a small plot of land, to a house, a barn, and a kitchen. The cowboy was a bachelor, intimate with saloons and poker tables; the settler was a family man, committed to building schools and churches. As Cain

Home on the range: chuckwagon, by A. A. Forbes (1862–1921).

slew Abel, the farmer would eventually overcome the cattleman on the open range, but not without a battle.

The fight between cattlemen and settlers was bitter, spreading beyond fists and guns. In legislatures, farming interests used quarantine laws, originally intended to curtail the spread of splenic or Texas fever, to hamstring cattle drives. When blanket quarantine laws were found unconstitutional in the 1880s, heavy inspection regulations took their place. No issue, however, was so complicated and symbolic as that of fencing. The nester wanted fences to keep out the cattle herds. The cattleman wanted fences, too, but he wanted to keep out the settler. The open range had been his preserve, and if settlement was allowed to break up the space, the cattle business would never be the same. But for the cattleman, fences also meant protecting cows from breeding with inferior strains, and so the fences supported the changing nature of the industry. Sometimes the ranchers ran their barbed wire across the open range, believing it really belonged to them, as in a sense it had.

The stockmen contended that the legislatures never understood their needs. Land laws for cattlemen were the same as those for farmers. The basic land units of section or quarter-section were fine for the plow, but they were bad for the cow — too small to provide a living for the men who herded cattle. Thus the ranchers rationalized illegal fencing. According to one estimate, there were 130 miles of illegal fence in Laramie County, Wyoming, alone. One town on the plains was completely surrounded by cattlemen's fences, leaving only two gates for townspeople to get in and out. The Congress finally declared fencing of the public domain illegal, but Washington was a long way off for enforcement. Instead, the differences between homesteaders and cattlemen were settled by guerrilla attacks with wire cutters and even guns.

As the industry changed, the cowboy increasingly became a distinct class of laborer, differing from the rancher, who either owned or managed for a larger corporation. The rancher was the "cattle king" or, as a muckraker would phrase it, the mogul or the baron. He made the decisions and reaped the profit. His actions affected American history, according to Lewis Atherton, while the cowboy contributed little. Helpless before the economic power of the ranchers, especially when the owners were combined into livestock growers associations, the cowboy-worker's only political recourse was to organize. The Knights of Labor had locals among the cowhands, and there were strikes for higher pay and better working conditions in the cattle kingdom just as there were elsewhere at the time. The first big cowboy strike involved seven of the largest ranches in the Texas panhandle in the spring of 1883. Three hundred cowboys held out for more than a year against the ranchers, paid gunmen, and Texas rangers, but they lost in the end. In 1886 a strike in Wyoming was more immediately successful at restoring a wage cut, but the leaders were all subsequently blacklisted. Nevertheless, these conflicts were not as disruptive as simultaneous industrial disorders in the East.

Perhaps the cowboy was too absorbed in his melancholy, too much a romantic sentimentalist, to appreciate tedious organization. Yet, in the Marxian context, he became a wage slave. Indeed, Marx's daughter, Eleanor, traveled in America with her husband, Edward Aveling, and found the cowboy to be precisely that. Their information came from Broncho John, handsome and blue eyed, who revealed to them that "no class is harder worked, none so poorly paid for their services." Aveling was smitten with the cowboys in Buffalo Bill's show, with "the ease and grace and simple refinement of these most manly men."[8]

The cowboy might, on the other hand, be a rustler, cattle thief, an outlaw against whom ranchers and virtuous cowboys could unite. The control of rustling could even be used as an excuse by big ranchers to eliminate the small competitor, as in Johnson County, Wyoming, in the early 1890s.

With vast grassy valleys among the Bighorn peaks, Johnson County was the heartland of the Wyoming Stockgrowers Association and home of its autocratic secretary, Thomas Sturgis. In this region of big operators, cowhands and farmers occasionally saved enough money to start a herd of their own. The stockgrowers association worried that herds begun in this way contained cattle that had been rustled or claimed when young and unbranded. Sturgis and his organization had spurred the territorial legislature in 1884 to pass the Maverick Bill, which declared every unbranded calf on the open range the property of the stockgrowers association. When the big interests caught suspects, however, they had difficulty getting them convicted, for juries were controlled by the local citizens, including farmers. More important, the growth of small operators, plus the incursions of farmers, threatened the association's control of the open range. The cattle barons readily concluded that all small owners were, by virtue of the size of their herds, thieves and rustlers. A local prostitute, Ella "Cattle Kate" Watson, took cows in trade and soon owned a handsome herd. She and her paramour, James Averell, were noisy in their denunciation of land monopolists, especially of the large growers who profited from the public domain. In 1889 Watson and Averell were lynched by a vigilante band.

The small growers faced real trouble, prevented as they were by the big herd owners from getting their cattle to market. Obviously the independent herders could not endure long periods without income, and so in self-defense formed their own organization. In 1892 they arranged to drive rather than ship their cattle east, avoiding the big interests and their railroad connections. Nat Champion, a former Texas cattle boss with a tough reputation, was to lead the drive. The big interests responded by hiring fifty gunmen who eventually ambushed Champion in a cabin along the Powder River, shooting him with three others. The local citizens were outraged, and hundreds of them gathered to hang the perpetrators; but the screams of the cattle magnates were heard as far away as Washington, and United States troops were sent to restore order. It is debatable whether or not federal intervention brought law and justice, for the cases against those who killed Champion and his friends were quietly dropped as the evidence disappeared bit by bit. In this Johnson County war the most powerful political forces in Wyoming stood in opposition not only to the rustler but to any cowboy individualistic enough to remain on his own.

A different kind of feud developed on the plains between cattlemen and sheepmen. The Spaniards had imported sheep, just as they had cattle, but the two husbanding operations never coexisted peacefully. From the cattleman's viewpoint, a sheep could not be trusted: if left alone, a sheep would crop the grass so short that the range would be ruined for cattle. The sheep is a small animal, less spirited than cattle, and thus shepherds need not be mounted. From his saddle the cowboy looked down in lordly disdain upon both the shepherd and the farmer. As the farmer had become a nester in cowboy lingo, the shepherd became a sheepman and his animal a woolly. Each of the new words was larded with appropriately damning adjectives. Cattlemen tended to consider the public domain their own preserve and thought their attacks on sheepmen were justified. It was easy for a bunch of mounted cowboys to terrify the sheepmen. One of the worst of these attacks came along the Green River, in Wyoming, where masked men tied the keepers and clubbed eight thousand sheep to death. Joe B. Frantz, historian of the cowboy, believes that "nowhere was the violence of the Great Plains more vicious than in the sheep-cattle feuds."[9]

The cattle kingdom was a masculine world, and out of it came a cult of masculine virtues. Women may have been idolized, but from afar; they were largely irrelevant to the cattle world. This image stands in sharp contrast to the women who actually lived and worked on the large ranches. The wife presided over the ranch house — the unifying symbol — and dispensed its hospitality. Lizzie Campbell of the Matador and Mary Goodnight of the Palo Duro mothered their cowboys, offering meals, staging dances, preaching admonitions, nursing the sick, and patching clothes. Nannie Alderson fed her cowboys their favorite dishes as they loitered in her kitchen. Other wives were less congenial, sometimes associating their cowboys with the likes of a rattlesnake. All of these women, though, unlike the woman in the cowboy cult, were strong human beings.

The cowboy, it is popularized, loved his horse far more than he loved any woman. Andy Adams called that affection "almost human." At least from the days of the Middle Ages, knights and crusaders have been lifted to the heights of bravado on the backs of their steeds. The horse gave the cowboy a boost in the pantheon of masculine heroism. Some analysts of the cowboy have wondered about homosexuality among these young men. Undoubtedly it existed, given the nature of the situation, but one fact is certain: the lasting appeal of the cowboy to Americans can be associated with a cult of masculinity. One of the most interesting followers of this cult was a future president of the United States who became enamored of the West, and especially of the cattle kingdom.

Theodore Roosevelt as rancher-cowboy, c. 1884.

Theodore Roosevelt had been an asthmatic, nearsighted child living in a wealthy household in a New York City brownstone. In his mid-twenties, frustrated by the pressures of the establishment, saddened and shaken by death in his family, and deeply disappointed in his desired political career, he faced what a psychologist might call an identity crisis. In 1883 he invested a fifth of his fortune in a cattle ranch in the Dakota Badlands near Medora, and by June 1884, seeking escape from his bundle of troubles, he had set himself up in a cabin on his Elk Horn Ranch and begun a new kind of life. He supervised the building of a herd and with his partners bought a second ranch, which he called the Maltese Cross, some twenty miles down the Little Missouri River. He loved these ranches — the smell of sage from the prairie, the pines, the river running near his porch. His nearest neighbor was ten miles away. His release from New York would seem to have been complete.

The cowboys laughed at his thin boyish face, his big teeth, thick glasses, and greenhorn vocabulary. It is hard to believe that he once purportedly yelled to his workmen, "Hasten forward quickly, there!" We can imagine his cowhands' reactions to the books on history and puritanism that he gave them. He stayed in the saddle, sometimes for thirteen hours a day, and slept soundly at night as he had not done in New York. Within a few months he was brown as the pine bark and thirty pounds heavier. He wrote home, "This country is growing on me more and more; it has a curious, fantastic beauty all its own."

For Roosevelt the rifle and the saddle were inseparable. "I am very fond of hunting," he wrote, "and there are few sensations I prefer to that of galloping over these rolling, limitless prairies, rifle in hand, or winding my way among the barren, fantastic and grimly picturesque deserts of the so-called Bad Lands."[10] Killing a deer provided the greatest excitement until he shot an elk, and that sensation was in turn superseded by the killing of buffalo. A ritualistic climax came with the slaying of grizzly bear — one brought down at some distance with two shots and another dropped with one shot at eight paces. His companions remembered his shouts of exultation ringing through the woods. When he returned to the East, he had crates of stuffed heads to adorn the hall of his house, and many of these trophies accompanied him to the White House where they vied for attention with the crystal chandeliers. His favorite shooting companions were "fearless and reckless," to him the manliest of virtues. The accolade was complete when he wrote, "The hunter is the archetype of freedom."[11]

For Roosevelt the cowboy was everything the image said he was — independent, bold, "fearless and reckless." He discerned a certain harum-scarum quality, but behind that was good fighting stuff, which he hoped to encourage. He obviously did not see cowboys as potential strikers. With reference to the Haymarket Riots, which occurred in Chicago in 1886 during an anarchist demonstration against police brutality, Roosevelt wrote, "My men here are hard working, labouring men, who work longer hours for no greater wages than many of the strikers; but they are Americans through and through; I believe nothing would give them greater pleasure than a chance with their rifles at one of the mobs." To Teddy Roosevelt straight shooting and fearlessness were American through and through and a defense, violent if necessary, of the status quo.

The West for Roosevelt was the truest America. The East would be saved only if it turned toward the West. If it, like expatriate Henry James, turned toward England, it would be effete, snobbish, and above all servile in its "dread of war."[12] In the Spanish-American War Teddy Roosevelt, leading his band of Rough Riders up San Juan Hill, was fearless and reckless, neckerchiefed and armed with a rifle, reveling in "the victory and gore" of the bully fight. He and his men were "the cowboy regiment" in full masculine array.[13]

According to G. Edward White, Roosevelt wished to be describing all Americans when he labeled the inhabitants of the Badlands as "overwhelmingly masculine. . . . Their masculinity is both a product of their environment and a prerequisite for success in coping with it."[14] Albert Beveridge, Henry Cabot Lodge, and Alfred Thayer Mahan — Roosevelt's friends and political allies — heartily agreed, extolling might and firmness and vigor and power, frowning on the armchair flabbiness of peaceful pursuits. In the same period and even in the same circles, artist Frederic Remington and writers David Graham Phillips and Owen Wister were publicizing the image. James R. McGovern has referred to "the virility impulse" of American Progressives.[15] The cult of American masculinity, however, lies much deeper than any political movement or any few decades in time. Engrained in the national mind, it is closely associated with our faith in the imperviousness of American power and is at least as pervasive as the cowboy in national imagery.

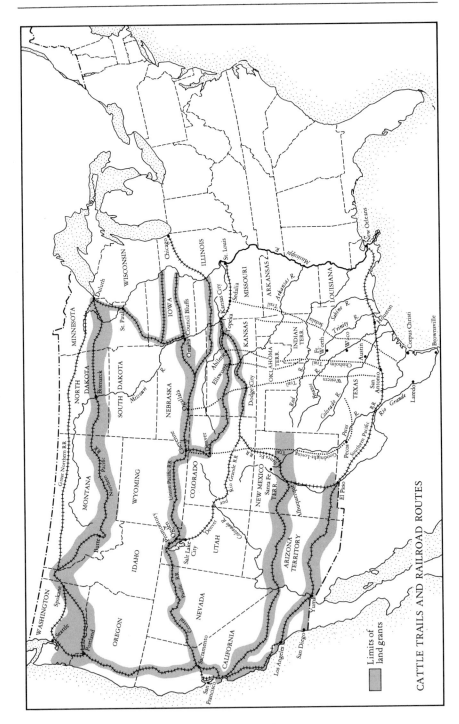

CATTLE TRAILS AND RAILROAD ROUTES

9

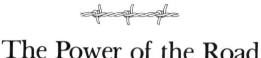

The Power of the Road

The power of American industrialism to exploit the underdeveloped West was nowhere more clearly revealed than in the building of the transcontinental railroad. The industrial index for late nineteenth-century America was based on steel production and railroad mileage. The railroads undergirded an exchange of products and persons and left money in many men's pockets. Wealth and power came to ride the rails. Bret Harte saw, in the ceremonies at Promontory Point in Utah Territory, the two engines (with overblown smokestacks and ox-sized cowcatchers) "Facing on a single track/Half a world behind each back."[1]

To the east lay post–Civil War industrial America, corporate and muscular; to the west, an isolated collection of individualistic trappers, miners, cowboys, and small farmers. Two worlds were only a golden spike apart!

The steel tracks marked the beginning of the end of the stagecoach, the prairie schooner, the horse, and the mule. Romantic and colorful perhaps, these all had to give way as the railroad, and with it progress, moved in. In the nineteenth century most people assumed that one measure of the good life was mobility. The golden spike symbolized progress and made earlier methods of transportation seem antiquated and primitive. Still, given the size of the population in the West before 1869, freight, mails, and people had been moving rather efficiently.

Much of the earlier system was based on federal government expenditures and subsidies. The main arteries originally had been sur-

Deadwood coaches, by J. C. H. Grabill, 1889.

veyed or explored by army engineers such as Frémont and Pike, and the army protected the caravans of goods and passengers that embarked on these roads. The Santa Fe Trail, for example, which began its busy life in the early 1820s, occasionally employed army escorts for its fleets of wagons, and the troops even went beyond the borders of the United States and across the Mexican plains. Equally important as a subsidy were government mail contracts. The first large-scale grant for mail service in the Far West went to John Butterfield and made possible a stagecoaching business of imperial design known as the Butterfield Overland Mail.

John Butterfield was one of a group of eastern self-made businessmen who jumped at the chance to capitalize on the need for transportation in the West. They included such near-legendary figures as Henry Wells and William Fargo. Butterfield, Wells, and Fargo all had begun separately as mail riders, coach drivers, or messengers for express companies. They rose to become agents and then owners or partners. In 1850 the three lives crossed when their respective companies merged into the American Express.

But that was in the East. When they turned their eyes toward the West, as most of the nation did following the Mexican conquests and the discovery of gold, Wells and Fargo combined to run stage lines between the mining camps in California. In 1857 John Butterfield received a government contract for $600,000 to organize a stage line between Missouri and California. The route he chose was called the "ox-bow" because it avoided the Rockies in a great festooned loop to the south, then proceeded up the California valleys to San Francisco. On the completion of the first run, President Buchanan wired Butterfield his congratulations, calling it "a glorious triumph for civilization." It was equally glorious for Wells, Fargo, and Butterfield, because they could receive passengers' fares from San Francisco to New York without losing a penny to rival companies.

Butterfield, a handsome, aggressive man, soon presided over a network that ran for nearly twenty-eight hundred miles, connecting St. Louis, Santa Fe, Denver, Virginia City, and San Francisco. Twice weekly a stage started in Missouri rather punctually and arrived in San Francisco twenty-two days later. The fare was $200 westward and less eastward because fewer people went that way. More than two hundred fifty swaying, leather-braced Concord coaches were tended by some eight hundred men.

In the early days of the Civil War, northerners forced Butterfield to abandon his southern loop and use the central road. There he was pushed into competition with another express and freighting company — Russell, Majors, and Waddell. Since 1855 this company had been engaged in the tedious, dusty business of hauling freight wagons over winding trails. Its claim to fame, however, rests not on this unromantic fact but on one lawless employee and one magnificent failure.

The employee was James Butler Hickok, who drove the stage on the Santa Fe Trail before he took up with Russell, Majors, and Waddell. For them he managed the stage along the Oregon Trail, roughly in the area of present-day Nebraska. Near the Rock Creek station, where Hickok presided, the company had bought some property from a man named David McCanles. Seeking payment one day in 1861, McCanles approached Hickok unarmed and was greeted by a deadly shot. No one seemed to doubt the act was murder, but the local justice of the peace was in the orbit of the company and Hickok was acquitted. His gunmanship served him well in the Civil War, in which he acted as scout and spy. After the war he took a turn as marshal in some of the Kansas cowtowns, among thcm Abilene, then returned to the army, subduing Indians with Sheridan and Custer. Hickok's apotheosis came in the Wild West shows of Buffalo Bill Cody, where he assumed the name Wild Bill. For a generation of boys the qualities of strength and aggressiveness turned a stagedriver-teamster-gunman-murderer into a minor god.

The aforementioned magnificent failure was the Pony Express, as legendary a phenomenon as Hickok. Once under way, the Express was speed incarnate. It covered 1,966 miles in an average of ten days, less than half the time of the Butterfield Mail. One hundred fifteen stations were provided for change of horses, and 120 riders mounted the relays. The horseman carried no guns, in an effort to conserve weight; speed was his only protection. "A little bit of a man," Mark Twain called one of them, "brimful of spirit and endurance." The mail pouches were kept slim by the cost of the letters — up to $10 an ounce. The Express lasted for less than two years, between 1860 and 1862, "like a belated fragment of a storm." But Americans have always loved its memory — so efficient, so organized, so dependent on the physical stamina of a rider alone against the elements.

It was the telegraph that killed the Pony Express, and partly as a result its parent corporation, Russell, Majors, and Waddell, went bankrupt in 1862. Ben Holladay foreclosed and took it over. For a short time after the Civil War, Holladay thus came to rival Butterfield. Holladay was not a Yankee businessman like the others, but after the war he had the sense to buy up surplus wagons and mules, and he managed to exert his southern charm sufficiently on Brigham Young to get preferential treatment in the Utah sector. It was a Holladay coach that Mark Twain rode when he came "roughing it" west. Twain delighted in the story of a boy who belittled Moses for the forty years he took to get the children of Israel across the desert: "Ben Holladay would have fetched them through in thirty-six hours."[2]

For all its color, the age of the western stage was short. Horsepower was already doomed. In the Northeast the transition to steam engines and steel rails was well advanced. States barely east of the Mississippi were already laced with rails. The Illinois Central was thriving, even advertising in Europe for settlers and allowing farmers to pay off mortgages with produce. Everywhere coaches were relegated to routes of minimal business. The corporations that bought out Ben Holladay and John Butterfield — Wells, Fargo, and Company in the West, and the American Express farther east — succeeded only because they monopolized the dwindling amount of staging. Henry Wells became president of a railroad, and Ben Holladay moved into shipping. The coaching age created comfortable fortunes for a few, but they were nothing compared to the fortunes ahead for the builders of the transcontinental railroad.

In 1849 a young politician by the name of William Gilpin addressed a mass meeting in Independence, Missouri. Among his listeners in that golden year one can imagine men whose thoughts wandered across the plains west to the mines. Gilpin's thinking tended in the same direction. He lambasted the Atlantic states for holding the West in bondage. The expansive force of its people could be stopped no more than could God's annual layering of rings on the forest trees. The East was dampening that force by diverting revenues to shipping and seaborne commerce rather than giving westerners cheap land from the public domain and, above all, allowing them to build a transcontinental railroad. Such an "iron path" would link East and West, bringing the ageless cultural artifacts of China — teas, lacquers, gunpowders — straight to the heart of America. Even if one took a strictly national view, Gilpin boomed, a railroad must join the two coasts like "ears on a human head." One might cringe at the rhetoric, but the dream was almost universal in the West. Only a few backward-looking, self-seeking interests such as the stage lines would begrudge the railroad.

By the time Gilpin spoke, there was no doubt that the transcontinental railroad would be built. The only questions were when, where, and how. At first there could be but one main line, and enormous economic profit would fall to the section, North or South, into which the rails would pour their loads. Some of the individual participants in the debate stood to gain from the decision. Senator Thomas Hart Benton, for example, owned land near the terminus of the central route, for which he fought mightily.

For a time it was hoped that the engineers could untie the political knots. Perhaps one route could be clearly demonstrated to be cheapest and others disqualified on purely practical grounds. In 1852 Congress appropriated $400,000 for the army to survey and determine the best route. After a year's work and the publication of thirteen volumes of details, the army in effect said there were seven practical routes, four of which were good ones — two in the North and two in the South. The hope for an apolitical solution thus died in 1853. Ten more years were needed to settle the question of the route, and then it was resolved only because one of the contending sections withdrew from the debate. By secession the South conceded the fight.

In 1862 Congress granted the West two of its most fervent wishes — cheap land in the Homestead Act and a transcontinental line in the Pacific Railroad Bill. Congress' purposes were clear: to tap the commerce of China, to supply miners and access their gold, and to transport farmers who would homestead on the public domain and whose produce would be carried back to feed the cities of the East. None of these could happen without the railroad.

The bill of 1862 tackled the question of how to build the railroad. It empowered two corporations, the Union Pacific and the Central Pacific, to construct (westward and eastward respectively) "a continuous railroad" from the hundredth meridian west to the Pacific

Santa Fe Railroad, Canyon Diablo, Arizona, c. 1900.

Ocean. The companies secured a four-hundred-foot right-of-way, two hundred feet on either side of the rails. They also received alternate sections of the public domain within ten miles of each side of the line, amounting to ten sections (or an equivalent of ten square miles) for each linear mile of track. Whenever necessary, the government agreed "to extinguish as rapidly as may be the Indian titles." To reduce financial risk, the legislation offered to loan the companies money for construction. Realizing costs would vary with the terrain, Congress scaled the loan from $16,000 per mile of level ground to $48,000 per mountainous mile, all in the form of thirty-year bonds at 6 percent interest.

This trinitarian subsidy of right-of-way, land grant, and loan did not spur the companies to action. By holding out for two years, they got the ante almost doubled. In 1864 the land grants increased to alternate sections within twenty miles of the track, amounting to twenty sections per mile instead of ten. On the loans the government took a second mortgage, reducing the companies' risk to nil. With little financial gamble involved and grand profits assured, the corporations moved forward to see which could build the fastest, get the largest subsidy, and engross most of the future commerce.

The Pacific Railroad Bills of 1862 and 1864 assumed that unaided private enterprise would not build the transcontinental line. Over most of the route between Missouri and California, population and markets were as sparse as trees on the Nevada desert. If society at large wished to bind together the coasts, like "ears on a human head," society would have to pay the cost. The government could have built the road itself, and the army corps of engineers probably would have done a good job. No one in the American Congress, however, entertained such "socialist" notions. There was no particular reason to question the policy regarding the loans. They were in fact eventually repaid in full with interest, though not without strong efforts to have them abrogated. The basic cost to the government was in land. About 45 million acres were granted to the Union Pacific and the Central Pacific alone. All western railroads received about 131 million acres, or roughly 9 percent of the public domain in 1850. Such largesse to one sector of the corporate economy may seem excessive unless one remembers that the land was valuable primarily after access and use. The great cessions of land from France and Mexico and the Mexican War itself could be reckoned roughly in dollars and cents. The cost of the public domain came to about twenty-three cents an acre, and the initial expense to the government for all the land granted to the western railroads came to about $31 million.

Such reasoning does not consider the potential value of the land, which was enormous. Society had a right to expect back some portion of the unearned increment. But the government's concerns were short range — the immediate transportation of men and supplies — and these were achieved. In the long run, however, society paid heavily, and a few men and companies reaped rich rewards.

Collis P. Huntington was the son of a Connecticut tinker, and inheritor of prudential virtues beginning with diligence and thrift. By the time he was sixteen he had made and, more important to his creed, saved $175, no small achievement in early rural America. Leaving home, he invested in a country store with his brother in upstate New York. He made money again, but not fast enough for his young ambition. At various times he tried peddling watches from a wagon like a proverbial Connecticut Yankee, foisting wooden nutmegs, selling butter in New York, and buying up unpaid notes at a discount in the South. In the selective frontier movement, it may not have been wholly coincidental that this kind of man looked west. Those who were more content, who asked less of life in a material sense, stayed behind keeping the country store.

Huntington joined the rush to California in 1849, choosing to go by ship via Panama. Like thousands of others, he was stranded on the isthmus for three months, clamoring for passage up the coast to San Francisco. During that time, shrewdly buying and selling whatever he could get his hands on, he increased his initial capital of $1,200 by nearly 300 percent. His waking hours, and perhaps even his dreams, were always dominated by an omnivorous sense of opportunity. Thus in the gold fields he immediately grasped the fundamental fact that fortune lay not in the bottom of a pan but in the pan itself. He looked back on his days with shovel and placer as his life's most monumental waste of time. Thereafter he took to supplying the needs of miners, charging what the market would bear. He pooled his resources with a frugal vegetarian, "Uncle Mark" Hopkins, and opened a store on K Street in Sacramento. In that tent-and-tenderfoot city they cornered markets on whatever they could, always hoping their corners might be on such crucial items as shovels.

In an upstairs room of his store in 1861 a group of men were called together by a zealot, sometimes known as "Crazy" Theodore Judah. It was not the first time Judah had spread his plans, surveys, and dreams before potential investors. These men, however, responded. Ignoring Judah, they later became known as the Big Four — the two store owners, Huntington and Hopkins, plus two others, Leland Stanford and Charles Crocker. They were physically big men, ranging from 200 to 240 pounds, and together totaled some 860 pounds. Eventually each of them pledged to buy $15,000 of stock in the company for which Judah had drawn the articles of incorporation, the Central Pacific Railroad.

In the East, the Union Pacific was capitalized at $100 million in shares of $1,000, and the government required that $2 million of the stock be subscribed before construction could begin. Under William B. Ogden, its first president, the company lacked investor appeal. Rumored costs of construction were as high as $30,000 per mile for the first hundred miles, and few could expect much return on a railroad that went "from nowhere to nowhere." The first $2 million were raised, however, by 1863, and construction began at Omaha before Christmas of that year. But it was not until a new president, Thomas C. Durant, hired General Grenville Dodge, and gave him absolute powers in the field, that the road began to take shape. Dodge hired the toughest men he could find, usually Irishmen, and established rigid discipline. His own shares of company stock were in his wife's name, and he reaped rewards more handsome than most generals in his position on temporary leave from the army.

The Crédit Mobilier, a subcontracting subsidiary corporation, en-

Building the Union Pacific in Nebraska, by A. R. Waud (1828–1891).

abled the leaders of the Union Pacific to make more money. The subsidiary could charge dearly for constructing the road, and the books of the Union Pacific would thus show little or no profit. Thomas Durant, heavily involved himself, hired agent George Train to see that Crédit Mobilier stock ended up in the right pockets. Recipients were not only company officials but also men like Schuyler Colfax, vice-president of the United States, and Oakes Ames and James Brooks, congressmen in a position to be "friendly" to the company. The unethical nature of the Crédit Mobilier was only part of a scandalous period. The Central Pacific had its own version of the same idea, known as the Credit and Finance Corporation, which was estimated to have taken at least $36 million in excess funds from the government. This kind of activity led Senator George Hoar of Massachusetts to denounce the railroad: "Every step of that mighty enterprise had been taken in fraud."[3]

Grenville Dodge, in hiring Irishmen, could tap a whole reservoir of immigration, which the railroads themselves encouraged by advertising in Europe. Employers in California had a harder time. The gold-rush hordes had melted away and labor there was dear. Crocker, in charge of construction, contemplated the importation of Mexican peons, the kind of cheap labor California always seemed to require for exploitation. Chinese laborers might have been even cheaper, but when

*Behind the ceremony: paymaster's care at Promontory, Utah, 1869,
by A. J. Russell.*

Stanford first advanced the idea of using them, he was laughed at.
The Chinese were considered too small and weak until someone remembered that their ancestors had built the Great Wall of China. A
few experiments were tried with small work gangs of fifty Chinese.
The results were so astounding that within six months two thousand
Chinese were at work on the road, and the company began importing
additional thousands from the Orient. Eventually the work force
was built heavily on the "Asiatic Contingent of the Grand Army of
Civilization," and ten thousand Chinese sweated over the tracks at
the peak of construction. Along some of the nearly impassable gorges
of the Sierras they picked away like ants against solid granite walls,
carrying the rock away in baskets — a job so difficult that, in spite of
their numbers, they were able to average only eight inches of laid
rails per day.

The Chinese in the Sierras held the record for the slowest pace.
The Union Pacific workers, in contrast, once laid ten miles of track
in one day. General Dodge encouraged competition whenever he

Union Pacific depot, Omaha, 1877.

could, not only between two rival companies but also between East and West, Irish and Chinese, progressive civilization and wilderness. A combative spirit spilled over into brawls when the two labor forces came into contact, and racist feelings about the Chinese and their opium smoking were given free rein. The rivalry resulted in slipshod work. John F. Stover has written: "The construction was often hurried with flimsy bridges, narrow embankments, and improperly ballasted track."[4] In the excitement of the contest two hundred miles of parallel work went ignored until the government stepped in and arbitrarily designated Promontory Point, Utah, as the site of the meeting of the rails, which came finally in the spring of 1869. (See map, p. 154.)

The construction of the railroad was a direct threat to the Indians. They were well aware of the significance of the tracks winding across the plains like an "iron snake." They likened the fumes from the locomotives to the acrid smoke of rifles and dreamed of the day they could blow their lungs free of them both. But they also knew that the smell of steel was not easily blown away. The "iron snake" brought with it hide hunters who could carry back buffalo skins by the millions, cattle cars to take away bellowing herds, farmers to stake out plots of wheat — they all spelled doom for the Indian. A

Deserted railroad town in Kansas, 1874.

year after the transcontinental railroad was finished, Red Cloud said, "The white children have surrounded me and have left me nothing but an island. When we first had all this land we were strong; now we are melting like snow on a hillside, while you are grown like spring grass."[5]

For the white man the railroad was little short of a miracle. A technological triumph, it was immediately utilizable. Tourists appreciated the physical comfort and ease it offered for getting across the thousand-mile span, especially when compared with travel by wagon and stage.

For the literary mind, romantic symbolism often draped the road. Joaquin Miller could discern poetry in every engine hurtling across the continent. Robert Louis Stevenson, traveling on the immigrant cars of the Union Pacific in 1879, captured some of the feeling:

> And when I think how the railroad has been pushed through this unwatered wilderness and haunt of savage tribes, and now will bear an immigrant for some £12 from the Atlantic to the Golden Gates; how at each stage of the construction, roaring, impromptu cities, full of gold

and lust and death, sprang up and then died away again, and are now but wayside stations in the desert; how in these uncouth places pig-tailed Chinese pirates worked side by side with border ruffians and broken men from Europe, talking together in a mixed dialect, mostly oaths, gambling, drinking, quarreling and murdering like wolves; how the plumed hereditary lord of all America heard, in this last fastness, the scream of the "bad medicine waggon" charioting his foes; and then when I go on to remember that all this epical turmoil was conducted by gentlemen in frock coats, and with a view to nothing more extraor-dinary than a fortune and a subsequent visit to Paris, it seems to me, I own, as if this railway were the one typical achievement of the age in which we live, as if it brought together into one plot all the ends of the world and all the degrees of social rank, and offered to some great writer the busiest, the most extended, and the most varied subject for an enduring literary work. If it be romance, if it be contrast, if it be heroism that we require, what was Troy town to this? But, alas! it is not these things that are necessary — it is only Homer.[6]

How can we understand such responses, especially in the face of the shoddy work, the tremendous costs, and the untested results? The transcontinental railroad was an old dream finally realized. The passage to India or the Northwest Passage had been found — if not exactly found, at least fashioned. The road meant, too, that the great territorial acquisitions of the West could, contrary to some fears, be assimilated into the nation. If there was guilt over these conquests, that guilt was momentarily hidden beneath the technological achieve-ment and submerged under visions of potential efficiency and profit.

Before the completion of the transcontinental line, a network of feeders began to extend outward from the main arteries. Railroad building was accelerating in all the industrialized nations, but in the American West the construction of additional mileage was encouraged by continuing government largesse. In 1863, for example, the Atchi-son, Topeka, and the Santa Fe received three million acres of the public domain. The Big Four incorporated the Southern Pacific, which together with other companies provided a line from California to New Orleans. That line received, by a congressional act of 1861, twenty sections per mile of track in the states and forty sections in the territories, in addition to its 1866 grant for the main route in California. The Northern Pacific through Montana and Idaho received land grants twice as large as those of the Union Pacific, though it re-ceived no loans. Still it had trouble until Henry Villard took over its direction and finished the construction in 1883. James J. Hill came too late for handouts — the government began entertaining second thoughts about subsidies — but he completed the Great Northern in 1893. By 1871, with land and bonds, the government had aided seventy-nine railroad companies.

It is hard to exaggerate the railroad's eventual control over the political and economic development of the West. The power stemmed from a welter of activities, depending on time, place, and opportunity. Practices included bribery of office holders and lawmen and regulatory commissions, discriminatory rates favoring certain customers or commodities, and the holding or pressuring of newspapers in order to manipulate public opinion. The name of the enterprise was free capitalism. One acquaintance of Collis Huntington captured the spirit by describing his friend as "tigerish and irrational in his ravenous pursuit. He was always on the scent, incapable of fatigue, delighting in his strength and the use of it, and full of the love of combat. . . . If the Great Wall of China were put in his path, he would attack it with his nails."[7]

The chief role of manipulating Congress and the judiciary fell to Huntington, who remained confident in his own righteousness while performing magic with his millions. "If you have to pay money to have the right thing done, it is only just and fair to do it," Huntington once wrote. "If a man has the power to do great evil and won't do right unless he is bribed to do it, I think the time spent will be gained when it is a man's duty to go up and bribe the judge."[8] As persistent as he had been selling watches from his wagon, he once sat for days in the office of the Secretary of the Treasury seeking the immediate delivery of bonds for the railroad. When Huntington announced that he was ready to continue his sit-in as long as necessary, the Secretary reluctantly surrendered.

Huntington preferred to work behind the scenes. Leland Stanford loved the limelight. He was governor of California for only two years, but they were crucial years for the Central Pacific. In 1885 his political ambition broke out again. As president of the Central Pacific he deliberately scuttled the railroad's candidate for the United States Senate in order to get himself elected. He served that term and part of another, remaining a senator until he died in 1893. Huntington never quite understood Stanford's lust for position. When Huntington heard that Stanford was running for the Senate, he wired, "I cannot believe it." A few years later, Huntington remarked, "Stanford is very clever in some things, but his strong point is his vanity."[9]

In settled regions rails simply improved existing commercial arteries. In the West, however, cities sprang up in the railroad's wake. Through this process the companies developed leverage. Not only could they make their own lands more valuable and hence reap subsidiary fortunes, but they could dictate where and how the cities would grow. Colton, California, for example, was created simply because another town, San Bernardino, would not grant advantages to the Southern

Pacific. In city planning, the San Francisco waterfront shows how doggedly the railroad could pursue its course. The Central Pacific bought five hundred acres of Oakland waterfront. Then it gradually purchased all the bay area's feeder railroads and their ferry slips. Finally it controlled the rim of San Francisco Bay, north, south, east, and west.

In rural areas the railroad could block development in other ways. With the government's land grants, for example, the railroads had the right to choose which alternate sections they wished. A deadline for the decision was seldom stipulated, so the companies quite naturally waited to see how development would go. Until the decision was made, no one could take up claims on any of the sections within twenty miles of either side of the tracks. Even after the company had made its choice, the railroad often would lease its land to an adjacent farmer, refusing to sell until prices had risen. The increased prices were, of course, largely the result of the famer's own labor.

From these few examples it is not hard to understand the hatred that flowed toward the railroad. For every poet who thrilled to the whine of the whistle through the night there was at least another who, in spirit, sat beside Thoreau at Walden Pond and quietly hated the Fitchburg Railroad for despoiling the environment. Thoreau knew the tracks connected him with society and would create their own mythology, but he sensed the worst when he wrote:

> We have constructed a fate. We do not ride on the railroad; it rides upon us. Did you ever think what those sleepers are that underlie the railroad? Each one is a man, an Irishman, or a Yankeeman. The rails are laid on them, and they are covered with sand, and the cars run smoothly over them. They are sound sleepers, I assure you. And every few years a new lot is laid down and run over; so that, if some have the pleasure of riding on a rail, others have the misfortune to be ridden upon.[10]

Nathaniel Hawthorne, who died five years before the completion of the transcontinental railroad, held similar worries about the future. In his allegorical story "The Celestial Railroad," steaming engines driven by demons take men not to heaven but to hell. Along the route at such stations as Vanity Fair people revel in prosperity and plenty as fat capitalists buy consciences.

Thoreau and Hawthorne were, of course, New Englanders reacting against the industrialization of their quiet towns. By the time the big western line was finished they were both dead, but what they had seen in New England began to take place in the West. There in 1869 late-budding industrialism took the form of a few mining smelters, some commercial depots, and the railroad itself. A protest against industrialism would come in the conservation movement, especially in the branch known as preservation, in the late nineteenth and early twentieth centuries. Farmers would rail against the abuses of the railroad. Meanwhile the railroads collected their due of resentment and bitterness. Henry George, in *Progress and Poverty* (1879), raised a fundamental question: Why should railroads benefit from increased land value while the growing society that had created the increase received little in return? Reflections, too, came in stories men told to one another — stories in which Collis Huntington had no more soul than a shark. The same men would chuckle at the tales of train holdups pulled by Jesse and Frank James, Sam Bass, and the Hole-in-the-Wall Gang. After all, the railroad had been stealing, and for a long time. In the legend of Jesse James one can see at least two currents flowing together — the western antilaw tradition and newer protests against corporate industrial power. A black cowhand, Nat Love, claimed to know Jesse well and wrote of the James boys:

> Their names are recorded in history as the most famous robbers of the new world, but to us cowboys of the cattle country who knew them well, they were true men, brave, kind, generous and considerate, and while they were robbers and bandits, yet what they took from the rich they gave to the poor. . . . And if they were robbers, by what name are we to call some of the great trusts, corporations and brokers, who have for years been robbing the people of this country?[11]

Was there any middle ground? To some the railroad was the achievement of the age, a monument to the perserverance and power of a people, and the men who built that monument were only a little lower than the demigods who wrestled in the shadows of Troy. To others the railroad was not a monument but a monster; the Frankensteins who created it were, in the words of the Sacramento *Union*, "cold-hearted, selfish, sordid men"[12] and the brave hearts were the outlaws who robbed the road of its ill-gotten revenue. To much of the East, the hero of the story was Collis Huntington; to a subtantial segment of the West, it was Jesse James.

10

Dugouts and Domesticity: Farming the Great Plains

"All human events *take place*," and a farmer, more than anyone else, is the product of his geography. In the East the land gradually had drawn him away from the peasant village pattern. Yet, as far west as Illinois, farmers were more than "a loose and accidental assemblage of atomized pioneers."[1] They had maintained networks of rural life. Economic and social ties still bound them. Even at a subsistence level they knew their success was related to barn raisings, barter, and the exchange of work. All aspects of the farmers' lives — intermarriage, politics, conversation at the local grist mill, camp meetings — were enveloped by the sense of a common place, by the home valley, the stream with its swimming hole, the picnic grove. Such rural life would be struck by shock waves of change as the farmer moved across the Mississippi.

Rudyard Kipling saw the prairies of America as a "ghastly monotony of earth and sky." "When the corn is in the ear," he wrote traveling through Minnesota, "the wind chasing shadows across it for miles on miles breeds as it were a vertigo in those who must look and cannot turn their eyes away." With the shady hedgerows of Devonshire, where Kipling had been educated, the contrast would indeed be great. The monotony he described was of the prairies, the fertile, grassy, rolling country, the agricultural heartland of the great Mississippi basin. Men, including Kipling, never tired of comparing the prairies with the ocean — unbroken horizons, long, green swells, a "sea of grass" across which prairie schooners sailed. Had Kipling been viewing the plains between the prairies and the Rocky Mountains, his vertigo might have touched on madness. There, the undulating grasses of the prairies became the short, tough cover of blue grama and buffalo grass. Robert Louis Stevenson found it a truly God-forsaken land. That was the area Major Stephen Long had labeled the Great American Desert, and with good reason. Rivers ran across it from the Rockies to the Mississippi, like rungs on a ladder, but they were hundreds of miles apart. The high mountains out of which the rivers flowed squeezed the moisture from the clouds and left the winds dry and pitiless. Little wonder that by the time of the Civil War farmers had gone no farther west than Kansas and Missouri, pausing before the barrier of the plains.

When men called it a desert, they imagined that it would be deserted of people; when they thought of people, they had in mind white farmers living the traditional agricultural life. Indians had lived on the Great Plains and farmed some of the region's valleys, but they were dismissed as wild nomads, and thus the land might still be thought deserted. Along with those "savages" existed the buffalo, but their immense numbers also indicated that the area was a desert, untouched by the white man's farming. For the region to become agricultural, the nomad and the wild beast had to go, but there was a transitional step — seminomadic cowboys introducing cattle onto the plains, supplanting the buffalo. The sparseness of the land seemed to indicate that grazing creatures and nomadic cultures were appropriate to the geography. But right or wrong for the land, the hunting ground of the Indian and the open range of the cattleman were anathema to the farmer, who wanted to straddle the land firmly, break it like a wild mustang, plow it, and make it do his bidding. He bore in his mind a myth, a pseudoscientific hope, that plowing and planting of trees would create moisture, that rain would follow the plow. It was as beguiling as the water witch's wand.

In 1931 Walter Prescott Webb, a Texas historian of the frontier, advanced the thesis that the plains were subdued by settlers only when technology allowed for adaptation to their peculiar conditions. In the East farmers were little concerned with water because rainfall was usually adequate; but their advancement on the plains rested on the availability of windmills and pumping equipment. In the East tilling could be done with iron or even wooden plows; on the plains the tough ground cover splintered wood and demanded steel. In the East the essential tool was the ax, for felling trees for clearings and splitting rails for fences; on the treeless plains the ax was of little use. There the farmers needed fences, perhaps more than ever, because of the vast distances and the threats of cattlemen's stampeding herds. They tried piling up mud in blocks, and the results, in addition to being ugly (as homely as a mud fence), were hopeless in spring rains. Plants such as cactus and Osage orange were deterrents but not strong enough to discourage bulls.

Sometimes adapting required innovating with what was given. The farmer was forced to build temporary shelters of sod blocks and to burn buffalo dung or chips for heat and cooking. The vast, level land called for big operations, far bigger than the clearings in eastern woods. Acceptance of bigness circled finally into technology, for the size of the job necessitated machines — threshers, harvesters, combines. In time the machines made possible deep plowing before the rain and rapid surface harrowing after the rain, techniques that came to be called dry farming. Webb considered these adaptations to be so fundamental that he called the 98th meridian an institutional fault line: "Practically every institution that was carried across it was either broken and remade or else greatly altered. The ways of travel, the weapons, the method of tilling the soil, the plows and other agricultural implements, and even the laws themselves were modified."[2] In the eastern woodlands, civilization stood on three legs — land, water, timber; west of the Mississippi, it was left on one leg — land — and it was not hard to predict that for a time it would topple. The Webb thesis is environmental determinism to the ultimate: he considered geography the prime cause and first force.

A modern interpreter of the West, David Potter, in *People of Plenty* cautions that we be careful not to overemphasize the land at the expense of the know-how and technology. An example of the importance of technology came in the work of Joseph Glidden, a farmer from De Kalb, Illinois, who patented in 1874 "a twisted wire with transverse spurs." He had devised barbed wire, a godsend for the farmer on the plains. Eighty million pounds of barbed wire had been sold by 1880, and twenty years later sales were averaging 297 million pounds per year. Barbed wire, produced in the factories of the East, challenged the assumption that the land determined all.

To ask whether geography or technology is more significant is to ask whether a glass is half full or half empty. One technological device, the windmill, stood above every Kansas farm like an ancient totem, inseparable from the life in its shadow; yet its wondrous pipes and blades were impotent without the water it sucked from below and without the prevailing winds that reliably swept across the plains.

Webb believed that the land and its peculiar technology reshaped the society and institutions subjected to them. Much did change, it

The unchanging roles of the farm woman.

is true. Land laws had to be revised to account for the differing situations of cattlemen and small farmers. New concepts of water rights had to be framed. It should be remembered, however, that these changes came slowly and falteringly and some institutions, such as capitalism, the family, and the forms of government actually were modified but little. For instance, a settler might for a time have lived in that remarkable adaptation to local conditions, the sod house, but at the earliest possible moment he built a large, clapboard structure whose cupolas would mingle comfortably with any small-town neighborhood east of the Mississippi. Into this house he moved his family, his Bible, his ledgers, the address of his congressman in Peoria, and his Brussels carpet from Sears Roebuck.

Technology usually was synonymous with machinery. For western farmers, especially those who owned the biggest chunks of land, machinery meant money, survival, and power. Leo Marx, in *The Machine in the Garden*, has described the overriding contemporary image of the machine as an engine of progress harnessing Promethean fires, subduing the wilderness, and carrying the farmer to his prophetic inheritance as lord of creation. Magazine editors, not the farmer himself, phrased the idea in that way. Farmers talked of yields in bushels and of mowers, gang harrowers, seed drills, and combines.

Such machines represented a long line of patent improvements that appeared one after the other throughout the nineteenth century. In some periods, however, the expansion of technology was more notable than in others. During the Civil War, for example, when the labor supply was dramatically reduced, there was a sudden increase in the manufacture of mowing machines. By 1890, with these and other implements, a ton of hay could be loaded from the field in five minutes. New reapers harvested grain more efficiently — seven times faster and with half the labor force. As a result of such speed, grain could be cut nearer to the time of perfect ripeness and maximum yield. In 1880 a new harvester could reap and shock twenty acres of wheat in a day, and the combine absorbed one man's easy labor where twenty men had worked much harder before.

When produce prices went up, more farmers came to the land and additional machinery was needed to allow expansion into less desirable areas. When prices went down, machines were still important because they reduced costs and permitted survival in the market. The pattern of plains farming became tied to eastern and world markets. An export economy called for larger and larger operations, so there grew in the region what have been called bonanza farms of thousands and thousands of acres. Wheat and oats were the great exports and, unlike cotton, were crops that benefited from the machine. These staples were adapted to the northern plains. The cycle was inexorable and plains farming became increasingly wedded to the machine.

The value of farm machinery produced annually in the United States between 1860 and 1900 rose from $21 million to $101 million. Some of the increase flowed into foreign markets, but one authority claims that American farmers spent $100 million for machinery in 1900. In any case, the staggering output suggests the importance of mechanization for success. By the end of the century, the average well-managed western farm required an estimated $785 investment in machinery. Add to this figure the costs of land, housing, food, and clothing for a holdover time until the first harvests, and it is easy to understand why a poor man was not a candidate for farming on the plains.

Most Americans have believed a contrary myth — that a poor farmer, if he had courage, stamina, and self-reliance, could move west, stake out a modest claim, and make a go of it. The myth rested on the availability of free land, boundless and fertile, and its basis was the Homestead Act of 1862. Supporting the idea of free land two years before passage of the act, Horace Greeley wrote:

> The one great point of superiority enjoyed by our countrymen over
> their cousins in western Europe is the facility wherewith every Ameri-
> can who is honest, industrious and sober may acquire, if he does not
> already possess, a homestead of his own; not a leasehold from some
> great capitalist or feudal baron, but a spot of earth of which no man
> may rightfully dispossess him so long as he shall shun evil courses and
> live within his means.[3]

Before the Homestead Act the principles of land policy had been
embodied in various preemption acts. Between 1804 and 1830, no
fewer than sixteen acts granted rights to special groups, and because
these were basically codifications of squatters' rights, threatening
the principle of revenue return for the public domain, general preemption laws were not adopted easily. In 1841, after the election of
William "Old Tippecanoe" Harrison to the presidency, the preemption principle was fully established. Any squatter on unclaimed
land could, when the land was surveyed and came up for auction,
exercise the first right to buy at the minimum price, usually $2 an
acre. However, the preemption laws did not disturb the fundamental policy that the public domain was to be a source of revenue.
Sooner or later the squatter, like anyone else, would have to pay for
the land he tilled.

Western idealists have always railed against that principle. The
public domain presented a precious opportunity, they never tired of
arguing, to structure the nation on the rock of small farmers working
their own land, proud and independent in their possession. Legislation to this end was introduced throughout the 1850s and was at
least partly related to a rising awareness of slavery in eastern cities.
The new Republican Party made an agreement possible. Although on
the eve of the Civil War substantial numbers of northern manu-
facturers worried that higher tariffs would hamper trade with the
South, a sufficient number believed otherwise, resulting in a northern-
western understanding. The West would allow the East to protect
manufactures by tariffs, and the East would in turn support free
land. A homestead act did indeed pass both houses of Congress in
1859, only to be vetoed by Democratic President James Buchanan.
The election of Lincoln in 1860 removed even the presidential
obstacle.

So, in May 1862, while Stonewall Jackson marauded the Shenandoah valley, and while spring wheat sprouted green in Nebraska, the
great Homestead Act became law. Titled "An Act to Secure Homesteads to Actual Settlers on the Public Domain," it took effect the
same day as the Emancipation Proclamation. Citizens over twenty-
one (including women heads of households), who had never borne

arms against the United States or given aid and comfort to its enemies, might file for up to 160 acres of surveyed public domain. They had to settle and cultivate the land for five years, after which they would receive full title; otherwise, the only cost would be a ten-dollar fee. The dream had become law, and for a hundred years Americans would believe that if things went bad, they could move west and take up a free homestead. In fact, by the mid-twentieth century, more than 285 million acres of the public domain were transferred from the government to private hands through the Homestead Act.

The dream, however, overlooked some critical points. First, more than 700 million acres were bought from, rather than granted by, the public domain during the same period — three or four times as many as were given free. Most farmers who went west did not homestead. Instead, they often took land under the preemption acts. Because surveyors worked slowly and the Homestead Act applied only to surveyed land, chances were great that a person would have to squat on the desired parcel and buy it later. Furthermore, land taken by the government from Indians was not available for homesteading but was reserved for cash sale, as were acres the government had given to the states. Huge grants to railroads were turned into salable tracts, highly desirable because the railroad was the only available link to wider markets. In fact, because of its distance from the rails, homestead land was usually the least desirable, and the homesteader would heartily agree as he hauled his wheat over endless miles through "loblollies" of encrusted mud.

The ideals behind the Homestead Act assumed not only that land would be free but that it would go directly into the hands of the small farmers without passing through land monopolists and speculators. But in fact the latter groups hardly disappeared. They could amass large holdings from the states, which were only too happy to cut prices for big buyers in order to turn their acres into dollars for schools and government needs. And there were fraudulent means, too. Dummy entries became standard jokes. Armies of men at speculators' biddings would take packing-case houses to quarter sections, satisfy the legal minimum, and then turn over the deed to a monopolist in exchange for a fee. Thereafter the little army of dummy entrants could push on their "houses," almost literally on wheels, while the speculator prepared to charge a good price for the land he had acquired. By these means speculation and monopolization of land were no less prevalent after the Homestead Act than they had been before. As an example of how successful such activity could be, Iowa speculators in the 1850s increased the average value

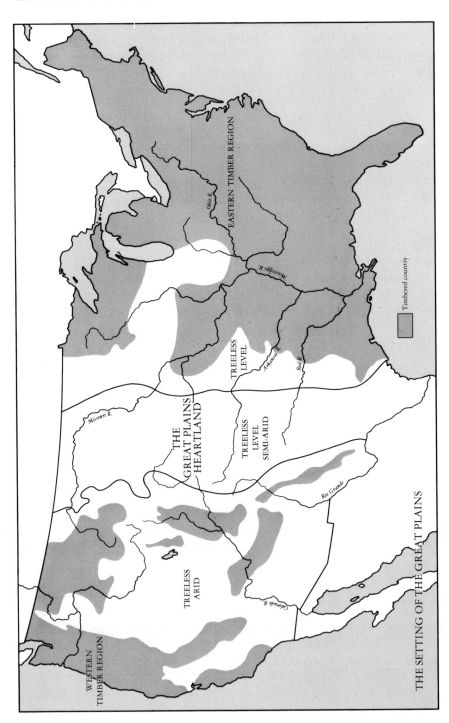

THE SETTING OF THE GREAT PLAINS

WESTERN TIMBER REGION

TREELESS ARID

THE GREAT PLAINS HEARTLAND

TREELESS LEVEL SEMI-ARID

TREELESS LEVEL

EASTERN TIMBER REGION

Timbered country

Missouri R.

Ohio R.

Mississippi R.

Arkansas R.

Red R.

Rio Grande

Colorado R.

of their holdings tenfold. The small western farmer still became as often as not a tenant on land owned by others.

The Homestead Act did not signal a significant change in overall policy. Historian Paul W. Gates has considered the legislation to be atypical, a misfit in a system that remained fundamentally unchanged and therefore blocked whatever ideals the act might have embodied.[4] Though he does not deny that hundreds of thousands of home-steaders profited mightily from the system, Gates cautions against too rosy a view of the government's largesse.

Not until the 1890s were cash sales of the public domain revised by Congress, chiefly through the reforming efforts of Representative George Julian from Indiana, and Land Commissioner William Sparks. These reformers were partly motivated by early attempts at conserva-tion. Reforestation was one goal, and between 1873 and 1891 under the Timber Culture Act, farmers could take 160 additional acres pro-vided they planted trees on a portion of the land. The impact of the act was not great, however. The beginnings of large forest reserves in effect instituted a policy of retaining large areas of public land for the public good. Curiously enough, more acres were taken up under the Homestead Act in the first part of the twentieth century than ever in the nineteenth, possibly because government cash sales were no longer available. The basic principles, nevertheless, were changing.

In the period following the Civil War the polarity of the settlement patterns between the rich and poor was evident. At one extreme was the sod house. It tended to appear first, like the prospector before the mining corporation, and it often sheltered hardship incarnate. When the poor farmer and his family (often a black freedman from the South, or an immigrant with a few treasured heirlooms fresh from the Old World) moved onto the plains, he could fashion a temporary dugout against a hill, or he could build a sod house. The tough, grassbound sod was sliced into strips about a foot wide, cut into bricks three feet long, and dragged to the site. They were placed edgewise so the walls would be three feet thick, forming an enclosure about eighteen by twenty-four feet. Two forked tree trunks held the ridgepole. Over the rafters went tar paper or sheeting, if the builder was lucky enough to have them. In any case the roof was finished by a layer of sod bricks, from which eventually grass and sunflowers would flourish. Because of its insulation, the room was cool in summer and warm in winter — warmer, that is, than the blizzards raging outside. The house was too heavy to be damaged by wind and too damp to be destroyed by fire and could be used as an animal shelter after the family moved out. However, the typical one window and one door provided little ventilation and little light. Dirt showered

Nebraska dugout, 1888.

from the ceiling. The soggy roof presented the constant danger of a cave-in. Even when intact, the roof leaked a thousand drips from a thousand secret cracks. Old Jules Sandoz brought his Swiss bride to a sod house in Nebraska, and during the first night, toward morning, it rained:

> The roof leaked a little at first, then more. Soon everywhere. Henriette sat on the wet straw tick all the next day with a purple umbrella over her head, crying noiselessly while Jules raged that there was no fuel. Plainly the white hands of his wife would be incapable of wielding a successful axe against the toughness of wet wood. So he plunged out, dragged in a fallen ash tree, and chopped it into appropriate lengths on the floor. At last he got the fire going and while one stoveful burned he dried another in the rusty oven, his socks steaming behind the stove. He made half a gallon of coffee and dug out the remainder of the crackers and cheese. As he pushed a cup toward Henriette he warned her that he was not the man to wait on a woman. She shook her head. She was not hungry.[5]

In contrast, the bonanza farms were flourishing by the 1880s in the wheatlands of the north central prairies and plains. In 1880 there were nearly three thousand farms, each more than a thousand acres, in the nine north-central states and territories. More than half of

Harvest hands on their way to the wheat fields, 1890.

these were west of the Mississippi, and by 1900, four-fifths of these giants were west of the spinal river. The Dakotas were the heartland. While the average lot was about seven thousand acres, Oliver Dalrymple's interests, for example, covered roughly a hundred thousand acres; others ranged between twenty and forty thousand acres. One of Dalrymple's fields alone stretched for thirteen thousand unbroken acres of rippling wheat. Gangs working on distant corners would not see each other for entire seasons. According to one tall tale, a plowman started in the spring, cut one straight slice across his farm until fall, and then turned around and harvested his way back.

The bonanza farms embodied vital counterparts of industrial capitalism — the application of machinery to mass production, absentee ownership, professional management, specialization, cheap labor. Not surprisingly, many of them grew from the corporate design of the railroads. After the panic of 1873, the Northern Pacific offered its far-flung acres in exchange for its own depreciated securities. Thus within two years after the panic the railroad had sold in the Dakotas 483,000 acres at $5 an acre. Twenty-three buyers accounted for approximately 304,000 acres, 63 percent of the total,

Steam harvester with twenty-five-foot swath.

mostly paid for with depreciated railroad bonds.[6] The new owners had no desire to settle on the land. They divided up the vast acres according to principles of efficient production and hired the best foremen and managers they could find. On each 10,000 acres they employed an average of 250 farmhands and paid them from $16 to $25 a month including room, board, and laundry. Sometimes the managers slowly acquired their own farms and ended with huge holdings. That was the way Oliver Dalrymple operated. Those who worked their own bonanza farms did best. Isaac Funk of Illinois, for example, initiated tenant farming in his area and died with an estate worth $2 million.

Companies with absentee owners did not always do so well. In fact, by the 1890s, though responsible for a vast increase in the amount of wheat produced in the West, they lost interest in their farming investments. Most absentee owners became land speculators and recouped their capital on the increased value of the land itself. Agriculture held too many risks, if not for the sod-house farmer, at least for the absentee corporation.

The stereotype of the yeoman independent homesteader is flawed. The chances were great that the farmer had to buy the land he really desired, and he was lucky indeed if he could get a good quarter-section for less than $500. Railroad land in western Nebraska in 1870 ranged from $6 to $8 an acre; comparable lots twenty years later sold for $25. Ultimately he would need $700 in machinery, and when in full swing he would be competing with operations ten or twenty times larger than his own. The results were translated into mortgages, indebtedness, and foreclosures, reflected in such slogans as: "In God we trusted; in Kansas we busted." In the words of one contemporary doleful ballad:

> How happy I am on my government claim,
> Where I've nothing to lose and nothing to gain,
> Nothing to eat and nothing to wear,
> Nothing from nothing is honest and square.
> But here I am stuck and here I must stay,
> My money's all gone and I can't get away;
> There's nothing will make a man hard and profane
> Like starving to death on a government claim.

Hamlin Garland, raised in Wisconsin, recounted some of the sad details in a story, "Under the Lion's Paw." The main character, Haskins, rents a farm that he could buy for $3,000, if he had the money. For two years he, his wife, and boy work long, dreary hours, but they do succeed. When the owner inspects the improvements Haskins has made, the price of the farm jumps to $5,000. When Haskins finally buys, he is forced to go into debt for the extra $2,000, which his own sweat had added to the value of the land. Ready to kill the eastern owner, he swallows his anger and returns to his newly mortgaged acres. Like a lion's paw the eastern businessman held the western farmer in bondage.

The railroad was once a symbol of promise for the settler. It advertised the beauties of the land. It sought out the farmer in the poverty pockets of Europe and gave him new hope. It promised him cheap transportation for his products and a link with the markets of the world. Gradually, however, the western farmer realized that the railroad engine was not to be his servant. The companies, it is true, did have peculiar problems on the plains. During peak harvest times, for example, they were forced to send empty cars westward to return eastward full. But rates in the West were far higher than could be justified by such added costs — two and three times higher per ton per mile than they were in the East. One company, Burlington, charged in the West four times what it levied east of the Mississippi. The reason for the high transport costs was the absence of competition and a general propensity to maximize profits. In the East losses were especially common — from rebates to favored shippers, from competitive rate wars, from reduced revenues over long hauls where competition kept rates low, from free passes for sympathetic judges and public officials. The burden of paying for many of these practices fell on the sparsely settled West. When the farmer groaned that he was paying the value of one whole bushel of corn or wheat in order to get a second bushel to market, he usually understated the case.

No one communicated the feelings of the farmer toward the railroad better than Frank Norris in his novel *The Octopus*. The wheat farmers of the San Joaquin valley in California had much in common with those of the Dakotas. In both places there was a high percentage of large bonanza farms with an umbilical dependence on the railroad. The Southern Pacific, led by Collis Huntington and Leland Stanford, monopolized the valley's transportation, embracing its access to markets like an octopus (an analogy used by Norris and his contemporaries). In the novel, company control of alternate sections blocked the growth of farms, reduced efficiency, or resulted in high prices when options to purchase came due. Thus, as in Garland's story, the corporation could reap the increase in value that the farmer himself had created. Furthermore, enormous freight rates were charged on machinery. In the Norris tale, a harvester was transported within sight of a farm but could not be delivered until it had passed through San Francisco and returned three hundred miles south. In this way an exorbitant short-haul rate could be added to the cost of transport.

In the climax of *The Octopus*, the Southern Pacific Railroad confronted the beleaguered, hostile farmer, driven to the point of violence. The railroad had to choose between two alternative routes. Population centers along the coast wanted the tracks to serve them. The railroad preferred to run through the inland valleys because of the greater availability of the public domain for their reimbursement. Secretaries of the interior had twice revoked and then reinstated the original coastal route. Farmers had moved into the San Joaquin valley and considered the land theirs by preemption. When the railroad finally received rights to the valley land, the farmers protested and sued in the courts, but the judges rendered for the company. Farmers formed vigilante bands, dressed as Indians, and raided corporate property. When armed men hired by the Southern Pacific came to evict them, they responded at Mussell Slough with guns on May 11, 1880. Eight men died in the battle. Seven settlers were arrested, five of whom were sentenced to eight months in jail and a fine of $300 each for resisting arrest. The local citizens honored them and gave them a splendid stay in jail, but the company kept the land.

The farmer on the Great Plains had feelings about the railroad as deep as those of the farmer in the San Joaquin valley. The tracks

Boosting South Dakota land, 1890.

were his public highway, and the government had an obligation to keep that highway available. Instead, the government and the railroad seemed to be allied against the farmer. Why did farmers so readily come to the plains? They came because of what Paul Gates called "insatiable land hunger," typical of rural, peasant, and agricultural societies. Advertisements by railroads and speculators led them to believe that millions of acres of rich, well-watered loam waited for their muscles and plows — free if they wished to homestead or for a pittance if they wished to buy. The propaganda was cruelly inaccurate, but the hope was unquenchable.

Consider the land which would someday form the long panhandle of Oklahoma. By 1889 the Oklahoma Indians had been forced to relinquish vast areas given to the Five Civilized Tribes fifty years earlier at the end of their trail of tears. On April 22, 1889, nearly two million of these acres were thrown open for settlement. At noon the cavalry was to fire a signal and the race for life and future would begin. The response was overwhelming. During March and April as many as a hundred thousand people swarmed to the line, setting up shanty towns and makeshift camps. These were the boomers, clad like Indians, some said, but with an unmistakable white man's gleam in their eyes. Some had followed that gleam too far, jumped the gun, and were hidden, ready to emerge from thickets to pounce upon their prizes at 12:01 P.M.; these were the "sooners." Part of the flurry was over good cheap land that had become hard to find elsewhere. But around this former Indian reservation, one magazine claimed, ran a "chain of enchantment." The chain was dropped on April 22, and the waiting thousands of "brawny noblemen of the West," on horse, wagon, buckboard, or buggy, whooped out on one of history's strangest races, each man certain that every starter was bound to win, each family's heart leaping at "the 'Realization Stakes' of home and prosperity."[7]

Agricultural success, there and elsewhere on the plains, could be achieved only after solutions were found to difficult economic situations; a gleam in the eye was merely a beginning. The farmer could prosper if he could either grow a high quantity per acre or earn a high price on what he grew. Thus owning fertile land was important, for a high price per bushel of wheat could be meaningless if yields were low, and vice versa. For example, in the Dakotas, prosperity for the farmer was based on a yield of twenty bushels of wheat per acre priced between eighty cents and a dollar per bushel. Below these figures, the farmer would likely go into debt. Immediately after the Civil War prices and yields were so high that farmers, rich or poor, optimistically bought too much land and too much machinery; they tended to overcapitalize. When prices fell in the panic of 1873, they suffered mightily. In the late 1880s, when drought and frost cut yields, they suffered again. Locusts in the young stalks, hailstorms when the wheat heads were heavy, rain at threshing time — such conditions farmers could not control or predict. Introduction of new strains of wheat — hard winter or Red Turkey — helped somewhat. Even these disasters would not have been so serious had prices risen as yields declined. But the western farmer sold in a world market; the railroads made that both possible and certain. As the century wore along, products from the Midwest were increasingly forced to compete with those from Argentina, Russia, and Australia. Prices tended to slip because of the competition, regardless of the local grasshoppers. After 1881 wheat did not again reach the level of a dollar a bushel until World War I; at some times, as in 1884 in the Dakotas, it sank to less than fifty cents a bushel.

After the panic of 1873, the western farmer remained in economic

Destitute farm family, Black Jack, Kansas, 1861.

distress until at least 1879. Eastern political leaders such as James G. Blaine were well aware of the agricultural depression, and some of them began to join western politicians in proposing overseas expansion of markets as a solution. Because American farmers were producing too much for home consumption, clearly new markets were essential. Beginning in 1877 the effects of an enormous increase in agricultural exports began to be felt, and by the end of the 1870s exports of meat and wheat had nearly doubled over what they had been ten years before. Thus the West could support Seward's purchase of Alaska, made in 1867 as a base from which America could eventually supplant England in the trade of the whole Pacific. The British controlled the supply of wheat, for example, from vast granaries such as Australia. The farmers of the American West were convinced that the price of their wheat was determined in Liverpool rather than in Fargo or Lincoln.

The British represented colonialism. The American farmer argued that his desire for overseas markets had nothing to do with politically enslaving other peoples. Quite the contrary, he wanted to see the area of freedom — that is, American freedom — extended everywhere on the globe. Thus in the Spanish-American War America expelled the Spanish imperialists from Cuba and gave the island political independence, in turn demanding economic privileges that might expand the American marketplace. There were peaceful means of overseas aggrandizement, as well. Even humanitarian distribution of food to famine-struck regions sometimes hinted of molding foreign tastes to the flavor of American food products.

By 1879 the great export bonanza of the 1870s had extricated the farmers from their long depression, and for the rest of the century they did not forget the reason for their release. Indeed, by 1898 they had convinced many eastern metropolitan businessmen of the soundness of expansionism. Thus grew, in the view of William Appleman Williams, "the roots of the modern American empire."[8] The farmer never convinced the industrialist, however, of the merit of his monetary schemes, even though they were related to expansionism. Because the British controlled the gold market, the substitution of silver for the gold standard would unseat the British. When William Jennings Bryan spoke for the farmer, he sought silver as the base for money: "You shall not crucify mankind upon a cross of gold." He associated this demand with reciprocal trade treaties and freer trade generally, so that the farmer could buy his manufactured goods, especially farm machinery, at lower prices.

Though businessmen in the East might eventually agree that the expansion of marketplaces was essential for American prosperity, they were not about to follow the agricultural leaders either into a substitution of silver for gold or into a system of free trade. The only supporters of these points the farmers could recruit were the workingmen of eastern cities. The two groups together sensed that their prosperity must be based on overseas markets, currency resting on silver rather than on gold, and an opening of trade to reduce the prices of manufactured goods.

Through these years farmers developed a sense of group consciousness. They read their own newspapers and journals such as the *Non-Conformist* and the *Western Rural*. They met in social organizations such as the Patrons of Husbandry (the Grange), where at meetings and picnics the men swapped yarns and aired their problems while the women exchanged recipes. Membership in the Grange numbered over eight hundred fifty thousand by 1875, and membership in various Farmers' Alliances, which took on more political overtones than the Grange, grew by 1890 to an additional one million. When farmers' factions won local elections, they could feel that their voices were being heard in legislative councils. Their excitement rose. The effect of William Jennings Bryan on a group, here seen through the eyes of Mari Sandoz, was electrifying:

[Bryan was] a mere stripling, an unknown young lawyer from Lincoln. He opened his generous mouth and the noisy audience before him quieted. Words flowed over them in a flood swift and clear as the Niobrara. . . . The speaker established the issues, swung into the tariff and ended on free silver, and when he sat down the crowd was still as a lull in a dry-land thunderstorm. Then in a frenzy of applause, the audience arose, climbed to the benches, and swept forward upon the prophet come to them. Never would these men see another such day as when the Panhandle first heard the young Bryan.[9]

From group consciousness emerged the Populist Party, which drafted its first platform in Omaha in 1892. Ignatius Donnelly, the sage of Nininger, Minnesota, set its preamble ringing with such phrases as "the fruits of the toil of millions," "colossal fortunes for a few," "tramps and millionaires," and "the outcries of a plundered people." The party nominated James B. Weaver for president. The child of a quarter-section homestead, Weaver had grown into a reformer worried about the strangulation of farmers by railroads and the widening chasm between the haves and the have-nots. Soon thereafter the depression of 1893 firmly cemented sentiments. The Populist revolt had begun.

In addition to Donnelly a marvelous crew of western spokesmen came to the fore, including Jeremiah "Sockless Jerry" Simpson, Kansas cattleman, and sad-eyed Mary Lease, also from Kansas, who purportedly asked plaintively that farmers raise less corn and more hell. Mrs. Lease's vision was filled with conspiratorial Jewish bankers and fearsome Englishmen. The future she dreaded would lie either in a region of anarchistic terror or in worldwide Russian despotism. One way to avoid such perils was to give the American farmer his due and to expand his marketplaces into Canada, Cuba, Haiti, Hawaii, and all over Latin America.

At the time the plans of the Populists seemed salted with radicalism, especially when they called for the nationalization of the railroads and freer trade; but Populist planks were more deeply cut from the ideas of Adam Smith than of Karl Marx. For a while some of their proposals, such as electoral reform, secret ballots, and income tax, set the nation's teeth on edge. Then they were co-opted by the Progressives, whose style was distinctly urban, with less of the Old West left in it.

Farmers had, nevertheless, made some political headway. Through local elections they had exerted enough pressure to secure the passage of state laws regulating railroad rates, and in the Supreme Court such laws had been decreed constitutional in *Munn* v. *Illinois* (1876). The progress was stifled in a later decision, *Wabash* v. *Illinois* (1886), but the national government then stepped in and proclaimed the propriety of such regulation in the Interstate Commerce Act of 1887. Locally and nationally, the legislation proved often ineffective, confusing, and illusory; yet it kept the farmer within the system. It held him from extreme radicalism or perhaps even from revolution.

Marxism was available to the farmer as an alternative to the Populist route. Edward Bellamy's Nationalist Clubs and Laurence Gronlund's adaptation of Marxism to American conditions, the *Cooperative Commonweath*, stirred Boston, New York, and San Francisco but never much interested the midwestern farmer. However, radical doctrines such as those of Henry George did make some headway there. Jerry Simpson and Hamlin Garland both championed the Georgist single tax. George wanted to place all taxation on the unearned increment in the value of land. Thus railroads would pay plenty for what they reaped on land speculation. Through such taxation the increased value would be returned to the society from which it had sprung. But Henry George was also more attractive to the discontented urbanites than to the farmers. The farmers' last great cry, radical or otherwise, was heard in the voice of the Populists.

In some ways the western farmer was not too badly off. Even the poorest sod buster could raise at least some of his food, unlike his factory-working counterpart. Agriculture, however, was a hard way of life, full of risks and calluses. On the plains, almost for the first time in history, the farmer was required to be virtually isolated from his fellows. Nowhere were the physical degradations more starkly revealed than in the role women were assigned on pioneer farms. Hamlin Garland looked upon his graying, wrinkled mother, old long before her time, thought back over her pioneer life, and wrote:

> My heart filled with bitterness and rebellion, bitterness against the pioneering madness which had scattered our family, and rebellion toward my father who had kept my mother always on the border working like a slave. . . . Was this the "fairy" land in which we were all to "reign like kings"?[10]

Beret, in Ole Rölvaag's classic *Giants in the Earth*, weighed down by unrelieved labor, came to feel the sky pressing upon her like a prison without even bars to break the horizon. Staying here, in the Dakota territory, these settlers in their sod houses would become as wild beasts, and "everything human in them would gradually be blotted out."[11] Beret slowly goes mad.

Isolation may not be the same as loneliness, and it is probably true, as Sandra Myres has said, that women were often surrounded by husbands, hired hands, and Indians but had few women friends.

Thus they felt intensely lonely, even when not alone. Actually, however, their own men were frequently gone — a fact that partially explained the more relaxed divorce laws in Western states.

The early success of most farms rested heavily on the shoulders of the woman, far beyond the stereotypic work in nursery, kitchen, and barnyard. She often sold butter and eggs, reaping cash in an economy chronically low on capital. Sometimes her work allowed critical time for the man to learn his own farm sufficiently to achieve some degree of success. When daughters were old enough they might be sent out for domestic service in the nearby town, but in such cases a frontier family from the East would probably have been more protective than would an immigrant family. In her journal Mollie Sanford, of Colorado and Nebraska homesteads, described the attempt of a hotel keeper to employ her teenage sisters. Although the family needed money, her mother was insulted by the mere suggestion of such employment.[12] On the other hand, experience with Bohemian homesteaders recounted in *My Ántonia* lead Willa Cather to conclude that immigrant girls sought work eagerly and so made all the difference between success and financial ruin on the farm back home.

A strain of independence in the wives of frontier farmers may have distinguished them from their urban counterparts. Jules Sandoz brought four wives successively to his Nebraska prairie. None of them was particularly submissive. One of them, Henriette, even built her own house, where she lived separately, allowing Jules access only when she wished. Before she was married, Elinore Stewart homesteaded her own land in Wyoming and remained enthusiastic about homesteading as a way for women to gain independence and security. None of these perceptive women held any illusions about the West, which they knew was a male-dominated society. Women often worked side by side with men and were desperately needed because of an overall labor shortage, but neither men nor women thought of the situation as anything but temporary. Their respective roles did not change in any real sense. Elinore Stewart may have done the mowing in a pinch, but she had to do it surreptitiously and fully expected her husband to forbid it as soon as he had hired a man.

It is not difficult to identify independent women in the West. What we need to examine, however, is how sensitively the role of women was being questioned. In the primitive conditions of the frontier, the woman's traditional role of mother, cook, and keeper of the hearth was usually reinforced. Perhaps release from such a role can come only when material possessions are widely distributed within a society and when the social fabric has been sufficiently disturbed, as by urban industry, to cause serious rifts in family life.

Women voting in Cheyenne, 1888.

Thus factory girls in Massachusetts may have been potentially far more revoluntionary than the Elinore Stewarts of Wyoming. In such a view the frontier would be a retrogressive force, one that strongly reinforced the traditional roles of the sexes.

The early legislation of woman suffrage in the West supports this theory. Often it has been assumed that the independence of western women caused a flood of egalitarian thinking and that men acquiesced in granting their helpmates the vote. Wyoming in 1869 was the first territory to grant women the ballot; Utah followed a few months later in 1870. In all, eleven western states granted women the vote before any state east of the Mississippi followed suit. While such leaders as Elizabeth Cady Stanton and Charlotte Perkins Gilman spent some time in the West, still, the focus of the women's movement, the ideological formulations and the political agitations, centered in the East.

The most reasonable explanation for the early western laws is that men in the West gave women the vote because women, confirmed in their traditional roles by frontier life, would reinforce the established

Puritan values and old traditions. In Utah, for example, women supported polygamy because they were committed to the Mormon Church and the puritanical virtues it enshrined. In its fight against polygamy, the federal government in 1887 suspended the new "liberal" women's suffrage, conceiving this move as the only way to bring change in Utah. Wyoming wanted, as Julie Jeffrey said, "not a new society but a tamed society." Political emancipation must not be confused with social or sexual emancipation.[13]

Erik H. Erikson offers some insight into the changing role of the pioneer farm wife. With her husband frequently away in woods and field, she became the disciplinarian and teacher of values. She assumed a rejective attitude toward her child in order to harden him for the rudely competitive frontier, but paradoxically, she also grew overly protective to ensure that her offspring would perpetuate values she feared were slipping from that primitive society. Consequently her role was expanded, and the transformation intensified its conservative quality.[14] Erikson's thesis fits with the general one that finds women in the West keenly committed to older values and mores. Industrialism and the city, not the western farm, opened new avenues for women.

The Great Plains proved for men and women alike a test of enormous magnitude. The environment was dry and treeless and aching with level loneliness. Crossing the "institutional fault line" demanded a new technology, complicated machinery, and intensive advertising and railroad promotion to induce farmers to try. If they failed, they could always move on in what William Appleman Williams called "the mirage of an infinity of second chances."[15] Thus another dose of restlessness was added, more evasion of social and personal responsibilities for the immediate community. Those who stayed fought long and frustratingly against corporate competition, railroad controls, and political intransigence. They learned strategies that climaxed in Populism and in the expansion of overseas markets. In the fight they felt again the western drive, which imbued them with a feeling of power. If men could outwit the wind, locusts, loneliness, corporate lawyers, Liverpool price manipulators, and still feed half the world with wheat and meat, who and what could ever stand in their way?

11

Plunder and Preservation

A man named John with untrimmed beard and hair to his shoulders, subsisting on bread and honey, came out of the wilderness with a call to "Repent, for the Kingdom of Sequoia is at hand." In spite of his eccentricities, John Muir might represent all those who in the late nineteenth century began to worry about the natural resources of the West.

Widespread concern was long in coming, though provocations had been apparent for generations. Early in the century the deciduous forests of the old Northwest (extending from Ohio to Illinois) were fast dwindling. Stands of beech and maple once stretched so deep and far that one could walk for days and never see the light of day. But to a farmer, quite understandably, trees were overgrown weeds, and he set about with sweat and determination to chop or girdle or burn them from his fields. Sawmills and pulp mills proved even more destructive than farmers. Fires carelessly ignited from their stacks killed off as many as twenty-five million acres of forest per year.[1] "Johnny Appleseed" Chapman, traipsing through Ohio, Indiana, and western Pennsylvania in the early years of the nineteenth century, tried in effect to replace the native forests with useful fruit trees. He and his contemporaries never questioned the basic American gospel of efficiency. Who could doubt that productive fields and orchards were preferable to natural forest? There were plenty of trees in other places, and it was obviously better to grow food than to preserve the woods.

The destruction of wildlife began with the beaver, whose habit of

Buffalo hunt, by Currier and Ives.

damming streams made him a model conservationist. As we have seen, the economics of fashion saved the beaver from extinction, but it was a close call. By the first quarter of the nineteenth century the sea otter of the Northwest coast had practically been eliminated. By the beginning of the twentieth century the fur seal had been reduced to 3 percent of its original population; only a Russian-Japanese-Canadian-American treaty saved the remainder. In some regions of California, grizzly bear and elk were hunted off the scene. Buffalo, once numbering anywhere from 15 million to 125 million, were efficiently reduced to about 800 by the late 1880s. The passenger pigeon was even less lucky. These sky-filling birds, veering and rippling from blue to purple in countless numbers, disappeared. They were consumed as squab at thirty to forty cents a dozen. Naturalist John Audubon knew a man who had killed as many as six thousand pigeons in one day. By the 1890s they were nearly extinct, and the last member of the species died in the Cincinnati Zoo on the morning of September 1, 1914. Egrets, herons, terns, eagles, whooping cranes, and condors have been saved only at the last minute from the passenger pigeon's fate.

The public lands of the country were not considered a resource to be husbanded and carefully allocated. Instead, 1,850,000,000 acres were distributed to provide revenue for federal and state governments, to assist corporations such as the railroads, and in the vague hope that the ownership of land — any land, no matter how unsuited to farming — would create a wise, stable citizenry. None of these purposes reflected any relationship between the varying qualities of the land and its appropriate use. The system of surveying square townships and sections was folly. The grid went down across rich bottomland, rocky uplands, hills and deserts, woods and prairies, streams and rivers.

In general, the right to exploit minerals and oil beneath the surface remained with the owner of the land, unlike practices in Latin America, where mineral rights generally remained with the state. Some mining methods — especially hydraulic mining, developed in California in 1852 — proved enormously destructive to the environment. Water, then readily available, was used in high-pressured jets to remove rubble and gold-bearing ores, a cheap and efficient method. It took no account, however, of the havoc wrought to streams and the valleys below as tons of mud and rocks buried plant life, including crops, like a chronic avalanche. Gusher oil wells had similarly disastrous effects on some areas as corporations sank as many wells as possible into new fields. One Texas gusher, as late as 1911, spewed 116,000 barrels of oil a day for nine days across soil, streams, and rivers.

It is wrong to condemn men for doing what later generations have learned not to do. Hydraulic miners did not relish the inundation of farms below, and oilmen did not cherish the waste of gusher wells. At the same time, we should not be blind to the fact that most of the waste was due to excessively rapid exploitation, to an economic system that placed all the premiums on fast competition, and to a laissez-faire government unwilling to protect the common good. Above all, the population at large believed in the myth of superabundance, as Stewart Udall calls it, or the cornucopian faith, in the words of William Vogt.[2] A generous Providence bred this faith. The continent was indeed rich — rich enough, for example, to mine more than half of the world's annual gold production almost overnight in 1849 and 1850, and to grow enough wheat to feed almost the entire world. Timber, oil, furs, and fish were seemingly too abundant to be worried about — especially since creation and capitalism alike gave Americans dominion over earth and sea and all that lived therein.

The physical drama, the sheer grandeur of western mountains and rivers, argued for protection, for some effort to keep the primeval beauty intact for later generations. The faint stirrings of such beliefs

Slaughtered buffalo near Cohagen, Montana, 1880, by L. A. Huffman.

were felt in the creation of Yellowstone as the nation's first national park. Fantastic geysers, irridescent pools, cobalt-encrusted springs, roaring waterfalls, striated canyons, quiet meadows and dense forests populated with wildlife, great lakes reflecting peaks between glistening glaciers — destruction of an area so unique would have affronted the Creator himself. Trappers' descriptions of Yellowstone might well have been considered hilarious western tall tales: geysers whose heads bumped the clouds, icy lakes adjacent to steaming pools where dinner could be boiled still on the hook. No skeptical easterner would take them seriously until they had been validated. Henry D. Washburn, surveyor general of Montana, took a party of scientists and local boosters into the region in the summer of 1870. So clearly did they realize that the tales were not exaggerated that around their camp fires some of the men talked of taking out claims to capitalize on future tourists, while others envisioned national protection.

The summer of 1871 witnessed the arrival of an impressive array of intellectuals to test the tales again. Ferdinand V. Hayden was a former New England schoolteacher. During the early 1870s he was pulling together various bureaus of the General Land Office into

Buffalo hunter stripping hides, by Paul Frenzeny and Jules Tavernier.

what would be the United States Geological Survey. Impulsive and excitable, he shrewdly foresaw the need to document the Yellowstone region and to provide visual proof of its geographical uniqueness. Accordingly, he brought with him two of the West's finest interpreters — William Henry Jackson, the photographer, and Thomas Moran, the painter.

The hope to preserve Yellowstone for public rather than private ends grew stronger after the expedition's return in the fall of 1871. Hayden wrote articles for newspapers and magazines. Legislators were particularly moved by Jackson's photographs. Jay Cook joined the cause, clearly thinking of profit from tourists traveling to Yellowstone on his Northern Pacific Railroad. On March 1, 1872, Congress created Yellowstone National Park, the "world's first, large-scale wilderness preservation in the public interest."[3] Two million acres were set aside "as a public park or pleasuring ground" for the American people. "Pleasuring grounds" were hardly in the national Puritan tradition. Thus the act might be viewed as a turning point in American intellectual history, and the fact that many congressmen

Mining near Nevada City, California, 1852.

vociferously opposed the measure only proves the point. In subsequent debates over funding for services and upkeep, congressmen denounced the park as "an expensive irrelevancy" and snorted at the government's entrance into "show business." Fortunately the majority followed a senator from Missouri who prophetically placed the park within the growing necessity for a "great breathing-place for the national lungs."[4]

A long road, however, lay between the creation of a national park and the curtailment of the massive attack by private interests on the resources of the West. The first serious challengers to the superabundance illusion were scientists with a high moral passion. John Wesley Powell, the best example, almost became an itinerant Methodist preacher like his father. By the time he entered Oberlin College, however, botany had won out over religion. He was not happy in college, resenting the dead hand of required courses. Not until he became president of the Illinois Natural History Society did his scientific future seem set. He volunteered for the Civil War and left the field as a major, but he had lost a forearm, amputated after the battle of Shiloh. The handicap hindered him but little. He took a teaching job as professor of geology in Illinois and managed to escort small groups of students on extensive field trips across the plains and into the Rockies. In 1869, with the financial support of the Smithsonian Institution, he led an expedition down the Colorado River through the Grand Canyon. He repeated the exploration in 1871. By then his scientific expertise and leadership qualities had attracted considerable attention, and he began to think of means by which the work of a naturalist might further the general understanding of the West. Consequently, Powell, like Hayden, helped combine a series of government agencies into the United States Geological Survey. Beginning in 1880, for fourteen of its formative years, Powell was director of the Survey.

Powell was, however, more than a naturalist and an institutionalizer. In his *Report on the Lands of the Arid Region of the United States*, written in 1877, he said that men and laws must be closely related to the environment from which they emerge. Because the American West encompassed regions of arid plain and waterless desert, thick forests and rugged mountains, the likes of which were unknown east of the Mississippi, the perpetuation of land laws drawn for eastern conditions did immeasurable violence to the relationship between man and his western environment. For example, the fundamental land unit in the East was the section (640 acres), one-quarter of which was the usual size of a farm sufficient in most eastern areas for keeping a family alive and reasonably prosperous. In the arid regions of the West, however, if land was irrigated, 80 acres were enough, and 160 acres too many, for one farmer to handle. If land was not irrigated and was used for running cattle, 2,560 acres would be required, sixteen times the space needed for a successful eastern farm. Even more important, land without water was worthless, a simple fact understood by Indian, Spaniard, and Mormon, but seemingly beyond the grasp of Washington legislators. The English principle of riparian rights (he who owned the banks of the stream was entitled to all the water he needed while other parts of a valley got none) was transplanted from the East into the West. Powell called for consideration of pure water as a scarce and precious resource to be carefully husbanded and allocated by the community for the benefit of society at large, not for a privileged few. To achieve this, the government had to transform itself into a planner of vital resources like land and water. Only then could the western farmer hope to become the self-reliant man rising in triumphant prosperity through the grace of labor and the baptism of his own sweat. By implication if not directly, nineteenth-century ideas of weak government, of the unregulated individual, of the corporation seeking profit rather than social good, all had to be superseded. "A complete revolution," Wallace Stegner called Powell's vision, "a denial of every cherished fantasy and myth associated with the Westward migration and the American dream of the Garden of the World."[5]

Only four years Powell's junior, another midwestern farm boy with a religious drive, John Muir, became a spokesman for forest and mountain as was Powell for the farmer and the land. In 1872 when Yellowstone Park was formed, Muir was living in Yosemite Valley, California, alone in a small cabin surrounded with snow and silence and the peaks he loved. The God he found in nature was unlike the God of his father, a strict Presbyterian Scot. Young Muir had been raised in Dunbar, where the Firth of Forth opens wide to the moods of the cold North Sea. Elder Muir, as stern as that sea, had required his son to memorize the Bible word for word, the entire New Testament and major portions of the Old Testament. One of his earliest tasks must thus have been to learn that on the sixth day of creation, God gave man dominion over nature. In opposition to this anthropocentric view Muir would set forth his message of preservation.

When Muir was eleven years old, in 1849, his family immigrated to America and took up residence on a farm in Wisconsin. The work of breaking the land very nearly broke the boy; he always contended that he was "a runt" as a result of overwork in his youth. Once he was nearly killed by mine gas as he alone chipped slowly away at the rock for the family well. The labor left little time for reading, which Muir desperately loved to do. His father had even imposed a strict rule of bed shortly after supper, a rule geared to make the farmwork physically bearable. The parental dictum said nothing, however, about rising early enough for reading before dawn's labor began. The boy devised a mechanism of clockwork, weights, and pulleys that thrust him upright in bed at three in the morning. Through such rousing he prepared himself in mathematics and classics to enter the University of Wisconsin on schedule with his contemporaries.

Education corrupts knowledge, Muir might have said, and absolutely formal education corrupts absolutely. An intellectual thirst so independent found irrelevant the requirements and prerequisites unrelated to his own personal yearnings for scientific understanding, and Muir left Madison for what he called "the university of the Wilderness." That school he never left. For the rest of his life he studied the natural environment — tramping from Canada to Mexico, traveling to Alaska and the South Seas, camping for years in his personal Walden, Yosemite, filling seventy notebooks with descriptions of bird calls, lizard tracks, cloud formations, glacial terrain.

He made a modest living on a ranch east of the San Francisco Bay growing grapes and cherries, but the life happily provided plenty of time to walk in the woods. Ralph Waldo Emerson, on a visit to Yosemite in 1871, slept indoors rather than outside with Muir, explaining that for him wilderness made a good mistress but an intolerable wife. For Muir, nature was wife, mistress, offspring, God.

Muir's ideas, pervading all his writings, began with nature as "a fountain of life" from which man is increasingly cut off by cities and civilization. For Muir the cure for man's troubles was a simple return to the wilderness; he found among sequoia groves "balm in these leafy Gileads." The destruction of natural beauty was a sin, an outrage against the divine harmony of all life. There was a mystical strain in Muir's view of nature, reminiscent of New England Transcendentalism, but Muir was not a sentimentalist. Nature and man were one, the evil and the ugly beside the good and beautiful. Muir, like Thoreau, recognized the scorpion and the fang in himself. The scorpion's poison, however, remained part of a natural cycle that included death. What Muir found reprehensible was not natural death, but a broad assault on nature, a senseless killing and destructiveness, through which man destroyed the very sources of life.

Though his hair grew to his shoulders and his beard went untrimmed, Muir did not withdraw from society but carried his message into business and politics. When sheepmen allowed their animals to overgraze and destroy the natural ground cover, he wrote articles about "the hoofed locusts." He thundered against the felling of forests and the wanton waste of wildlife. More than any other man he was responsible for reserving the Yosemite as a national park in 1890. In 1892 he helped organize the Sierra Club, dedicated, among other things, to enlisting "the support and cooperation of the people and the government in preserving the forests and other natural features of the Sierra Nevada Mountains." He served as its president for twenty-two years.

By the 1890s the winds of Progressivism in the nation brought a climate warm to the principles of conservation. The "gospel of efficiency," an honored tradition in America, fit comfortably beside the conservationists' principle of using resources wisely.[6] A few businessmen, lumbermen, and stock raisers could easily take a stand against wastefulness. Most of these interests, however, lobbied against such an attack on free enterprise, and consequently it was not easy to persuade the government to freeze conservatonist principles into law. The first Forest Reserve Act in 1891 empowered the president to set aside wooded areas in which logging could be carried on only under regulations. The purpose of the legislation was not clearly stated, though it was generally assumed that exploitation of timber and water resources would be curtailed. President Benjamin Harrison set aside thirteen million acres; President Cleveland, twenty-one million; President McKinley, seven million. However, much of this land was returned to the public domain. The struggle had only begun.

In 1903 John Muir took the president of the United States on a camping trip into the Yosemite. Teddy Roosevelt loved it. The two men slept out overnight, happily waking under a blanket of fresh snow. Around the camp fire Muir scolded Roosevelt about game hunting, asking when he was going to grow up. But the message of conservation went much deeper and Roosevelt knew it. Muir may have been a thorn, but other less-intense preservationists were more influential upon Roosevelt. During his administration, from 1901 to 1909, an unparalleled array of conservation activity took place.

In 1902 he pushed through Congress the Newlands Act, allocating water resources and creating irrigation projects. The bill passed three months before John Wesley Powell died. Thirty irrigation projects were instituted, and three million acres of arid lands were reclaimed for agriculture before Roosevelt left office. Oil, coal, and phosphate lands were withdrawn from the public domain in order to forestall, at least temporarily, their engrossment by corporate monopolies. One hundred fifty million acres of forests were reserved, creating 138 new forests in twenty-one states. Four wildlife zones became refuges for large animals and fifty-one for birds and small animals. Roosevelt found a device — his power to create national monuments — to protect areas such as the Grand Canyon, the petrified forest, the Olympic peninsula, and Mount Lassen until some of them could become national parks. Before he left the presidency, four national parks were added (Crater Lake, Wind Cave, Mesa Verde, Platte), making a total of seven. Another law to gladden John Muir's heart was the requirement of fees to be paid by stockmen and shepherds who fattened their "hoofed locusts" on the public domain.

Roosevelt transferred the administration of national forests from the Department of the Interior to the Department of Agriculture, where his chief lieutenant in conservation, Gifford Pinchot, served. Pinchot, a Connecticut Yankee, was only twelve years old when Powell wrote his report on the arid lands in 1877. Later, as a young man, Pinchot studied forestry in Europe and spent more than thirty years as professor of forestry at Yale. What land conservation was for Powell, timber protection was to Pinchot. The two men disagreed, however, on the role of government in conservation. Powell came to fear government as potentially corrupt. Pinchot championed strong government to prevent corporate transgressions. Muir and Powell

*The Big Three of conservation: Pinchot left of Roosevelt, Muir at right;
Sequoia Grove, 1903.*

cajoled; Pinchot quietly manipulated the bureaucracy. The years
1907 and 1908 saw a high-water mark of conservation with a national
White House conference and a Congress that thought of itself as
peculiarly dedicated to the protection of the environment. The Taft
administration, World War I, and the 1920s saw the disappearance of
all the momentum. It would be several generations before the movement reached the point at which Pinchot had left it in 1910.

With men like Muir, however, the issue by the end of the century
had moved beyond conservation. Increasingly, Muir saw that man
must not only allocate wisely but must also see beyond utility. Man
lives in a subtle balance with nature, as the spoke of a wheel or part
of a rim. The weakening of any segment, even temporarily, weakens
the whole. The chemical balances of carbon dioxide and oxygen, of

heat and light, of living populations and food supplies, become difficult to repair when technology upsets the harmony. Muir began to call for what would later be termed preservation, rather than conservation. He was carrying forward the ideas germinated in the creation of Yellowstone National Park in 1872, though little appreciated at the time, and he was asking that a halt must be called to technological, engineering, and utilitarian goals unless they could somehow be related with the larger balance of nature.

Answering Muir, Pinchot never wavered from his contention that nature should be in the service of man. Resources had to be wisely used in order to extend their utility. There was no logical reason why a forest should not be viewed as a crop, to be harvested and replanted. The damming of a river to provide a reservoir of life-giving water and power benefited man far more than did the preservation of another river and valley, no matter how deeply a few sentimentalists might glory in the primeval loveliness.

The story of the Hetch Hetchy Valley illustrates the conflict between utilitarians and preservationists. It was Muir country, a "little Yosemite" valley within the national park, with sharp glacial walls and meadowed floor. Muir wrote of it as "a grand landscape garden, one of Nature's rarest and most precious mountain temples. As in Yosemite, the sublime rocks of its walls seem to glow with life, whether leaning back in response or standing erect in thoughtful attitudes, giving welcome to storms and calms alike."[7] Some two hundred miles to the west lay San Francisco, where offshoots of a gold rush, Pacific shipping, and a transcontinental railroad had combined to build a metropolis. Engineers seeking a dependable water supply for San Francisco fastened upon the Hetch Hetchy Valley as the best place to impound the water. It was the cheapest source. There were other possibilities. But could not a lake, even though man-made, be as beautiful as a valley? John Muir loudly answered no. A national park was itself sacred. Besides, to drown a place of such beauty would be akin to bulldozing the Yellowstone or draining San Francisco Bay. In newspapers, magazines, and Sierra Club journals, he labeled the dam supporters "temple destroyers" and "devotees of ravaging commercialism." The dam grew into a symbol of American materialism and overriding business values. Dollars seemed more important than waterfalls.

Pinchot, a leading proponent of damming the Hetch Hetchy, spoke of "the benefits to be derived from its use as a reservoir." Engineers continued to claim that a dam there was the only practical solution to metropolitan San Francisco's thirst. President Roosevelt vacillated, supported Pinchot, then just as he left office turned away from the dam. For more than five years, the arguments pro and con flew. They were complicated, and Muir's position was by no means the only morally defensible one. Making this same point, Holway Jones, historian of the Sierra Club, claims that the full story remains to be told. But whatever the complexities behind the long series of congressional hearings, the final decision came under Woodrow Wilson in 1913, and work on the dam began. By 1923 nine miles of the Hetch Hetchy Valley were covered with water.

John Muir died a year after the Hetch Hetchy decision, deeply saddened by his final defeat. Preservation had lost to conservation; the engineers and the gospel of efficiency had won again; and Muir's call to "Repent, for the Kingdom of Sequoia is at hand" sounded hollow and contrived.

The West had contained such abundance that it had encouraged waste, unexamined growth, and an illusion of an inexhaustible cornucopia. With the leadership of men such as Muir, Powell, and Pinchot some progress was made toward lessening the wastefulness, especially during the administration of Theodore Roosevelt. But the failure to preserve the Hetch Hetchy exposed the fundamental cleavage between the philosophies of conservationists like Pinchot and preservationists like Muir. Neither doctrine, however, fared well in the business-oriented, corporate-dominated 1920s. The Depression, the New Deal, and, later, pollution alarms in areas such as Los Angeles, New York, and Lake Erie were necessary to place conservation and preservation high on the nation's agenda once more.

12

The Ethnic Frontier

The frontier provided the fuel for the melting pot to blend American nationality. St. Jean de Crèvecoeur, a French-Canadian immigrant and settler, writing just before the American Revolution, looked into the "forlorn hope" of scattered settlements and saw a "promiscuous breed" of people who, while subduing the wilderness, were transformed into a new race, the American. Through the metamorphosis the prejudices of Europe were left behind, sloughed off like the skin of an onion. Walt Whitman said of the idea: "Your characteristic race, here may be hardy, sweet, gigantic grow, here tower proportionate to Nature, here climb the vast pure spaces unconfined."[1]

The melting-pot metaphor described a situation in which people of various nationalities allowed themselves to be blended together in order to create the new American identity. It was based on the assimilation of northern Europeans such as Swedes and Germans who settled in the midwest. Merle Curti in his study of a Wisconsin county observed truly cordial relations between foreign-born, non-English–speaking immigrants and native-born Americans, even though many decades passed before the newcomers achieved political equality.[2] "Racially" distinct groups — people of greater physical and cultural identity, such as Indians, blacks, Mexicans, and Orientals — encountered special problems. For them assimilation was frequently no more than acquiescence to the white majority's demands that the minority conform to the prevailing Anglo-American culture. "Minority" is in a few instances a misnomer, for the groups in question stood, in some local situations, in the majority. The words "race" and "minority" connote attitude as well as number. The extent to which minority groups were excluded from the dominant society was determined in part by continuing patterns of racism, which would not allow conformity to succeed, and in part by the minority's unwillingness to conform. It is conceivable that in the earliest phases of frontier development, relations between races might have rested more on an individual basis and acceptance might then have been the norm. During the first few years individuals in the racial minority were in high demand because of their special frontier skills — Squanto teaching the Pilgrims to plant fish in the cornhills, French trappers living with Canadian Indians, Mexicans teaching the first miners the techniques of the placers. But such periods were extremely short — a few years for the Massachusetts Indians, only a few months for the Mexicans in the gold fields. Thereafter the racial minority typically was frozen into a lower-class position, excluded from potentially lucrative jobs such as mining, and permanently assigned to the ranks of unskilled labor.

It may be that class lines developed first and that racism emerged later as a justification for exploitation. In this view, the early frontier years might be seen as a period in which the economy was immature, class divisions imprecise, merchants not yet committed to their stakes in store and saloon, land speculators not yet on the scene, and the labor force drifting and unidentifiable. Indians could then be what they apparently were to many fur trappers — individuals to be loved or hated as individuals. On the other hand, it is thoroughly possible that racist assumptions had earlier origins, particularly relative to blacks in America. The short period of minority usefulness simply abated for a time what would ultimately assert itself in class barriers. Whether racism entered the picture before, after, or simultaneously with the maturing and structuring of social systems is probably unanswerable; but once it emerged, it remained.

If we consider the continental sweep of white relations with the native American Indians, at only a few rare times did it seem likely that an amalgamation or blending of the races could take place. The union of native and Spaniard into the Mexican stock, the acceptance of French fur trappers by Algonquians, the broadly multiracial settlement of Chicago in the early 1800s, the heyday of Cherokee acculturation in Georgia in the late 1820s — these events suggest that more might have been hoped for; the extermination of natives in the Caribbean and racial warfare on the Great Plains were not inevitable. Indian cultures, however, were tough and varied from the long-established urban pueblos on warm mesas in the Southwest to the determined survival of Eskimos on the frozen rim of the Hudson

Bay. But the United States government, from the administration of George Washington to that of Herbert Hoover, demanded total cultural capitulation from the Indian. The melting pot was not an option. Indian proposals for separate statehood, which would have amounted to political as well as cultural pluralism, were never seriously considered. Conformity to white culture was mandatory, though often eₙ ough it fell afoul of basic racism. One is left with the kind of fatalism to which Herbert Blalock comes at one point in his book on minority relations: in the competition for power, which is fundamental to race relations, native races pitted against European technology were predictably annihilated or expelled; the weaker and less useful the minority became, the more likely was its destruction.[3]

During most of the nineteenth century the federal government was willing to deal with tribes on the assumption that all Indian tribal organizations were alike and that a treaty consummated with chiefs was binding upon all members. In his first contact with Indians in the New World, the white man, carrying with him the prevalent Machiavellian ideals of government, consistently treated the Indian as having the powers of a Renaissance prince. Subsequently the government reasoned from nineteenth-century notions of political democracy: the Indian must conform to patterns established by the majority and embrace other elements of the modern political system such as private property, landownership, capitalistic agriculture, and representative government.

Until the Civil War the thrust of the treaty system was to keep the Indians moving west until gathered in one large reservation — not a coequal state, but Indian Territory, like all territories under the direct control of the federal government. The domain was the Great Plains — vast and dry as summer winds — still considered economically worthless as Major Stephen Long had proclaimed it in 1820. Into this land the remnants were herded — Shawnee, Delaware, Ottawa, Huron. Removal could not leave its perpetrators proud. The worst instance was the removal of the Five Civilized Tribes. The Cherokee, Choctaw, Chickasaw, Creek, and Seminole had been granted large reservations in Georgia and Tennessee, had dutifully settled into an agricultural economy, welcomed missionaries, and published a newspaper as part of their cultural revolution. But whites coveted their lands, especially when gold was discovered in them.

Georgia moved to extinguish the rights of the Indians by declaring them aliens. The Supreme Court responded in *Cherokee Nation* v. *Georgia* (1831) that the Indian was not foreign but a distinct political society within, and was part of, the United States. Buried in Justice John Marshall's words was the implication that the Indian might

Sequoyah with his Cherokee syllabary.

someday take his place as an equal member of the prevailing society. Congressman David Crockett rose in the House of Representatives and said he could not vote for Cherokee removal and still answer to his God. In 1832, the Supreme Court tried to protect the Indians again, in *Worcester* v. *Georgia*, but Georgia, President Andrew Jackson, and the army all had different ideas. Instead of protecting the Cherokees under the court decision, General Winfield Scott in 1838 began removing them and their other regional allies to the Great Plains.

They were forced to walk or provide their own transport from Georgia to Oklahoma over what the Cherokees came to call the Trail on Which We Cried. One out of four Cherokees died of cold, hunger, exhaustion, or disease. For all, there were graves of kin along that sad road. Locked on the reservation, generations of Indians fell into bitterness and even resorted to fratricide. Sequoyah, deviser of the Cherokee alphabet, and in white cultural terms perhaps the finest intellect the Indian peoples have produced, walked silently into the Mexican desert and was never heard from again.

The system of large reservations protected by treaty was shattered by the Mexican War, California gold, and the Oregon Fever. Hordes of white men had to push across Indian land, and the way the prob-

Indians at Ft. Laramie, Wyoming, 1868: attributed to Alexander Gardner.

lem was to be solved became clear by 1851. At Fort Laramie, as many as twelve thousand Indians gathered to hear government proposals to grant passage to immigrants across their lands. The Indians received in exchange grants and promises that were never honored.

After the Civil War the Great Plains were no longer considered useless. Indeed, technology was about to make them the garden of the world — a garden rich with grain. The price of wheat shot up during the Civil War. To the Sioux the influx of farmers was a new kind of white man's gold rush. In 1868 that tribe was forced to sit down with army officers again and to accept a sadly diminished reservation. For them there was no melting pot, no assimilation, less and less land — only exclusion. But there would be thirty years of desperate Indian resistance.

War on the plains lasted from 1861 to 1890, well over a generation. There were moments of victory and defeat for particular tribes, among them the Cheyenne and Sioux. There were lulls in the fighting and then renewed battles over different provocations — miners, immigrants, railroads, massacre, counter-massacre. But substantially the war was between the white man and the Indian for control of the Great Plains.

The army was an instrument of national policy, though its liaison with the Department of the Interior, in which the Bureau of Indian Affairs was housed, was consistently weak and pitiful. The reservation system fundamentally disturbed Indian patterns of food gathering, making government assistance necessary and thereby opening the door for graft. Despite the cries of humanitarians horrified at the decimation of a people, the army responded to the demands of western settlers who wanted the Indians out of the way. The army sometimes used the Indians as scapegoats, falsely interpreting tribal actions as evidence of "Confederate plots." In 1861, for example, the Navajos were subjected to their own trail of tears. The army, worried that they might prove a military threat as southern sympathizers, commissioned Kit Carson to remove the entire tribe from its villages in the canyons of northern New Mexico and Arizona to internment at Fort Sumner in eastern New Mexico. The Indian wars were used by ambitious officers as avenues for their own personal advancement: no battles meant no honors, acclaim, or promotions. The army was at the center of a vicious spiral of hatred, one level of fury escalating into a tier of bloodletting. The highest levels of command of the army should have been held accountable for not protecting Indians against white settlers. Though lesser officers and enlisted men often sympathized with the native, there is not one significant example of the army protecting the Indian under the law.

One irony in the course of western racial relations was the use of black troops to fight Indians. William Katz has estimated that 20 percent of the troops in the West were black.[4] The black 24th and 25th Infantry and the 9th and 10th Cavalry were commissioned by Congress immediately after the Civil War. The units conveniently absorbed freedmen. Blacks were segregated, received less pay than white soldiers, and were commanded by whites. The black cavalry accepted the name "buffalo soldiers," a designation used respectfully by the Indians, with reference to their hair. The black troops rated good marks from the army for discipline, courage, low rate of desertion, and high morale. Frederic Remington bivouacked with them for a few days one summer and patronizingly drew them as comic characters, especially when confronting face to face "heap big Injuns." Theodore Davis, another artist on the scene, agreed that they were disciplined and their morale was high, but contended that the reason for this was that the white officers were "of the proper stamp." The black man, according to Davis, enjoyed the "sport" of killing Indians.

So why should not the white man encourage him?[5] Settlers were often not so sure. Protection from savage Indians was one thing, but protection by armed black men was quite another. Old Jules Sandoz in Nebraska, through the writings of his daughter, Mari Sandoz, described townspeople bristling at the presence of black soldiers in their streets and beginning to wonder if they did not prefer the Indians.[6]

But with black soldiers or white, the immediate task for settlers was to get rid of the Indians. Colonel John M. Chivington, a Methodist elder in the local Colorado militia, felt precisely that way. He claimed that the Cheyennes during 1864 had attacked white settlers on three occasions, although the Indians and Chief Black Kettle pointed out that the incidents had been initiated by white soldiers. Chivington took no stock in Indian viewpoints, just as he rejected Major Edward Wynkoop's designation of the Cheyennes as "superior beings."[7] Chivington made his position clear: "I have come to kill Indians, and believe it is right and honorable to use any means under God's heaven to kill Indians." He was consistent; on another occasion he dismissed the morality of shooting Indian children with a memorable phrase, "Nits make lice," and he was not the first to entertain the idea.[8]

Black Kettle was led to believe that his Cheyennes would be safe in camp at Sand Creek, within the precincts of Fort Lyon, Colorado. Their presence, however, continued to irritate Coloradans such as Chivington. Nagged by rumors of an Indian outbreak, his volunteers surprised the camp at sunrise on November 29, 1864, while most of the young warriors were away on a hunt. No Cheyenne ever forgot that day. Black Kettle held firmly to a United States flag and a white banner of truce; many of his people huddled around him. Some women desperately exposed their bodies so the troops would not mistake them for men. At least 105 women and children and 28 men were killed. George Bent, a half-breed Cheyenne living in the camp, estimated greater fatalities, and Chivington, reflecting his disposition, boasted that his men killed nearly 500. Until the massacre at Sand Creek, the Cheyennes had been divided on the issue of cooperation with the government. The killings settled the matter in favor of guerrilla warfare and any other means necessary to drive the white man from their lands.

Some Cheyennes fought in the north with the Sioux, and others could be found beside Comanches and Arapahos in the south. In 1877 the government cajoled and coerced them onto the Oklahoma reservation. Some broke loose, were hunted, caught, imprisoned, and

Battle between Blackfeet and Assiniboines at the fur trade's Ft. McKenzie on the upper Missouri, by Karl Bodmer, 1833.

escaped. A remnant was eventually assigned to Red Cloud's Sioux reservation, where in resignation they gambled, drank what whisky they could get, and dreamed.

The Poncas, unlike their Cheyenne neighbors just to the south, were a good example of what happened to tribes that adapted rather well to white culture. Under the leadership of their chief, Standing Bear, they had converted to Christianity, settled on farms, and generally befriended the whites. But the government's policy called for all Indians to be removed to reservations, and accordingly in 1868 they were assigned land in a portion of the Sioux reservation. They protested removal, as had the Cherokees. Some friendly whites helped them to bring their case to court. The government contended that Indians were not persons under the law and that legal protection did not apply to them. The judge, however, sternly dissented:

> The Poncas are amongst the most peaceable and friendly of all the Indian tribes. . . . If they could be removed to the Indian Territory by force, and kept there in the same way, I can see no good reason why they might not be taken and kept by force in the penitentiary at Lincoln or Leavenworth or Jefferson City.[9]

The judge declared that Standing Bear as a person under the law could not be moved without his permission. Understandably fearful that the decision would undermine the reservation system, the army and the Department of the Interior chose to interpret the judge's decision as referring only to Standing Bear himself, whom they allowed freedom. The others were moved to Indian Territory.

In the far Northwest, the chief of the Nez Percé had been converted to Christianity and had been willing to lead his people to a pastoral life on the Wallowa reservation. When settlers protested that the green Wallowa valley was being wasted and could be put to better use, the government agreed and induced a minority of the tribe to accept a smaller portion. Thus the original treaty was broken and caused the elder chief to toss away his Bible. Subsequently his son, the young Chief Joseph, inspired one of the most dramatic resistances in Indian history. From July to October 1877 he led a retreat that took his band of 650 men, women, and children into three full-scale engagements against the army while maneuvering over thirteen hundred miles. In Montana they headed north, hoping to find asylum in Canada. Some fifty miles from freedom, they were surrounded. After five days of watching his people freeze and starve, Chief Joseph surrendered. From depths of feeling, he spoke words of undying beauty:

> Tell Captain Howard I know his heart. What he told me before I have in my heart. I am tired of fighting. Our chiefs are killed. . . . The old men are all dead. It is the young men who say yes and no. He who led the young men is dead. It is cold and we have no blankets. The little children are freezing to death. My people, some of them, have run away to the hills, and have no blankets, no food; no one knows where they are — perhaps freezing to death. I want to have time to look for my children and see how many I can find. Maybe I shall find them among the dead. Hear me, my chiefs, I am tired; my heart is sick and sad. From where the sun now stands, I will fight no more forever.[10]

Meanwhile, the Sioux under Red Cloud had achieved impressive military victories, which led in 1868 to their receiving in perpetuity the Great Sioux Reservation, stretching from the Missouri River westward through the Black Hills of Dakota. The Sioux had fought to preserve their rights to the adjacent Powder River country of Montana, but the terms of the treaty deliberately left sovereignty vague. In spite of his victories, and hoping in the long run to save the lives — if not the spirit — of his people from further white incursions, Red Cloud led many of the Sioux onto the reservation. He stood in contrast to young Sioux militants such as Crazy Horse of the Oglala band and Sitting Bull of the Hunkpapa, who continued to live in freedom along the Powder River. Crazy Horse was a young chief clear in

Custer's last rally, by John Mulvany, c. 1881.

his distrust of the whites; he refused to participate in the "piecemeal penning" of his people.[11] He continued to follow the buffalo, as his fathers had done, and to smell the sweet grass of the plains as he willed. Sitting Bull, a shaman as well as a chief, also believed that compromise with the whites led nowhere. Although lamed by a Crow bullet in his younger years, he remained an active warrior, a constant thorn for the army, and a threat to the whole reservation system.

The complete breakdown of the 1868 agreement began with two developments — the plan of the Northern Pacific Railroad to build across the Powder River country and rumors of gold in the Black Hills. A flood of whites to the area was assured when Colonel George A. Custer trumpeted news of the gold discovery. The Sioux rallied in protest and, in the ensuing conflicts, Crazy Horse and Sitting Bull emerged as leaders of the resistance.

In June 1876, with leaves full in groves along the Powder River and the nearby Rosebud and Little Big Horn, Sioux braves numbered more than four thousand. Two army regiments marched against them, led by General George Crook and General Alfred Terry, each with slightly more than a thousand troops. In the first major contact along the Rosebud, Crazy Horse and Crook fought with roughly equal

*Sioux version of the field of battle at the Little Big Horn,
by Red Horse.*

numbers. Though each side claimed victory, in fact Crook was im-
mobilized for nearly a month.

The players were ready for the most famous, if not most significant,
moment of the war for the plains — Custer's last stand. General Custer's
7th Cavalry, a part of Terry's army, numbered about two hundred
men, including a few civilians. In an action that must be included
among man's most stupid heroics, Custer, disobeying orders to wait
for reinforcements, charged the Sioux. Neither Custer nor any of his
men saw sundown on June 25.

From the standpoint of Indian history, as Vine DeLoria has implied,
Custer died not only for his own sins but for those of his people.[12]
He sought personal acclaim, the kind bestowed by the nation on
those who sought out Indians and took care of them permanently.
But indirectly he was also the instrument of many western interests —
the men of the gold rush to the Black Hills, a rush he helped create;
railroad investors who saw their Northern Pacific tracks rusting because the Sioux would not lay down their arms; cattlemen who saw

the plains ready for expanded herds from Kansas and Texas; settlers bearing seeds of wheat and hollyhocks and dreams of neat furrows across the earth. Compared with the seriousness of Sitting Bull, who felt that his people must have the buffalo country or perish, Custer with his flowing hair, red-top boots, and grandiose ambition may seem faintly ridiculous. But placed among the figures he represented, Custer was an historical force of immense magnitude.

Ironically, Custer's last stand within a few months turned into the last major stand of the Sioux. The Indians were defeated the following winter by General Crook. In the freezing January of 1877, Crazy Horse's village was scattered by General Nelson Miles, but not until May did Crazy Horse surrender to Crook at the Red Cloud Agency in Nebraska. Rumors understandably flew that he would not remain on the reservation. When the army tried to arrest him, he offered just enough show of resistance to provide the soldiers with a pretext for bayoneting him. Crazy Horse died within hours.

Sitting Bull had meanwhile escaped with a few followers across the border into Canada. He petitioned the Canadian government for food and land. Worried about its own Indian problems and the precedent such action might set, Canada refused. Thus he was forced to return to the United States, where he was made a prisoner. The government allowed him to go off for a while with Buffalo Bill's Wild West Show, parading in his sacred feathers before the thrilled capitals of the eastern seaboard and Europe. To the Sioux and most other Indians, however, he remained a dignified and beloved spiritual leader.

With the military threat ended, the government could afford to listen to philanthropists and such idealistic reformers as Helen Hunt Jackson and T. A. Bland, who for years had called attention to the ill treatment of Indians. The Dawes Act of 1887 resulted. It provided that, with the discretion of the president, reservation land might be allotted to individual Indians, each family receiving a 160-acre farm. These could not be leased or sold within twenty-five years of allocation. All surplus reservation land was opened for sale to whites. Thus while the act was in effect, total Indian holdings were reduced from 138 to 47 million acres. The act provided also that the individual Indian would become a full-fledged citizen of the United States. Though both philanthropists and government agencies touting individualism considered it the height of benevolence, the Dawes Act was ultimately the means for undermining Indian culture.

Under this same individual philanthropic approach came efforts to educate the Indians as laborers in the white economy. Carlisle Indian School in Pennsylvania was founded in 1879 by a former Indian fighter, Lieutenant Henry Pratt. The first Indians brought there were

Sioux, raising some tribal suspicion that, in case of renewed hostilities, officials might use their children as hostages. The girls were given white names, dressed as Victorian ladies, and taught to play the piano. The boys were organized like the army and drilled in uniforms. It is not hard to imagine the emotions of Spotted Tail, the Sioux chief, when he first visited the school. He immediately removed his sons and took them back to the reservation at his own expense. The whole episode recalled Mark Twain's rueful proposal that the country kill off half the Indians and educate the others to death.

With active resistance less and less feasible, the Indians responded, as the oppressed often do, with an outburst of visionary energy. The Ghost Dance movement was the final flame of hope before long resignation. It recalled Tecumseh's brother Tenskwatawa, the Shawnee prophet, whose one eye blazed with expectations for the eastern tribes in 1811. Eighty years later, the period of the Ghost Dance marked the beginnings of the peyote cult, based on hallucinations induced by the peyote plant. Like the Ghost Dance, it too provided an escape into a world of visions fast becoming the only alternative to active resistance. Quanah Parker, for example, fiery Comanche chief, once led as hostile a band as ever threatened whites on the plains. After some bitter battles he surrendered and spent thirty years trying to persuade his people to adjust to white culture, holding all the while, however, to the peyote vision.

The Ghost Dance, like the peyote cult, was built upon feelings epitomized by the Cheyenne chief Little Wolf on a sacred bluff above the Platte:

> Off by himself on an isolated point the third day of the fasting, the chief looked out over the grey, snow-patched prairie for one whole sun's passing, throwing his eyes back over all the long Cheyenne trail. . . . And now this long sorrowing with all their hearts on the ground. But with wisdom they might pass this trail also, this hard Cheyenne autumn and its frozen winter. . . . Beyond it must be a new springtime, with grass for the horses, with the geese flying north overhead and children laughing in the painted villages.[13]

The Ghost Dance emerged with the shaman Wovoka, who rekindled an earlier awakening among the Paiutes of Nevada. During an eclipse in 1888 he was transfigured by visions and felt himself inspired by the Great Spirit to speak to all Indians. They must act as brothers but never resort to violence. He foresaw a day when the white man would either be washed away by floods or covered with a wave of rich earth once trod only by Indians. With the white man would be buried the implements he had brought — guns, whisky, manufactured clothing. All the great Indian warriors killed by the white man would return.

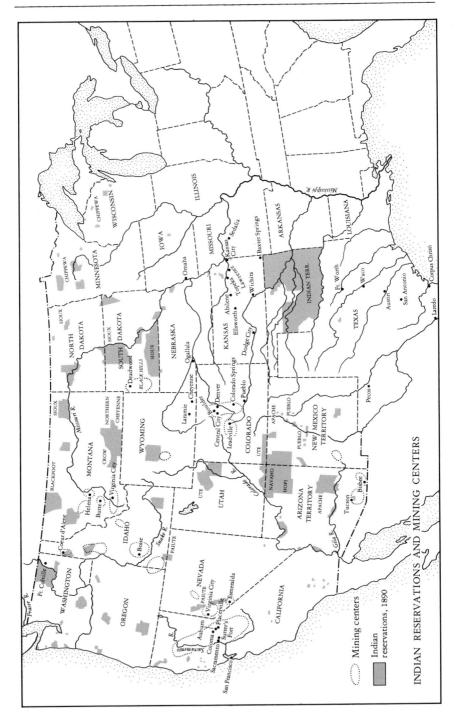

INDIAN RESERVATIONS AND MINING CENTERS

Mining centers

Indian reservations, 1890

Living Indians would be suspended as the crest of earth cleansed the world, or clad in their white ghost shirts they would dance, keeping themselves above the sacred soil in the company of the returning spirits. It was a revitalization movement with historical counterparts among the oppressed everywhere in the world.

Wovoka's followers developed the message into a ritual that included five days of worship by slow dancing and meditation. Impractical, illusory, beautiful in its simple pathos, rich in spirituality and racial memory, a message of brotherhood weirdly flowering from the depths of despair, it spread rapidly among the tribes throughout the Far West.

Sitting Bull, still leading the Sioux, sent emissaries to Wovoka to learn the message. When they returned, he was interested but worried about the possible reaction of the white man. Indian agents called the cult anti-Christian, and the army began to arrest Ghost Dancers. Indian sympathizers asked why the army was not also arresting Seventh-Day Adventists, who waited in similar fashion for the imminent coming of their messiah. The army obviously feared another outbreak of resistance. These worries were shared by nearby settlers, and one Nebraska farmer described newspapermen sending east jittery stories of Indian atrocities.[14] In December 1890, when Sitting Bull sought permission to go to Pine Ridge to meet the new messiah, the local agent used the request as a pretext for claiming that the aging chief planned to escape and ordered his arrest by agency police. Sitting Bull's friends and his seventeen-year-old son tried to protect him, but after a skirmish, eight men lay shot, including Sitting Bull, dead in the cold.

In late December, a few days after Sitting Bull's death, a band of Sioux moved north from Pine Ridge, fleeing the scene. Custer's old regiment, the 7th Cavalry, was sent to apprehend them, which they easily did in the freezing cold at an encampment on a creek called Wounded Knee. With four new efficient machine guns trained on them, the Indians were disarmed. Somehow a shot was fired, causing the army to open fire on the men, women, and children in the camp. Before the Sioux warriors were wiped out, they managed to kill twenty-five whites. Frantic women and children were pursued, then shot. More than two hundred Sioux lay massacred and bleeding on the snow. The spirit of Red Cloud's remaining people, once proud in the bravery of Crazy Horse and Sitting Bull and revived by the Ghost Dance movement, was thus obliterated under the winter clouds at Wounded Knee. On the day after the massacre, Jules Sandoz rode to the site:

From a hill to the north he looked down upon the desolate field, upon the dark piles of men, women, and children sprawled among their goods. Dry snow trailed little ridges of white over them making them look like strange-limbed animals left for the night and the wolves. Here in ten minutes an entire community was as the buffalo that bleached on the plains. . . . There was something loose in the world that hated joy and happiness as it hated brightness and color, reducing everything to drab agony and gray.[15]

The first decade of the twentieth century brought an intensification of the cultural erosion already well advanced before the end of the Indian wars. Attitudes toward native Americans remained hostile among settlers who came into closest contact with the Indians. One Iowan described people of the nearby reservation as "worthless as so many tamed wolves." When Indians moved away from the tribe into cities, they frequently fell into menial occupations and "permanent pauperdom." In the early 1920s Washington ordered reservation dwellers to cut their hair, and at least one group of resistors were handcuffed as they were shorn. Black Elk's words were reality: "The nation's hoop is broken and scattered. There is no center any longer, and the sacred tree is dead."[16]

In the early twentieth century, revivals of Indian culture emphasizing intertribal solidarity often circulated around peyote, a drug derived from a Southwestern cactus and taken in a ritual to induce hallucinations. The most important support group was the Native American Church, formed in Oklahoma City in 1918. It became a springboard for Indian political activity. In 1934 the so-called Indian New Deal, the Indian Reorganization Act, was the result of a vigorous superintendent of Indian affairs, John Collier. It instituted a return to tribal organization, but did not address the serious problems of disease, mortality, and poverty among the tribes. After 1917 Indian population ceased its long decline, but neither peyote nor New Deal could fully restore Black Elk's broken hoop.

Blacks contributed to every phase of western development, as trappers, explorers, cowboys, soldiers, settlers, and city laborers. The nineteenth-century myth of the West, however, does not include them in any of these roles; the myth is wholly white. The exclusion of blacks from the legends suggests the extent to which they were excluded from the benefits of expansion. In short, with the exception of a few unusual times and places blacks were no more assimilated into western life than they were elsewhere in America.

For example, many more blacks were engaged in the fur trade than is realized. At the managerial level, a few (usually West Indians)

"Sign Language" by Frederic Remington, 1889.

worked their way down the St. Lawrence to Montreal or up the Mississippi to St. Louis. The proverbial French Canadian voyageur frequently bore Negro blood in his veins. In the American fur trade in the nineteenth century the black man tended to be a menial, a cook or servant, and often a slave. York, for example, on the Lewis and Clark expedition, was in bondage to William Clark. Occasionally a black trapper such as James Beckworth, whose West Indian mother was a slave, would rise to an important entrepreneurial position. But this tended to occur when the fur trade was not economically mature. As corporate structures were established and social patterns solidified, the black man found himself relegated to the ranks of unskilled laborer.

Blacks were sometimes used by the whites to fight the Indians, but on some occasions blacks and Indians felt a common cause. Some Indians bought and held black slaves. The relationship tended to be a happy one, with the slave admitted into full fellowship within the tribe. Fugitive slaves often were welcomed into Indian tribes, along all southern frontier regions from Missouri, through Texas, to Florida. The Seminole tribe in Florida, for example, achieved a separate tribal identity as a result of its amalgamation with blacks in the eighteenth century. Providing a haven for fugitive slaves, the Seminoles continued to undermine the institution of slavery. Seminoles were the target of southern fears of both the Indian and the black. As a result the three Seminole wars spanning the years from 1816 to 1842 were peculiarly vicious. Their intensity may be judged by the American losses of fifteen hundred during the last eight years of the fighting alone.[17]

The issue of slavery in the West exposed deep patterns of racial prejudice. Antislavery efforts often were motivated by hatred and fear of the black man and a desire to see him contained in the South and excluded from the West. "This government was made for the benefit of the white race," wrote a Michigan editor in 1861.[18] As new territories and states faced the question of inclusion or exclusion of slavery, widespread desires surfaced not only to avoid slavery but to keep out free blacks as well.

In Oregon in the spring of 1844, the issue had not yet been written into law when a black man, James Sauls, was arrested and jailed. He had an Indian wife and threatened to instigate an Indian uprising if he was not released. Sauls himself was persuaded to leave the area, but his threat so chilled Oregonians that, according to their provisional constitution, not only was slavery excluded but free blacks were to be whipped periodically until they quit the territory. Blacks were a bad influence on Indians, settlers reasoned, and it was far easier to keep them out than to rid the region of Indians. In December 1844 the law was modified so that any free black man in the territory would be bound to a master as an apprentice for a short time, after which he had to leave. The exclusion law, though unenforced after the Civil War, remained on the statute books as late as the 1920s.

In California, until about 1848, blacks seemed to be accepted as individuals, but when the gold seekers descended, racial prejudice rapidly emerged. The first governor, Peter Burnett, had come down from Oregon, where a few years before he had been a prime mover in antiblack legislation. In California he campaigned for governor on a similar platform, publicly avowing that blacks were drunken and improvident. Burnett and his followers were unable to get exclusion written into the constitution of 1849, so it became the prime order of business for the first legislature. "The principle is no doubt correct," wrote Burnett, "that when a state, for reasons satisfactory to itself, denies the right of suffrage and office to a certain class, it is sometimes the best humanity also to deny the privilege of residence."[19] Exclusion was narrowly defeated, but legal restrictions, such as the bar against blacks' testimony in court, remained in effect until late in the Civil War.

In Oregon and California sentiments emerged, as they did in prac-

"Rescue of Corporal Scott" by Frederic Remington.

tically every territory, around the problem of slavery. Antislavery feeling was directed at keeping blacks out and was part of a much larger phenomenon of prejudice. The social disruption of emancipation sent blacks westward for the first time in sizable numbers. In typical western enterprises — cattle raising, Indian fighting, the settlement of the plains — blacks and whites worked side by side. In Texas, former slaves quite naturally took their place beside the white cowboy. Subsequent myths have ignored the fact that an estimated one-fourth of the total number of cowboys were black.[20] Likewise the black's role as Indian fighter with the army was far greater than his proportionate strength in the population.

On the other hand, a small proportion of blacks tried their hands at settling and farming on the plains. Homesteading was a new experience for most of them, for legislation and court action had generally denied preemption rights to free blacks on the public domain.[21] In spite of most slaves' experience at farming, postwar recommendations, including some from the Secretary of the Interior, that freedmen be granted agricultural land from the public domain were seldom

One-Horse Charlie (with cigar) and Shoshone Indians, Reno, 1886.

taken seriously. "Perhaps never in American history," writes V. Jacque Voegeli, "has the federal government had a better opportunity both to mitigate racial intolerance in the South and to emancipate the freedmen from the heritage of slavery."[22]

Nevertheless, without encouragement or special consideration, blacks, sometimes called Exodusters, did move to the plains. Benjamin Singleton, for example, a former slave, organized groups of poor, black farmers in the South and led them into Kansas and Nebraska. They were not always welcomed; one hundred of his followers were driven out of Lincoln in 1879. But in spite of restrictions on voting and other discouragements, large numbers of blacks came. According to one estimate, from fifteen to twenty thousand blacks settled during 1880 in Kansas alone. Only one-third of them brought teams and equipment, which helps to explain why so many became hired laborers and transients. But entire communities sometimes remained intact, such as Nicodemus, Kansas, founded in 1877, and Boley, Kansas, founded in 1889.[23]

For most blacks, the greatest economic opportunities lay in the

Ben Hodges, cowboy and rustler, Dodge City.

city, largely because demands for unskilled labor there were unusually high. In the urban environment white hostility was intensified by proximity and competition for jobs. Mifflin Gibbs, a black man who went to San Francisco from Philadelphia in 1850, found that white construction workers would walk off when they saw a black man on the job. He opposed poll taxes directed at poor minorities, and he raised petitions of protest, which went unheard.[24] Even social exclusion could go to extremes. Angie Debo tells of a white doctor who had to live ten miles out of town, presumably because he had a black wife.[25] Blacks who moved to cattle towns very soon found themselves segregated and victimized by the kind of discrimination that made it almost impossible to convict or even prosecute a white man for the murder of a black.[26]

No matter where one looks in the West, in areas largely peopled from the South or in regions populated from the North, attitudes toward the black man were not notably different. It is hard to believe that an educated and responsible man like William Allen White, the Kansas editor, would exhibit so little sensitivity, even late in the century. His reaction was no more than amusement when, at a city celebration, blacks walked out as the band played "All Coons Look Alike to Me." Though a liberal reformer, White obviously misunderstood the emotions of this racial minority. His position suggested that sources of prejudice were not sectional or urban, not southern, western, or rural. They lay deep in the national experience.

The Mexican is the product of a variety of cultures. The Spaniard had conquered the Indian and had then partly absorbed his way of life. Thus by the time Mexico declared its independence from Spain, its people had hammered out a distinctive culture. Within a decade after the American conquest of the Southwest, the Mexican majority, at least in California, was reduced to a minority by the flood of Anglo-Americans. During the period of transition the Mexican, like the Indian, clung tenaciously to major elements of his own culture, such as the Spanish language and the Catholic Church. The Anglo culture, steeped in Puritanism, legalism, and rationalism, demanded conformity. The Mexican did not adapt, and he was relegated to positions of low economic and social status. However, the unskilled labor of the Mexican was essential, particularly to agriculture. Unlike blacks, who lived and competed in close proximity with the white man, Mexicans lived apart in farming communities. They were socially less threatening and thus may have suffered a shade less from prejudice than did the blacks. Nevertheless, Mexican and Anglo cultures remained polarized. The Mexicans continued to think of the Anglo-Americans as marauding and materialistic. The Anglos, in the 1850s going through one of their worst periods of nativism and anti-Catholicism, continued to label Mexicans lazy and shiftless. According to the Treaty of Guadalupe Hidalgo, Mexicans who wished to remain in ceded territory would be allowed all the rights of citizens of the United States and would be "maintained and protected in the free enjoyment of their liberty and property." The decades to come made a mockery of that guarantee. In mines in California, for example, when the Mexicans were no longer needed to give advice about mining techniques, they were driven out of the camps, taxed as "foreigners," and refused legal recourse. In these circumstances it was hardly surprising that a Mexican girl in Downieville, known only as Juanita, was hanged for the killing of a white man after a mockery of a trial.

The Mexicans had long been tied to the land, especially in California, where their way of life was so based on the cattle ranch. In order to establish title to the land under the new government, intricate procedures were required. The United States Land Commission sat from 1851 to 1856. Enormously complicated by claims of squatters and

Mexican muleteers, 1845.

by inconsistencies between Mexican and United States law, the decisions facing the commission were anything but simple. In California, out of 813 claims covering some thirteen million acres, 604 claims of nine million acres were confirmed. However, the process was long, averaging seventeen years per case, and great losses came from the need to sell in order to pay lawyers' fees. The large landholdings were fair game for the hordes of Anglo-American settlers pouring into the new territories.

One consequence of exclusion and hostility was social banditry, the frequent response of a persecuted minority in times of social disruption. Robbing the rich to give to the poor, the social bandit was a criminal only in the eyes of the state. To most of the people from among whom he sprang, he was virtue itself. The dream behind his action, as in the case of the Ghost Dance with the Indians, was the symbolic destruction of the establishment and the revival of a lost past.

Counterbalancing innumerable Anglo lynchings of Mexicans, a variety of Mexican bandits, such as Tiburcio Vasquez and Three-Fingered Jack, roamed the countryside, usually robbing the Anglos.

Romance and the social bandit: Joaquin Murieta as Robin Hood.

The most famous of these was Joaquin Murieta, a semifictional hero who combined the exploits of at least five actual men. Facts were less important, however, than the legend, which was finally distilled by Yellow Bird, a Cherokee Indian, in 1854. Yellow Bird's book was a beautiful example of one persecuted minority finding meaning in the story of another. Yellow Bird told of Murieta unobtrusively working his mining claim when he was driven off by Yankees. Later he was publicly whipped for his brother's crime of horse stealing and, while tied, forced to watch as his mistress was raped. Murieta's vow of revenge echoed the frustration of California's oppressed Mexicans.

The Murieta legend instilled fear in the Anglo community. The governor of California himself placed a bounty of $1,000 on the outlaw. Harry Love, a former Texas Ranger, rode with a posse on Murieta's trail. He found a small group of Mexicans around a camp fire, shot their leader, and brought back his head as that of Joaquin Murieta. The head was pickled in whisky and displayed to thousands. But to California's Mexicans, Murieta had not been killed; in a real sense he would never die.

A thousand miles east in Texas and only five years later, another cultural hero emerged whose actions were more historic than legendary. Juan Cortina was the son of a displaced landed family. Feeling keenly his people's plight, he assumed the role of Robin Hood, stealing from the Anglo rich to give to the Mexican poor. He once wrote: "To me is entrusted the breaking of the chains of your slavery."[27] In 1859 Cortina and a hundred men raided Brownsville, the only center of American strength on the lower Rio Grande. The raiders shot three Americans, released all the prisoners in the jail, and then retreated to a camp, which began to attract flocks of frustrated Mexican-Americans. Cortina eventually was defeated in a battle with the United States army in which sixty of his followers were killed, but he retreated across the border and continued his raids. A band of Texas Rangers crossed the boundary early in 1860. Though they killed thirty Mexicans, they did not capture the leader. Cortina himself was silenced only after Colonel Robert E. Lee was sent by the United States army with instructions to cross into Mexico if necessary. Under this threat of invasion, Mexico imprisoned Cortina in 1875, effectively ending his rebellion along the border. Two hundred forty-five men had died, testimony to the fact that racial discontent along the Rio Grande had moved beyond social banditry to the level of guerrilla warfare.[28]

Mexican-Americans in Texas sometimes found themselves supported by other minorities, notably Indians and blacks. The latter were usually escaped slaves seeking asylum along the border and willing to fight against their former masters. The Indians on their part were beginning to retaliate against white penetration of their lands. The Mexican-Americans had inherited a tradition of hostility from two wars and in addition were becoming aware that Anglo law was undermining their power as landowners. The three discontented peoples did not always work in concert, but neither were they as distant as historians sometimes imply. A raid on Corpus Christi in 1849, for example, is sometimes described as an Indian foray, but actually it included escaped black slaves and Mexican-Americans as well.

One indication of this discontent is that Cortina first directed his activity against a city, Brownsville, virtually the only place in the region where Anglos were to be found. Most Anglos there were not yet landowners but were recently arrived merchants. But new economic forces were developing. Soon railroads would be spreading a commercial, industrial economy into the Southwest. Movements like that of Cortina were based partly on premonitions that the new commercial and industrial power would threaten the Mexican-American position.

Meanwhile, industrializing influences were creating larger and larger agricultural units, just as they were on the bonanza farms of the northern plains. Faced with the need for agricultural labor, Anglos turned to Mexican-Americans as the next ethnic group to be exploited for this purpose. Farm labor rapidly became the occupation most open to the multitudes of Mexican immigrants entering the Southwest, especially during the first quarter of the twentieth century. The new migrants, though a completely different class from the older landholders, could harken back to men such as Cortina and Murieta who had fought for their people. More recently César Chavez in California and Reies Tijerina in New Mexico, like their early counterparts, continue to seek ways for Mexican-Americans to partake more fully in the dominant society without losing their identity.

The Chinese were notable for maintaining their cultural identity. They first came to the California gold mines in appreciable numbers about 1851, chiefly to earn money but also to escape social and economic upheavals at home. Coming as temporary sojourners, they intended to return to China as soon as their savings warranted. From 1848 to 1854, forty-five thousand Chinese arrived; in 1854, eight hundred forty landed in San Francisco in a single day.[29] Most of them came under a Chinese-controlled contract labor system in which the immigrant worked out the cost of his transportation. The arrangement made it possible for a few Chinese contractors or associations to govern practically every aspect of their countrymen's lives in America. Even after the worker had completed his obligation for transportation, his dependence persisted. Labor, housing, social clubs, temples, joss houses, opium dens, and brothels were all managed by a complicated web of companies, clans, guilds, tongs — all serving the needs of isolated, lonely men far from home. Almost none of the men brought wives; the first three years of the migration brought only sixteen Chinese women.

Although the social system was complex, it was at the same time a coordinated network with lines of power concentrated in five (later six) companies. These in turn were ruled by the most stable merchants in the community. The highest echelons, however, could not, or did not, impose peace on the total group. Among the five companies there were not only feuds but sometimes actual warfare. Overt outbreaks, generally misnamed "tong wars," diminished after the 1860s, and even tighter monopolistic control by the companies followed. Taken as a whole, the Chinese enclave, a separate world, living, worshiping, and fighting within itself, was one of the least assimilated and least acculturated societies ever to exist in America.

Chinese and whites working in the gold fields, Auburn, 1852.

During their first decade in this country most Chinese worked in the mines, about 75 percent of them by the early 1860s. But the Chinese miners were not restricted to California, and they spread inland early. Enclaves of Chinese miners were evident in camps as far from the coast as Montana. In the second decade there was a shift away from mining; railroads discovered the value of Chinese labor. The Central Pacific ultimately hired ten thousand Chinese to lay the transcontinental tracks. Mining and railroad construction predominated until the 1880s, after which the Chinese tended to be employed in manufacturing — especially cigars, shoes, and textiles — an occupation in which they experienced less discrimination. In California, before the turn of the century, half of the labor force engaged in manufacturing was Chinese. By 1890 they had also become a dominant part of California's agricultural labor force.

Changing occupations often were accompanied by changing goals. Intentions to stay gradually replaced the desire to return to China, especially among the second and third generations. For example, three

Chinese gambling den, San Francisco, 1875.

Chinese families migrated to the mines of Butte, Montana, in the 1870s, all as sojourners. By the twentieth century, the original migrants all had returned to China, but only five of their children had emigrated. The others stayed in Butte. In the third generation, interestingly enough, the older pattern recurred; a few Chinese went back to Asia, but a larger percentage dispersed to other parts of the United States.[30]

White prejudice, however, did not seem to change, even though it had been related to the sojourner status of the Chinese. There is always ambiguity in human emotions. The Chinese were sometimes seen as representatives of the oldest of cultures and as wise as Confucius. Other ideas, however, aroused deeper, more negative feelings. The Chinese were so different that they seemed unassimilable into any Western society. They were considered inscrutable and devious. They were thought to engage in unspeakable vices and barbaric customs. They labored for a pittance and thus held down the wages of Anglo-American competitors.

Efforts to rid California of Chinese began early. The California Foreign Miners' License Tax had been imposed in 1850 before the Chinese came, and in most mining camps the tax was eagerly extended to them. Exclusion from some types of work, such as railroad construction, waited until Chinese labor was no longer needed but came quickly in periods of economic distress when competition for jobs grew acute. Once exclusionary feelings were afoot, however, actions went beyond the immediate economic causation. Taxes were often directly discriminatory, as when Los Angeles placed a heavy fee on launderers and vegetable peddlers, knowing that practically everyone engaged in these jobs was Chinese. Such laws were facilitated by the prohibition of Chinese testimony in court. When a white man was presumably killed by a Chinese in Los Angeles in 1871, the omnipresent anti-Chinese feelings promoted a massacre in which fifteen Chinese were hanged on makeshift gallows.[31] The Chinese community reacted violently, raised money for court fees, and threatened to walk off their jobs, before tempers cooled.

Elsewhere, labor unions had acted to bar Chinese from membership. Municipalities engaged in similar practices. Great Falls, Montana, for example, was able to exclude Chinese so effectively that not until World War II was a Chinese restaurant possible, and even then the restaurant opened only because servicemen from a nearby army base were hungry for chop suey.

The most serious movement against the Chinese was closing immigration to them. Organized labor, especially the Workingmen's Party of San Francisco, made exclusion a crusade. When the Chinese were still working hard on the completion of the transcontinental railroad, the Burlingame Treaty with China in 1868 had pledged an open door for immigrants. As labor mounted its campaign, especially after the panic of 1873, the Burlingame Treaty was the butt of the criticism. A bill in Congress to abrogate the treaty in 1879 got all the way to the White House, where it was vetoed. In 1880 a treaty regulating Chinese immigration provided that the United States could "regulate, limit, or suspend such coming or residence, but may not absolutely prohibit it." In 1882 the Chinese Exclusion Act suspended Chinese immigration for ten years and thereafter was extended until the 1940s. Clamor from labor unions in California had produced national policy.

Historians have generally assumed that the federal government reluctantly reacted against the Chinese after strong pressures from western states like California. In this view, the Northeast and Midwest did not harbor substantial anti-Chinese feelings. Mary Coolidge, for example, wrote two volumes in 1909 on Chinese immigration, the standard work for nearly two generations. She contended that Americans' first reaction to the Chienese was warm and friendly and that several decades passed before anti-Chinese feelings developed. Thereafter, in Coolidge's opinion, California engaged in a conspiracy

The Denver anti-Chinese riot, 1880.

with the federal government to get the Chinese excluded. Other scholars, most recently Stuart C. Miller, have shown that the racist view of the Chinese was prevalent in all sections of the country and existed when the Chinese arrived. In short, he claims, an unfavorable image and even contempt for the Chinese dominated nineteenth-century American thought.[32] The unique islands of culture shaped by the Chinese in America were never free of misunderstanding and hostility, but it is probably true that external prejudices were minimized as long as Chinese labor was essential to the economy as a whole. Thus the difference in attitude was slight, and when the Chinese labor was no longer needed, the gloss was easily removed to expose the more persistent forms of racism.

Because Japan barred emigration until well after the middle of the nineteenth century, the Japanese came to the west coast much later than the Chinese. Not until the 1890s did they arrive in significant numbers, and in the following decade 22,000 came. By 1920, however, there were 111,000 Japanese in the United States, of which nearly 93,000 lived along the Pacific coast, with 20,000 of these in Los Angeles County.[33] Like the Chinese, the very earliest groups were mostly men who hoped to return home. Much more quickly than the Chinese, however, Japanese women and families began to come. This fact made a crucial difference, for the family became a prime social control.

Within a tightly knit community of Japanese families, there were associations common to all Japanese communities; their function was protective rather than economic. The overcrowded island of Japan had required intensive agricultural methods, and in America the Japanese quite naturally continued to use those techniques. They pioneered in the irrigation of vegetable crops in order to supply an early or all-year market. By 1919 they accounted for nearly half of the farm labor in California, and in some crops, such as celery, they came to practically dominate the market. In the fishing and canning industries they also rose rapidly. Their Horatio Alger successes are the economic counterpart to the aphorism one Japanese-American used to describe his people, "Scratch a Japanese-American and find a white Anglo-Saxon Protestant."[34]

Antipathy toward the Japanese surfaced early. Their culture was alien, so the arguments went; they were incapable of adapting to democracy; their low standard of living drove down wages. Labor unions barred them. They were disliked as a group. In 1900, James Phelan, the mayor of San Francisco, quarantined all Japanese, along with Chinese, regardless of their health, as carriers of bubonic plague. Anti-Japanese pressures resulted in 1908 in the curtailment of immigration through the Gentleman's Agreement with Japan, and, going further, California laws in 1913 and 1920 prohibited land ownership by Japanese nationals. The land laws were not effective because second-generation Japanese, automatically United States citizens, could assume legal ownership. Consequently, attention moved to Japanese exclusion, and all immigration was cut off in 1924.

In this discussion of racial minorities in the West, several groups have been excluded — Germans and Scandinavians in the Midwest and Irish, Italians, and Poles in large cities. If a racial minority is defined as an ethnic group competing for power in the prevailing society, then these groups are certainly part of the story. Yet, most of these people represented not racial, but only cultural, differences; and even the cultures were not generally conceived as alien to the dominant society.

However selected and defined, no racial minority became assimilated into American life in any appreciable way. Even if we assume for the sake of argument that the melting pot was a reality, we must admit that the frontier did not assist assimilation. Open land was not the magic ingredient the westerners thought it would be. Advertising frantically for settlers, the West seemed ready to welcome anyone. But in fact it was hospitable to none but its own narrowly defined kind. When outsiders of color arrived, old antipathies surfaced, and westerners cried for restrictions on immigration with almost as much frenzy as they had called for settlers. If there was a time when frontiersmen worked to break barriers of racial animosity, it occurred in the earliest period, before social and economic patterns solidified.

A variety of causes laid the foundations for racial conflict. A minority might cease to be useful in the development of the region, as did the Mexicans in the first years of the gold rush. A racial group might too successfully compete for scarce jobs in the labor market and, like the Chinese, threaten to undercut union wage scales. A minority's cultural differences might be so great that, like Indians and Orientals, they appear unassimilable. One or more of these conditions developed early in most western communities.

Before the racial conflict was well under way, a few individuals were admitted to the benefits of the prevailing society. But in time, usually a good deal later, the minority coalesced and then faced violent resistance. The prevailing culture frequently hardened its long-felt prejudices into bars against individuals and the group, and the resulting conflict brought exclusion and in extreme cases, such as that of the Indian, virtual annihilation. Somewhere in the latter phases, the excluded minority, with rare exceptions like the Japanese, sank into passivity and fatalism, interpreted by the prevailing society as racial characteristics. Messianic cults, like the Ghost Dance or the Black Muslims, sometimes based on drugs, have typically arisen from such fatalism. Because the minority was relegated to the lowest economic and social levels, race and low class became interchangeable and reinforced one another. Poverty among minority peoples became endemic. In poor housing and with minimal opportunity, in slums, ghettos, barrios, across the railroad tracks or a highway, the excluded minority found itself "always on the other side of something."[35] On the "other" side of the Mississippi or wherever the frontier existed, hopes for assimilation of racial minorities were justified only in the earliest period of an immature economy.

13

Preachers and Teachers

THE KINGDOM OF GOD IN THE WEST

Frontier life, like rural life everywhere, was filled with hard work, isolation, and stultifying tasks, especially for women. The natural elements seen by romantics as lovely — boundless skies, billowing grain as far as the eye could penetrate, the soft warmth of a wood-burning stove — were hardly considered romantic by those who lived constantly with them. To people bound to work beneath the sky, battle for grain against great odds, drudge for hours over the wood-burning stove, monotony and isolation brought intellectual stagnation and walled-in minds. The result was a craving for mental stimulation, a desire to hold fast to old ways, and a search for acceptable emotional outlets. Efforts to meet these human needs influenced American Protestantism enormously. For any religious denomination, the appropriateness of its response to frontier conditions determined its impact on American life.

Emotionally starved frontier people took readily to evangelistic revivalism, which sought to rekindle the simple purity of a direct experience with man's creator. The roots of evangelical revivalism ran back through the eighteenth-century's Great Awakening in colonial America. The "new lights," as those who had been saved called themselves, tried to create situations in which direct communication with God might be experienced. Early in the nineteenth century, beyond the Alleghenies, the same tendencies produced the circuit rider and the camp meeting.

Circuit-riding preacher, by A. R. Waud, 1867.

The circuit rider, with his Bible for a lance, rode forth to thwart isolation and protect the faithful. The idea seems to have come from the first Methodist bishop in America, Francis Asbury, at about the turn of the century. Circuit riders lived on the hospitality of farm wives and tried to keep a schedule that included preaching every day of the week except Monday.

Peter Cartwright, the archetypal circuit rider, was raised on the Kentucky frontier in a region known as Rogues Harbor. His father had participated in a Regulator movement that tried to clean up the neighborhood, but he seems to have been unsuccessful, judging from the conviction of one of Peter's brothers as a murderer. Peter himself was a lusty, aggressive youth until the age of sixteen, when at a camp meeting the spirit of God descended and he was converted from wayward ways to Methodism. After licensing by the church, he began in 1803 his life as a traveling preacher. At first he covered wide circles of Kentucky, Tennessee, Ohio, and Indiana; he later moved to Illinois, where he could speak more freely against slavery. In all, for nearly seventy years and fourteen thousand sermons, he relentlessly

Methodist camp meeting, c. 1849.

made his rounds, referring to himself as "the Lord's breaking plow." His huge head and burning eyes suggested the energy that this "muscular Christianity" required. A circuit rider's wife, Julia Lovejoy, wrote from Kansas in 1858:

> Some of them have been through "war and flood," now shivering with cold, then pinched with hunger, fording dangerous streams, or wading through the water hip high; now swimming a swollen creek with horse and buggy, or grappling with the angry waves, that were bearing off its precious burden [his box of books], and leaving one shoe in the bed of the creek, ne'er to be "fished up by hook and line," and thus drenched to the skin, riding miles in wet clothing! Now this is no fiction, but the actual experience of one whose aching head I have this hour been endeavoring to alleviate.[1]

The camp meeting, the frontier form of revivalism, emerged from what is sometimes called the Second Great Awakening among backwoodsmen in Kentucky and Tennessee. It grew into a true frontier institution, like the missions of the Southwest. People traveled long distances to a meeting, bringing the whole family by buckboard to a central place. Prepared to stay for days or weeks, they became a closely knit camp arranged in a circle of tents and buggies, with cooking fires within easy reach of one another for chatting and gossiping. The central clearing was the focus of activity. A rough shed covered rows of benches seating as many as two thousand people. Sermons lasted for hours. Their emphasis was on personal salvation, fear of hell fire, and hope of the cool, sweet mercy of God. The promise of an ever-present Providence must have comforted people living in physical danger. The supernatural was acceptable, and though the preachers were smart enough to recognize the emotional counterfeit, they also understood the value of true feeling.

The gospel was sung in ways to gladden John Wesley's heart. Wesley had entreated his followers to sing lustily, and they responded by making Methodism, especially in its camp meeting form, a vividly vocal religion. Although there were dozens of printed hymnals, variations on the songs were legion, with local additions and spontaneous combinations in typical folk tradition. The hymns captured the most striking images from the Bible — golden streets, starry crowns, parting waters, "When the stars begin to fall, you'll see the moon ableeding." They sang, too, of a spiritual battle against "the world, the Devil, and Tom Paine." There were also martial images — a holy war, the sword of truth, trumpets heralding the soldiers of the Cross. But the battle was basically personal, and the songs were adapted to individual experiences, as each person enlisted, if not to fight, at least "to shout old Satan's kingdom down": "Come to Jesus, come to Jesus," was softly sung as individuals with tears in their eyes and new conversion in their hearts moved forward to the mourners' bench. This clearing on the frontier was like Jordan: "There's a great camp meeting in the promised land." And how sad the parting: "Till we meet again, till we meet again, God be with us till we meet again." And finally came the return to lonely lives:

> Farewell, my friends, I'm bound for Canaan,
> I'm traveling through the wilderness.
> Your company has been delightful,
> You who doth leave my mind distressed.
> I go away, behind to leave you.
> Perhaps never to meet again;
> But if we never have this pleasure,
> I hope we'll meet on Canaan's land.[2]

At such times, God was indeed near. The millennial quality of Protestantism in nineteenth-century America must be related to this close feeling between man and God. Sarah Royce, for example, traveling with her small family across the wilderness, saw God descend to her in a burning (American) bush, as he had to Moses on Sinai. In his *Kingdom of God in America*, H. Richard Niebuhr describes this millennial quality — the confidence that when Christ walks again on earth he will come to Americans on American soil: "To an ever increasing extent they turned from the expectation of heavenly bliss to the hope of a radical transformation of life upon earth." The doctrine of the coming millennium in America was secularized, nationalized, and used to justify war, beliefs in racial superiority, and capitalism: "It is in particular the kingdom of the Anglo-Saxon race which is destined to bring light to the gentiles by means of lamps manufactured in America."[3]

As the nation readied itself along the Alleghenies for the trek westward, four Protestant denominations seemed best prepared to lead the march — the Presbyterians, the Congregationalists, the Methodists, and the Baptists. The Presbyterians — Scotch-Irish hunters, fighters, and small farmers — had long been associated with the frontier. Some of the first western revivals took place in Presbyterian areas, but the church itself grew reluctant to engage in such excesses. This reluctance may have been due partly to a respect for education. Presbyterians demanded a trained ministry, even as early as 1735 when William Tennent set up his "log college," which would later expand into Princeton University. But the supply of educated ministers would never keep abreast of the demand, and that fact, coupled with severe strictures against drinking and gambling, gradually robbed the Presbyterians of their strength.

The Presbyterians, however, were part of a united front for missionizing the frontier. In 1801, they joined with the Congregationalists in a Plan of Union to coordinate and expedite their respective efforts in western expansion. In general, however, the Congregationalists suffered from the problems that held back the Presbyterians in establishing a wider following.

The Baptists, too, began with something of a frontier tradition. Roger Williams might be considered a frontiersman as he fled Massachusetts and established his wilderness home among the Indians of Rhode Island. Baptists were strengthened by the Great Awakening, but not until the nineteenth century did they become a major American denomination. They believed education was fine but was hardly a prerequisite for godliness. A lay preacher was as likely to effectively spread God's word westward as was a trained minister. There were internal bickerings over the need for education and salary for ministers, but finally the Baptists came to allow, if not encourage, an untrained, unsalaried clergy.

By the early nineteenth century Methodism had thrown off the taint of its English origin and had become a highly nationalistic denomination. The first bishop, Francis Asbury, strengthened his institution so it would be able to function on the frontier. Peter Cartwright, along with dozens of other circuit riders such as James Finley, William McGee, and William McKendree showed one way in which the church met frontier conditions. Circuit riding and camp meetings were innovations that helped the Methodists become the chief American denomination. By 1900, Methodists numbered nearly five and a half million; in that year the Baptists counted four and a half million, the Presbyterians only one and a half million.

The frontier contributed greatly to the splintering of American sects. True, the doctrine of the priesthood of all believers and the tendency away from a hierarchical organization inclined Protestantism toward schism. But, just as capitalism and Protestantism were congenial, the frontier with its myth of individualism and self-reliance was a most agreeable environment for Protestant leanings.

Alexander Campbell once hoped to counter the splintering effects of the frontier by unifying Protestants, but he succeeded only in creating another denomination. Campbell, a Scotch-Irishman, preached among his Presbyterian countrymen on the frontier. In one of his soul-searching moods, he threw over Presbyterianism to become a Baptist. More and more convinced that the Second Coming of Christ was near, he admonished against worldliness, including political activity. He believed disunity among Christians was intolerable and hoped that a new translation of the Bible might provide a rallying point. Campbell's version of the New Testament appeared in 1827. His teaching led to a new denomination, especially after 1833, when the followers of Campbell and Barton W. Stone joined together as the Disciples of Christ. Eighty years later the sect counted a million members.

Although the frontier produced schism, this is not to say that it was a liberating or innovative force in religion. In doctrine and policy the West probably pushed heaviest in the assertion of conservatism and preservation of old religious values. Jesuits, Franciscans, and Dominicans on the borderlands of New Spain devised new approaches to the missionization of natives. Circuit riding and camp meetings were other adaptations to a frontier location. They did not, however, affect doctrines. According to Will Herberg: "The story of American Protestantism is the story of a religious movement following the advancing frontier and subduing it, periodically crystallizing it into established denominations, yet always in some way breaking through them again."[4]

Frontier conditions in the upper Hudson valley between 1820 and 1850 produced frenzies of religious enthusiasm — an intriguing mix of revivals, divining rods, revelations, utopian experiments, spiritualist rappings, and seances. This basin between the Great Lakes and the Finger Lakes, extending to western Massachusetts and Vermont, was a natural passage for westward migrants, and thus its population, like people on most early frontiers, tended to be transient. The Seventh-Day Adventists, the Mormons, and a host of lesser denominations emerged from the fires of enthusiasm.

William Miller, a quiet searcher of his own soul and the Bible, was a product of this "burnt over district." He early convinced himself that the Second Coming of Christ was near but did not reveal his prophecy until 1832. He hesitated to mention an exact date but felt the final judgment would come either before the end of 1843 or by the vernal equinox on March 21, 1844. He soon had a large following with revivals, newspapers, and a group of organizers. The believers purified themselves in preparation, by paying debts or by divesting themselves of possessions. After March 21, 1844, another date was set, and again Millerites climbed hills in their white ascension robes to await their Lord and the end of time. The long vigil brought midnight but no messiah. The "Great Disappointment" sent droves of Millerites to other religions, but those who remained faithful carried on the adventist creed.

Nothing emerged from this area as important to the American West as the Church of Jesus Christ of Latter-Day Saints. From almost the beginning the Mormons were a beleaguered people, locked in a tension between their own religious vision and the inability of frontier society to tolerate differences. Conflicts, persecutions, murders, war — all forced them to move west from place after place. Thus Mormons became a peculiarly frontier people, and the interplay of their theology and the frontier made them a case study in the persistence of tradition.

Joseph Smith, founder of the Mormon Church, was moved as a boy of ten from Vermont to a farm in upstate New York. As a teenager young Joseph was troubled by conflicting claims to religious truth, and he prayed for guidance. In the revelations that followed, he was led to Mount Cumorah near Palmyra, New York, where, by his own accounts, he dug from the ground a set of thinly hammered golden plates covered with hieroglyphs. With the aid of special tools and instructions, Smith translated the plates into the Book of Mormon, first published in 1830.

It told of one of the lost tribes of Israel, which, after captivity in Babylon, wandered to the shores of the New World. The leader of the tribe, Lehi, kept alive the old teachings and his people prospered. On his death, his kingdom was divided between his two sons, Nephi and Laman. The Lamanites drifted from the old ways and degenerated;

the Nephites prospered, especially after Jesus appeared to them following his crucifixion in Jerusalem. The Lamanites and Nephites fell to fighting, and in a climactic battle reminiscent of Armageddon, the Nephites were utterly destroyed, save for two, a father and his son. These, Mormon and Moroni, recorded on golden plates the story of their people, plus segments of doctrine from the New Testament reaffirmed by Christ in the New World. To the new Church of Jesus Christ of Latter-Day Saints, the Book of Mormon was a scripture equal in authority to the Bible. Believing in the continuous unfolding of revealed truth (as have most Christians), Smith and his successor Brigham Young subsequently compiled their new revelations into published form as *Doctrine and Covenants* and *The Pearl of Great Price.*

On some issues the Mormons did not differ from other Protestants. In their affirmation of the covenanted community, they have been described as modern Puritans, and in this respect one should not forget Joseph Smith's New England roots. Other Mormon beliefs, however, set them apart, especially polygamy, and these differences forged a distinctive community on the frontier.

In 1831, the year following the appearance of the Book of Mormon, the new church and its young founder (Smith was twenty-six years old) began their migration westward. They settled temporarily at Kirtland, Ohio, but Smith searched farther and proclaimed the New Zion for his people to be in Jackson County, Missouri, close to the Missouri River in the region now dominated by Independence and Kansas City. The locale was becoming the threshold for the great migrations to Oregon and California. When Smith called his saints to "Gather ye out from the eastern lands" to Missouri, he unwittingly threw them into contact with a transient multitude. Meanwhile, twelve hundred of them moved to Jackson County within two years. Their community was laid out like a New England town — central common, neat streets, outlying farms. The doctrines of stewardship and consecration were clarified by practice and continuing revelations. All goods were held in trust from God, and when anyone owned more than he needed, the surplus was consecrated for those less fortunate. The Mormons were hammering out doctrines that placed the survival of the group above that of the individual.

Church policies were inevitably influenced by the social environment of Missouri. In their attitudes toward blacks, the Mormons smacked of New England and abolitionism, but Missouri was a slave state. Anxious that their future in Zion be secure, Mormons justified slavery, using rationalizations from the Old Testament. On the other hand, no Mormon ever denied the Christian doctrine concerning the equality and brotherhood of all men. Blacks became members of the Mormon Church, and by 1837 at least two free blacks had been admitted to the priesthood.[5]

The Mormons tended to do business among themselves, excluding and alienating outsiders. Small incidents led to major confrontations. In 1833 mobs roamed around Jackson County, broke up a Mormon printing press, and tarred and feathered a leading Mormon. In cold November, mobs drove out the saints and burned their property. They regrouped in Kirtland, Ohio, and even added to their numbers so that by 1836 there were three thousand of them. Needing capital, they organized a bank, using inflated land values as a basis for their currency. During the panic of 1837, the bank collapsed, causing a new crisis. Some Mormons left, disillusioned. Most followed Joseph Smith to a new settlement at Far West, Missouri. Once again through hard work, consecration, and with all surplus going to the needy, nearly ten thousand saints were reunited.

In Missouri once more, remembering past troubles there, Smith began to advise against admitting blacks to the priesthood. The policy did not appear in print until 1842 and was later incorporated into *The Pearl of Great Price.* This early practice became doctrine and remained intact through subsequent generations. Mormons continued to hold slaves, though by 1850 in Utah the number of slaves was only twenty-six.

The Mormons' next move, in 1839, to the banks of the Mississippi in Illinois was the last before they went to Utah. With new vigor they set to building again, and the new site, which they christened Nauvoo, soon boasted a hotel and their first large temple. By 1844, twenty-five thousand saints were there. Some Mormons looked back on these days as the happiest of their lives. With prosperity came a slight weakening of the old doctrines of consecration and stewardship, which began to be interpreted more in the manner of a joint-stock corporation than as holdings in common. Perhaps the most significant outgrowth of this period, however, was the belief in and practice of plural marriage.

On July 12, 1843, at Nauvoo, Joseph Smith issued a "new and everlasting covenant," which leaned heavily on Old Testament precedents and allowed Mormon men to take more than one wife: "If any man have ten virgins given unto him by this law, he cannot commit adultery, for they belong to him, and they are given unto him: therefore he is justified."

Mormon polygamy has been exaggerated and misunderstood. Even in its heyday in Utah it was not widely practiced. Not more than one out of ten families was polygamous, and even in those the great

Martyrdom of Joseph and Hyrum Smith, 1844.

majority involved only two wives. Men with large numbers of wives were in the hierarchy of the church or were among the wealthiest Mormons. Thus, Brigham Young, who married twenty-seven women and fathered fifty-six children, was hardly typical. Sometimes marriages were wholly charitable acts, as when John D. Lee at the age of thirty-five took into his household a woman of forty-eight and later married at one time a widowed mother and her three daughters.

Polygamy was undoubtedly the most important single cause of hostility toward the Saints. Ann Eliza Young wrote an exposé in which she charged: "There is fault somewhere. There is worse than that. There is positive sin; and in her heart of hearts, no woman of them all believes it to be right."[6] The Republican Party, newly founded, included in its 1856 platform reference to "those two relics of barbarism — polygamy and slavery."

Two federal laws in 1862 and 1874 prohibited polygamy, but the Edmunds Act of 1882 was the first legislation to stipulate severe penalties. The Supreme Court upheld the constitutionality of these acts, but the laws all applied solely to the territories, much as the Emancipation Proclamation covered only the states in rebellion.

Mormon polygamy: a Utah farm family, 1865.

What was being said to the Mormons was simply that polygamy had to go before Utah could be admitted as a state. The Mormons conceded in 1890 by abolishing polygamy in practice, though not in theory. It had been a long and bitter struggle, which the Mormons would always regard as one more evidence of implacable frontier hostility toward their religious beliefs.

Persecution of the Mormons reached its zenith at Nauvoo. In June 1844 Joseph Smith and his brother Hyrum were shot by an enraged mob of vigilantes. The continued success of the Mormons had been one cause for new bursts of hostility. There were also waves of schism within the church, especially following Smith's promulgation of polygamy in 1843. After an autocratic act against the schismatics, Smith and his brother had been jailed in nearby Carthage, partly for their own protection. The mob had its way, however, and thereby gave to the saints not only two hallowed martyrs but the necessity to move once more. So the Mormons would sing:

> We'll find a place, which God for us prepared,
> Far away in the West;
> Where none shall come to hurt or make afraid;
> There the Saints will be blessed.

Brigham Young grasped the leadership and began careful plans for a migration, including the choice of a site in Mexican territory beyond the Rockies.

This remarkable relocation of tens of thousands of people, beginning in early 1846, was made in stages, and advance parties set up way stations along the route, the biggest being winter quarters in Nebraska. By 1852 twenty thousand Mormons were around Salt Lake; thirty years later, there were one hundred fifty thousand. Their cooperative theological penchant was pressed into constantly expanding enterprises, such as the creation of community water supplies in the new, arid region. Increasing numbers of missionaries were dispatched to Europe, especially to the industrial towns of England and the farms of Scandinavia, calling converts to Utah where lay both religious and economic hope. The church defrayed some of the expenses of the passage, but in return it expected individual initiative and group cohesion. Between 1856 and 1861 handcart brigades were organized in which men pulled small carts like oxen, drawing their children and belongings across the plains.

The Mormons in Utah developed a strongly practical and communal way of life. Most of Brigham Young's revelations, and certainly his leadership, concerned economic matters. Smith's early doctrines of stewardship and consecration were coupled with a sort of Horatio Alger ideal: every herdboy expected to become a prosperous patriarch. The Mormons' economic system was in fact a bootstrap operation. No foreign or eastern capital was available to the Mormons. Nevertheless, sugar beet factories and mining smelters to which labor was assigned from a pool of poor migrants were set up. A new version of the Puritan theocracy emerged. The church became the owner of mercantile outlets, sugar and woolen factories, a bank and a life insurance company, and a major stockholder of railroads. That the church should so succeed was proof of God's blessing, especially since the saints sought lives of sober cooperation and brotherly devotion. Divorces were rare and jails were underpopulated. Critics called the Mormons' system dictatorship, and they were partly right, but the shared social vision had happily wedded a communitarian theology with the needs of the frontier.

Unlike the Mormons, the Roman Catholics, it is often assumed, never adapted well to frontier conditions; they remained with the Jews in the urban ghettos of the East. Reflection reduces this theory to no more than half-truth. In some western areas it would be more accurate to say that the Protestants, far from simply rushing into a vacuum, pushed the Catholics aside. Vigilance committees in the mines and the cattle country tended to be Protestant, and their victims tended to be Catholics, especially Irish and Mexicans. Catholics once dominated the fur trade, inasmuch as French Canadians provided its backbone. Irish Catholics built the central part of the transcon-

*Catholic missionary techniques: Father Nicolas Point's journal,
Rocky Mountains, 1840s.*

tinental railroad. Catholic missionaries, such as Father De Smet, out-
did the Protestants in the Oregon country. In all the areas that once
belonged to New Spain or Mexico, Catholicism predominated until
the coming of the Protestant flood.

Actually, Catholics pioneered as farmers westward from the Atlantic, as did most religious groups, though admittedly in small numbers. Bishop John Ireland of Minnesota never tired of urging urban
congregations to move from man-made cities to the God-created
countryside.

Judaism was hardly a frontier religion, yet the "steady trickle" of
Jews westward should not be ignored. Trappers, miners, land speculators, but most often merchants, the Jews moved from one trading
center to another following the lines of prosperity. Though they
comprised only one-half of one percent of the population in the
Northeast, they represented as much as one and a half percent in
many western areas. The population of Los Angeles in 1850, just
over six thousand, included eight Jews. All were recent European immigrants living in four adjacent houses, and all but one were young,

*Father Point's Indian converts under the Immaculate Heart of Mary,
Rocky Mountains, 1840s.*

unmarried, and occupied as merchants.[7] In some frontier situations,
without synagogue or burial privileges, Jews had to travel long distances to visit graves of their dead. Nevertheless, men such as Rabbi
Isaac Wise of Cincinnati, before the Civil War, considered the West to
play a major role in the liberalizing and Americanizing of Judaism.

Whatever the contributions of the Catholics and the Jews to the
westward movement in the nineteenth century, their religions were
not in the primary thrust. The rapidly moving frontier was a Protestant phenomenon. It may not be wholly coincidental that Protestantism also proved congenial to modern capitalism. The Calvinistic
ethic of work, the "calling," and the virtues of prudence and self-
reliance were well-suited to both capitalism and the frontier. The
Methodist and Baptist churches best understood rural conditions and
adapted their policies to sparse settlements. The Jews remained in
widely spread mercantile centers and a few mining camps, while the
Catholic church worked best in the stable institutions of urban life.
Exceptions abound, but none destroys the essential fact that the
nineteenth-century American frontier was fundamentally Protestant.

In preparing for the coming Kingdom, the Protestant churches played a strong social role in maturing western communities. The Calvinist doctrine of the calling impelled men and women to civic life. The fact that the churches demanded lay participation in their own adjustment and growth on the frontier meant that members brought experience in getting things done through committees and boards. The churches were way stations between a political vacuum and the social participation associated with middle-class respectability. "Yes, my friends," said an aging Peter Cartwright, "for seventy long years amid appalling difficulties and dangers, I have waged an incessant warfare against the world, the flesh, and the devil and all other enemies of the Democratic party."[8] In at least Cartwright's mind, political and religious responsibilities were indistinguishable. The social horizons may have been circumscribed by capitalist ethics; no one, except the Quakers, paid any attention to the rights and plight of Indians or workingmen. Yet through philanthropy for the poor, support of missionary causes, and general creation of religious institutions, western churches became sources of social action.

Julia Lovejoy hated much of her life in frontier Kansas — the harsh weather, the estrangement from her former home, and particularly the presence of snakes, which she feared and abhorred as if they were truly, not merely metaphorically, Satan himself. But she also held a deep, personal religious belief, a Calvinist's conviction of God's calling, the internal Protestant energy so supportive of the nation's political expansion. And she never hesitated to express that conviction, overcoming all her doubts and fears: "We are glad we came to Kansas, to labor for truth and justice, and we shall triumph."[9]

SCHOOLS

What a society wants its children to know reveals what that society wants itself to be. By the middle of the nineteenth century, American education had become a creed, a common faith, a catechism of true belief, largely because people believed it served a crucial social function. The reconstruction of society on the frontier exposed vital economic and political wants, which schools could meet. The primitive West needed to be transformed into a sophisticated society, rough individuals into refined citizens. The job was not easy, and the tensions created along the way were enormous.

Education serves two principal constituents — the individual and the society — that may be seen as lying at opposite ends of a continuum. Every educational institution strives to serve the entire spectrum but in emphasis is oriented toward one end or the other. The individual and society are themselves divided about what they expect from schooling. Education of the individual is based on external standards, rigidly determined to produce a properly educated person. On the frontier, curricula founded on classical Greek and Latin led to the study of traditional subjects at many levels. Education of the individual also had an internalized purpose, with standards springing from the child or student, differing from one to another, in an open curriculum of wide choice.

The social purpose of education may be similarly divided between the intention to keep things as they are, a static vision, and the intention to change the social forms in a continuing, dynamic way. As society in the West became complicated, the change was mirrored in the educational system — both public and private — from elementary grades to the university.

Before the coming of formal education, frontier people, like rural people everywhere, relied on churches, intensive reading of the Bible, and above all, folk traditions growing out of extended family relationships to teach the young what they needed to know. As the nineteenth century progressed, the family remained an important source of education, though to a lessening degree. It gave the farm boy training in how to be a farmer and the farm girl a confirmation of her role in the kitchen. The apprentice system, though nearly extinct, might be seen as an extension of the family. The master was obliged to act as surrogate father to the apprentice in moral supervision as well as in vocational instruction. In the face of a multiplicity of denominations and faiths, any one church was unlikely to provide widely acceptable schooling. In the West, as everywhere, the family, the master-apprentice system, and the church proved inadequate, and the school picked up the obligations unfulfilled by the other institutions.

Thus grew support for public schools. The principle behind seventeenth-century laws in Massachusetts calling for every community of reasonable size to provide a school at public expense was accepted, except in the South, where there was a notable lack of concern. But questions of finance and control remained unsettled. The states might have shouldered the burdens of public education. In the Land Ordinance of 1785, they had received a boost in the provision that section 16 of every township would provide funds for education. In practice, however, the monetary results were mixed. A few states such as Michigan used their reserves well, though the schools were not fully free, but such states as Ohio and Indiana sold these lands too soon and too cheaply and found that resource rapidly dissipated. States could tax directly for education, but there was universal reluc-

Sod schoolhouse, Oklahoma Territory, c. 1895.

tance to do so. Efforts at state support usually met with the same lack of success that greeted John Swett, the most notable early state superintendent of schools in California, who energetically proclaimed that "the wealth of the state must educate the children of the state."

Though they remained unwilling to tax, states were creating bureaucracies to control education. Horace Mann had led in the founding of a school system in Massachusetts in 1837. Western states, drafting new constitutions, followed Mann's lead. In Michigan in 1837 and in California in 1850 school systems were born with the state itself. These bureaucracies, run by professional educators, worked to standardize and professionalize pedagogy, textbooks, curricula, teacher training, and certification. But because the states refused to tax, making it necessary for schools, if they were to be free, to be financed by districts, fundamental control remained at the local level.

Western communities faced high initial costs. Building a schoolhouse in a small struggling village could be a heavy expense to the few individuals involved, especially since after the 1860s new homesteads were exempt from taxation. Residents in the little hamlet of Galesville, Wisconsin, were shocked to learn in the 1870s that their first schoolhouse would cost $6,400, yet they went ahead with construction.[10] Galesville's county supported education at about the level of much older but comparatively rural communities in Vermont.

If education is "an instrument of deliberate social purposes," as Bernard Bailyn has said, what were the purposes driving the local boards of citizens who controlled the schools?[11] Primary elements in the old social-economic-religious order were slipping away and needed to be retained. The school was responsible for keeping the child loyal to the nation, aware of his moral responsibilities, and assured of his place in the economy. Jacksonian Democrats had injected into American thought the hope that the common school would become the instrument of equality, that it would stamp out elitism and destroy the marbled foundations of privilege. But education faced new conditions in the West. There were new challenges on the frontier — often as specific and practical as building from materials at hand, adapting windmills for pumping water from great depths, writing laws for the cattlemen holding immense acreage. Members of the local school board, men grappling with these immediate problems, could reason that they knew best what services to offer, what ideas to inculcate.

For such a social purpose, the one-room schoolhouse hardly seemed effective. The barren rooms usually seated children on rough boards, with a teacher's desk in front and an inefficient wood-burning stove near the center. A pail, a broom, and a tin cup likely took the place of educational equipment such as maps and blackboards. "Not one line of grace, not one touch of color relieved the room's bare walls or softened its harsh windows," wrote Hamlin Garland of his school.[12]

Intellect and formal education were not the prime qualifications for the teacher. Even if he were so qualified, he soon learned that a firm hand was more important. The young teacher in Edward Eggleston's *Hoosier Schoolmaster*, having reviewed his classical knowledge in fear of the interview for the job, was in the end asked only, "Can you take it?" A trustee explained why the teacher's position was open: "The boys driv' off the last two and licked the one afore them like blazes."[13] Frequent turnover appeared in practically all the records. The usual teacher's disposition was stern. One teacher combined his own personal escape, getting drunk every Saturday night, with a routine whipping of the whole class on Monday morning. Excessive, yes, but not an inappropriate act to flow from the Calvinist ethic. Whipping was widespread; in one code, for example, whispering brought two stripes or lashes. Students' ears were pulled until they were swollen. There were also myriads of variations on the dunce cap and ridicule as punishment. Sometimes a child had to wear leather spectacles with small peepholes, making him turn his whole head to

"One-Room School" by W. L. Taylor, 1900.

look to the side and thus becoming a laughing stock.[14] Lucy Huntington in Wisconsin remembered her frontier school as "a place to drive out all the poetry and the spirit of the mind."[15]

Although the physical setting, the schoolroom itself, was poor, certain tools like the McGuffey Readers proved extraordinarily effective. Between 1836 and 1920, one hundred twenty-two million copies were sold, with uncounted users per copy. The books were divided into six grades and selections were progressively difficult. The Reader became for the schools what the Bible was for the individual — a vast, unifying depository of stories, legends, poetry, drama, and history. The advanced Readers had portions of Shakespeare and long passages from Longfellow; Rip Van Winkle was there, and Little Nell, and the barefoot boy with cheek of tan. Hamlin Garland, reminiscing about his frontier school, remembered how with McGuffey "I forgot my squat little body and my mop of hair and became imaginatively a page in the train of Ivanhoe, or a bowman in the army of Richard the

"Snap the Whip" by Winslow Homer (1836-1910).

Lion Heart battling the Saracen in the Holy Land."[16] Twentieth-century conservatives have idolized McGuffey Readers, finding their decline somehow related to a decline in American morals. In the 1920s Henry Ford subsidized a new printing, hoping for reinstatement of the book in schools.

Ford's action was revealing, for the McGuffey Readers taught what the nineteenth-century business community wanted. Richard Mosier has titled his book on the Readers *The Making of the American Mind.* Diligence and honesty, hard work and religious devotion, such qualities were extolled and urged upon the individual. The Readers also illuminated important social goals, implying that a ruling and leisure class were prerequisites for the development of art and culture, and the most obvious purveyors of cultural authority were those whose hard work in business had carried them to the top. In their opinion, undisciplined democracy was a fearsome force, especially with universal suffrage in the air, for in that democracy might be found both Hugh Idle, the laggard who had ended in poverty, and Timothy Toil, who had worked hard and earned the social and political authority now due him. Envy of the rich was vain and mean; poverty was the result of laziness, not the fault of any economic or social system. The established institutions provided ample ways to better the lot of anyone committed to the sanctity of private property, willing to work hard, and possessing an uncomplaining disposition.

The West did not figure heavily into the history McGuffey extolled. Only a few western figures such as Daniel Boone appear in the Readers. The West as a theme in American experience actually did not enter any elementary textbooks until after Frederick Jackson Turner set forth his thesis in the 1890s.[17] Far from being actors in what would later become the great national epic, rough frontier libertarians were more likely to be seen as threats to the established order, destructive of the fundamental respect for private property, supposedly anchored by education.

COLLEGES

The religious denominational college was as much a part of the Anglo-American westward movement as was the covered wagon. Donald G. Tewksbury has written that the American college is a truly indigenous frontier institution, the agent of a rapid cultural and religious advance. No other nation has ever founded so many small colleges in such a short span of time.[18]

One hundred eighty-two colleges founded in America before the Civil War survived into the twentieth century. Of these, the Presbyterians were involved in the founding of forty-nine, and thus Princeton, the chief Presbyterian center, was the true "mother of colleges." The Methodists inaugurated thirty-four; the Baptists, twenty-five; and the Congregationalists, twenty-one. The Catholics came next with fourteen, most of which were in urban centers. New frontier denominations responded to the same urge to educate. The Disciples of Christ, followers of Alexander Campbell, had established colleges in Kentucky, western Virginia, Ohio, and Illinois by 1850.[19]

In general, the religious colleges followed traditional curricula and forms of achievement, heavily infused with the classics. Rigid requirements in philosophy, Greek, and Latin rested on the assumption that knowledge and mental agility were transferable from one subject to another and that the sharpening of young minds on Cicero and Augustine would produce strong citizens and good businessmen even on the frontier. These colleges assumed that American society was good, that it needed little change, that it was endangered only by foreign, misguided ideologies, and that the curriculum would protect against such ideas.

Near the junction of the Missouri and Mississippi rivers in Illinois, the elms and ivy of Shurtleff College were not unlike those of hundreds of other small denominational colleges in the West. The name

Shurtleff College, Illinois.

came, typically, from an eastern donor who had given $10,000 toward his own memorial. The founder was a far more interesting Baptist circuit rider, John Mason Peck. Peck has been called the Reinhold Niebuhr of his day because his social vision ranged so broadly. He was indeed a man of the world, loving the outdoors and a pillow of saddlebags. In western society, however, he sensed trouble. The rowdies he saw around him in St. Louis suggested dangerous "rampant egalitarian impulses" in the West. Morality and community harmony could be preserved only when teachers and ministers were well trained and institutions created. Peck was a democrat; he believed all men should be schooled, to control their leveling tendencies. Westerners needed to be shaped, productively channeled, made happy in their work, and dedicated to the church and state of which they were a part. "The mind must be trained," Peck wrote, "to the habits of thinking; to logical reasoning, to readiness of speech; to systematical arrangement of gospel truth, and to a practical application of Christian duties."[20]

In the 1820s, Peck opened a seminary, which was renamed Shurtleff College in 1835. He wrote in his memoirs that the influence of the rowdies was vastly reduced, and the beauty of orderly traditions had taken their place. Like many denominational colleges, Shurtleff sought state aid, but unlike others, did not receive it, largely because Peck's own Baptist Church was split over questions of training ministers. Yet Shurtleff stood its ground, facing west across the great spinal river, a bastion against the dangers of an anarchic society.

A more direct answer to western problems was the rise of the state university — expansive, practical, contemptuous of the East, burdened with a multitide of ambiguous goals, yet with a fixed social purpose. Higher education was to rely little on European models. Crèvecoeur's new American found his college, and it lay, as might be expected, in the West. Frederick Rudolph concludes that the flowering of the state university was a consequence of the westward movement, and from its beginning in the Midwest it was consistently designed to cope with frontier conditions.[21]

Before the Civil War, state support of higher education was often directed to what would later be termed private institutions. Both the University of Ohio (1802) and Miami University of Ohio (1809) were created by the state and received state funds, but the state was not able to control them directly, and Presbyterians in these particular cases moved into the vacuum. The Dartmouth College case in 1818 established a pattern in which the state had no direct voice in policy, even while providing funds; control rested with independent boards of trustees. State schools before the Civil War could be directed by the group that dominated their boards. In spite of the ambiguity, twenty-seven institutions received state support before 1860.[22] The passage of the Morrill Act in 1862 drew a much clearer line between state and private colleges.

Justin Smith Morrill, senator from Vermont, had for years been drafting bills seeking a better use for the public lands — namely for higher education. The Morrill Act gave to each state for each member it had in Congress thirty thousand acres, the returns from which were to be used to support colleges that would offer training in agriculture and mechanical arts. These land-grant colleges were to teach, as a dean of the University of Missouri later said, "the science of higher production."[23]

Opposition to the land-grant colleges came from most private schools, which sensed correctly that some of their support was threatened. The Morrill Act opened a period in which states withdrew funds from the most clearly sectarian institutions, found new ways to support and control existing schools such as Michigan and Ohio, and created new state colleges. Eventually there would be sixty-nine state universities. The small, private college took refuge in its appeal as a training ground for individualists, to be sharpened in battle with

Michigan State faculty, 1890-91.

Cicero and Virgil. Support increasingly came from the new business elite — self-made men who cherished the dream of nurturing more of their own competitive kind and who feared the rise of socialism. Their social purpose was very different from that on which the state universities were embarked.

For the state institutions — Kansas founded in 1865, Illinois in 1867, California in 1868, Nebraska in 1869 — the watchword was utility. Classical studies were neglected, though not ignored. "The tendency of the land-grant institutions," writes Rudolph, "was to enthrone the practical and to ignore the traditional." The effect of the impetus for mechanical arts was to thrust science and engineering to the fore. Applied science achieved a position it had never known before at the college level. "All true education," said the University of Michigan's president in the 1850s, "is practical."[24]

Agriculture, however, did not fare so well, at least in the beginning. Boys who came to college from the farms tended to be anxious to get off the land and into the city; those who remained at home were not at all impressed by the "fancy farmer" turned out by the new courses. Thus enrollments in agricultural courses were small, and

*Joseph Le Conte (1823–1901) lecturing at the
University of California, Berkeley.*

agricultural admissions standards were drastically lowered. The Hatch
Act of 1887 changed the situation by providing federal funds for
scientific agricultural studies and by adding agricultural extension
services so that results in hard practical terms could be transmitted
directly to the farmers. Thus in the 1890s the study of agriculture
dramatically expanded and took its place among the practical contributions of the land-grant colleges.

The state universities vitally affected the lower schools, for the
universities increasingly dictated how they wanted their entering students prepared. In the East private academies continued to train
students for the private colleges, but in the West there were too few
academies and the public schools fell heir to the job. One result was
the supremacy of the public high school in the West. The university
indicated the courses it would accept for admission, and the high
school fell into line and offered them. Western universities accepted
more subjects for admission than did eastern universities. By 1900,
when similar movements were belatedly afoot in the East, California

recognized thirty preparatory areas, while Yale, relatively liberal in this respect, accepted only thirteen.

Inasmuch as it was building anew, western education faced little friction from existing institutions. Thus it responded more readily to forces promoting science, technology, and utility. In the same vein, it is sometimes assumed that the West provided an innovative impetus for the education of women on an equal basis with men. It was felt that equality of the sexes was a natural outgrowth of women's increasingly vital contributions to the work of the farm. The admission of women to Oberlin College was "the first authentic instance of women being able to obtain a college education equivalent to that of a man."[25] Founded in Ohio in 1833, Oberlin had been associated with much of the ferment of its time. Rebelling students from nearby Lane Seminary had moved to Oberlin as part of their protest against slavery. Oberlin admitted black students early and offered a pioneer curriculum in manual arts. In 1837 it enrolled four women, and four years later three of them were granted bachelor's degrees. Oberlin continued to offer a "ladies course," typical of programs in many schools — housekeeping, needlework, the appropriate aspects of gardening and textiles — but the four women studied history and philosophy along with the men. Antioch College, also in Ohio, under the presidency of Horace Mann admitted women on an equal basis in 1852, the year of its founding. Nevertheless, before the Civil War the vast majority of women in college were enrolled in "ladies courses," and no more than half a dozen institutions offered them an education equal to that provided for men.

The state university in the West, that bulwark of utility, provided women with their greatest avenue toward equal education. The University of Minnesota admitted women when it opened in 1851, as did Iowa in 1855 and Kansas in 1865. By 1870, eight state universities were admitting women — the three that had begun coeducationally, plus Wisconsin, Indiana, Missouri, Michigan, and California. Generally, women were subject to special regulations. At Missouri a guard was required to escort them to class. Among the eight no more than two hundred women attended, at a time when three thousand women were enrolled in all courses at the secondary level.[26] Still, a beginning had been made.

Some of the reasons for admitting women were purely practical. President James Fairchild of Oberlin College believed that the presence of women would have a beneficial effect on the men — the transformation of rowdies into gentlemen. The Civil War and the immediate postwar period caused a drop in enrollments, and administrators hoped that women might take up the slack. More influential was the coeducational makeup of the public school system. If college preparatory high schools were coeducational, it was a gross inconsistency to block women from continuing their education. At the same time an enormous demand rose for female teachers in the elementary schools. By the 1830s, women were supplanting the Hoosier schoolmasters, both in one-room schoolhouses and in larger graded schools. By 1870 two out of three teachers in the United States were women. They were found better at the job and, more important to business-minded school boards, were willing to work for less money than men were. If women were to train the citizens of the future, even while only men could vote, how could they do so without an equal chance at education?

The West wanted and needed to be enmeshed with the nation, and the educational system was geared to that social purpose. The McGuffey Readers may have opened broad European literary vistas to Hamlin Garland, but no one could deny that their dominant concern was with American patriotism. By the 1880s, states such as Wisconsin demanded that all instruction be in English, an antidote to nonnationalist sentiments. The denominational college might be thought broader in its classical curriculum, but most American denominations had grown more proud of their American connections than of their European roots. In any case, soon dominating the educational scene, state universities leaned heavily toward nationalism. They were born creatures of the federal government; federal funds continued to support many of their programs, such as agriculture, and the government, through the Reserve Officers Training Corps, used them as recruiting grounds for its armed services.

The most intense nationalism is rooted in deep local attachment; thus even the regional qualities of the state universities may have strengthened nationalism. The Midwest as a region grew to be almost synonymous with its Big Ten. For generations, much more than football provided the feeling that the Mississippi valley was producing the sturdiest, most independent, most typical American. Some of the greatest western regional writers were associated with state universities — Frank Norris and Jack London at California, Willa Cather at Nebraska, and John Muir at Wisconsin. It is hardly coincidence that Frederick Jackson Turner, the West's greatest interpreter, emerged from the University of Wisconsin.

Yet for all its achievements, western education can hardly be viewed as a bearer of intellectualism and culture. Long after the frontier period was over, practicality and utility were more often the dominant notes than were scholarship, intellect, and creativity. Richard Hofstadter, discussing anti-intellectualism in America, found that what most nineteenth-century Americans considered important about an artist was his successful career upward, not his art. To most people widespread artistic activity signaled a nation's decline into effeteness — witness Italy during the Renaissance.[27] Certainly the schools of the West taught that strength and practicality, rather than scholarship and the arts, were the foundation of the nation's power. Piety, hard work, honesty, and diligence were all held in higher respect than intellect, and state universities did not encourage intellectualism for its own sake. The social purpose of education in the West was to bring the region into line with overall patterns of national development, cementing a rough egalitarian population with the traditions of the nation. Indeed, the university often was considered a bulwark against "foreign" ideologies. The president of the University of North Dakota put it squarely: "We must educate our young men of today so that they will not become the mad socialists of tomorrow."[28]

The schools and colleges continued to preach self-reliance and the prudential virtues so important to the Calvinist ethic and the business community. Practical concerns freed the curriculum from its rigid attachment to classical tradition, but curricula nevertheless remained strict enough to repel such creative spirits as John Muir, Jack London, and Frank Norris, none of whom submitted themselves to university requirements for long. Only with later progressive educational movements would the schools try to start from a different point in their process of socialization, leading ultimately to concern with individual differences and internal direction of students in a dynamic, rapidly changing social order. This transformation would come later and would be the product of an intellectual, urban climate, not the outgrowth of rural minds preoccupied with an active frontier.

14

The Search for Community

In Sinclair Lewis's *Main Street*, when Carol Kennicott first walks into Gopher Prairie, Minnesota, the houses of the whole town huddle before her, scarcely more impressive than a hazel thicket: "There was no dignity in it, nor any hope of greatness. . . . It was a frontier camp. It was not a place to live in, not possibly, not conceivably." The people were as "drab as their houses, as flat as their fields." Feeling its plainness and flimsiness, she walks through the town, from one end to the other; the tour takes thirty-six minutes.[1] A different kind of woman, Zona Gale, looked back on a similar town, Portage, Wisconsin, with quiet affection. Her main street was called Daphne, and it held memories of tulip beds and twilight bonfires, with people concerned enough to help one another through illness and hard times. Zona Gale would say that people like Carol Kennicott sought the front door of life — a brass and polished knocker and a fan-vaulted window — and that the small town was like a back door, or perhaps a side door, to existence.[2] The two views may be reconciled if we think of the small town in three ways — as a search for community in a scattered, fractured population; as the perpetuation of a religious pattern while uniformity of belief rapidly deteriorated; and as a fervent localism struggling against strong national tides.

The small town was closely related to the frontier and was not a later, separate development. According to Lewis Atherton, the small town was "spawned by an agricultural frontier"; he claimed that the history of the northern plains is largely "this history of its towns."[3]

Richard C. Wade considers the towns a spearhead of expansion, a holding action for the farmers and settlers to come. He sees in frontier society both a rural and an urban force, each supporting and servicing the other. Both elements were essential in transforming "the gloomy wilderness into a richly diversified region."[4] In any case, the small town was a focal point in the Western story, a community growing out of scattered social fragments.

Wichita, Kansas, exemplified the varied economic strands that could be pulled together in the founding of a town. At the confluence of the two main branches of the Arkansas River, it had once been a campsite for Indians and traders. The Osages, however, were relieved of their land in that region between 1864 and 1869. Settlers meanwhile had moved in, already claiming preemption rights. Speculators accompanied them, first in the corporate guise of the Wichita Town and Land Company, set up in 1868. At one time two rival promoters claimed separate plots of land, vying for merchants and buyers to form the true nucleus of the community. Potential investors were impressed with the location athwart the Chisholm Trail, and they dreamed of all the cattlemen who would need supplies and refreshment on the dreary drive to Abilene. Boosters bet too on the coming of the railroad, and when the Santa Fe tracks were laid into Wichita in 1872, the town's boom began. Through the railroad, wider markets opened for the farmers thereabouts. Deflated by the depression that followed 1873, the town nevertheless grew because of the influx of poor farmers seeking jobs. The population, which in 1869 had numbered no more than three hundred, rose by 1875 to the respectable size of twenty-five hundred, and before the town celebrated its centennial, it would increase to a quarter of a million.

There was a basic sameness to Gopher Prairie, Portage, Peoria, and Wichita. "Main Street," as Sinclair Lewis said, "is the culmination of Main Street everywhere." The identical block pattern, ignoring the terrain, was borrowed from Philadelphia because it was regular and sensible. Everywhere were the same false fronts for dry-goods store and post office, saloon and livery stable, church and schoolhouse. From the Mississippi to the Pacific, the towns were like little corn-hills — some tall, some short, some with more ears and kernels than others, but from a distance indistinguishable.

The sameness was the product of common drives to escape isolation and to avoid anarchy. The need for community bred commonality. The schoolhouse was built at public expense, and it served a variety of public ends. It was easily converted into a party room for dances, which a small town loved. It was a rostrum for traveling lyceum speakers and for community debates. It could be used for lodge

Saturday morning in a midwestern town, 1874.

meetings, if the Masons had not yet built their own hall or if the saloon was not yet available.

The community was cemented by festivals, intensely local yet everywhere the same — Christmas and the 4th of July, the coming of the circus, and a harvest celebration, perhaps the most sentimental of all. The harvest reminded men that their town was still close to the farm, recalled its emergence from the raw land, when "for the first time in all the brooding ages the prairie landscape stretched field after field, bearing this crown of ordered beauty."[5] That the country and field bordered so closely was clear to William Allen White, a representative product of the midwestern town. Reminiscing about Eldorado and Emporia, the Kansas towns in which he was raised, he recalled the prime influences on his youth, the true centers of his learning — the house where he learned to read and absorbed the attitudes of his parents; the barn, full of life and activity; and, above all, the river and the woods, rich in nature lore, educating him in "wisdom, the rules of life, and the skills which had survival value in the world of

The main street of a boom town: Chestnut St., Leadville, 1881.

boyhood." Alongside these, what the school taught seemed super-ficial.[6]

A prime element of community was the newspaper, subscribed to by practically everybody and probably read more avidly, if not more frequently, than the Bible. Alexis de Tocquieville had recognized in the 1830s that Americans were addicted to newspapers. By late in the century, White claimed, the daily or weekly journal had become a major industry in every town.[7] It related gossip, the arrivals of visitors, plans for the harvest celebration, and generally created an illusion of a homogeneous society leisurely pursuing progress along a serene and confident path.

Personal accounts of small-town life in the West are often filled with a sense of determined aspiration, of history in the making, of participation in an enterprise with a rich future built upon self-confident expectations. Angie Debo puts words into the mouths of the early settlers of Prairie City, sternly and unquestionably prophesy-ing the time when "there will be such a big star on the American flag it will splash the blue off to the bounds of infinite space."[8] When Lord Bryce, the British professor and diplomat, visited Bismarck, North Dakota, in the 1880s, he was struck by the way men saw their community, not as it was in the present but as it would be ten, twenty, fifty, even a hundred years in the future. With an air of ceaseless haste and a "fire in their heart," time was too short and present achievement too little.[9] But Bryce, stressing the feeling for the future, overlooked the strong sense of the past that helped build an overwhelming inwardness and confidence. William Allen White, only slightly later than Bryce, invoked the spirit of the past as he looked forward:

> This town is the fruit of great aspiration. And we who live here now have a debt to posterity which we can pay only by still achieving, still pursuing; we must learn to labor and wait, even as they learned it who built here on this townsite when it was raw upland prairie. It is well to think on these things.[10]

This was an editorial, not a sermon, and White reflected the entrepreneurial sensitivity that saw its own advantage in every step of what was lovingly called progress.

This booster fetish for the future at times revolved around the designation of county seat. In Kansas there was once an actual battle with guns for possession of the county records. Free buildings were often used as bait. Mud slinging occurred frequently, with local editors calling rival towns "bug infestations" and "manure piles." Eminence, Kansas, even hired Bat Masterson to protect its interests in an election, but the town lost to Ravanna which boomed for a short time, then fell into ruins when the county moved its center elsewhere.

On the New England frontier when a community was born the foundation lay in a covenant as old as Abraham, in which God agreed to be with and protect his people while they in turn cooperated to bring his kingdom to earth. The community was a sacred enterprise, reaching down to the smallest detail of helping one's neighbor when in trouble or gone astray. This spirit, when infused with charity and faith, may be the highest social motive known to man. The ideal of the small, close-knit community was carried deep in the minds of most frontiersmen, especially those from New England and the Old Northwest. Certainly it was clear in the thoughts of Zona Gale as she described Friendship Village, where no one became sick or distressed without immediately receiving community assistance. The covenant signed by every member of the Buck Run Church in Kentucky spoke loudly and clearly: the congregation solemnly agreed to "watch over each other in brotherly tenderness," to edify one another, to succor the weak, to bear each other's burdens, and to hold in common all "hands and hearts."[11] When the congregation was effectively synonymous with the community, as in the innumerable Mormon towns throughout the Great Basin, the covenant was indeed a powerful social instrument.

Other types of community, however, had always existed. Without a covenant, for example, the cumulative community simply grew, unplanned. A trade route, a crossroads, some natural advantage — any of these circumstances might start the process, stimulate services and economic relationships, and thereafter expand. St. Louis grew from a trading post, Denver from a mining camp, Wichita from a cattle trail. This pattern was by far the most prevalent.

Even the covenanted community in the West seldom worked in its ideal form. Charity often ceased to be founded on common religious assumptions. Frederick Russell Burnham, who lived in a Midwest small town in the 1870s, thought most people spent half of their time trying to reform someone else in a quiet fervor of "intolerant religiosity."[12] This oppressive, narrow morality — peeping through keyholes — was the cause of Carol Kennicott's rebellion. It was what Caroline Kirkland referred to when she wrote that anyone who wanted privacy in her small town was labeled proud or something worse: "Of all places in the world in which to live on the shady side of public opinion an American backwoods settlement is the worst."[13] It was the community without the deep spirit of the covenant and Puritanism without religion. What had once been action infused with community responsibility under a God of judgment became the exaggerated individualism of self-appointed moralists.

One of the persistent myths of small-town life pictured a homogeneous, classless society in which anyone with ambition, thrift, and diligence could easily move upward. In reality, society was highly stratified. Clearly identifiable was an upper class of businessmen and local officials, who were almost always the chief property owners. In western cattle towns, for example, no more than 20 percent of the population — entrepreneurs, managers, and officials — owned from 75 to 80 percent of the property.[14] The group was composed of large landholders and highly successful businessmen on the one hand and small shopkeepers and professional people on the other. Even in these developing societies, family background was important in the top social echelons. The lower classes were divided between workingmen, transients, and drifters, and indigenous ethnic groups such as Indians, blacks, and Mexicans, who generally stood isolated at the bottom. A typical midwesterner who claimed that no class lines existed in his town later admitted he could easily place every person in a category such as upper crust, better sort of worker, or people who lived like animals. A class system obviously existed in his mind, though he was reluctant to confess it.[15]

If the myth of classlessness had any factual basis, it would be in the existence of vertical mobility, allowing a flow from low to upper status. Very early in frontier communities, class lines were vague, occupational openings were everywhere apparent, and social mobility must have been noticeable. But after the early years, though the myth of classslessness persisted, reality changed. Distinctions hardened and the chance of movement between classes diminished. Carl Bridenbaugh described a similar pattern in the growth of towns in colonial America, many of which were frontier towns. After a short period of fluidity, "class lines tightened and society crystallized into easily recognizable categories of better, middling, and poorer sorts."[16]

Facts on the subject are difficult to find, but in Trempealeau County, Wisconsin, such a conclusion was confirmed by Merle Curti in *Making of an American Community*. In the initial period, between 1850 and 1860, the surge of economic expansion opened opportunities on every side; in the next decade the doors began to close. In a sampling of 126 townspeople from 1870 to 1880, of those who did not retire and were classifiable only thirteen rose and seven fell.[17] Evidently, by 1880 Trempealeau citizens were no longer significantly mobile. Richard Wade found the same pattern — a short period of egalitarianism followed by a rapid closing of the class doors — in all the frontier towns before 1830 stretching along the Ohio valley from Pittsburgh to St. Louis. Even in the supposedly wide-open brawling cattle towns of the plains — among them Wichita, Dodge City, and Ellsworth — a careful scrutiny by Robert Dykstra has uncovered the same relatively early growth of class rigidity. The cattle towns harbored an unusual number of teenagers elbowing their way into the labor force, but after the first few years their strength and vitality were seldom sufficient to break the barriers into the entrepreneurial levels.

These examples imply for the West what Stephen Thernstrom concludes for the nation: the man who rose from rags to riches was exceptional. A Harvard background or its equivalent mattered; the frontier opened no appreciable number of positions at the top. At the lower ranges Thernstrom found a different picture. More upward mobility was observed at these levels, especially if the acquisition of property is considered a sign of it. Men did earn sufficient money to save and buy, creating an illusion of improving status, though the actual effect of such acquisition on occupation and class standing might be minimal.[18]

Don Doyle in a detailed study of Jacksonville, Illinois, found that the fastest growing groups were unskilled (such as domestic servants or railroad workers) and skilled (such as blacksmiths or masons) laborers, not the professionals and businessmen at the top. To move upward most people had to move elsewhere. Among those who remained, social mobility in the town's early decades was as high as 30 to 50 percent. Jacksonville, however, was unusual in this respect. As the figures indicate, the upward movement was never anything like the waves of opportunity touted by western boosters.

Toward the end of the nineteenth century the atmosphere in small western towns seemed increasingly uneasy. Cohesiveness had degenerated into narrow morality. The industrial promise of linking farm and market had not been fulfilled; the railroads clearly served only eastern capital. Conflicts within the community grew more overt, especially as depressions such as those following 1873 and 1893 exposed the vulnerability of the lower classes, which had been ignored. Newspapers that had concealed trouble in order to create illusions about their communities' strength for investment grudgingly admitted the existence of discord. The hardening of class lines bred dissatisfaction. As Dykstra said of the cattle towns, social conflict was the rule, not the exception.[19] Most intellectuals fled the town and began to describe their former environment as smug, prejudiced, sterile, and joyless, as did Thomas Wolfe in *You Can't Go Home Again*.[20]

Some of these feelings exploded in Populism and Progressivism. But the causes were deeper than politics in any narrow sense. Robert Wiebe has argued that the trouble stemmed from small-town America's resistance to change. Dedicated to prudential virtues and "the good old days," townspeople saw industrial values as corrupting and oppressive and sighed, in the words of Vachel Lindsay, "for the sweet life wrenched and torn by thundering commerce, fierce and bare."[21] True, towns often courted industry in the hope of creating more jobs and revenue in their own precincts. But monopolies beyond their control, large-scale corporations, and intervention by the federal government corroded individualism. Turning inward, they developed an intense localism as a shield against unwelcome change. They lashed out against immigrants as un-American, especially after they realized the frontier was ending and would no longer work its purportedly magic transformation of foreigners into new men. Self-determination for the local community became the watchword of the small town as it faced the end of the frontier.

Not all communities survived such crises of identity and direction. The frontier has always known ghost towns — derelicts of depleted resources, changed trade routes, or warped visions of speculators. Wade tells of hundreds of urban centers that died along the Ohio valley in the frontier period. Even those with such glorious names as Town of America and Rising Sun dwindled into memory. Iowa alone had more than two thousand abandoned towns, villages, hamlets, and country post offices in fewer than one hundred years.[22]

Some towns did grow into cities — St. Louis and St. Paul, Denver and Dubuque, Seattle and San Francisco. Thernstrom has identified 101 communities that grew by 100 percent in the 1880s alone.[23] This growth was fed by investors and speculators, by land booms and busts, by chambers of commerce. The city was a western attraction in its own right, holding out prospects of profit and prosperity in a growing metropolis. More important, urban growth came because of moves from farm to city, especially during periods of agricultural distress. But the attraction never weakened; drab and shabby, city streets to young farm boys were thrillingly hectic and comparatively regal. For every urban worker in the East who moved to the West, at least ten people pulled up their rural roots and settled in a burgeoning city. All kinds of qualifications must be made on a view of the West as a safety valve for the East, but everywhere the city was unquestionably a safety valve for the discontents of the countryside. Once begun, the movement sustained itself; the city was intoxicated with growth, with a belief that greatness was synonymous with size and that quantity was the prime measure of progress.

In the transition from small town to city, however, size was not the only determinant. The impersonal quality of life was a more important hallmark. When the post office required a street name on the envelope and a number on the door, the letter boy no longer needed to know the occupant's name, and with the name went the color of hair and gossip about an evening in a long-gone summer. The shift between town and city could be sensed when citizens turned over responsibility to a bureaucracy. When a volunteer fire department was supplanted by a paid, organized force, the town qualitatively changed. Similar shifts in responsibility affected police protection, supervision of utilities (especially maintenance of streets), zoning for housing, and concern for public health. The new impersonality came to be cherished as insulation against snooping.

In the city, class proportions shifted. Workers became far more numerous and usually ethnic groups expanded. William Allen White remembered when the railroad, representative of all industry, came to his town. But the interesting thing was White's first sight of a black man, or rather a whole crew of them, sweating over the rails, sufficiently unusual to a small-town boy of eight to cause him to imitate blacks at work. Even in the 1830s cities such as Cincinnati were beginning to legislate against their black populations in housing.

New ecological problems arose. Grass and trees disappeared; overarching elms and maples characterized the small town, but hardly the city. Surprisingly early, the waterfronts were ruined and lovely stretches of river turned into eyesores. Into blighted sections moved transient populations, bringing with them Barbary Coasts and red-light districts that caused the small town to turn its back in shame. It had a right to be shocked, for the city was where its sons and daughters were going, especially if they aspired to literature or the arts.

Except for some minor flashes in mining camps, the city brought culture to the West. Nevertheless, the small town, so neglectful of intellectual values, was conscious of its rootlessness and tried to "husband the cultural graces." To imitate the East meant to provide theaters, libraries, lyceums. The small town wanted these things, as it wanted jigsaw scrolls on its verandas. But despite this apparent interest, the arts were distrusted. The small town was not for men who hungered after Bach or thrilled to a sudden change of key in a Mozart sonata. Those men, or their spirits, died like the father in Willa Cather's *My Antonia* with their broken violins beside them. Another of Cather's characters, Henry Merrick, a gentle young man who watched sunsets instead of keeping the cows from the corn, fled to the city to become a sculptor; he was hated by the townspeople because he had spurned their values. If an artist remained in Everyville, he might become a recluse, lost in fantasy, as was Enoch Robinson, the rejected painter in Sherwood Anderson's *Winesburg, Ohio*, who resorted to imagining persons with whom he could talk, only realizing as an old man the intensity of his loneliness.[24]

Generally, painters and musicians exiled from Main Street could find some congenial life, though seldom much, in the city. Mark Twain, child of a small town, had to go to San Francisco to "simper and air his graces" at the opera. As a matter of fact, opera in America grew out of French culture in New Orleans and spread its way upward along the Mississippi through cities like St. Louis long before it settled into urban life in the eastern part of the nation. A good many western cities, however, put on airs by calling their local theater an opera house when in reality the show was no more than vaudeville.[25]

The western theater was more entertainment than culture. It sprang up among bored miners. Edwin Booth and Lotta Crabtree acted in tent theaters before wildly enthusiastic and even discriminating crowds years before they achieved fame elsewhere. Along the Mississippi and Ohio rivers, the theater was a waterfront institution, smacking of all the wickedness it had known in Restoration England. Yet even the Mormons of Salt Lake had a thriving theater by 1865. Raucous or dignified, the stage provided a cultural dimension that Gopher Corners had never enjoyed.

The small town produced some literary lights — Hamlin Garland, Mark Twain, Edgar Lee Masters — but the city gave them publishers and a forum. And the city itself added a host of writers — Frank

Theater in Cheyenne, 1877.

Norris, Jack London, Bret Harte, Henry George. Much of the West's awareness of itself as a region, its self-conscious bluster and its dogged defiance, comes from urban literary figures.

Cities thrived and culture emerged partly because the West was a mecca for tourists. Travelers came by the thousands, most of them rich. Europeans were particularly attracted, fascinated by an increasingly romanticized vision of rugged wilderness. Prince Maximilian of Wied, who hunted in the Rocky Mountains as early as the 1830s, ushered in a long line of German travelers. English and Scottish visitors were so plentiful that they became stereotypes. Their compatriots' large investments in cattle and mining were not unrelated to these travels. Wealthy easterners came for reasons of health: Francis Parkman on the Oregon Trail and Richard Henry Dana sailing to California were forerunners of that strain. They enjoyed themselves and wrote books about their experiences, thus publicizing the region.

The railroads had been ridiculed for building from nowhere to nowhere. After the first lines were created, they began to generate traffic through pamphlets, posters, agents, and handbills — an early example of advertising creating demand. An important step in the

Dining car on the Union Pacific, 1870.

late 1860s was the advent of the Pullman sleeper car, the luxurious palace on wheels so appealing to the wealthy. These rolling hotels, paneled in mahogany, their lights shaded with Tiffany glass, brought travelers comfortably to the great western tourist resorts. The first of these was the Hotel del Monte, built by a subsidiary of the Southern Pacific Railroad amid the cypress of the Monterey peninsula. In the 1880s hotels sprouted all over the West — the Antlers in Colorado Springs, the Del Coronado on the San Diego Bay, the Banff in the Canadian Rockies, El Tovar on the rim of the Grand Canyon. One visitor pointed out that whereas European hotels were a means to an end, in the American West hotels were an end in themselves. Guests spent days playing polo, riding to the hounds, lolling in warm baths, driving in lovely carriages through scenic grounds. At dinner people dressed as if they were going to the opera in London.

Tourism in the late nineteenth century was a means of bringing the wealthy West. The less affluent travelers came in their wake, generally waiting for the automobile. Still, tourism affected all classes, for the workers of nearby cities supplied the goods and services. The traveler made a difference in western history, just as other transients

Olympian Hotel, Tacoma, Washington, c. 1891.

had influenced it — restless miners, land-grubbing speculators, and riverfront drifters.

Tourists were also potential investors, precipitating at least two great land booms in western metropolitan areas. In the 1880s, the completion of competing transcontinental railroad lines such as the Santa Fe dramatically reduced passenger rates, and hordes of people were channeled into such urban centers as San Francisco and Los Angeles. In southern California, suburbs and land subdivisions mushroomed. Grandiose tourist attractions such as the entire city of Venice, replete with canals, gondolas, Italian-costumed orchestras playing airs from *La Traviata* on the beach, and a simulated St. Mark's Square with a doge's palace, made it possible to combine in one place tourism, health-treatment, and land speculation. English tourists, erstwhile country squires, became ranchers not only of cattle but of walnuts and oranges. The land boom and tourist pattern was repeated in the 1920s.

The impersonality of the city, the transient nature of tourism, and the speculative quality of land booms did not contribute to the quest

for community. The construction of model utopian societies, however, was a counterthrust relatively minor in its effects, yet illuminat-
ing by contrast. At least two hundred communitarian experiments
were started in America in the nineteenth century, and at least 75
percent of them were on the frontier of their day. Utopian ideas and
residents of the communities came from Europe and the East but
were related to the frontier because open land challenged men to
experiment. Inasmuch as men went west to start over, plan a new
life with greener futures, so these groups dreamed of ways for human
beings to live harmoniously.

In a short period of six weeks, beginning in May 1825, eight hundred people descended on a little Indiana frontier village. They were
disciples of Robert Owen, but in their heads swarmed ideas that had
been supported by Jacobin and Pietist alike — nothing less than
equality and fraternity and brotherhood — to be spread from New
Harmony, Indiana, around the world. Though Owen's dreams had
begun in a Scottish factory town, on the American frontier they
could grow without having to push through the detritus of custom.
The communards held most goods in common, and the profits of
their industry were reaped by the community. But Owen called for
much more. On July 4, 1826, his version of the Declaration of Independence drummed from society three evils — private property,
religion, and marriage. It would indeed be a new world. Two thousand people finally came to New Harmony. They were intelligent,
farsighted, well-intentioned men and women — educational reformers
such as William Maclure, women of strength and vision such as
Frances Wright, and scientists such as Thomas Say. The community
lasted for two years; the dreams never died.

As a congenial environment for experimentation, the West was
used by followers of Charles Fourier, French bachelor-dreamer-
fanatic. According to his preachings, an age of harmony was coming,
and the cooperative community was the harbinger of that future. In
the 1840s and 1850s thirteen Fourierist communities were set up in
Ohio, Indiana, Illinois, Michigan, Wisconsin, and Texas. The most
successful of these, the Wisconsin Phalanx, lasted six years and claimed
a profit of 108 percent on its original investment.

Another group of Frenchmen, steeped in the writings of Henri
de Saint Simon and Etienne Cabet, tried their luck in Texas along the
Red River in 1848. These Icarians, a name they took from Cabet's
novel *Voyage en Icarie*, believed that if men lived communally,
modern industrialism could abolish the evils of inequality. In good
frontier fashion they were victimized by land speculators and so
moved north to Nauvoo, Illinois, with considerably less capital but

*New Harmony, Indiana: site of Owen's experiment five years later,
by Karl Bodmer.*

abundant hope. There they took over the town the Mormons had
vacated three years before. In 1852, they began their migration to
Iowa, where for generations they lived a rewarding communal life,
even spawning a satellite colony in California.

Colorado, following its mining booms, witnessed a rash of reformist settlements that included such causes as the urban poor, women,
diet, and temperance. The latter drive lay behind the Union colony
that established Greeley. Its four hundred abstaining members arrived
on their twelve thousand acres in 1870. They labored on cooperative
irrigation and fencing and formed an orchestra, library, dramatic
society, newspaper, hotel, and singing groups. They claimed not to
drink, smoke, or swear, but within a year cracks appeared after an
outsider erected a saloon. When speculators bought in, deeper divisions grew, and the colony soon reverted to little more than a normal
frontier town.

In the state of Washington between 1895 and 1906 socialist followers of Theodore Hertska established several utopian colonies
under the name Equality. Likewise San Francisco socialists led a
band of communitarians into the Kaweah Cooperative Commonwealth in the foothills of the Sierra Nevada. Between 1885 and 1890

they underwent the transports and tribulations of communal life until the federal government commandeered their land for national forest and national park. In 1914 a brilliant young Los Angeles socialist, Job Harriman, organized a group of men and women discouraged by the quality of life under the competitive strains of capitalism. At Llano del Rio they soon brought pear trees to blossom from Mojave Desert sand, symbolizing what true community could accomplish. Most of these later efforts grew from conditions in western cities — Seattle, San Francisco, and Los Angeles. With the growth of urban and industrial society, the West was breeding the same circumstances against which eastern and European communitarians had earlier sought release.

The religious quest for community was, of course, much older than the need for justice in an industrial society. Indeed, the Puritans claimed that their covenanted community was a most significant social reorganization. Before the American Revolution, before the line was drawn between church and state, communitarianism was almost wholly religious. In the eighteenth century, waves of German Pietists sought communal life in America as part of their understanding of brotherhood. The Shakers came to America at about the time of the Revolution, and their communitarianism was based on mystical revelations that elevated their first prophet, Mother Ann Lee, to the level of a deity. Although the nineteenth century brought secular communitarianism to the fore, it by no means saw the demise of the religious variety. The Hutterian Bruderhof, or Hutterite Brotherhood, was rooted in the sixteenth-century Reformation but migrated to Canada to pursue its quiet devotion to communism. It branched southward across the border into the Dakotas and Iowa in the 1870s and has continued to expand, now numbering well over a hundred communities. In the 1840s a mystical Pietist, William Keil, preached of the need to live simply, close to the land and to God. He founded two communities that eventually garnered hundreds — one in Bethel, Missouri, in 1844; the other in Aurora, Oregon Territory, in 1856.

Religion and ethnic culture often intermingled in the communal life. Swedes, for example, under a Lutheran heretic, Eric Jansen, migrated as a group in 1846 to build sod houses and dugouts at Bishop Hill on the Illinois prairie. Germans, following revelations of Christian Metz and Barbara Heinemann, set up an island of ethnic culture at Amana, Iowa, in 1855. They achieved economic fame with woollen blankets and later added their communal name to refrigerators and freezers. Not until the Great Depression of the 1930s did their communitarianism break down into a joint-stock arrangement. But before that, five generations had found meaning in a community which went beyond anything the western small town could replicate.

The Mormons gave to the frontier some of its warmest examples of the covenanted community, especially under the leadership of a parent organization, the United Order. Orderville in southern Utah became the best known, growing from an initial 150 people to 700 between 1875 and 1880. These communards, considering themselves one large family, ate, worked, played, and worshiped under "the gospel plan," as it was called, in the life-style of the earliest Christian apostles. A "United Order bugler," like the angel Gabriel, joyfully called them to each of the daily rounds. In harsh frontier conditions they achieved virtual self-sufficiency, producing artists and musicians as well as blacksmiths and farmers. Nearby mines ultimately created distractions of wealth too strong for some of the young, and the federal government's prosecutions for polygamy in the 1880s removed their leaders to hiding or jail. Yet at its height, harmony dwelt in Orderville, and almost every reminiscence of the community, according to historian Leonard Arrington, recalled "the closest approximation to a well-ordered, supremely happy Christian life that was possible of achievement in human society."[26]

A new bloom of communal activity began in the late 1960s and was centered in two western regions — New Mexico and northern California to southern Oregon. These modern communes, which continue to use a frontier environment as an alternative, remain commentaries on the faults of prevailing society. Man continues to seek community — a just society based on economic and political equality and characterized by warm human relationships. Communitarians may have understood this goal only too well, but other people — isolated trappers and miners, small-town busybodies, lonely walkers of city streets — also understood it when they found themselves without it. The frontier, in its early exaggerated sense of individualism and in its later headlong rush toward urbanization, may often have been a valley of digression, an unfortunate experience in the search for community.

15

The Western Hero

Half man, half god, "with a piece of sunrise in his pocket," so Constance Rourke saw the western hero.[1] He was a god because he realized impossible goals, a man because he was earthy and close to fundamental American experience; his piece of sunrise was moral righteousness. He was at once regional and universal, violent and gentle, boastful and modest, lawless and honorable, competitive and compassionate, savage and civilized. Like Proteus, he assumed different forms. For James Fenimore Cooper he was Leatherstocking; for Owen Wister, the Virginian; on the movie screen, Gary Cooper or Tom Mix; on television, Wyatt Earp; in the dime novel, Seth Jones or Buffalo Bill; under the circus tent, Wild Bill Hickok; as a social rebel, Jesse James; as a woman, Annie Oakley or Calamity Jane; in oral tradition, Davy Crockett or Mike Fink; in the North, Paul Bunyan; in the Southwest, Pecos Bill; on the Great Plains, Febold Feboldson; for the Indian, Geronimo; for the black, Deadwood Dick; for the Mexican, Joaquin Murieta. As a hero he revealed what a great many people were or wanted to be.

Paul Bunyan looms over the oral tradition of the once heavily timbered Old Northwest. In the tallest of tall tales, his size was prodigious. His ox, Babe, born in the winter of blue snow, drank dry the Mississippi. The top three stories of his hotel were hinged to allow the moon to pass. His dragging pick gouged the Grand Canyon of the Colorado. His sweat on a hot day formed the Great Salt Lake.

Bunyan was only one of a crew of regional whoppers. The Great

Plains cradled Febold Feboldson, an unconquerable Swede who overcame the tribulations of the prairies. He triumphed over razor-sharp blizzards and summer suns so hot they popped the corn still on the cob. One spring, when the fog was so thick it was drinkable and seeds in the earth could not decide whether to grow up or down, Febold cut the fog into great strips and buried them along the roadside, and every spring the ditches are still full of water.

Pecos Bill was a towering counterpart in the Southwest. His rope, which stretched from the Pecos to the Rio Grande, could lasso the lightning. He fenced Arizona as a calf pasture and raised his horse Widow-maker on nitroglycerin and barbed wire. The only time Pecos Bill was thrown was while riding a cyclone.

Sometimes the hero developed from a historic figure, such as Davy Crockett or Mike Fink. Here are some of the basic facts of Crockett's life: he was born in Tennessee; became a local politician; served in the Congress from 1827 to 1831 and again from 1833 to 1835; changed his political allegiance from the Jacksonian Democrats to the Whigs, who made him the object of a publicity campaign intended to win backwoods support. Mike Fink's life can also be traced, though much less completely. He was raised on the Pennsylvania frontier, where he acquired his skill with the rifle. He drifted to the Ohio and down the Mississippi, working as a riverboatman. Later he trapped for the Rocky Mountain Fur Company. Among a collection of scoundrels, Fink might have been the worst, "a lying, sadistic, foul-mouthed braggart, a teacherous and murderous psychopath."[2]

When Crockett and Fink moved into legend, as they did through oral tradition, almanacs, and newspaper fillers, the exaggerated qualities of Bunyan and his friends quickly crept in. Davy Crockett, far from the halls of Congress, fell in love with a country girl but wanted relief from the ridiculous feelings because, like an illness, they constrained his action. He had heard of machines that generated electricity and cured arthritis, and decided to try something similar but more natural and direct. Standing in the clearing of the woods in the midst of a ferocious storm, he opened his mouth to the heavens and dared the lightning to enter his vitals. When a bolt obliged, Davy was somewhat shaken; the lightning coming out the other end took his trousers with it. For several weeks he could eat his food raw, as it was cooked on the way down. But he was cured of love and could go his way in freedom.

In legend, Mike Fink could drink a gallon of whisky with no effects. He fought at the drop of a hat, drubbing those who did not laugh at his jokes and fighting just to keep his joints from getting "marrow dried." He could take the keelboat *Light Foot* through the worst rapids of the Ohio, standing like Hercules at the helm, his steady eye and iron arm steering it away from every rock. In ancient Greece he would have been a Jason. He was a river god, "one of those minor deities whom men create in their own image and magnify to magnify themselves."[3] Mike Fink often entered stories beside Davy Crockett, the two in monumental competition. Each had his own gun. Davy's was his Betsy and Mike's was Bang-all — identifiable, personalized like Arthur's sword Excalibur and Siegfried's Nothung.

The western hero in legend is a man of excess. He is a creature of the tall tale and fits comfortably in that form of humor. He knows no moderation, in gunplay, drinking, or fighting. He is motivated by a competitive spirit that lures him on the violent aggression. He is wasteful of game and natural resources. Restless, impatient, he needs no one around him because he is self-sufficient. He is individualism personified, standing outside of society or demonstrating that society is irrelevant. His strength and power stem from his continuing bout with the forces of nature. Alone against the wilderness, he is supreme.

In formal literature there is no better model of the western hero than Owen Wister's *The Virginian*. Published in 1902, it was the product of Wister's western experiences in the 1880s, and it became one of the most influential and widely read American novels.[4] A socially conscious mother had forced Wister to study music in Europe and at Harvard. In his twenties, his health collapsed, and to recuperate he retreated to a Wyoming cattle ranch in 1885, one of the last great years in the heyday of the open range. The West was a revelation to Wister, the wilderness fresh like Creation: "The ancient earth was indeed my mother and I have found her again after being lost among houses, customs, and restraints."[5] Wister returned east at the end of the summer, but between 1885 and 1900 he made fifteen trips west. He began writing stories and short novels about the cattle country, and the work, along with the spring air of Wyoming, seemed to cleanse his spirit. But his writing was done in the East, and after he published *The Virginian*, he did not return to the plains. When he was invited to visit Wyoming later in his life, he refused, fearing to find social and economic changes that would destroy the ghosts of the past.

The world of those ghosts, the setting of the western story, was filled with innocence, freshness, and beginnings. The initiative, the energy, and the aggressive action were all masculine. Wister called the cattle frontier the great playground of young men. But it was far more than play. It restored health, as it had for Wister himself, and it re-created men as self-reliant individuals. Underscoring self-reliance is the Virginian's namelessness. Beyond the reference to Virginia, his

Christian name is given but once, and we learn precious little of his background. As with all western heroes, the vagueness of his past requires the reader to judge the man solely in the present.

The individualistic hero stood out starkly against the setting. He was at home in a natural backdrop, lost and uncertain before an unnatural one such as a town. Hell's Hinges, the dusty settlement in the 1916 William S. Hart movie of that name, had to be literally and symbolically burned to the ground before the hero and heroine could walk happily together toward the western mountains. Medicine Bow in *The Virginian* was insignificant, isolated, perhaps even temporary, a "wretched husk of squalor." Its buildings stood as weak facades against the strength of the wind. Such towns were "forever the same shapeless pattern, more forlorn they were than stale bones." But above and beyond was the atmosphere of crystal light, serene, pure, "a space across which Noah and Adam might come straight from Genesis."[6]

The setting thus emphasized the natural man as a golden sunset might focus attention to a bird flying across it. The plumage of civilized society is no longer evident. At times the story physically wraps this natural man in nature, as when the Virginian rolls in the dust, insulating himself from the restraint of civilization. At another time the veneer is stripped away by fever. Badly hurt, he is nursed by Molly Wood, his love, in her cabin. In his delirium he raves wildly, all inhibitions gone. In this state he might be expected to curse and to speak basely of sex. But, with his deepest thoughts and instincts exposed, the natural man is found to be pure.

The purity of his intentions toward woman should not conceal the fact that the western hero placed her on a pedestal, distant and untouchable. The westerner does not admit women to his world; that is, he does not allow them to step down from their elevation: "Never speak ill of any man to any woman. Men's quarrels were not for women's ears." In his scheme, good women were to know only a fragment of men's lives.[7] In the story the woman represents the East — culture, schools, and religion, all of which are effete, superficial, and unnatural. The good woman never understands the westerner. She is seldom, if ever, a Scarlett O'Hara or a Becky Sharp — that is, a strong woman who knows far better than men what is really going on and controls events through her own machinations. In the western story the fallen woman, the prostitute, can understand a man, but she does not represent the East. She has forsaken culture, entered the man's world, and so has found her place, like the hero, in the West.

In the man's world of fighting, card games, and business transactions, bystanders and friends must not interfere. Even the law is suspect, and only mediocre people would resort to legal protection when the issue is man to man. Yet even in this lawless, masculine world, a code governs violence. The hero must not shoot a man in the back, and he must not shoot an unarmed man. More important, however, is the reluctance that precedes the hero's resorting to violence. The Virginian, for example, knows that he must someday kill Trampas, the villain in his story, but the gentle side of the hero controls his actions for nearly five years. The reluctance provides time for honorable purposes to be established.

Honor, indeed, is the only justification for violence. Robert Warshow calls the western hero the last gentleman and his story the only literary form in which the concept of personal honor remains strong.[8] Honor triumphs over friendship as the Virginian allows his best friend Steve to die in a just lynching. The hero may not understand his own motives, and certainly he has difficulty verbalizing them, but he nevertheless knows what must be done. His internal gyroscope keeps him on the honorable course without rationalization. Action takes the place of words. The Virginian, for example, has committed himself to his inevitable confrontation with Trampas. He struggles to explain his reasons to Molly but cannot do so to the satisfaction of either of them. "Can't you see how it is about a man?" he finally asks. "It's not for their benefit, friends or enemies, that I have got this thing to do." With these confused words the self-reliant individual with his unexpressed certainty walks to his rendezvous with violence.

The western hero has assumed so many shapes that it would be foolish to think that his essence could be conveyed through one novel. James Fenimore Cooper at the beginning of the nineteenth century created one of the greatest western figures, a frontier trapper and scout who moves from youth to death through a long series of novels and has different names as he goes — Leatherstocking, Deerslayer, Pathfinder, Natty Bumpo, Hawkeye. But Cooper did not call his scout the hero. That title went to the young dashing man who carried off the girl. Henry Nash Smith has pointed out that Cooper, bound by the social and literary conventions of his day, could not allow the scout to be the hero because he was not of genteel birth.[9] Thus Cooper's plots revolve mechanically around young white officers of good birth and pale young ladies who are likely to swoon when the going gets rough.

Twentieth-century readers of *The Last of the Mohicans*, for example, have little interest in Duncan and Alice, technically the heroes. Instead they turn to Cora, the mulatto — strong, resourceful, and attracted to an Indian, "the noble Uncas nobly in love with the

Beadle and Adams dime novel, 1896.

nobly dark Cora."[10] More fascinating is the hunter-scout, whose name in *The Last of the Mohicans* is Hawkeye and to whom we would gladly assign the title of hero. He is brave and honorable, the natural aristocrat. Like the Virginian, in his heart he knows what is right because he lives close to nature. He acts vigorously in the service of a higher purpose. Standing between the Indian and the white man, he represents the best of both. In a later novel, *The Prairie*, he dies seated, facing west in his final lonely confrontation with nature. "I am without kith or kin in the wide world!" he says self-reliantly. "We have never been chiefs; but honest, and useful in our way. I hope it cannot be denied we have always proved ourselves."[11]

Cooper's hunter-scout, only slightly changed, entered the broader realms of American popular culture through the dime novel. Erastus Beadle with his brother Irwin and his partner Robert Adams set out to apply the techniques of mass production to publishing. The house of Beadle and Adams was not the first to offer cheap, paperbound novels, but it did initiate issues in series and in large numbers. In 1860 Beadle printed the beginning of the so-called dime novels,

Malaeska: The Indian Wife of the White Hunter. A few stories later, *Seth Jones or the Captives of the Frontier* proved that the publisher was on a successful course; it may have sold as many as four hundred thousand copies.[12] Novel followed novel in series after series, though each story was complete in itself. In 1865 the normal printing for any one dime novel was about sixty thousand copies. During the first five years alone total sales ran to five million copies. Some authors eventually churned out as many as six hundred novels.

Seth Jones, the first great success, was set in the late eighteenth-century frontier settlements of New York, a locale familiar to readers of Cooper. A white girl had been captured by Mohawk Indians, and the climax of the story was her rescue by the hunter-scout Seth Jones. Seth was a lovable, downeast Yankee type who knew the wilderness, including its native inhabitants, as he knew the back of his hand. Because most dime novelists wrote so fast, they had little time for revision, and they had to know in advance what was acceptable both to the publisher and to the reading public. The stories thus reflected what a good number of authors believed to be the nation's taste. The stories gauged what most people felt was true and important about the West, and, in the words of Henry Nash Smith, the dime novel became "an objectified mass dream."[13] Admittedly there were advertising campaigns. *Seth Jones*, for example, was ballyhooed by thousands of placards bearing only the words "Who is Seth Jones?" But advertising was yet too young to be a substantial molder of opinion.

Although it was not the only setting, the West was by far the most popular. Of the 3,158 dime novels published by Beadle and Adams between 1860 and 1898, two-thirds took place in the trans-Mississippi West.[14] The trapper or hunter-scout, the lineal descendant of Cooper's Leatherstocking, was at first the favorite character. The outlaw and the soldier eventually joined the roster, but after the 1880s the cowboy overshadowed them all. Thus Seth Jones and his counterparts, such as Kit Carson, Davy Crockett, and Daniel Boone, were increasingly upstaged by such cattle-kingdom characters as Big Foot Wallace, Deadwood Dick, Wild Bill Hickok, Calamity Jane, and Buffalo Bill Cody. Unlike Leatherstocking, these westerners were clearly heroes; Cooper's worries about genteel upbringing tended to be ignored. The dime novelist seemed intent on giving the impression of historical truth. He loved to use real people as subjects. But he was not overly scrupulous in his attention to truth. Beadle warned his authors to avoid "repetition of any experience which, though true, is yet better untold."[15]

Calamity Jane was one of the real women who became fictionalized in the dime novel. Her full name was either Mary Jane Canary or

James Butler "Wild Bill" Hickok, 1869.

Martha Jane Canary. Her mother was a prostitute, and Calamity herself was an alcoholic. At seventeen she was wearing pants and consorting with railroad construction crews. A bit later she was banished from General Crook's expedition against the Sioux when a colonel found her swimming nude with the men. These are the kinds of true details that Beadle claimed were "yet better untold." The dime novel made Calamity Jane lovable and kindhearted. Like her real self, however, the fictional character could outride, outswear, and outshoot the men. She could stand on a running horse bareback and light a cigar. She was, indeed, a violent woman, unlike any feminine character in Cooper's novels. Nevertheless, the dime novelist who wrote about her had to wrestle with the requirement of gentility in the heroine. Of course, Calamity Jane may not be considered critically a heroine, but she and other violent women in the dime novels are allowed status through devices revealing the lingering influence of Cooper's social conventions. Sometimes the woman's violent role is found to be only a disguise; or perhaps, like Calamity Jane, she is in the end shown to be capable of dropping her western lingo for the faultless English of an eastern school.

None topped Buffalo Bill Cody, the prince of all dime-novel heroes. The first story dealing with him, *Buffalo Bill, King of the Bordermen,* was published by the firm of Street and Smith, but the

William "Buffalo Bill" Cody in performance, c. 1905.

author, Edward Z. C. Judson (alias Ned Buntline), subsequently wrote nearly two hundred Buffalo Bill novels for Beadle and Adams. Buntline was not alone; Prentiss Ingraham wrote nearly as many. In these stories Buffalo Bill was skilled in techniques of wilderness survival — "the greatest scout of the West" — and he was uncharacteristically temperate in food and drink. Honor motivated all his actions, whether rescuing white women from dastardly attacks by Indians or protecting other women's virtue by vows of high purpose. As the number of novels grew, the fictitious details multiplied and Buffalo Bill's exploits in the service of honor became more and more daring, just as his flair for costumes burgeoned from embroidered silk shirts and buckskin pants to black velvet and gold braid.

William Frederick Cody was himself such a showman, such a ham actor, that he did his best to live the role in which the dime novel had cast him. His experience had included plenty of raw material for histrionics. As a boy he had worked on the supply train of the army's expedition against the Mormons. He tramped to the Colorado gold rush and rode for the Pony Express. He scouted for the army in cam-

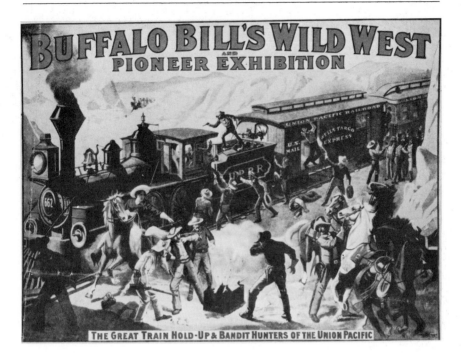

The promotion of the West through entertainment.

paigns against the Comanches, Sioux, Kiowas, and practically every other plains tribe. His nickname derived from a job in which he hunted buffalo to feed railroad construction gangs. In 1872, he hit his stride as actor and producer in a play, *Scouts of the Plains*, written by his friend Ned Buntline. His wild west show was organized in 1883, and by then Buffalo Bill was a national hero. The wild west show was the dime-novel western come to life. The characters of one merged into the cast of the other. Illusions of the novels became flesh and blood, and Buffalo Bill was the Great White Father with flowing hair and velvet breeches on the Great White Horse.

The show began with an overture played by thirty-six "cowboy" musicians wearing flannel shirts, slouch hats, and moccasins. Laced throughout were exhibitions of shooting and riding. Annie Oakley, the sweetheart of all the shows, would enter trippingly throwing kisses, and then her rifle would begin to crack. She hit glass balls and clay pigeons and especially little three-by-five-inch cards thrown high and then sliced by her bullets. The cards were printed with a picture of her and a big red heart, and after they were shot she threw them to the delighted audience. Buck Taylor, King of the Cowboys,

"Little Sure Shot" Annie Oakley.

clung to bucking broncs and led a troop in square dances and Virginia reels on horseback. The Pony Express was demonstrated, and the Deadwood Stage Coach made a simulated run. But the highlights were the spectacles. An immigrant train, complete with oxen and mules, was attacked by whooping Indians and then rescued by the cowboys. A herd of buffalo came through for the buffalo hunt. A settler's cabin was attacked by savagely painted Indians. Sometimes Custer's last stand would provide the climax, showman Cody further immortalizing showman Custer.

During the season of 1885 Sitting Bull toured with the show. He signed the contract partly because he had seen Annie Oakley the year before and had taken a liking to her. He named her Little Sure Shot, and their relationship appears to have been a warm one. But it was difficult for the audience to accept the great Sioux chief into the show's context. After all, he was Custer's enemy; he was the embodiment of Buffalo Bill's troubles when he had scouted for the boys in blue. When Sitting Bull came on in his great ceremonial feathers, he was occasionally hissed, and, in spite of his respect for Annie, he did not sign another contract. Most of the $50 he made a week, he gave away to bootblacks and urchins around the show. He was unable to understand why wealthy white men allowed such poverty in their society.

By the turn of the century, and certainly after Wister published *The Virginian* in 1902, the basic pattern of the western story was set. But its popularity had only begun. Street and Smith had started their monthly pulp magazines, which simply took the story patterns from the dime novel and broke them into groups of monthly installments. In any listing of the progeny of the dime novel, Zane Grey must certainly be accorded a high rank. Grey, a bored New York dentist, published his first book in 1903 but did not hit his real stride until 1912 with *Riders of the Purple Sage*. Lassiter, the cowboy hero, rescues his love from Mormon perfidy and takes her to a secret canyon where nature enfolds them in its embrace. The book has sold at least 1.8 million copies. Grey wrote fifty-four westerns, including *The Thundering Herd* and *The Code of the West*. In one twenty-year period his sales topped 17 million copies, a record only exceeded later in the century by Louis L'Amour.

The motion picture picked up the theme of the western with as much gusto as had the dime novel. Indeed it is hard to imagine the history of the film without the western. *The Great Train Robbery* of 1903, one of the earliest full-length narratives, coupled forever the motion picture and the western hero. Edward S. Porter, its producer, was probably aware that the Union Pacific train crossing Wyoming in 1900 had been held up by a well-known group of bandits, the Wild Bunch. He made his film, though, two thousand miles away in New Jersey, on the tracks of the Delaware and Lackawanna, and it therefore may be considered, like the lithographs of Currier and Ives, an eastern interpretation of western history. In *The Great Train Robbery* came the first close-up in film history; it was, interestingly enough, of a westerner pointing his gun straight at the audience. Porter made other westerns, including *Rescued from an Eagle's Nest*, in which a baby is stolen by an eagle and taken to its eyrie high atop a peak in the Rockies. The heroic father must scale the mountain and then do battle with the villainous bird to save his child.

The first identifiable film star to assume the mantle of the western hero was Bronco Billy Anderson. In a span of a few years after 1908 Bronco Billy starred in nearly five hundred short westerns, which drew freely on yellowing dime novels for their plots. In this same period, just before World War I, David W. Griffith directed the first of his western landmarks, *The Last Drop of Water* and *Fighting Blood*. In the early 1920s William S. Hart worked with Griffith to bring epic qualities to the western. The best example was *Tumble-*

weeds, in which the Oklahoma land rush became a spectacle in the best tradition of the wild west show. The genre was ready for the showmanship of Tom Mix, who was as clever as Buffalo Bill at thrilling audiences. Mix, like Cody, held western credentials of his own. An army man, cowboy, marshal, Texas Ranger, and rodeo star, he moved naturally through such films as *Chip of the Flying "U"* and *Sky High*.

The 1920s also saw the emergence of Gary Cooper who, in movies such as *Nevada* and *Fighting Caravans*, used the stories of Zane Grey rather as Bronco Billy Anderson's films had capitalized on dime novels. Perhaps Cooper's most memorable role was as the greatest western hero of them all, the Virginian, a film made in 1929. Walter Huston played Trampas, and the classic shoot-out between the two could be heard as well as seen, for the film was one of the first with sound. Off and on for nearly thirty years Cooper continued to play in westerns — *The Plainsman* (he played Wild Bill Hickok), 1937; *The Cowboy and the Lady*, 1939; *The Westerner*, 1940; *The Unconquered*, 1947; *Distant Drums*, 1951; to mention a few. In one of his last great westerns, *High Noon*, the climax was nearly identical to a corresponding scene in *The Virginian*, which Cooper had immortalized thirty years earlier.

During and after the 1940s John Ford placed his stamp on film westerns. By then the form had grown sophisticated enough to adapt subtly to a director's changing philosophy. Early films such as *My Darling Clementine, Wagon Master*, and the first version of *Stagecoach* betrayed Ford's feelings that the West had worked a good influence on the white character and that the Indian was a bloodthirsty savage. But a far different note emerged after the 1950s in *The Man Who Shot Liberty Valance, Two Who Rode Together*, and *Cheyenne Autumn*. Ford's views of Indian culture had softened, and his attitude toward the white frontiersman had soured.

A less romantic approach to the American past may explain the rise in the 1960s of tongue-in-cheek westerns like *Cat Ballou, Butch Cassidy and the Sundance Kid, Little Big Man*, Robert Altman's *Buffalo Bill and the Indians*, and Mel Brooks' *Blazing Saddles*. Even though tarnished, the basic themes of the western — self-reliant individualism and personal honor — remained indestructible in these films.[16]

The western became America's national epic and the westerner the national hero. The modern nation-state requires that its people be aware of some uniqueness in their past, something that sets them apart from other nationalities and unifies discordant groups within the population. The western story dealt with an experience to which

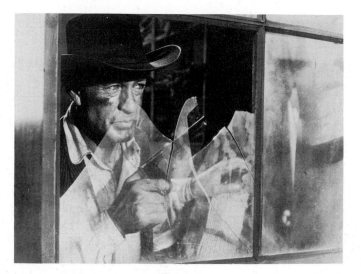

Gary Cooper in High Noon, *1952.*

all regions of the country could relate. The Civil War was also a shared event, but the western avoided the divisiveness of that conflict. Neither North nor South could embrace a symbol springing from the history of the other, but both could cherish such an embodiment of the frontier as the cowboy. For a variety of sound historical reasons the western theme was right for a national epic. The federal government, like a mother, had created the West — first by fighting wars of expansion and then by parceling out the public domain. Thereafter the federal government nourished and protected the area through army exploration, subsidies for transportation, encouragement of settlement, and the general promotion of economic development. Eventually the nation turned to its matured offspring for the symbols that would hold its other parts together.

The appeal of the western, however, went beyond the United States, striking the sympathies of Germans, Frenchmen, and Englishmen, sometimes as much as those of Americans. Karl May, a German who died in 1912, wrote almost as many western novels as Zane Grey, and his continuing character, a western trapper called Old Shatterhand, had a devoted following along the Rhine. Earlier in the 1840s and 1850s Friedrich Gerstäcker preceded May with German westerns, including *The Outlaw Hunters* and *The Terror of the Mines*. Mayne Reid, a monocled, yellow-gloved Irishman, composed stories such as *White Squaw* and *The Scalp Hunters* in London and Buckinghamshire. In France, Oliver Gloux (better known as Gustav Aimard) included in his westerns, among them *The Prairie Flower*, fanciful details such as ostrich hunts among the plains Indians. Though a few of these men spent time in America, most of their readers were European.

Part of the explanation for the appeal of westerns may well lie in the psychological realm. The strong male character carrying a gun could have sexual implications. Psychologists also have suggested that as the role of women broadened in the twentieth century, both men and women looked with nostalgia to an unquestionably male-dominated society. The masculine world of the cowboy has attracted adolescents rebelling against the authoritarian controls of their child-hood. The western cult of masculinity thus in several ways might be explained in terms of the modern psyche.

Much clearer to a historian, however, is the yearning of modern society to escape from an impersonal, pluralistic, and complex age. "The refugee from the accelerated pace of Eastern America," wrote Karl May, "can find solace in the suspended world of the frontier."[17] In a time when puzzling and controversial social problems are inter-minably analyzed, the western story presents clear distinctions be-tween right and wrong. The western tells of a day when options were still open. In a day when practically every decision leaves nagging doubts, with grays and uncertainties, the western presents issues in black and white. In an era of delayed action, rational investigations, and agonizing appeals, the western offers (with only a decent period for suspense) quick action followed by indisputable results.

New themes have crept into the stories — the hardships and monot-ony of western life (as in Tom Lea's *Wonderful Country*), the irre-sponsible shiftlessness of frontiersmen (as in H. L. Davis's *Honey in the Horn*), the psychology of violence (as in Walter Van Tilburg Clark's *The Ox-Bow Incident*). But these are only sophisticated glosses on the basic code of the West. In the final scene of the movie *Shane*, little Joey cries out to his departing hero, growing small against the magnificent Teton peaks, "Come back, Shane; Shane, come back." William S. Hart, watching with his friends as a cattle herd ran off at the approach of Oklahoma settlers, intoned solemnly, "Boys, it's the last of the West." And Gary Cooper closed his television memorial "The Real West" with a soft nostalgic thought: how wonderful to start the whole westward movement over again. Through each char-acter a majority of the American people called symbolically for a return to the sense of boundless natural power with which the legen-dary western heroes were so well endowed, for a rebirth of trust in the individual's inner truth and certitude, which the Virginian so confidently held, and for a recurrence of the western's predictable situations, in which violent action would usher in the triumph of personal honor.

16

The Image of
the West in Art

John Bartlett, chief commissioner to survey the Mexican boundary, sat in the crotch of a mesquite tree in 1852 and sketched the pueblo ruin before him. He had a parasol propped in the branches above, but even so the temperature was 104 degrees. Dripping perspiration warped his sketch paper as he tried to capture the scene exactly as it was. The crinkled spots were nothing, however, compared with the changes that would come when the artist transformed his sketch to a finished sepia drawing. Proportions were changed, the terrain was radically revised, and shadows were flung across the page to give an illusion of depth.

The episode bespeaks much about art and the American West. First and most obviously, the artist, when he was on the scene, faced immense physical difficulties. Bartlett suffered heat and mesquite thorns; elsewhere there was cold, wind, dust, glare, or rain. Second, Bartlett, like so many others, strove to achieve documentary accuracy. Finally, psychological, social, and esthetic values screened artistic behavior and triumphed over photographic representation.

As if he were standing in a hall of mirrors or in a whispering gallery, the artist creates images, impressions, and evocations. "Each form conjures up a thousand memories and after-images" in him as well as in his viewers.[1] Intertwined is the artist's instinctive urge to paint what he "knows" rather than what he "sees." So Robert Penn

Warren envisioned the mind of the painter John James Audubon, watching a great heron rise from the cypress swamp in the bright red dawn:

> Thought: "On that sky it is black."
> Thought: "In my mind it is white." . . .
> Dawn: his heart shook in the tension of the world.[2]

Utilitarian purposes long dominated American art, especially when artists first moved into the far stretches of the West. They sought to document scientifically the new land, trying, as Tocqueville said of all Americans, "to discern the object which engages their attention with extreme clearness."[3]

A good example was Samuel Seymour, who drew for Major Stephen Long's expedition of 1819 and 1820. Seymour was the first official artist on a western exploring expedition and initiated a series of artists who would be enlisted in the cause of science. He was specifically assigned to paint Indians, to choose landscapes for their "beauty or grandeur," and to ferret out any subjects "appropriate to his art."[4] Through these instructions, Seymour was invited to apply his own artistic imagination and style to the documentary job at hand. Although not a great enough artist to take fullest advantage of the opportunity, he became sufficiently excited about some events — such as his first view of the Rockies and an Indian council — to endow drawings of particular scenes with a vitality beyond mere record.

The marriage of art and science was a constant in western exploration from 1820 at least until 1880. Titian Peale, from the family of Philadelphia artists, traveled as a naturalist with Major Long, but his drawings of animals and plants proved more than biology. John C. Frémont on his expeditions of 1845 and 1848 engaged Edward and Richard Kern, two brothers from Philadelphia, to interpret his journey visually. The Kerns were scientists, having worked with such men as Henry Schoolcraft and Samuel Morton in great institutions, among them the emerging Smithsonian. But they were no less artists, having exhibited in distinguished salons such as the Academy of Fine Arts in Philadelphia. In both circles the fact that they had tramped the western wilderness brought them esteem. When Catlin said that the wilderness was the true school of the arts, the Kerns would have rejoined that it was also a good school of science; indeed, they would have said that one important purpose of art is to serve science. This is not to say, however, that the Kerns' paintings were beyond personal interpretation. Richard, for example, in redoing his field sketches, repositioned an Indian pueblo in order to create an illusion of space and order missing in real life. He would change the eye level in an Indian kiva to convey an impression of architectural strength quite different from the fact. Furthermore, their sketches in final form in the printed reports had passed through the hands of eastern lithographers. When details were missing in a sketch, the lithographer would supply them. The costumes of Pueblo weavers, for example, emerged in the prints rather like those of medieval artisans. Though suppositions distorted the pictures, tens of thousands of Americans accepted them as scientifically accurate.

George Catlin has been acclaimed as an accurate portrayer of the plains Indians before they were contaminated by white influences. His drawings of tribes such as the Sioux and the Mandans were filled with details of bone necklaces, buffalo robes, and eagle feathers — delights for future anthropologists. But behind the artifacts are the Indians themselves, gazing with noble dignity. The portraits are rich in character, showing magnificent figures before the white man degraded them with whisky and the reservation system.

As a young man, Catlin had watched an Indian delegation walk through the streets of Philadelphia. He called them "lords of the forest" and was so impressed that he resolved, "Nothing short of the loss of my life, shall prevent me from visiting their country, and of becoming their historian."[5] Enthusiastically in 1832 he started up the Missouri River. He spent three months getting to the mouth of the Yellowstone and sketched practically every Indian he met on the way. That was the first of many jaunts over the next five years, alternating with periods of studio work, during which he transcribed his sketches into finished paintings.

Catlin's aim, however, was more than recording; he hoped to spread a message about the vanishing Indian. He opened an Indian Gallery, a traveling exhibition including more than three hundred oil portraits and two hundred scenes, plus some live grizzly bears and pantomimes of Indians scalping. The show was a sellout as far away as London and Paris.

Catlin also wrote a good deal about his consuming interest, and his prose, pompous and labyrinthine, reveals his preconceptions: "Man in the simplicity and loftiness of his nature, unrestrained and unfettered by the disguises of art, is surely the most beautiful model for the painter — and the country from which he hails is unquestionably the best study and school of the arts in the world."[6] At times the Indian for Catlin is a poet lost in grief for loved ones or a philosopher deep in contemplation or a Greek god of lithe and agile limb. Catlin admits that he is bound to his Indian subject in a "mystic web of sympathy." It is indeed hard to imagine Catlin as an objective observer. True, he admits cruelty and greed are to be found in the character of some of the Indians, but such admissions appear to be afterthoughts or no more than foils against which he can mount the model of the noble savage. He considered the Indian mind "a beautiful blank on which anything might be written."[7] This natural man greeted white civilization with a Lockean *tabula rasa*, and Catlin would have imprinted it with white civilization. There would be no melting pot in which both white and Indian cultures equally contributed and adapted to one another. Rather, Catlin believed, the Indian should embrace the goals of Chestnut Street in Philadelphia or Beacon Hill in Boston. He found it a dreadful shame that the only civilized people the Indians normally met were the dregs of society known as frontiersmen.

The most appealing scene of native life Catlin could imagine was an Indian man "smoking his pipe, under his own humble roof, with his wife and children around him, and his faithful dogs and horses hanging about his hospitable tenement."[8] Catlin regretted that in the natural state the Indian did not know the efficacy and justice of civilized laws or "the light and the grace that flow from Christian faith."[9] It is clear that Catlin found the highest good not in Indian, but in white society, particularly in an agrarian society firmly rooted in private property, monogamy, and Christianity. Although he was filled with sympathy for the native Americans, he was in fact no better endowed with the objective qualities needed to evaluate their culture than were the soldiers concurrently herding Cherokees from Georgia to Oklahoma.

Karl Bodmer was the first of many artists to translate the American West into a European image. Bodmer's patron in the West was Maximilian, prince of the small southern German principality of Wied. Maximilian's royal mind had been tuned to natural science. The prince had examined the jungles of Brazil in 1815; and when he turned his attention to North America, he sought the best-trained artist. His choice was Bodmer, a Swiss who prepared for his assignment by examining every western collection available, among them the works of Samuel Seymour and George Catlin. Maximilian and Bodmer arrived in the West only a few months after Catlin, and they remained for nearly two years. Bodmer, a master craftsman, was far more skilled than Catlin. Yet into his portraits crept the trappings of Near Eastern exoticism, and his Indians sometimes appeared suspiciously fiendish.

Alfred Jacob Miller, with Catlin and Bodmer one of the earliest delineators of the plains and Rockies, studied as a young man in Europe. Returning to America, he set up a studio in New Orleans, from which his reputation must have spread up the Father of Waters to St. Louis. There in 1837 a Scottish nobleman on leave from the British army, Captain William Drummond Stewart, prepared for

Hidatsa Indian, Leader of the Dog Dance, by Karl Bodmer, 1833.

another adventure in the Rockies, which he had been enjoying since about 1833. He added Miller to his entourage. They traveled the North Platte, the Sweetwater, and South Pass, the route that would be designated the Oregon Trail less than a decade later. The most memorable of Miller's drawings, however, were not of scenes along the route but sketches of the fur trade in its palmiest days. In his field drawings, mountain men set traps, spun tales around camp fires, rested in the shade at noon, bartered for Indian brides, caroused at rendezvous. In general, Miller gave the mountain man as much detailed attention as Catlin had given the Indian. These first hand sketches were recopied, time and again, on large and small canvases in his studio, each with additional subjective intrusions. In *The Trapper's Bride*, the horse became a steed, the father a distinguished patriarch, and the trapper an eager young husband. Miller typically continued to work from his sketches for decades, though he never returned to the West.

The 1840s sharpened the European interest in the American West as an exotic whetstone for the imagination. Paul Kane had been intrigued by Indians as a boy in York, Canada, but his compelling desire to paint them was unsatisfied until 1843, when he first saw George Catlin's Indian gallery in London. He had steeped himself in Rome and Florence, and the Swiss Alps had enraptured him, but nothing hit him as hard as the image of Catlin's Indians. Catlin convinced him that the Indians were fast losing their primeval state in the face of white cultural subversion. By 1845 Kane was heading for western Canada, traveling by canoe with the fur brigades of the Hudson's Bay Company. In the following year in Fort Vancouver he watched the Oregon Treaty being signed. He played backgammon with Peter Skene Ogden, crossed the new boundary for a visit to the Whitman mission, and in the summer of 1848 started the long trip back to Toronto, carrying more than four hundred sketches of Indians, fur posts, and majestic western scenes.

Kane passed the next years of his life translating his sketches into finished oils, much as a sculptor fashions a figure from rough clay into polished marble. In the process he gave more dramatic stripes to medicine men, embroidered more handsomely chieftains' robes, and reassembled artifacts from various times and places for better effect. His horses became taller and more Arabian. His sketch of an Indian buffalo hunt was modeled after an engraving of an Italian hunt scene. Kane often added neutral grays and dark browns to give the effect of works by old masters. Foreboding cloud banks were piled into some skies, and day scenes were transformed to night so the moon and camp fire could throw weird shadows. These versions were bought by the Canadian government, hung in the Houses of Parliament, and later were prominently displayed in the National Gallery.

A careful reading of Kane's prose suggests that his artistic interpretations of the Indian should be viewed cautiously. He found Indians to be "invariably dirty" and hence intolerable to the white man.[10] Time after time he erroneously implies that chiefs exerted immense power over their tribes; he imputes to them a position that he might assign to princes of Britain. In Kane's view the Indian medicine man was a charlatan, a necromancer, who humbly admitted that his powers would have little effect on the white man. He believed that Christian missionaries, particularly Methodists, calmed the Indian's fierceness, moderated his intemperance, and implanted true wisdom in his heathen mind. Yet for all Kane's ethnocentrism, he was sympathetic to the Indian. He went out of his way to point out that Indians were not cannibals. He was willing to understand the women's practice of leaving the tribal circle during menstruation, though he delicately referred to "certain stated periods" after which the woman returns to "health."[11] His view of the Indian was infused with ideas of romantic love. He shows Indian swains playing plaintive flute songs outside the wigwams of their beloved and tells long tales of young maidens waiting through the years for the return of lost warriors.

In the same decade Rudolph Friedrich Kurz was painting the West. "From my earliest youth," he wrote in his journal, "primeval forest and Indians had an indescribable charm for me." He determined to devote his whole career to forests, wild animals, and Indians.[12] His friend and countryman Karl Bodmer told him to prepare himself better for the American West, so he went to Paris! In 1846 he finally embarked for New Orleans, only to find that a war stood in the way of his destination. He went north, got a job with the American Fur Company, and ended up along the upper Missouri near Fort Union at the mouth of the Yellowstone. His excitement at painting Indians overshadowed mosquitoes, bedbugs, smelly rooms in the fort, and a tedious job as a clerk. These discomforts are described in his journals but not in his art.

Kurz never transferred his sketches into finished paintings. When he returned to Switzerland, he fell into a prolonged illness. His sketches thus give us some insight into the way preconceptions can work, even in the field. In one case he refused to paint an Indian girl because she was not wearing her hair as he thought she should. Because she was in mourning, her long tresses had been cut, and so she was written out of history. He took a special liking to certain tribes. The Crows became his favorites, and he concentrated on them at the expense of others. Kurz did, however, paint Indian ponies accurately, with their big bellies and their shagginess, ponies Bodmer and Miller had turned into Arabian steeds.

The romantic climate of opinion dominated art from late in the eighteenth century until the middle of the nineteenth century, the period in which the American Far West was being interpreted for the first time. Some assumptions about the frontier had been long evident — the individualism of the pioneer, the nobility of the Indian, the glories of the wilderness — but generally these themes waited until the romantic period for their fullest artistic expression.

Before the Renaissance no one had considered painting a mountain or a forest for its own sake worth a man's time. In the seventeenth century the projection of meaning into nature was forecast in the painting of tortured rocks with which the Dutchman Joachim Patinir framed an agonized St. Jerome. Patinir's contemporary Jacob Ruisdael delighted in the cool rush of water through a dank glade. But the painter the later romantics looked back upon with the most relish was Salvator Rosa, a seventeenth-century Italian whose somber sienna

"Last of the Mohicans" by Thomas Cole (1801-1848).

tones could not hide his emotional view of nature. In England in the eighteenth century, Philippe de Loutherburg began to paint moody skies charged with drama, and he was followed by the young J. M. W. Turner, whose early canvases are electric with storms overpowering man. The works of the Frenchman Eugène Delacroix in the early nineteenth century may have marked the height of the romantic movement in painting. He was selected to illustrate a French scientific expedition into north Africa, but his resulting art bears little stamp of the mundane reality of exploration. Instead, he painted lions and tigers red in tooth and claw, horses leaping from the sea, and jungles shimmering in mystery.

The first full-fledged American romantics were members of the Hudson River School — Asher Durand, Thomas Cole, and Frederick Church, to name a few. In Durand's *Kindred Spirits*, the painter and a poet stand on a rocky outcrop, meditating on the leafy glen beneath them. Thomas Cole roamed through similar clefts in the Catskills, and his paintings bristle with jutting peaks that challenge the clouds for domination of the sky. Nature for him was as often savage as it was benign. This is seen in his treatment of Niagara Falls. As a matter of fact, Niagara came to symbolize the whole Hudson River School, for it was painted almost ritualistically. In most versions an infinitesimal man stands on the brink of the falls facing the cataract, presumably feeling anew the strength of natural forces.

As the country moved west, a group of painters formed along the banks of the Mississippi. Among these artists was Carl Wimar, who had come to St. Louis from Germany as a lad of fifteen. A shy boy, much enamored of Indians, he was occasionally mistaken for one. When beginning to draw, he could not hope to study art until good fortune struck: his mother had been hospitable to a wayfarer, and the stranger on his death willed her enough money to send the boy to Europe. So Carl returned to his homeland, seeking his artistic grail in Dusseldorf, which had become a minor mecca for American artists. There he trained with Emanuel Leutze, an American émigré and painter of *Washington Crossing the Delaware*. Wimar discovered that, even six thousand miles from the scene, he had not forgotten his absorption with the Indian, and Leutze encouraged him to paint western and Indian subjects, though he had to strain his memory for details. The titles suggest the subject of his work: *The Capture of Daniel Boone's Daughter, Captive Charger, Indians Attacking an Immigrant Train.*

Upon returning to St. Louis in 1857, he continued his work, penetrating the Far West aboard riverboats of the American Fur Company, rather as Kurz had done earlier. But the tenor of his work continued as it was in Germany. In general his subjects remained dramatic, often chosen from historical events. Wimar perpetuated the view of the frontier as a region laden with moral impact for its inhabitants.

Before Wimar left Dusseldorf, another St. Louis painter, George Caleb Bingham, arrived there. Bingham quickly became part of the circle, writing home that his teacher Leutze treated him like a brother. He had already painted the first version of one of his most famous pictures, showing Daniel Boone escorting settlers through the Cumberland Gap into the clear light of Kentucky. This was the kind of historical drama Leutze loved, but Bingham went far beyond the historical movement, conveying stalwart frontier qualities sharpened on the stone of the wilderness. As a result of their intimate contacts with the natural world, Boone and his friends symbolized immense courage and unconquerable faith in hard work and the cleansing of the raw West by civilization. Bingham executed other canvases of the same scene, one measuring thirteen by eighteen feet, which he entered in an American competition for the best work illustrating the history of the West. Interestingly enough, Leutze also entered the contest and won the prize for his preliminary drawings of *Westward the*

"The Abduction of Boone's Daughter by the Indians"
by Carl Wimar (1828-1862).

Course of Empire Takes Its Way, later to grace the walls of the national capitol.

Bingham did not stay as long in Germany as Wimar had, and Leutze also returned to America after nearly twenty years in Dusseldorf. In 1858 Bingham was back along the Mississippi. He began to paint genre scenes, everyday life as he saw it around him. But that is not to say that his works were realistic in any narrow sense. Nature still infused his scenes, and natural qualities were evident in the simplicity of the men he painted. River mists evoked the loneliness of trappers; quiet currents provided a backdrop for rough men venting simple emotions by dancing and gambling; slowly moving waters defined the cast of characters — transients loitering and drifting along the backwaters of the frontier.

Wimar, Bingham, and Leutze thus carried Hudson River concepts of nature to the banks of the Mississippi and the Missouri. One might expect that, in the transition, regard for the esthetic canons prevailing in the East and in Europe would have changed, perhaps freeing artists from their attachments to European ideas. But this particular road west involved a detour — intellectually as well as physically — to Dusseldorf. In Germany, ideas of the West were affected by earlier expectations, and the Mississippi School remained fully in the context of romanticism.

Another continental jump led to the zenith of western romantic interpretations — the Rocky Mountain School of painters. The Civil War was over, the nation had settled its sectional problems, or so it hoped, and artists took a long look at the nation's dimensions. The most grandiose western features, the Yellowstone and the Grand Canyon of the Colorado, caught their view. Niagara, the Catskills, the Hudson, even the Mississippi, were dwarfed by the jagged peaks and blue rivers of the Far West.

No one captured the spirit of the grandiose as well as Albert Bierstadt. German by birth, he had been raised amid the bustle of sailing ships in New Bedford, Massachusetts, and was only twenty-one when his first painting was exhibited in Boston. He studied in Europe and, while there, sketched castles on the Rhine and hiked among the Alps. His first chance to see the American West came in 1858, when he accompanied General Frederick Landers on a survey party westward from St. Louis. Entranced with what he saw, he left the expedition to tramp and sketch through the Wind River Mountains and the Shoshone country. In 1860 his first Rocky Mountain pictures were immediately and overwhelmingly successful. In England his paintings soon brought higher prices than an American artist had ever received.

With his friend Fitz-Hugh Ludlow, a wealthy opium smoker, Bierstadt returned to the West, sketching the Colorado Rockies, the Great Salt Lake, Oregon, and California. Success enabled him to build a thirty-five-room house overlooking the Hudson River at Irvington and to set up a second studio in San Francisco. From there, on excursions into the Yosemite and Hetch Hetchy valleys, he absorbed material for some of his most gloriously romantic canvases, enormous in square footage, grand with overreaching peaks and bands of water gleaming between dark forests. But all was not well in the relations between the American people as an art audience and the long-standing marriage of western painters with European romanticism. Europe had embarked in other directions, notably toward French Impressionism. Bierstadt fell out of favor, especially with art critics, and sold fewer and fewer paintings. When he died in 1902, the year of Wister's *Virginian*, his huge canvases were assigned to the nation's attic.

More than twenty years after Bierstadt first saw the West, Thomas Moran was introduced to the Grand Tetons and the Yellowstone country. Moran was thirty-four years old and as well steeped in English romanticism as Bierstadt had been in its German form. He delighted in reading Robert Browning and Arthur Young. He was a friend and

"Yosemite Valley" by Albert Bierstadt (1830–1902).

correspondent of John Ruskin, critical monarch of English romanticism, who overcame his antipathy to Americans long enough to implore Moran to move to England. In London, Moran was intrigued by the emotionally freighted early paintings of J. M. W. Turner. These English influences immediately preceded his journey west with Ferdinand V. Hayden's surveying party in 1871. In the Yellowstone and the Grand Tetons, Moran's excitement was boundless. Back in his studio, he flung his canvases over entire walls and, like Bierstadt, gave to western space its image in footage. Hayden had also brought along a photographer, William Henry Jackson, whose prints, along with the paintings of Moran, were instrumental in persuading Congress to create Yellowstone National Park.

Moran and Bierstadt together carried the romantic concepts of nature to their ultimate in size and grandeur. For them the western landscape was sublime and awe inspiring. Man stood in the presence of nature as in a Gothic cathedral, tuning his muted senses to the infinite beauty. Moran's *Grand Canyon of the Yellowstone* might be interpreted as a stained-glass window, each small piece of color transmitting an aura of mystical reverence. Like the glass, these paintings are not photographically real; Moran once said that literal transcripts from nature are worthless. Nature was glorified and worshiped at a time when Americans were first seriously considering the preservation of their western landscape from man's depredations. The small man in the foreground of the paintings who so needed nature was at the same time building railroads and hotels.

Later in the century, in contrast with the Rocky Mountain School, painters such as Frederic Remington de-emphasized the elemental grandeur of nature and stressed instead the human qualities called forth by the grimness of the wilderness. In paintings such as *Night Wolf* the animal, threatened by the dark surroundings, stands forth like a courageous man in self-reliant independence. Remington was the chief exponent in art of the rugged western individualist.

His mother had wanted him to be a businessman in the manner of Rockefeller or Carnegie. However, after seven different jobs in eighteen months, he fell ill. His aversion to industrial society lasted the rest of his life. He had developed a love for the outdoors, skill in horseback riding, and marksmanship. Thus prepared, he went to Montana in the early 1880s and discovered the West to be his natural environment. Sight unseen he purchased 320 acres in Kansas for a sheep ranch. His three years there included some happy times. Like a boy, he joined in pranks, throwing spitballs at bald men and going on larks as far south as Mexico. During this time he found that his real talent and joy lay in drawing. This awareness, combined with financial distress on the ranch, caused him to return to New York in the summer of 1885.

Concurrently, public opinion in the East was focused on the army's campaign against Geronimo, the Apache militant. Because Remington had once crossed the Mexican border and therefore knew more about the Sonoran and Chihuahuan terrain than any other artist, he was asked to illustrate articles about Geronimo and the campaign for *Outing* magazine. One pictorial success followed another, and before long he was New York's resident expert on the West, drawing for *Harper's* and *Century* as well as for *Outing*. Another claimant for the title of honorary westerner, Theodore Roosevelt, was captivated by Remington's sketches and asked him to illustrate his forthcoming *Ranch Life and the Hunting Trail.*

Bierstadt had entered the rarefied *beau monde* of art; Remington remained outside that realm, reflecting far more of the popular imagination. Between 1888 and 1890 paintings and bronzes poured from his studio. His paintings brought tens of thousands of dollars, and he never lacked purchasers. Toward the end of his life he could even indulge in the histrionics of burning piles of his canvases, as a robber baron might light cigars with ten-dollar bills.

"The Scout" by Frederic Remington.

Remington rivaled his friend Roosevelt in living up to the cult of masculinity. His apparent distaste for women was reflected in his paintings, where among hundreds of male subjects no more than four women ever appeared. He believed masculine strength came from conflicts with nature, the individual against drought and wind. In *Friend or Foe*, a lone rider strains his eyes to identify a barely visible speck on the bleak horizon.

Remington treated the Indian as if he were a part of hostile nature, an abrasion against which the Anglo-Saxon could prove his mettle. In the summer of 1890, the artist marched with General Nelson Miles when the army massacred a remnant of Sioux at Wounded Knee. Aware of the bloodshed of women and children by the hundreds, Remington nevertheless thrilled at the subsequent passing of the troops in review, as if they had on that day proved their manliness. In his view, Indians as a race were no better than foreigners.

With his distaste for eastern industrial society, Remington lumped the Indian together with the immigrants then pouring into factories of the East. He wrote to a friend: "Jews, Injuns, Chinamen, Italians,

"In Without Knocking" by Charles M. Russell.

Huns — the rubbish of the earth I hate — I've got some Winchesters and when the massacring begins, I can get my share of 'em, and whats more, I will."[13] In his paintings of lonely cowboys looking out over a rough-cast nature and of cavalrymen riding to the attack, bugles shrill, pennants proud, Remington proclaimed man triumphant over nature and the Anglo-Saxon male dominant over "lesser" peoples.

Remington had a counterpart in Charles M. Russell, who liked to be introduced as a Montana cowboy rather than as an artist, and who would have loved Remington's designation of "man with the bark on." Like Remington, Russell was raised in a wealthy family from which he escaped to the outdoors. He ardently read western dime novels and was filled with notions about the West. When at the age of sixteen he left his St. Louis home, he met a trapper who introduced him to the Judith Basin in Montana. Russell never lost his love for that country. For eleven years he worked as a horse wrangler, but during this time he also began to draw and paint. After he married, his wife so successfully managed the sale of his work that he could settle down comfortably in Great Falls.

Russell conceived of the West in terms of complete freedom, which was for him nothing more complicated than an absence of restraint. He intuitively sympathized with outlaws and believed the Indian was once noble because he had been free. Sometimes Russell tried, almost humorously, to capture Indian viewpoints, as his painting *Indians Discover Lewis and Clark* suggests. Russell projected a simple, boyish West, and his popularity as an artist shows the extent to which most people were in tune with the chord he struck.

If one moves only the short step from Russell to the world of prints by Currier and Ives, that sympathetic chord for the free, individualistic, simplistic West is even more dramatically sounded. Take, for example, the Currier and Ives print *The Rocky Mountains: Emigrants Crossing the Plains*. Lithographed in 1866 from a painting by Fanny Palmer, this print was widely sold and seen in barber shops, saloons, hotel rooms, and in the parlors of rich and poor alike. The Rocky Mountains transcend all human experience, surpassing Bierstadt. Blue glaciers mirror a stormless sky over meadows as green as Elysium. Amid lush foliage only one dead tree remains to feed any lingering romantic's melancholy. Full-bellied oxen pull wagons containing men and women, properly paired. They seem not to notice the Indians whose wigwams stand a scant hundred yards away, and the Indians look on in idle curiosity, neither threatening nor threatened. Hardly a detail in the entire view is what we would now call factual, yet Currier and Ives, like scientific draftsmen earlier in the century, were consistently extolled for their "meticulous accuracy."[14] Perhaps it is enough to say that accuracy, like beauty, remains in the eye of the beholder.

The twentieth century finds nature neutral — as constructive as destructive, as usable as unmanageable, as ferocious and bloody as serene and gentle — in short, amoral and unrelated to human motives. The nineteenth-century artist saw no such neutrality. Nature was charged with meaning and gave men moral purpose. The fury of nature instructed men to fight back; the raw energy of a storm provided the requisite power. Softer moods exposed the values of peace and tranquillity; the moist warmth of a meadow in Indian summer imparted contentment and acquiescence. Mountains taught humility; rivers, persistence and determination; spring leaves, joy; autumn foliage, gratitude and fruitfulness. Nature at the very least aroused in men elevated thoughts and inspired the pleasures of contemplation.

Nature's moods are so varied and so extreme that awesome tensions result. The soft summer sky is at another time gloweringly black; the smooth river breaks into the churning rapids; level plains are ridged with sharp peaks. The tensions in these opposites are like electric charges that can be wired to man. The tensions, then, can also illuminate in some mystical way man's own dichotomies — his limitless dreams beside the realities of his accomplishments, his weakness before the magnitude of the universe, his evanescent life versus eternity, and ultimately and starkly, life against death. The western artist depicted these tensions and their relations to man in a thousand ways. Sometimes the technique was to position human figures as if they, like the viewer, were drinking the essences from nature. Often figures were in the close foreground and were relatively small, dwarfed by the giant natural forms before which they stood. The skies could be split between heavenly blue and portentous black. The light on the scene could be dramatically focused, generally in bands of bright sunlight alternating into the distance with dark shadow. And, the most frequent detail of all — a twisted dead tree would stand among the fullblown leaves of summer. One nineteenth-century author put the point in words: "The world of Man is a mixture of contrarieties. The source of his sweetest enjoyments is often the fountain of his bitterest anguish."[15]

The morality of nature is the most persistent theme in paintings of the West. The buffalo hunt — the most compelling subject for the western artist — proclaimed that man could conquer beast. The scene was as full of human glory as were Renaissance paintings of Saint George subduing the dragon. Against the buffalo, however, man was not aided by God or by the righteousness of a maiden's cause. He was elemental man, raw muscle; thus Indians were frequently the buffalo hunters.

The western setting provided contrasts more dramatic than painters had yet known, exceeding the Alps and the burning Sahara. These extremes, through the magic of art as well as nature, imbued western man with limitless energy. Recipient of such strength, he could be stopped by nothing. No Holy Grail, no Excalibur, could endow him with more confidence. Consciousness of inexhaustible power may well be the most significant aspect of the western image. When the Indian was sympathetically portrayed by Catlin, his vigor stemmed from his closeness to nature. In the same way, the white man might become strong and self-reliant. Men like Remington interpreted the Indian strayed from nature as "rubbish." In that situation, the white man, who had become the natural man, might righteously destroy the Indian. Self-righteousness thus reinforced the consciousness of power so dominant in western art.

17

The Frontier Experience
in Retrospect

A TRANSIT AND AN IMAGE

"It gradually occurred to me," writes Arthur K. Moore, "that some of the more troublesome, not to say harmful, attitudes of the present were traceable to presumptions about man and society which noisily declared themselves on the frontier."[1] Two of the most obvious burdens we bear are an excessive reverence for individualism and a moralistic view of nature. How we inherited these ideas may be apparent if we first extract from the frontier experience certain determining aspects — the rapidity of its growth, the dynamism of its expansive force, its violence, and its disdain for authority. From each of these have grown controlling assumptions about the American character, reinforced by myth and memory.

The American westward movement was unusually rapid. Generation after generation of participants and observers were impressed by the quick transformation of wilderness into populous urbanized regions. Hester Prynne spoke the words of Hawthorne when she mused how recently her bustling village had been only "a leaf-strewn desert."[2] Within an individual's lifetime empty frontiers became the congested cities of Springfield, Independence, Salt Lake City, Spokane, San Francisco. In 1853, feeling the tempo, a news correspondent in St. Paul observed, "ten years is a lifetime here, and twenty, time out of

"The Rocky Mountains: Emigrants crossing the plains"
by Currier and Ives.

memory."[3] Americans subdued almost an entire continent from the Appalachians to the Pacific in little more than two generations.

Easterners such as Daniel Webster delighted in contrasting their compact farms and easily bridged streams with the boundless prairies and measureless rivers of the West. These comparisons did not take into account other equally large frontiers such as Siberia, the South American pampas, and the Canadian or Alaskan vastness. For all its ruggedness and aridity, the West was a reasonably hospitable environment and lent itself to rapid development. The members of the Lewis and Clark expedition, for example, never came near starving, whereas similarly well-planned explorations into the heartland of Australia and Africa brought to their members death by hunger and thirst, tortuous fatigue, and wild insanity. Quantities of people seemed always ready to stream into the American West, jostling for the best land, willing to endure hardships and disappointments. If they failed, they could try elsewhere, playing the incredible American game that William Appleman Williams has called "an infinity of second chances."[4]

The American frontier was unusual in creating a climate of inces-

"Madonna of the Prairie" by W. H. D. Koerner (1878–1938).

sant war. Pioneers battled Indians from the 1620s to the 1890s. Cattlemen fought sheepmen, farmers fought cattlemen, mine workers fought mine operators, outlaws fought railroads, and vigilantes roamed through the story underscoring the barbarities. Distant authority was often suspect, and local officials were respected but little more. In contrast Canadian frontiersmen submitted to the delegated judicial powers of Hudson's Bay Company and later of the Northwest Mounted Police. In spite of the geographical similarities between the American and Canadian frontiers, Canadian westerners in general were more orderly and respectful of central authority than were their American counterparts, and their frontier developed more slowly. Consequently in Canada there were fewer instances of violence against minorities, fewer Indian wars, and infrequent vigilantism. In this contrast can be seen the influence of a people's history on their subsequent acts. Americans had fought a revolution against central colonial authority. They had written into their laws, as in the Northwest Ordinance, prohibitions against new colonialism. Their nineteenth-century West was settled in a period of capitalistic laissez-faire: let men alone so that the competitive laws of the market can produce the best forms of society. Furthermore the great migration from western Europe, composed of many nationalities — Germans, Scots, Irish, French, Scandinavians — contrasted with frontiers such as Australia's, where settlement was overwhelmingly British.

With the four distinguishing characteristics of the American frontier in mind — rapid growth, dynamic expansion, violence, and disdain for authority — men have long considered the frontier dominant in American history. In the early nineteenth century Alexis de Tocqueville remarked: "This gradual and continuous progress of the European race towards the Rocky Mountains has the solemnity of a providential event; it is like a deluge of men rising unabatedly, and daily driven onwards by the hand of God."[5] Jefferson understood the impulse when he shelved his constitutional scruples to buy Louisiana and when he dispatched Lewis and Clark on their mission. Whitman sang toasts to the "lands of the Western shore, to the new culminating man, to you, the empire new." Emerson, too, recognized the importance: "Luckily for us, . . . the nervous, rocky West is intruding a new and continental element into the national mind, and we shall yet have an American genius."[6]

The nation, however, had to await Frederick Jackson Turner for a full-blown theory on the meaning of the frontier. As a young man Turner had studied Phoenician voyages and the restless thrust of trappers on American waters. Then in 1893 in the stale air of a historical convention he proclaimed in poetic prose the primary significance of the American frontier: "The existence of an area of free land, its continuous recession, and the advance of American settlement westward explain American development." The seeds may have come from Europe, but the plants had grown fresh in unexpected form:

> To the frontier the American intellect owes its striking characteristics. That coarseness and strength combined with acuteness and inquisitiveness; that practical, inventive turn of mind, quick to find expedients; that masterful grasp of material things, lacking in the artistic, but powerful to effect great ends; that restless, nervous energy; that dominant individualism, working for good and for evil, and withal that buoyancy and exuberance which comes from freedom — these are traits of the frontier, or traits called out elsewhere because of the existence of the frontier.[7]

More than molding character, Turner saw the West as a unifier of the nation, welding together various stocks and regions and encouraging an aggressive nationalism that fed on its own expansive energies. At the local level the frontier nurtured forms so democratic that the long evolution of Anglo-Saxon self-government paled in importance beside the force of the American wilderness.

Then the frontier closed, its influence ended. In 1890 the Census Bureau declared it could no longer designate the boundaries of the frontier by means of population statistics. Previously it had been able to draw a line demarking areas of settlement having population greater than two people per square mile. By 1890 the best of the cheap land was taken. The pulse of expansion, the rhythm of the frontier line moving west, would become myth and memory. What, Turner asked, would happen when the pulse no longer beat? The momentum of the long continental expansion would probably propel America into acquiring an overseas empire. At home increasing concentrations of wealth would face the rising power of organized labor, producing an intensification of class struggles. Politics would turn more and more to socialistic solutions as the tide of individualism slowly ebbed.[8]

Acceptance of Turner's thesis was based on the remarkable accuracy of his predictions. The frontier theory became part of American intellectual history. It was eagerly championed not only by historians but by the reading public. Earlier, in the 1880s, Hubert Howe Bancroft's thirty-nine volumes of western narrative history had enjoyed remarkable popularity. Turner's ideas brought such works a new aura, the halo of an all-embracing interpretation. The West had not been a place of escape, a preface to more important things, an uncouth aberration. The West had been a central, governing force in the national spirit. Before the acceptance of the Turner thesis, the West had not been considered fit for college study. It did not even creep into the lower schools and the McGuffey Readers, except in an occasional Indian story. After Turner, study of the West became as academically acceptable as that of the North and the South.

Turner defined the frontier in a confusing variety of ways — as an area of free, open land; as a line of population density; as a recurrent transition from primitive to complex society; as a spirit or climate of opinion that could be called forth even in the urban East. Partly because of their ambiguity, his theories fit the mood of romantic nationalism. In later and more sobering times, especially during the Great Depression, scholars began to wonder if Turner had not distracted the nation from more pressing questions. Instead of drawing attention to international affairs, the thesis allowed a sentimental wallowing in the nation's domestic history. Instead of facing the reality of class hatred, it posed a Horatio Alger individualism at odds with economic trends. Instead of examining the problems of industrialization and urbanization, it directed attention to a rural wilderness and a primitive social process.

Turner saw the process as a part of evolution, and his theory assumed progress from the simple to the complex. For him the frontier was a region in which staunch Europeans transfigured a reluctant native environment. Historians in the 1980s, especially Howard Lamar and Robert Berkhofer, place the word *process* in a different context, and see the frontier far less ethnocentrically; they view it more as an interaction among various peoples. The original environment was never empty, and progress was by no means inevitable.

Not unlike the scholars, the nation at large has never made up its mind about the meaning of the frontier. Daniel Boone could be seen as an heroic individual, fleeing corrupt society, or he could be the Promethean bearer of civilization to the uncouth wilderness. A pioneer, if he lived far enough away, could be extolled as the true leather-stockinged nobleman of nature, or, if he lived nearby, could be dismissed as a drifter and a libertine with dirty fingernails and a wide range of bodily smells.

When concentrating on the fiction as opposed to the fact, most Americans have emphasized the individual frontiersman. The frontier for them was comprised of the prospector, trapper, and cowboy rather than the company or labor union; the circuit rider rather than the cooperative missionary societies; the Pony Express rather than the long Santa Fe caravans. Like Hester Prynne, the westerners' "intellect and heart had their home, as it were, in desert places,"[9] isolated, lonely settings for the Thoreaus, Boones, Ahabs, and Hawkeyes of our dreams. On the frontier could grow Mark Twain's river pilot, "the only unfettered and entirely independent human being that lived on earth," withdrawn but lordly and commanding.[10] In general this westerner might be called a new Adam, "the authentic American as a figure of heroic innocence and vast potentialities, poised at the start of a new history."[11] Individualism has been the most widely assumed product of the frontier experience — an assumption that has governed people's behavior and changed American history. When defined, individualism is associated with self-reliance, self-sufficiency, independence, laissez-faire, freedom from restraint, loneliness, selfishness, egotism, eccentricity, isolation. Its opposites are community, mutual dependence, tradition, social responsibility, socialism.

The word *individualism* emerged in the nineteenth century, and one of its earliest uses was in Toqueville's *Democracy in America*. The timing is interesting in view of David Riesman's description of nineteenth-century man as the inner-directed person, seeking justification solely within himself, governed by a psychological gyroscope that set his course and limited his behavior.[12] In a slightly larger context, B. F. Skinner has identified the individualist as "autonomous man," a construct of the humanistic and romantic traditions.[13]

Skinner contends that the self-directed, free-willed individual has led us to the brink of destruction, that ideas such as freedom and human dignity have outlived their purpose; society must turn away from them in order to survive. From Skinner's point of view, to continue to extol legendary frontier values would be suicidal. Whether western harshness forced people to individualistic self-reliance or toward group cooperation, they thought the frontier dictated individualism, and much of American history has been affected by that assumption.

Two ideas associated with the assumption have been capitalism and Protestantism. Max Weber's classic insights into the growth of these two movements, each reinforcing the other, may provide an interesting comparison with a congenial relationship between the West and Protestantism. Some of the essential tenets of Protestantism — the direct relation between man and God, the personal interpretation of the Bible, the priesthood of all believers — were peculiarly relevant to isolated, lonely people embarked on a supposed sea of self-reliance. The camp meeting with its emphasis on individual conversion, the circuit rider alone battling wind and rain, and the splintering of sects whenever there were new visions — these were all indeed individualistic.

Yet frontier religion was heavily communal, training community leaders in youth groups and aid societies. These groups were strongly nationalistic, as well, for the kingdom of God in its transplantation had become Americanized. The messianic age might begin on the new frontier, just as Christ had first appeared on the frontiers of Rome. The Mormons believed that Christ had already revealed himself in the New World, and it is noteworthy that this group was the most communal of religious people.

Frontier individualism was impregnated with a philosophy of the inner man. Looking sincerely within himself, the individual found a law higher than man, and he was commanded to obey that statute before all others. The doctrine worked if one started from the same assumptions. But where the frontier became pluralistic, the theory often led to violent repression of one group by another. In the face of this doctrine the covenanted community as an opposing idea broke down into the self-appointed moralism of the small town. At its worst, the acceptance of the supremacy of the inner law bore the unfortunate fruit of irresponsibility to the group. What does it matter what others think or need if one knows that he is right? On the frontier, the defense of this higher law was frequently an excuse for violence. Coercive physical force is easy to exert when buttressed by the certainties of self-righteousness. Thus vigilantes, in addition to their other purposes and methods, assumed a "shoot first, ask questions later" attitude, and their approach could easily intensify self-righteous racial conflict.

Land policies are also related to the individualistic myth, though again, facts stand at wide variance with the assumptions. What was more important in keeping farmers pouring westward than the availability of fertile land? Other nations — Spain, Mexico, Australia — gave food, clothing, livestock, and money in addition to land in order to lure people toward the frontiers; yet these subsidies were often ineffective. In America land hunger was believed to be a self-generating force that coursed through American history without artificial stimulation, moving the Boones, Austins, Kelleys, and Donners out onto the trails.

In the seventeenth century the English gave land hunger a special twist by emphasizing permanent settlement by entire families. Consequently, the English Crown grew peculiarly protective of citizens' rights. Thus desirable political climates, as well as land, attracted non-English people, and the Scotch-Irish and Germans, some of the most typical frontiersmen, flowed into the back country. The British tried to keep land hunger from upsetting Indians and fur traders, but the pressures were so great that anyone in America could have predicted that the policy would not be effective. Even during the years of the American Revolution, men such as Daniel Boone and Richard Henderson climbed the ridges and claimed chunks of rich valley beyond. The impulse rose throughout the nineteenth century. It peaked in the 1820s in Texas, in the 1840s in Oregon, California, and Utah, in the 1870s on the Great Plains, and again in California in the 1880s.

The momentum stemmed, first, from the policies of the federal government in distributing land, its most compelling resource. The policy called for direct allocation to individuals, but the government soon found it desirable to sell to land companies. Revenue was important. The government planned to profit from the land, practically eliminating for decades the need for taxes. The escape from taxation might be labeled a social goal, and public ends were also served in allocations of land to states to cover their expenses, especially in connection with education. But long-range purposes, such as recreation, better planning of waterfronts, and preservation of forests and minerals, were seldom implemented, though they could have been through land policy. With hindsight, one weeps at the lost opportunities to protect natural beauty.

The government always talked as if its first and only land commitment was the buttressing of its sturdiest independent citizenry, the stout yeoman farmer, through granting him free or cheap land. By protecting rights of squatters and later by passage of the home-

Thomas Moran at work in the Grand Canyon, c. 1904.

stead laws, the government actually practiced its professed ideals. More often, however, the nation allowed large corporate speculators to stand between it and the small farmer. The land speculator was ubiquitous in the American West, fueling the dynamics of expansion while belying national ideals. Land hunger was also the product of advertising. The land companies whipped up desire, just as the railroads did later. Nor was the government quiet. It supported, for example, expeditions of exploration and then freely distributed elaborately illustrated reports. The individualistic myth thus overlooked the role of highly organized companies and governments in encouraging the dynamics of land settlement. Howard Mumford Jones suggests: "Indeed the thesis could be defended that from the landing of Columbus to the latest rise in the cost of houses American history can be 'explained' by the scramble for real estate."[14]

Speculation, inasmuch as it sought profit and not long-term responsibility, was one wellspring of frontier restlessness. Like the telephone man in *The Glass Menagerie*, the westerner fell in love with long distance. Every miner knew that the best strike was just over the mountain. Unless diverted by city lights, every farmer might exchange his hardpan for the next green valley. Only the Pacific would break that set of temptations. "Restless, restless were the gods and always in motion," wrote Stephen Vincent Benét.[15] The spirit was suggested by Charles Dickens when he contrasted the American stagecoach drivers' rousing call "Go ahead" with the English counterpart, "All right!"[16] To Dickens the shouts symbolized American restlessness in contrast with quieter English stability.

Much of the movement stemmed from factors beyond the West; mobility was everywhere the nineteenth century's measure of progress. Mass motion was given high priority with the doctrine of the safety valve. Turner did not emphasize the theory, but his followers claimed that movement westward relieved tensions in eastern centers, making it harder to hold down wages and providing an escape from harsh labor conditions. In a series of studies during the 1940s social scientists showed that workingmen did not so use the West. Nearly $1,500 was the amount of capital needed to set up a western farm, an enormous sum for the average factory hand. Furthermore, because of skill and temperament the factory worker did not readily take up the plow.

Theorists have, however, subsequently introduced a revised model. They now see in the West a psychological safety valve that convinced the Horace Greeleys of the East, rightly or wrongly, that laborers could go West, and this belief affected men's behavior. Moreover, a single leap from an eastern factory to an isolated western farm was not the only move possible. The first man may have moved only a few miles, displacing another who moved a hundred miles further, and so on, in a long series of small steps.

Another safety valve functioned in rural areas, as farmers moved to the city. In all the situations, a selective process was at work, for the dynamics of the movement tended to leave behind responsible and committed people who valued their human and physical environment too much to leave. But whatever the ramifications, the product was a general restlessness, which in turn was disruptive of responsibility to the community. That San Francisco remains the suicide capital of the nation may be related to the general disquietude. When the movement was blocked, the result could be personal frustration, even tragedy.

Geographical activity should not be confused with social mobility. The Horatio Alger myth pictured young men moving freely upward in a fluid class structure with wealth and status for all who practiced diligence and thrift. Such mobility undoubtedly prevailed in the earliest stages of developing economies as society moved west. Very early, however, as soon as the church and the school and the bank were built, probably no more than ten years after the founding of any community, social and economic mobility for a great majority became a dream — widespread, but still a dream.[17]

Regarding the impact of the frontier on American institutions, Turner saw three strong thrusts — individualism, democracy, and nationalism. The first two are closely related. By democracy Turner usually meant mass participation in the decision making of a society; each individual was significant in his own right in a one man, one vote way.

Western communities in their earliest phases enjoyed widespread political participation, while the individualists gathered in mass meetings, as democratic as a Greek city-state. In the context of highly practical needs such as protection from wolves or probate of a will, a remarkable amount of self-government did sprout through the frontier. In many situations — wagon trains, caravans, fur brigades, mining camps — leaders were quickly removed when ineffective. Often the result was disruptive, and the group broke into wrangling parts. When stability was achieved, the individualistic phases of democracy tended to be over. As mature economies developed, popular sovereignty excused the action of the few in gaining control over others, and the process was often associated with vigilantism. Participation thereafter remained the habit and privilege of the rich and powerful; racial minorities and propertyless transients were excluded. The myth persisted that the frontier would forge a homogeneous, democratic society, though in fact control tended to rest with a restricted class. Such citizens were white, Protestant, anti-intellectual, and staunch in their belief in frontier democracy.

One would think that an individualistic impulse might be innovative, with personal differences directing change in basic ideas and institutions. On the frontier, however, it is not easy to find tendencies toward breaking with the past. What posed as reform was seldom substantial; rather it was often a transfer of power from group to group. Farmers in revolt and Regulators rarely wanted new institutions but only more protection under existing ones. In religion the frontier produced a few adaptions, such as the circuit rider and the camp meeting, but old policies and doctrines were reinforced by fears that they might be lost. Women first received the vote in two western states but not because of motives of egalitarian reform: Wyoming wanted to attract settlers, and Utah needed to protect Mormon institutions from the threats of Gentile men. Some improvements in women's status came in education but were overshadowed by the western cult of masculinity. The role of wife and mother crystallized in the pioneer process. Buffeted by uncertainties and determined to remain capitalists, Christians, and patriots, frontiersmen were fearful of losing their

Frederic Remington in his New York studio, 1905.

heritage, and they called on the holy name of tradition far more often than they invoked the spirit of innovation.

If characterized by individualism, the frontier period must be considered to have been much shorter than generally supposed. Within a few years individualistic miners and cowboys were surrounded by large smelters, corporations with heavy foreign investments, the extensive controls of stockgrowers associations. Democratic aspects of claim law, such as prohibition of absentee ownership, applied only to first claimants, and any subsequent holder could work the land or not work the land as he pleased. Committees that actually cleaned up criminal environments were soon replaced by vigilantes acting on less savory motives of racial, political, and economic control. In San Francisco that transition took place in five years, between 1851 and 1856. Almost as quickly on other frontiers, sod houses were replaced by frame and carpet, classless populations became structured, and the violence of homicidal shoot-outs in cowtowns settled down to a statistically normal rate. What persisted was not the fact of the individualistic frontier but the myth of its glory, and that myth became America's most cherished tradition.

The American West enveloped and reinforced the assumption that nature was an embodiment of morality. The wilderness was a teacher for man and a source of his most important truths. In the words of Wordsworth:

> One impulse from a vernal wood
> May teach you more of man
> Of moral evil and of good
> Than all the sages can.[18]

On this side of the Atlantic Wordsworth was echoed in literature by Emerson ("In the woods we return to reason and faith"), Thoreau ("We need the tonic of wilderness. . . . We can never have enough of nature"), Cooper ("This book of nature I can read, and I find it full of wisdom and knowledge"), and in history by Francis Parkman and John Muir with their haunting passion for the wild.[19] Howard Mumford Jones called it the second discovery of America, when men saw that "the voice of God spoke in the thunder of Niagara, on the heights of American mountain ranges, in the elemental power of American rivers, the endless sweep of prairie, desert, and great plains."[20] The feeling was allied with individualism, for nature spoke most clearly to the lone figure. The West was the lost garden for humanity, and, in the words of John G. Neihardt, "groping for the old Adamic dream, he found his patterns in the tree and stream."[21] The pastoral idyll was like a Bierstadt painting, with an isolated figure turned toward the towering truth, the cool springs, or the cloud-filled romanticism of his heartland.

Romantic writers believed in the moral content of nature, but the majority of western men placed a higher priority on monetary profit from nature's resources. Sir Ferdinando Gorges, one of the earliest Englishmen in America, revealed the motivation: "Let us come a little nearer to that which all harken unto and that forsooth is profit."[22] People believed nature had to serve their will instead of mankind's blending into the eternal primal soul. The forests and the prairies and the lakes, as Greeley put it, "must be tamed to hear and heed his voice."[23] Such discrepancies between ideals and behavior are not unusual in history, and so it may not be too surprising to find the actions of settlers in the West at odds with the romantic respect and love for the wilderness.

Arthur K. Moore calls the frontiersman a "grotesque jest" on the initial ideals, "for the actual pioneer displayed few of the qualities predicted of men living close to nature, and the defective culture which they erected in the fabled garden disappointed even modest expectations."[24] In the beginning the Indian had disturbed the environment very little. After the European invasions, the efficiency of

"Song of the Talking Wire" by Henry Farny (1847–1916).

steel and technology made the control and disruption of nature feasible and commonplace. The myth of superabundance — that the West was an inexhaustible cornucopia — paved the way for irresponsible use, especially in the presence of the profit motive and faith in progress. Rich land, forests, oil and mineral aggregates, and clear waters were designated private property subject to the will of individuals, and, as Walt Whitman saw them, men "in the name of Christ and trade . . . deflowered the world's last sylvan glade."[25] A parade of bird and animal life — passenger pigeons, beaver, fur seals, antelope, buffalo — passed before this voracious review. To replace the buffalo, the white man raised cattle, subsequently shipped the animals to distant markets, and so destroyed the plains' ecological cycle of birth, death, decay, and regeneration.

Boasting of additional progress, farmers straggled onto the prairies with barbed wire, windmills, and steel plows. The spirit of Johnny Appleseed marched with them: hemlocks were weeds and forests must die so that apple orchards might bloom. Joyfully accepting the romantic agrarian myth, the simple landowning farmer believed that he personified the virtues of honesty, diligence, and self-reliance. To encourage such farmers was the least the government, even a laissez-faire government, could do; hence the Homestead Act.

John Wesley Powell carried into the Southwest the banner of concern for natural resources. He tried to persuade the nation that laws and customs must be adapted to each changing natural environment. John Muir championed the preservation of undisturbed wilderness, the temple in which the soul is enriched and enlarged. Yet Muir died a sad and defeated man as the lovely Hetch Hetchy Valley in the Sierras filled with dammed waters. The romantic view of nature never died; in the twentieth century, movements back to the land, including renewed interest in Alaska, have become the logical inheritors of the ideas of Powell and Muir.

Though there was ambiguity in the two concepts of nature — in submission to nature's truth and in bending of nature to human will — there is one point at which the two converge. Whether being bent or doing the bending, man is the recipient and expender of power. The frontier infused people with a sense of energy and strength to effect great ends. The self-confidence of those who built cities within a lifetime, who conquered arid plains, who scaled impassable mountains, who felled the largest trees, was not easily reined. Their jokes were long spun tales of the impossible, and in the end Davy Crockett metaphorically stood astride the world. After grappling with and conquering the vaulting, spatial immensity of the continent, Westerners were filled with a consciousness of power, a certainty that nothing could stand in the way of the American pioneer. That feeling may help explain some of the overconfidence, even arrogance, that America continues to exhibit to the world community.

Nature was exploited through capitalism and the application of the principles of private property. According to Howard Mumford Jones, "The notion of individual ownership is in flat contradiction to the emotional appeal of the uncharted forest, the unfenced range, the trackless mountains, and the open sky."[26] Yet the doctrines of private property were too much in the wind to be transcended. Capitalism emerged in Europe at about the same time that America was colonized. The Spanish conquistador was an example of the budding competitive breed. In New France, precapitalist, feudal institutions crumbled long before they collapsed around the Bastille. Many of the first English settlements were supported by a joint-stock company, the economic institution that two hundred years later brought cattle to the plains and smelters to the mines. The fur-trade rendezvous in the Rockies was an application of private profit to the distribution of goods and services. The American frontier was transformed because the East and Europe invested in it. The competitive spirit, seen in men such as Grenville Dodge, building the transcontinental railroad, provided the steam and the energy. Education encouraged faith in a driving individualism that would somehow work for the good of society.

One capitalist, the farmer, was caught in a vicious web. His life was isolated and hard; the more he mechanized his operations, the larger his acreage became. He was forced to rely on exports and suffered from price fluctuations determined in distant shipping centers. The industrialized East, protected by tariffs, charged him dearly for his machines, and the railroads sometimes took as much as half of his product for freight rates. The farmer, however, knew how to protest. He had learned from Nathaniel Bacon and Daniel Shays, men who took the law into their own hands in good frontier fashion. But agriculture was seldom radical enough to propose any basic change in capitalism. The Populists called for the nationalization of the railroads, and Henry George proclaimed vaguely socialistic ideas. But the farmer tended to seek more, not less capitalism, especially if overseas markets could be expanded to his advantage. Economist Walt W. Rostow has suggested that the extent and the limits of governmental activity in the West should be studied as a desirable model for underdeveloped regions throughout the world.[27]

Economic development was facilitated by a close relationship between government and science. Western state universities encouraged engineering and practical subjects rather than the classical curriculum. The federal government supported agricultural extension services, which carried research directly to the farm. Thus the wilderness was rapidly transformed for human use.

In the end the frontier united the nation. The central government had nurtured the West in many ways — by granting it political equality through statehood, subsidizing its economic development, and showering the abundance of nature into its private hands. It opened the public domain for agriculture and the cattle industry. Army engineers surveyed for roads and railroads. Federal policies balanced the export of gold to help import steel, which ultimately built western railroads. After the Civil War the nation sought in haste a new identity, one that had to be forged in the West because the North and South had drunk too much of bitterness. The frontier was an available epic in which both the North and the South had participated. As a Missouri newspaper expressed it in 1858, "The extreme Southerner, the Virginian, the Yankee, recognize each his own image in the many-sided man of the West. They feel they have certain affinities for him, though they have none for each other."[28]

Strip the frontier of its racial ugliness, forget its insistent irresponsibility, and drape the whole in self-reliant individualism, moralizing nature, and fervent nationalism, and America had found its image — beautiful as a redwood forest, honest as a cowboy, powerful as Paul Bunyan, and independent as Davy Crockett at the Alamo. The frontier might have been racist, but it did not tolerate slavery. It might have been decentralized, but it vigorously supported federal legislation for its own economic development. It might have sought promotion from the central government, but it loudly condemned regulation. It might have called for an expansion of foreign markets, but it did not condone colonialism. It might have thought of its rapid expansion as a manifest destiny, but it fought and screamed to make certain that destiny moved in the direction the West desired.

The frontier became our "road of destiny," as Willa Cather expressed it. "Whatever we had missed, we possessed together the precious, the incommunicable past."[29] The pioneer transit, with its recurrent cycle of growth from primitive conditions, motivated by and continually selecting its own myths and legends, pervaded American life and will continue to color tomorrow.

THE TESTAMENT OF VIOLENCE

Violence is a product of the political system of all dynamic societies, especially if it is defined to include threats, intimidation, compulsion, and coercion, as well as more overt forms of physical force. It is unusually evident in a proudly competitive environment such as the American frontier and, among the disadvantaged, may be associated with the growth of group identity and awareness of their potential power. Against such challenges, the established order reacts coercively, violently. To consider violence senseless, criminal, juvenile, factional, fanatic, or un-American, and go no further, is to miss deeper understanding. Tocqueville perceived this when he wrote:

> If ever the free institutions of America are destroyed, that event may be attributed to the omnipotence of the majority, which may at some future time urge the minorities to desperation and oblige them to have recourse to physical force. Anarchy will then be the result, but it will have been brought about by despotism.[30]

A study of violence should involve a careful examination of the context in which it occurs. This is particularly important on the frontier, where the epithet *violent* has been attached mainly to villains and misfits. The good, according to the myth, resorted to violence only with the most extreme provocation. A second look may reveal the inadequacy of this cliché.

If we assume that Americans have an inclination toward violent action, to what extent has the frontier contributed to that propensity? The natural setting was wild and placed a premium on physical toughness. The cult of masculinity that grew up around the cowboy was basically an acknowledgment that strength was required for success. Life on farms, on ranges, and in mines made muscular energy an asset. Action was enthroned over intellect.

More importantly, frontier society was permeated with fear and doubt. Primitive conditions threatened established social values. In the period of exploration and first contact, the wilderness could be a glorious experience, as it was for Frémont. Yet living day after day listening to the monotony of the winds and scratching out a living could produce not glory but fear of being stripped of civilization. Frustration grew from cultural deprivation. Frequently, though not as often as we like to think, the forms of law and order were missing: lack of authority feeds fear. Furthermore, on the frontier nearly all civilians were armed. Few societies have allowed such unrestricted ownership of firearms. The gun on the cabin wall within easy reach, whatever its value as a hunting tool, meant that any meeting could quickly become an armed mob. When Parkman moved west across the Missouri and bade adieu to the principles of Blackstone's *Commentaries*, he recognized that the foreigner, Mr. Blackstone, had been supplanted by the very American Mr. Colt. Even so, the pervasiveness of weapons was probably less a cause than a symptom of conflict.

It makes a difference whether violence is in defense of established norms or in quest of new values, whether it is to defend an elite or to champion an outcast minority. From any viewpoint, the violence of farmers in revolt must surely be distinguished from the violence of an army fighting Indians. Values and context may be better seen if we separate unofficial from official violence.

Unofficial group violence or vigilantism may be defined as organized, extra-legal activity. Richard Maxwell Brown identifies 326 vigilante organizations in American history and believes that a complete list would undoubtedly reach 500, excluding lynching mobs.[31] These organizations are known to have taken 729 victims. In the Far West between 1849 and 1902, Brown isolates 210 vigilante movements. California provided the model; Montana, the deadliest single episode; Texas, the largest number. Only Oregon and Utah suffered little or not at all from vigilante fever.

Just as Americans have often talked peace while encouraging violence, so have they praised the law while extolling vigilantism. The South Carolina Regulators of the 1760s were widely lauded for their effectiveness. By the 1840s excesses in Illinois and the Ozarks had given the local counterparts of the Regulators the taint of anarchism. In San Francisco the designation was changed from Regulators to Vigilantes, and the movement's righteousness regilded the idea for a half-century.

Lynching of John Heith, Tombstone, Arizona, 1884.

If unofficial group violence is typified by the vigilantes, individual violence should evoke an image of a lone man, hard knuckled, standing at the end of a dusty street, about to face an equally isolated individual man to man. Whether he is a trapper, a miner, a cowboy, or a marshal, he walks alone toward his timeless and violent rendezvous with evil. In the image, the struggle is stark, primitive, internal, and personal. It is not political, social, or economic, not tinged with class pressures, workingmen's ideas, or businessmen's motives. When we examine this tradition with some attention to historical accuracy, however, we discover that individual violence, like that of groups, mirrors a multitude of tensions in the social structure. Harold L. Nieburg writes, "Disturbed and distraught persons . . . are both the victims and the heralds of social change."[32]

The social bandit, like Jesse James and Joaquin Murieta, appears in myth and legend. He was the frontier's Robin Hood or primitive rebel, as Eric Hobsbawm calls him.[33] He was strictly rural and pre-capitalist, autonomous, highly romantic, even millennial. Because presumably he robbed the rich and gave to the poor, his crimes were crimes only in the eyes of the wealthy or the state; no genuine democrat would consider him guilty. Honorable, young, unattached, ephemeral, he represented the weak against the powerful. And when he finally met his end, he was brought down through betrayal within his circle, the law coming too late or in a bungling fashion. Often, reports of his death were considered false, for how could a man who was the spirit of the people die?

Adding history to legend, we find that this bandit arose out of social turmoil. Joaquin Murieta sent terror into the hearts of the prosperous Anglo farmers of the San Joaquin valley in the 1850s. In that period, Mexicans were suffering the first consequences of their newly reduced status following the conquest of California. They were losing land and social position, and their future seemed bleak. For them, Murieta's violence was sweet revenge.

Jesse James translated in a roughly analogous way the hates and frustrations of thousands of people who had suffered in the Civil War at the hands of the Union army. He fought the dragon of the railroad, which symbolized not only the North but corporate wealth and industrial power as well. The story of Jesse James verifies the claim of Hobsbawm that the social bandit is an eternal peasant, raising a cry for revenge on whoever oppresses the poor. In some way the oppressor will be curbed. The bandit's act may seem futile, but, Hobsbawm warns, such violence may become epidemic against a prevailing society that finds itself "in a condition of abnormal tension and disruption."[34]

In this connection, the effect of war on crime should not go unnoted, as illustrated in hundreds of cases, those of Jesse James, Joaquin Murieta, and John Wesley Hardin (a gunman and former Confederate) among them. The excessive brutality of the Civil War is generally recognized, more so than that of the Mexican War. The fighters between 1846 and 1848 often used guerrilla tactics — the method of the Texas Rangers — and the hit-and-run attacks on both sides during the march to Mexico City. The Mexican War could account for some of the attitudes of veterans toward Mexicans. In the nation at large there was a marked increase of prison commitments following both the Mexican and Civil wars. In the year after the Civil War, violent crimes increased 50 percent. The 1867 annual report of the Kansas State Penitentiary indicated that of 126 convicts, 104 were veterans and 60 of these believed their service in the army marked the beginning of their criminal turn of mind. Facts were equally disturbing in New York, Massachusetts, Kansas, and Pennsylvania.[35] Philip D. Jordan calls violence on the frontier after both the Mexican and Civil Wars "epidemic."[36] In the West a war against Indians was fought throughout the frontier period, undoubtedly having a continuing effect on individual crime.

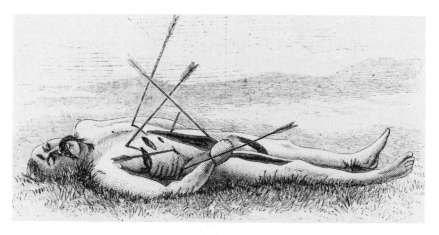

Body of a sergeant, Kansas-Colorado Indian Wars, 1867.

Crime among minority groups often resulted from confusion and misunderstanding about what the law actually was. Indians hardly accepted white law. Former Mexican nationals likewise faced a new set of statutes based on unfamiliar principles. For example, under Mexican law a salt lick in the Guadalupe Mountains near the border in Texas was communal property; all men could lead their herds to it without cost or interference. When Anglo law was imposed on the area, the salt lick fell into private hands, and charges were immediately levied on its use. Mexicans were understandably furious, and violence erupted.[37]

Law enforcement on the frontier was a confusing welter of terms and jurisdictions. Powers were unclear and overlapped one another like shingles on a shanty of inconsistency. A town's peace officer might be called policeman, constable, or marshal; sometimes he was elected, sometimes appointed by the city council. Counties traditionally used the title sheriff, though occasionally towns, too, adopted it. The federal marshal was appointed by the president and acted as an arm of the United States district court. These officials supervised jails and hunted criminals, but their functions varied considerably and sometimes included sweeping out the courtroom, cleaning the streets, and, most important, collecting taxes. The federal marshal's duties embraced army desertion, mail theft, and crimes committed on Indian reservations. There was plenty of room for chicanery, particularly when communities deliberately hired criminals for their lawmen, assuming that it takes a killer to catch one.

On more than a few occasions the confusion led law officers to oppose and fight one another. On October 26, 1881, in the nearly legendary shoot-out at the O.K. Corral in Tombstone, Arizona, Virgil Earp, serving as both town marshal and deputy United States marshal, had enlisted as deputies his brothers Wyatt and Morgan and John "Doc" Holliday. John Behan, appointed by Territorial Governor John C. Frémont and allied with the rival Clanton faction, acted as county sheriff. Seeking to arrest the Clanton gang, Virgil and his deputies approached the corral, while Sheriff Behan tried to prevent the officers from doing what they considered to be their duty. The gunfight followed, and immediately afterward the sheriff moved in to arrest Virgil, a federal and local officer, along with his deputies, on charges of murder. The Earps and Holliday were later cleared. Because of such occurrences, law enforcement was too conflicting and antagonistic to be generally respected.[38]

Violence exercised by the government is, for the historian, difficult to interpret. We tend not to consider the coercive nature of government as violence. Government legitimizes its power through law, and, whatever its social utility, the legal system tends to obscure the coercion involved. Then, too, as with all violence, official or otherwise, judgments can be made only in the context of purpose. If we assume the legitimacy of unionizing and collective bargaining, the use of military force at Ludlow and Coeur d'Alene was unjust. The ultimate test of the legitimacy of official violence is the extent to which it serves the long-term needs of the people, especially when one group seeks new status relative to other groups. Success breeds acceptability.

The problem of context can be further illustrated by the sad story of violence between the government and the Indian. Although Washington acted with popular support and although the army may only have implemented legitimate power, the violence exercised against the Cherokees in the removal from Georgia to Oklahoma, to cite one case, must nevertheless be considered unjust. The Cherokees were not part of the American political system; they could not vote, they could not testify in court; most of their appeals to public opinion were fruitless. It is not improper to describe them as a dispossessed minority seeking admission to the political structure. The Cherokees were educated, spoke English, read newspapers, elected intelligent spokesmen, had settled down to agricultural pursuits, and successfully raised cotton on plantations with black slaves. They were what Richard E. Rubenstein calls "a domestic group denied the privilege of citizenship."[39] Such groups have been admitted to the political system, but only when the prevailing structure was sufficiently racked with doubts and factionalism to open the way to reorganization. Alas, the Indian was never faced with such a possibility or presented

Execution of thirty-eight Sioux: Mankato, Minnesota,
December 26, 1862.

with such a wedge. Laborers and some immigrant groups succeeded; the black man and the Indian did not.

The Texas Rangers, a local example of official violence, was a group first formed by Anglo settlers in Mexican Texas in the 1820s. The force became official with the birth of the Lone Star Republic, and it acted as a guerrilla band along the border during the Mexican War. After the Civil War it regrouped into two branches, one to fight Indians to the north and the other to patrol the southern border with a special eye on Mexicans. Rangers were not above crossing the Rio Grande if necessary to get their man, and on one occasion they even tangled with the Mexican army. Though they gained a reputation for shooting before all the evidence was in, most of the community blessed them when they brought back criminals such as Sam Bass and John Wesley Hardin. For a Texas Ranger, violence toward Indian, Mexican, and rustler was as natural as branding a calf. In the diplomatic words of a leading Texas historian, the Texas Rangers "seldom gave any Mexican, whether a national of the United States or of Mexico, the benefit of the doubt."[40]

One reason westerners supported such rangers was fear of anarchy. Curiously enough, government policy, or lack of it, was largely to blame for this alarm. In the heyday of laissez-faire and the minimal state, the nation never saw fit to institute a territorial police force comparable to the Royal Canadian Mounted Police. Such a body might have impartially executed the law and at least occasionally protected the Indian as well as the white. Instead, central force was exerted only if absolutely necessary, when situations had grown out of hand; witness of the national guard shooting at already enraged miners. The vacuum of order was an excuse and a symptom, and it resulted in upheavals that undermined justice.

Once again, we see how hard it is to separate the frontier from a larger context. The nineteenth century, especially after the Civil War, was a discordant period for the nation. Three presidents were shot within four decades. That fact underscores the tendencies erupting in all segments of society — in vigilantism, against organized labor, and with the Indian, to mention a few. The frontier, however, played a more influential role than that of reflector or projector of the national psyche. It lent respectability to certain kinds of violence and so offered excuses and cover-ups for social groups, including the government, to parade their barbarities as righteousness.

18

The West in Our Time

James Michener focused on Colorado for his novel *Centennial* (1974), but in effect he recounted much of the history of the West. He himself was a Pennsylvanian who had taken a job in Denver, where he became caught up in the "fire and fury that characterized life in the West." He was struck by the people he met — taller (he wondered if that was because they ate more salad); intellectually less speculative, though at the same time willing to accept new ideas; and vitally aware of their mission to build a subnation within America. The future of that region, Michener concluded, was beyond the imagination of any single individual.[1] The history of the modern West may well require a composite of many such individuals. The dozens in the pages that follow will provide a start. They will tell a story of increasingly rapid growth in population; of expanding industry associated with science and technology; of automobiles and planes and an intensified concern for the environment; of politics moving from Progressive desires for reform to more recent conservative fears of change; of a society as pluralistic as a gold-rush mining camp but far more dedicated to a variety of religious values and artistic expressions. Michener might have said that the West in the present, as well as in the future, is already beyond the imagination of any single individual.

ECONOMIC AND POPULATION GROWTH

Take, for example, the imagination of Amadeo Peter Giannini, founder of what would become the largest private bank in the world. This tall, massive, lumbering, deep-voiced, stubborn tyrant of a man knew how important money was to the small investor, and he envisioned making it available on western, not eastern, terms. In good frontier tradition, his orientation was to the land; it was farmers he first sensed were in deepest need.

Giannini had been raised in the 1870s on a forty-acre orchard in fruit-growing country near San Jose. When the family moved to San Francisco, the teenager remained far more interested in the produce business — the crates of lettuce and peaches in the predawn markets — than in school. By the age of nineteen he owned a third of his stepfather's firm and was buying whole future crops directly from the farmers. Not only was he appreciative of the earth and its bounty, but he was coming to know the uses and power of money.

At the age of thirty-three he left the produce business and entered a savings and loan bank. San Francisco was then the financial capital of the West, providing loans for ranchers, miners, and lumbermen all over the hinterland (though usually to the wealthy ones, and at high interest rates). Giannini wanted to offer small loans to individuals at reasonable interest, and to do so, he set up his own Bank of Italy in 1904. Small depositors were encouraged, and there were enough of them to bring him one million dollars in the first two years.

In the earthquake of 1906 most San Francisco banks saw their vaults sink into hopeless ruin. Giannini managed to cart out of the burning city $80,000 hidden under the fruit crates of his old produce firm. While the city burned, he reopened his bank for full operations in another building, reemphasizing his reputation for providing safety for small depositors and lending to small borrowers in distress. By the end of 1906 he had doubled his depositors and his assets.

Giannini extended his philosophy, initiating branch banks, which he called "money stores," so that local farmers and businessmen could have easy access, and be in contact with local managers and personnel. By the 1920s he had increased his branches to nearly a hundred.

While he tried to avoid speculative land booms and oil risks, Giannini supported and nurtured some new industries, such as motion pictures. He lent funds for the first nickelodeon in San Francisco in 1909. Eventually he had invested some $50 million in the films of Douglas Fairbanks, Charlie Chaplin, Harold Lloyd, and Walt Disney.

In 1930, seeking greater respectability and a broader base for expansion, the Bank of Italy became the Bank of America. Within a few years it had grown to be the fourth largest in the nation. Its parent corporation owned other banks in Arizona, Nevada, Oregon, and Washington. Just after World War II the bank surpassed the Chase Manhattan Bank of New York in number of depositors and

*Foundations of growth: Henry Kaiser (second from left)
and fellow contractors at Hoover Dam, 1935.*

assets, and thereby became the world's largest. The achievement had
taken forty-one years in the life of Amadeo Giannini. Before he died
in 1949, vitally aware of the electronic future emerging from the
inventions of World War II, he still could smile and say, "the West
hasn't even started yet."[2]

Just before World War I, while Giannini was finding opportunities
in banking, a young Henry J. Kaiser was foreseeing the need for highways in Vancouver, in the Pacific Northwest. In 1914 the automobile
was already wheeling its way into the virtual transformation of the
land, and until the late 1920s Kaiser sharpened his skills in large-scale
construction by creating roads for Henry Ford. Kaiser was an
energetic, smiling German who would work eagerly for sixteen hours
a day. His genius at organization was tested and proved in the 1930s
when he led six companies in the construction of the Hoover Dam.
Thereafter his name became permanently linked with western water.

He was instrumental in the construction of the Bonneville and Grand Coulee dams on the Columbia River, as well as a second dam on the Colorado (the Parker) and the Shasta Dam in northern California. To supply the latter, he built the largest cement plant in the world at Permanente, near San Jose. In the 1930s Kaiser's construction firm was responsible for the massive concrete pillars from which the San Francisco-Oakland Bay Bridge was suspended.

As World War II threatened, Kaiser turned his attention from concrete to steel. Although steel had long been produced in the West, primarily at Pueblo, Colorado, the total production was negligible. The pressures of World War II changed the market situation dramatically, and early in the war, mills rose at Houston and Daingerfield, Texas; Geneva, Utah; and Tulsa, Oklahoma. In April 1942 at Fontana, California, Kaiser broke ground for his mill. The Kaiser plant's first priority became the production of the huge prefabricated plates for the hulls of merchant ships, high on the list of urgent wartime necessities. He once said, "I'm a builder, and if you call yourself a builder you ought to be able to build anything."[3] Thus to highways, dams, and bridges, Kaiser added steel and ships.

In the first months of the war his shipyards rose at San Pedro, Seattle, and four centers around the San Francisco Bay. Before the war was over, he was part of a fourfold increase in western steel production and could therefore finish each Liberty Ship in only twenty-five days. At one time in 1943 a ship was rolling down one of Kaiser's launching ways every ten hours. More than 300,000 civilian employees, including women and minorities, paved the way for the postwar ascendency of manufacturing in areas such as California and Texas. Kaiser had lured his work force from all over the country, using time-tested western methods, such as ballyhooing the climate. But he also offered subsidized medical care. His Kaiser-Permanente Health Plan, now independent, remains one of the strongest health maintenance organizations in the nation, covering well over a million people.

Kaiser died in 1967 in Hawaii, the new western state he had come to love in his later years. His life was a mural of western industrial growth. His projects were most often government sponsored and financed, but that fact, too, was integral to the western story. Federal agencies had been underwriting western development from wagon roads and army surveys to the land-grant universities and agricultural experiment stations. By the 1970s western states were receiving major proportions of the defense and aerospace contracts. Arrell Gibson has pointed out that in 1972 his state of Oklahoma paid through various forms of taxation to the federal government $1,600,000,000 while it received from the federal government $2,800,000,000.[4] Yet Kaiser, like so many western individualists, was the man who grasped the opportunities as they came his way, and in the process he founded an industrial empire.

Howard Hughes, a tall, lean Texan, was another legend in his own time, and his rise, like Kaiser's, was made possible by the phenomenal western population growth. Houston, where Hughes was born, mushroomed from 138,000 in 1920 to more than 1,300,000 in 1976, when Hughes died. At the age of nineteen he inherited the Hughes Tool Company, maker of oil-drilling equipment. His youthful imagination was caught, however, not by black gold, but by the wild blue yonder. By the time he was thirty, he had set a world aviation speed record, 152 miles an hour. In his forties he was designing and flying experimental planes. A near-fatal crash in 1946 did not stop him in the following year from piloting the maiden (and sole) flight of his *Spruce Goose*, a plywood monster, the largest plane ever built.

Meanwhile, he was putting his money — a lot of it — where his heart was. He founded Hughes Aircraft in 1932 at the age of twenty-seven. The firm prospered less from the production of his planes than from satellites and weapons-guidance systems. In the 1950s he controlled the stock of Transcontinental World Airways, but, accused of mismanagement, he sold his TWA shares for $546 million. Much later, in 1970, he bought what became Hughes Air West, which carried passengers and freight throughout the sun belt.

Like many another young man, Hughes had dreamed of making movies, so he turned to Hollywood in the 1920s. At the age of twenty-two he assumed direction of a film he had been financing, *Hell's Angels*, a story of World War I aviators. Before it was completed in 1930, the film was transformed into a "talkie." Jean Harlow, at that time an unknown, replaced the original star. In 1946 Hughes's second major film, *The Outlaw*, based on the life of Billy the Kid, was promoted by unusually sensational advertising of its star, Jane Russell. In 1948 he purchased an entire studio, RKO, which under his leadership nearly went bankrupt.

From his youth Hughes had been called the bashful millionaire, but his bashfulness was only part of a strange personality. As he became older, his fear of germs and death became obsessive, and he increasingly withdrew from social contact. He was seldom seen, even by his closest associates. From his penthouses, however, the investments continued. In 1967 after the sale of his TWA stock he began buying property in Las Vegas and Reno — such hotels and casinos as the Desert Inn, the Sands, the Silver Slipper, and Harold's Club. By the time he died in 1976, he was one of the wealthiest men in the world.[5]

The life of Howard Hughes was, indeed, a modern western tall tale. But it also embodied industrial and demographic expansion. Personally colorful, he was only a minor member of a crew of aircraft industrialists, a group that spread across the West from Texas to Washington, men such as Donald Douglas, William E. Boeing, John K. Northrop, and Allan Lockheed. When Hughes dabbled in films, his base was the entertainment factory that California was fast becoming in the 1920s. From his hermitage in Las Vegas, he presided over part of the western tourist industry that stretched from those gambling tables in Nevada to the dude ranches of Phoenix, the ski slopes of the Rockies, and the beaches of the Pacific and Gulf coasts. Tourism was what Earl Pomeroy has called "the search for the golden West." It was an industry of princely proportions that helped make Howard Hughes a billionaire.

Like his entire fortune, Hughes's airlines and factories were grounded on the phenomenal population boom in the West. In the region from the Rocky Mountain states westward, the population increase per decade since 1900 has been double that of the national norm, with the exception of the 1960s when it was slightly lower. From 1900 to 1910 the West jumped by 66 percent while the nation rose only 21 percent. All figures dipped dramatically during the 1930s with an equally sharp increase following World War II. Neil Morgan has noted that in one decade, between 1950 and 1960, the states west of the Rockies grew by a number equivalent to the population of all the New York boroughs combined.[6] It was a mobile and restless population, true to its western forebears, now carrying more passports than the Americans of any other region. And it was a population ranging between the very young and the retired and elderly. Many of the latter had swelled the suburbs around Los Angeles, Phoenix, and Dallas.

Generally the West was prepared for that great migration where water and power were concerned. Henry Kaiser's part in the damming of the Colorado and Columbia rivers certainly helped. Out of the early conservation period had come the flowering of irrigation projects and the reclamation of arid lands. The inspiration of John Wesley Powell and the warnings of John Muir were felt anew. A good example was the advantage taken by such men as George Chaffey in the diversion of Colorado River water into the lower Colorado desert. The Imperial Valley thus created would ultimately shelter big farms producing fruit and vegetables practically the year around. As we have seen, the Newlands Act of 1902 provided federal money for such projects throughout the West. One of the earliest such diversions — water from the Truckee River to Nevada farms and ranches — caused Pyramid Lake nearly to wither away. As the lake was the economic and spiritual base for the Paiute Indians, the results were tragic, and the law, even to the Supreme Court, has provided no relief. Similar conflicts have appeared throughout the water-hungry West.

Up until the 1970s the government still hoped to limit its water delivery to farms under 160 acres, but small farms were failing, especially in the agricultural slumps of the 1920s and 1930s. The economic pressures for larger farms were so strong that by the 1970s the size of the average farm in the West had risen to 1,500 acres.

Agribusiness, though never a major tenant of western acreage, grew more and more important this century. We have seen its roots in the Dakota bonanza farms and in syndicates running such huge operations as the King Ranch. Large-scale corporate farming began to spread throughout the West whether in wheatland, corn belt, or fruit orchard. The Di Giorgio Company, for example, not only owned more than 50,000 acres but marketed its products under the S & W and Treesweet labels. It ran its farms from board rooms in San Francisco and raised capital on the New York Stock Exchange, and in 1947, reached an annual income of more than $18 million. Its tamarisk-lined 11,000 acres near Bakersfield housed six hundred farm workers, an equal number came in by the day, and hundreds more were hired at peak seasons. Anglos, Mexicans, and Filipinos who worked there were segregated in their housing and dining. These were Western agribusiness laborers described by Carey McWilliams in *Factories in the Field* (1939), punching a time clock, working at piece or hourly wage rates, living in a shack or a company barracks, and lacking all contact with the real owners of the factory farm.[7]

In the past, big ranches and corporate mining had brought strikes of working men to the corrals and smelters. As business organized to control its markets, labor continued to seek direction of its own product, the labor supply. We have already seen how the Knights of Labor unionized cowboys and how violent were the strikes of miners at Coeur d'Alene and Ludlow. The Western Federation of Miners trained one of the West's leading militants, a one-eyed giant of a man, Bill Haywood. In 1905 Big Bill led his miners into the Industrial Workers of the World. The Wobblies, as they were called, appealed to laborers forgotten by the major unions, such as lumberjacks in the northwestern forests, and especially migrant workers on the big western farms. The Wobblies believed that only force would bring down the managerial elite, but they added songs to their violence and so tended to be immortalized in such ballads as "Joe Hill": "Said Joe, 'what they forgot to kill went on to organize.'"

Joe was actually Joel Hillstrom, a good-looking radical Swede, who joined the IWW in 1910 and became its troubadour. His best known song was "The Preacher and the Slave" in which the establishment minister could offer no more to the slaving worker than "pie in the sky by and by." In 1915 Joe was convicted of murder. The firing squad turned the handsome blond into a martyr, for the union always believed that the execution was motivated by desire to squelch organized labor. Hill's last words to Bill Haywood were, "Don't waste any time in mourning, organize!" By World War I, Wobblies numbered more than 100,000, including 20,000 farm workers stretching from the wheat fields of the Midwest to the fruit orchards of California.[8] But far too radical and anarchistic for American labor, the Wobblies faded from the scene in the late 1920s.

Not until the 1960s did migrant farm labor find another champion, César Chávez. In the Great Depression, César's father had lost his small farm near Yuma, and the family, including five children, joined the caravans of pickers following the ripening crops. Moving and working, the boy attended more than thirty schools, never reaching beyond the seventh grade. As a young man in the Mexican barrio of San Jose he was inspired to join the Community Service Organization in a drive to register Mexicans for the vote. After 1962 the skills he had learned were applied to the organization of agricultural workers. His United Farm Workers led their first strike against the grape growers beginning in 1965. It included a nationwide campaign for all sympathetic consumers to boycott grapes, and the effects were felt as far away as England and Sweden.

With the philosophy of Thoreau's nonviolent civil disobedience and the techniques of Mahatma Gandhi, Chávez dramatized the situation with a long fast, broken by a communion in the fields during which Robert Kennedy knelt beside him at the altar. In the spring of 1966 the growers, including the Di Giorgio Company, began to buckle.

Chávez, too, can illustrate the complexity of western economic life; his subsequent major strike in 1970 was not just an action against the lettuce growers, but also an internecine labor conflict with the Teamsters Union. And if he carried some of the flair of the Wobblies, he embodied even more the deeper feelings of the Mexican people. The spirit of Murieta and Cortina was never far off. Chávez's support was also related to an unprecedented Mexican-American population growth. In California alone, Hispanics increased in number from 368,000 in 1930 to 1,426,000 in 1960.[9]

César Chávez (flanked by wife and brother) leading rally, 1975.

Similarly intricate economic and social interweaving can be traced in the environmental movement, much of which can be seen through the life of Stewart Udall. Arizona, with its pine and aspen forests, saguaro deserts, and such glories as the Grand Canyon, might well instill worries that economic and population growth would destroy the West's natural grandeur. Stewart Udall was one such anxious Arizonan. His grandfather, a polygamous Mormon bishop in the 1880s, had helped transform an area around St. John in northern Arizona with dams, reservoirs, and cooperative irrigation. His descendants became a clan of office holders, the largest in Arizona history, including two state supreme court justices and two mayors of Phoenix.

When Udall was thirty-eight years old, he followed this family tradition by his election to the national Congress. He fought for the return of 100,000 acres to Arizona National Forests, for desalinization projects, and against water pollution. John F. Kennedy (who called conservation "the highest form of national thrift") appointed him Secretary of the Interior in 1961, where he served until 1969. His first act was an eighteen-month moratorium on the sale of public lands. He became a strong advocate of hydroelectric public power, especially for domestic and rural consumers. He proposed newer and more efficient uses of coal. During his administration he set aside eleven new wildlife refuges. A Republican political opponent called Udall "the greatest secretary that has ever held the office."

"The modern land raiders," Udall wrote in *The Quiet Crisis* (1963), "like the public-land raiders of another era, are ready to justify short-term gains by seeking to minimize the long-term losses. 'Present the repair bill to the next generation' has always been their unspoken slogan." Ecology would undercut these despoilers by "the land ethic of tomorrow," which should stress, as it did with Thoreau, "the live-and-help-live logic of the great chain of life."[10]

PROGRESSIVE TO CONSERVATIVE POLITICS

Issues such as federal assistance to the economy and the conservation of western resources required political action. Perhaps, then, it is not surprising that the West in the twentieth century should take a place increasingly near the center of national politics. At the turn of the century many westerners already were leading the way. It was the Progressive period, and the greatest Progressive of them all was Theodore Roosevelt, who as president of the United States never forgot his restorative, youthful years as a Dakota rancher. The ranks of Progressive leaders were disproportionately peppered with westerners such as Robert La Follette of Wisconsin and Hiram Johnson of California. The "Oregon System," which came to stand for Progressive experiments nationwide, was an inheritance from William S. U'Ren from the Portland area, a Republican Progressive who saw enacted women's suffrage, direct election of senators, workmen's compensation, and the initiative and referendum. A more powerful western voice came from Idaho, beginning shortly after its admission as a state in 1890.

William E. Borah achieved national reputation in 1906 as the state's prosecutor in the trial of Big Bill Haywood, who had come to personify the Wobblies and radical labor. Haywood was charged with conspiracy in the murder of Frank Steunenberg, former governor of Idaho, who took a promanagement stand. Clarence Darrow, who defended Haywood, succeeded in getting him acquitted. Borah's position was ambiguous, for, like many Republican Progressives, he opposed monopoly, especially in the form of the railroad. He consistently tried to curb the excessive powers of big business, yet was also opposed to organized labor, at least the militant variety. At the same time, Borah was a silver-tongued orator for silver interests, and represented Idaho in the U.S. Senate for thirty-four years. From 1906 to 1940 his unusually rich voice was raised in behalf of the direct election of senators, the income tax, and the creation of the Department of Labor.

In these reforms he was supported by a network of western Progressive activities. In his state of Idaho, women had gained voting rights in 1896, the result of a movement led in the Northwest by a lively persuader, Abigail Scott Duniway. We have already seen how the pressure to grant women the vote had its earliest successes in western states such as Wyoming and Utah. Charlotte Perkins Gilman was attending Women's Congresses in San Francisco in the 1890s. By 1914 all but one state west of the Rockies had granted women the vote, while only one state east of the Mississippi had done so.

In the twentieth century the West has sent four presidents to Washington — Herbert Hoover, Lyndon Johnson, Richard Nixon, and Ronald Reagan (not to mention such hopefuls as Henry Wallace, Alfred Landon, Barry Goldwater, Wayne Morse, Mark Hatfield, and Jerry Brown.) Perhaps it is the ex-western movie star, the ranch owner who loves to ride horses and chop wood, who bespeaks most of modern western politics. For one thing, Ronald Reagan, in becoming governor and president, was the product of political campaign managers. The firm of Whittaker and Baxter of San Francisco, whose clients included Richard Nixon, was one of the earliest packagers of politicians, but Reagan chose the Los Angeles firm of Spencer and Roberts. With Reagan their job was not easy, for in 1966 when he ran for governor of California he had never held a public office.

Born and educated in Illinois, he had worked as a radio sportscaster before going to Hollywood in 1938, at the age of twenty-six, to become an actor. Most of his movie roles were in westerns, the genre that, with the influence of Gary Cooper and Tom Mix, was at the height of its popularity. The political stance Reagan exhibited in the Screen Actors' Guild was decidedly to the left. As he began to make money and purchase California land, he turned further and further to the right. By the time he became governor in 1967, he promised to reduce the cost of government, in his words to "squeeze and cut and trim." His position was not unlike that of the individualistic cattleman of the nineteenth century, who was perfectly willing to allow the government to provide him with the open range but opposed to taxation for social purposes. In similar fashion Reagan vigorously opposed the federal government's 160-acre limit on the users of water from federal projects, while at the same time denouncing

*The politician as westerner: President Ronald Reagan
at his Santa Barbara ranch, 1981.*

Chávez and the grape boycott by the farm workers. In his two terms as governor he continued to crusade against social welfare (his heaviest cuts were in the fields of mental-health care and higher education). Social welfare was for Reagan "a cancer eating at our vitals." In the 1970s he took that crusade to the national level and in 1980 was successful in gaining the presidency. As president he was able to extend the 160-acre limit to 640 acres, reversing the Newlands Act of 1902. This move reflects much of what has changed in the West and much that has remained the same.

THE PLURALISTIC SOCIETY

If politicians such as Borah and Reagan illustrate the West's rising political significance, it is equally true that political life has reflected a changing society. Barbara Jordan, for example, was a notable Texas representative in Congress, but her life also has paved the way to a more active role for the black people in the West.

Barbara Jordan was raised in Houston, Howard Hughes's home-town, but instead of inheriting a fortune she was raised on one of the few paved streets in the Negro section. Her father was a preacher and her family good churchgoing Baptists, but the most important influence on Barbara came from her maverick grandfather, a religiously independent junk dealer. He kept her in money, because, unlike her sisters, she was willing to help him sort rags. He read her the diction-ary and "Songs of the Blood Washed," and told her that the world was not a playground but a schoolroom.

In her all-black schools she did not question segregation, but her high school debate team raised the issue of integration in her mind. Traveling with the team, she endured the dreary round of segregated motels and drinking fountains, and the back doors of restaurants. Her skin was very dark, and from all sides came the message that black was bad. She saw little hope for change, but while still in high school she announced that she would become a lawyer.

Her debate coach at Texas Southern University in Houston en-couraged her, and she enrolled at Boston University Law School. She enjoyed entering the front doors of Boston restaurants. It was a heady time, shortly after *Brown vs. Board of Education*, in which the Supreme Court had struck down the doctrine of separate but equal. She knew it would take more than a court decision. Some people had to push, and the ones who could make it in the white world could best do the pushing.

After passing the bar in both Massachusetts and Texas, she prac-ticed law in Houston out of her parents' dining room. At the same time she entered local politics and began to receive standing ovations on her speeches for social reform. She ran for the Texas House of Representatives and lost twice, being told that she had too much against her — her color, her sex, and her broad shoulders. Still, she persisted. Her first election to the Texas Senate came only after re-districting, which followed civil-rights agitation. The year was 1966, and she was the first black woman in the Texas legislature.

Though she shed many a tear at the assassination of John Kennedy, it was Lyndon Johnson and his civil-rights emphasis that led her into national politics. After he left the White House, he helped her directly in local campaigning. "You will always be my president," she told him.[11] She was elected to the national Congress in 1972.

Johnson had suggested she serve on the Judiciary Committee, and hence her national visibility in 1973 as that committee sat before television cameras in hearings on the impeachment of President Richard Nixon. These hearings, which led to the resignation of Nixon over the Watergate scandal, revealed Barbara Jordan as a cool, rational,

*Political pluralism Texas style: Barbara Jordan and
Lyndon Johnson, Houston, 1971.*

thorough mind in a crisis situation. She had come a long way from
sorting rags with her grandfather in Houston, to leading her people
and representing her state of Texas. And one might add that the West
had come a long way in designating a black woman from Texas to sit
in official judgment on another westerner who was also the president
of the United States.

During Jordan's political career, the black population in the West
was skyrocketing, especially after World War II. A good example was
southeastern Los Angeles, an area once called Mudtown and later
Watts, which between 1945 and 1965 increased by 600 percent.
Disease, death, and unemployment rates all remained stubbornly and
tragically higher for the black people. On August 11, 1965, a hot
smoggy day, mobs of black people in Watts erupted. For four successive days and nights angry mobs fought with police and the National
Guard, looted white stores, and burned hundreds of buildings within
a forty-mile radius. Thirty-four people were killed in the Watts riots,
and racial conflict had reached a new level of violence in the West.

Western blacks spoke out for what became known as "Black Nationalism," the militant assertion of Negro power. It spurned integration as a trap; separation was championed. Black culture was distinct and beautiful, not to be watered down by integration. Another black woman in the late 1960s represented this radical position. Angela Davis was born late in World War II of an educated black family in Birmingham, Alabama. Both her mother and father were teachers, her mother holding an M.A. degree from New York University. They provided her with a childhood of church youth groups, Girl Scout meetings, and piano and clarinet lessons. As a young person she was motivated to join pickets in protest of segregation.

Much of this life she put behind her when she went to Brandeis University in Boston to study French literature, where she graduated Phi Beta Kappa. During her senior year at Brandeis she studied with Herbert Marcuse and was excited by his amalgam of Freud and Marx. Marcuse, a refugee from Nazi Germany, was becoming the philosopher of the New Left, claiming that the counterculture, in spite of its non-working–class status, was one of the few fists that might break through the established economy. Marcuse sent Davis for postgraduate study in Frankfurt, where she was further radicalized. While she was in Europe, Marcuse moved to the University of California at San Diego, and so in 1967 she followed him to California.

In the 1960s the West was proving to be the bellwether of both extreme conservatism (witness Ronald Reagan) and of extreme social protest (with such leaders as Angela Davis). Youths and hippies, in disturbing numbers, were rebelling against established systems. Students at Berkeley were barricading streets, pelting police, and demanding free speech in order that the Vietnam War might be stopped. New Leftists were decrying the quality of life around them: excessive competition, workers alienated from their work, gross materialsim, and moral breakdown. The prevailing society, though strong in gun power, had lost its heart and soul. Davis, taking her lead from Marcuse, felt that black people, because they were held in bondage, might lead other revolutionaries on the road to social change. In any case, there was no reason for blacks to integrate into a dying culture.

Davis was only one voice in the Black Power movement. It included, among others, Malcolm X and Eldridge Cleaver with their moving autobiographies, Huey Newton and Bobby Seale with their militant Black Panthers, Stokely Carmichael and his Congress of Racial Equality. Perhaps the high-water mark of this movement came in 1970 at San Rafael near San Francisco Bay. Three black convicts had been accused of murder in connection with a riot at Soledad Prison. At an unrelated trial, a protesting brother of one of the Soledad men initiated an armed incident in which one prisoner escaped and four men were killed, including the judge. Some of the guns used had been owned by Angela Davis. She contended that arms were necessary for blacks in a violent society, and a jury acquitted her.[12]

Davis never represented more than a minor fraction of the black people of the West. Barbara Jordan was a far more central role model, as were Ralph Bunche, black Los Angeleno and recipient of the Nobel peace prize in 1950, and Tom Bradley, first black mayor of Los Angeles and gubernatorial hopeful in 1982.

If the black people were divided in their approach to social change, the Indians were no less so. In the 1960s and 1970s they, too, had a radical faction. Vine Deloria, a Yankton Sioux, laid the foundation. After receiving a Lutheran divinity degree and a law degree from the University of Colorado, Deloria began writing controversial books about the Indian people. In *Custer Died for Your Sins* (1969) he pointed out that unfulfilled expectations cause human grief, "and we have had our share." The first step to free the Indian from cultural oppression, he said, would be to educate the white man from the myths in which "he has clothed us for so long." As for the Indian, "until we can once again produce people like Crazy Horse all the money and help in the world will not save us."[13]

The American Indian Movement, or AIM, was founded in Minneapolis in 1968 to protect drunken Indians of the ghetto from police brutality. Calling for a return of sacred Indian traditions, it thereafter expanded rapidly throughout the West, placing the slogan "red power" beside "black power." Its culminating demonstration came in 1973 with the occupation of the historic site at Wounded Knee. The Indians were armed with rifles and demanded an investigation of the Bureau of Indian Affairs and its treatment of the Oglala Sioux in the context of the nation's 371 broken Indian treaties. The U.S. Army besieged the two hundred Indians at Wounded Knee and unlawfully introduced armored tanks, helicopters, and grenade launchers onto the reservation. Supporters got through, however, including Angela Davis and a delegation from the Communist Party. A national poll indicated that a majority of Americans supported the Indians at Wounded Knee. Eventually a peace treaty was signed in which the demonstrators claimed a victory; but the investigation brought little change. The Indians remained, as Deloria wrote, "a nation overwhelmed by the inevitability of history."[14]

The communal strain of the social protest that rose in the West in the late 1960s was likewise atypical but symptomatic. The hundreds of communes that formed in those years, particularly in New Mexico, in Colorado, and on the Pacific slope, criticized the Establishment by experimenting with cooperation. San Francisco was a seedbed. Among countless others sheltered in the city was Stephen Gaskin, a gaunt figure with wire-rimmed spectacles, who had come to San Francisco fresh from the Marines after the Korean War. In time, he taught a popular course in which he inveighed against the oppressive power of the modern state and the work ethic, calling instead for a life of personal fulfillment. His message blended Zen and Yoga and mystical Christianity. In 1970 he led two hundred of his followers in vans and old busses on a singing, lecturing, meditating tour of the West. When they returned, they decided to settle down together. The best, most affordable land they could find was in Tennessee, and there on seventeen hundred acres southwest of Nashville they founded The Farm. They shared possessions, ate as vegetarians, and worked hard in their fields, soon producing enough sorghum and soy beans to sell. Work was a meditation: "It's just you and the dirt and God," said Gaskin. By 1977 they numbered seven hundred adults and three hundred children. In their simplicity and hard life they probably are closer to the frontier than many westerners who wear the superficial trappings.

Angela Davis and Stephen Gaskin represent the commentators and critics of society, the moths that bat their wings against the sources of energy. The mainstream of that energy held to old ways, as it always had in the West. Most twentieth-century Americans attended not Stephen Gaskin's type of meditation group, but traditional churches and synagogues. Some western religions, such as Mormonism, that had once been radical departures, settled into a conservative establishment in this century. Joseph Fielding Smith, nephew of the Mormon prophet, became First President of the Church of Jesus Christ of Latter-Day Saints in 1901. Until he died in 1918, he worked hard to bring the Mormon church out of its polygamous and communitarian past into more conservative religious ways.

The Roman Catholic Church veered little from its well-trodden paths. Despite the substantial number of Mexcian-Americans traditionally in its parishes, the church long delayed incorporating that group in its hierarchy. That change occurred, however, in San Antonio, Texas, in 1970, and was happily greeted by southwestern Mexicans via television all the way to Los Angeles. Father Patrick (Patricio) Flores was elevated to the bishopric in a mass that included mariachi bands and an epistle read by César Chávez. Nine years later, after a short time as bishop of El Paso, Flores returned to San Antonio as an archbishop. He called on American Catholics to identify more closely with Hispanics, now more than a quarter of the membership of the American Catholic Church. "They are a people to be loved," he preached, "and a people to be respected." Their cultural values, framed by the family and a devotion to all persons from the elderly to the unborn child, kept them close to traditional religion and especially to the multicultural Catholic Church.[15]

So the pluralism of western society reached a new pitch, especially after World War II. The old demands for assimilation seemed to be quieting as minorities claimed greater rights within the mainstream and, on rarer occasions, sought to become proud, independent islands within that mainstream. Women, as is seen through Barbara Jordan and Angela Davis, were part of the new assertiveness. It is conceivable that their role will aid unification within the flux of pluralism.

CULTURE AND THE ARTS

The West sloughed off its frontier but remained a region. Like all other regions in the modern world, it became increasingly torn between national homogeneity and the desire to remain distinct. This latter pull dominated the arts. Regionalism grows from a sense of place, a love of the land — the quiet satisfaction from rippling wheat or quaking aspen or purpling desert hills. It assumes that places infect their people, coloring their speech, their attitudes, and their dreams. Out of that regionalism has come a western cultural voice as strong and dominant as a prairie wind. Such cultural voices are based on a sense of the past, and it is not coincidental that the twentieth century has seen the rise of major western research collections: the Huntington Library in San Marino, the Bancroft Library in Berkeley, and the Newberry Library in Chicago.

Regional culture, even in the restricted sense of the fine arts, is often supported by a popular expression of pride and distinctiveness. The twentieth-century West has frequently heard such tones. A good example would be Woody Guthrie, whose folk songs lamented the dust-bowl farmer and the Depression poor, but whose idiom could have come only from the southern plains.

From the same area came Will Rogers, the cowboy philosopher who symbolized the West throughout the 1920s and 1930s. Rogers never tired of reminding people that he was born a Cherokee in Indian Territory before it became Oklahoma. He learned riding and roping as a cowhand in Texas and on his own family ranch. As a young man, he signed with various Wild West shows, billed as the Cherokee Kid, and by World War I had toured South Africa, Australia, and New Zealand. By then he had perfected his trick-roping act and to it had added bits of pithy humor in a southwestern drawl. Playing this role he starred for years in the Ziegfeld Follies. In the 1920s he

The popular image of a region: Will Rogers, 1920s.

moved to motion pictures and was also in demand as a lecturer, on radio, in magazine articles, and for his "telegrams" boxed on the front page of newspapers. There was in his image much of the West's tall-tale braggadocio: Colorado was a "grand-stand seat" on the world; any European country could be lost in a Texas cotton patch; and Texas was the only place where you could find hot and cold running oil. His words were liberally laced with western optimism: to try to restrain the West now would be "like spitting on a railroad track to stop a train"; "if Oklahoma does in the next twenty-two years what we have done in the past, why, New York will be our parking space."[16]

The fine arts have become even more sensitive to regional nuances. Who understood regionalism better than the father of modern architecture, Frank Lloyd Wright? His first awareness of the earth came during work on his uncle's farm near his home town of Richland Center, Wisconsin. He never forgot that earth, even while in Chicago during his twenties. Assisting the great American architect, Louis Sullivan, he came to practice an organic concept in which a building

Regionalism in the arts: A Frank Lloyd Wright prairie house, 1907.

should extend its place, growing from its own surroundings. He founded and led the "prairie school" of young Chicago architects, seeking an architecture in which human beings would be linked to nature. "I loved the prairies by instinct as a great simplicity," he wrote, and he wished to let human habitations stand, not upright, but "comfortably and naturally flat with the ground."[17]

In 1911 Wright began the creation of Taliesin, Wisconsin, a farm and studio and community in which he applied the new principles. Later in his life he became attached to the southwestern desert and built Taliesin West in the saguaro uplands northeast of Phoenix. Its roof angles followed the slopes of the mountains, its jagged points suggested the spines of cactus, the stones of its walls came from its own site, its colors were those of desert sun and the reflection of mauve sunsets on sand. He took apprentices into his Taliesins, east and west, teaching a total way of life in which architecture was only part of a whole. It was the same message that another architect, Paolo Solari, would unfold in his creation of Arcosanti, a model city environment also in the Arizona desert. These were suggestions of a widespread regional architecture.

While Frank Lloyd Wright was perfecting his prairie style, a strong-willed young woman on the plains of Nebraska left home to teach school. It was 1913; she was seventeen and had just finished the eighth grade. To pass the rural teacher's examination, she had sneaked into Rushville, fearful of her father's wrath. She would later immortalize her parent as Old Jules Sandoz, but at this point Mari was happy to escape that domineering curmudgeon of the Nebraska frontier. Following a disastrous marriage at eighteen, Mari moved to Lincoln, supporting herself and eventually attending college. With fifty thousand people, a symphony orchestra, and a theater, Lincoln was like an opening blossom for this wiry girl from the sand hills. She called it home for the rest of her life.

Mari Sandoz hoped to become a writer. Her model, one of the few American writers she ever admired, was Willa Cather, who had preceded her at the University of Nebraska before the turn of the century. Cather had learned, above all, to write of the place on the earth that was her own, Nebraska, close to the frontier on which Mari Sandoz was raised. In Cather's *O Pioneers* (1913) Mari undoubtedly identified with Alexandra Bergson, a fiercely independent woman of immigrant stock who battled for a place among frontiersmen.

Mari's first struggle was to prove her own intelligence even to herself, since her father Jules had been so certain of women's inferiority. Her desire to share knowledge, and particularly to bring her region to the attention of the world, became intense. "I must guide and inspire and lead and compel," she wrote. It is not surprising that she became a far better historian than a novelist.

Lincoln in the 1920s sagged with the depressed agricultural economy. Mari took various small jobs, all the while trying to write short stories, which produced only a growing pile of rejection slips. She subsisted on tea and the free sugar and crackers on cafe tables. One editor commented that her work was too gloomy, resembling a Hamlin Garland view of the farmer in Dakota, and she began to wonder if her father had been right, if artists and writers were the maggots of society.

Then in 1926 she won a contest for a story about Sand Hills, her homeland. Shortly afterward, the death of her father inspired her to write his life, and for years, through bank failures, dust bowl, and days in which she came close to starvation, she worked to complete *Old Jules*. Her father emerged from its pages as a cantankerous, hateful, stubborn man beating his wives and children into submission or insanity, while working the wild land of the Nebraska panhandle to produce at his bidding. Mari inherited much of his overpowering independence. Still, rejection slip after rejection slip, opened in her tiny upstairs room in Lincoln, left her discouraged, malnourished, and tubercular.

When her luck changed, it was like a spring flood on the Niobrara. In 1935 *Old Jules* won a prize, found a publisher (Little, Brown and Company), and was chosen by the Book-of-the-Month Club. To the last, however, as cantankerous as her father, she fought with her editors over details. Easterners did not care enough about the West, she complained, to make the effort to understand it.

Her next most important book was a biography of the Sioux chief Crazy Horse, a history that combined her own sense of place with the Indian love and reverence for the land. She had come to share the mysticism of Crazy Horse, and she appreciated that feeling especially in a man who could fight against monumental odds. Crazy Horse was indeed a mythic hero — for the Sioux in the days of Sitting Bull, for Vine Deloria in the context of AIM, and for Mari Sandoz as a woman writer struggling to identify herself with a region. Just before she died in 1966, Mari wrote *The Battle of the Little Big Horn*. It was a short, moving, anti-Custer book about what may have been Crazy Horse's finest hour. It may also have been Mari's literary and historical best. As a reviewer said, the words raced along "like raindrops making light running sounds over the dry earth of the prairies she knew so well."[18] This might have been an epitaph for Mari Sandoz, one that western writers from Hamlin Garland to John Steinbeck would appreciate.

Paintbrushes, not words, raced along for Georgia O'Keeffe, even from her youth in rural Wisconsin. She was an alert but quietly observant child with dark skin inherited from her Hungarian mother. Never gregarious, she spent most of her life wearing loose Old World clothing, almost always black. Somehow in the heartland of Wisconsin she was inspired to become an artist but kept her desire to herself, since art was apparently a man's profession. She loved the prairies, which she considered the most normal part of America. But many years later, when Frank Lloyd Wright asked her to live in Taliesin, she discovered another part of the West where she wished even more to be.

First, however, came her rendezvous with the art world of New York. After a series of family moves and misfortunes, she found herself in the big city continuing her drawing and painting. In a lucky break, some of her starkly sexual charcoal drawings came to the attention of Alfred Stieglitz, the pioneer photographer and wealthy connoisseur, and he showed them in his gallery. In her search for a living, she took a job as drawing instructor in Amarillo, Texas. Amarillo was a rough boom town in 1912. Boarding in a small hotel frequented by cowboys, she became entranced by the vast open spaces that surrounded the town — "terrible winds and a wonderful emptiness." That feeling was intensified in her next job at West Texas State Normal College in Canyon, south of Amarillo. She tried to

Regionalism in the arts: "Ranchos Church, Taos, New Mexico"
by Georgia O'Keeffe, 1930.

open her students' eyes to the glory of a sunrise and the importance of art in their hard lives.

One summer she vacationed in Santa Fe, New Mexico, and immediately adopted that area as her spiritual home. "From then on," she later wrote, "I was always on my way back." She had been sending her drawings and paintings to Stieglitz in New York, and he admired them. When she returned to the city, their relationship deepened. The two became lovers and were married in 1924. As the wife of Stieglitz, she became intimate with the New York art world, but remained her strong-willed, silent, black-clad self.

At the age of forty-one her restlessness won out, and she again headed West for a summer in New Mexico. She stayed in Taos at the sprawling establishment of Mabel Dodge, wealthy patroness who had in the past hosted such figures as Willa Cather and D. H. Lawrence. O'Keeffe's studio was a small adobe under cottonwoods by a stream, with piñon smoke rising from a fireplace in the corner. It all fitted the simplicity of her paintings of bright desert and dark mesa. She worked alone, ignoring the art colony that Taos had become since the turn of the century. In the fall of 1929 in New York the usual mad tempo plus the Great Crash contrasted with her New Mexico paintings of plain adobe walls or stark black Penitente crosses against an azure sky. In subsequent New Mexico summers she discovered bleached animal bones on the shimmering desert floor and turned them into a series of paintings, symbols of transient life and untouchable nature. Of the natural scene around her, she quietly affirmed, "This is my world."

When Stieglitz died in 1946 and she had buried him, O'Keeffe, at sixty-one, returned to New Mexico permanently. Eventually she lived in two houses — beside the plaza of the hilltop village of Abiquiu and in an adobe she had bought on the edge of the Ghost Ranch nearby.

In her eighties she became nearly blind, though her general good health continued thanks to years of attention to her diet — organic vegetables, fresh milk and eggs, wild herbs — and a massage technique called Rolfing. In the 1960s her land turned violent with the Mexican uprising led by Reies Tijerina, who was trying to restore Anglo land thefts to the Mexican people. But O'Keeffe remained aloof, more concerned with the texture of cottonwood limbs. When she could no longer see them clearly, she still painted, using her minimal peripheral vision, tape for guidance, and assistants to read the tubes' colors. In her nineties she remains a quiet, aggressive, determined woman. "I have always known what I wanted," she explains. And she has always had the willpower to get it. She abominates the steel monstrosities that carry high tension wires across her pink mesas. Still, she can say of her valley, "sometimes I think I am half mad with love for this place."[19]

CONCLUSION

What a medley, these twentieth-century westerners! Amadeo Giannini, Henry Kaiser, and Howard Hughes amassed fortunes made possible by rapid industrialization, high technology of air and water and highway, and an enormous growth of an ever-restless population. Some of that technology, as with Kaiser's dams, and some of that population growth, as in the big cities, have caused ecological scars and concerns. The environmental issue has persisted from William E. Borah to Ronald Reagan. Yet the political mainstream has seen the slow shift from a predominantly Progressive and reformist bent in the early century to an increasingly conservative color in recent years. At the same time, the West felt strong tensions from the demands of its minorities, as communicated through César Chávez, Barbara Jordan, Angela Davis, and Vine Deloria. Yet through them all have come the voices of regional loves, the artistic genius of people such as Frank Lloyd Wright and Georgia O'Keeffe, holding their region dear.

Think of all these westerners, not so much as leaders, but as people who have taken advantage of the peculiar social and economic conditions of the modern West. As leaders they have been aggressive and persevering, but that can be said of leaders anywhere in the world. On the other hand, as westerners, they have cherished a unique region of the earth and have succeeded because they have related to its particular qualities.

Western diversity is both vertical and horizontal. Vertically it piles up a towering jumble of ethnic customs, political persuasions, and economic classes. Horizontally it spreads in subregions as different as the northern plains, the arid Southwest, or the coastal shelf. What holds this diversity together as the West? First, there is the common historical experience of pioneering, producing what Carl Becker called the conformity of individualism that springs from the memory of shared hardship. Second, there is a western style, the one Michener so quickly observed in his move to Denver, which may include a greater hunger for salads, but is usually described in terms of casual dress and friendly greetings. That style is expressed more deeply, however, in regional architecture and literature. Third, there has been the perception of a difference, based on half-truths, such as wider horizons and freedom from established ways. That perception is firmly grounded in a sense of place. So the West is an historical memory, a living style, and a regional perception. The diversity comes within these three.

Georgia O'Keeffe described a New Mexico day as the "loud ringing of a hammer striking something hard."[20] At bottom the West has always been hard — stubborn people exploiting a tough land with restless, reckless violence. In time that hardness became memory and, combined with what was left of the land's grandeur, it gave westerners a regional awareness that will probably never die. The hammer blows of industrialization and modernization have played a role in remolding that tradition. These were no more than extensions of a process reaching back to the first steel plow breaking the plains. However, the forces of modern growth have become all-encompassing. Even the battered Indian, the native westerner, has been swept up in them, his population swelling, his warriors lost in the urban dance. Meanwhile the West continues its noisy transfiguration — as a region still echoing its frontier past.

Notes

1
Dancers and Shadows: A Reflection

1. Nathaniel Hawthorne, *Twice-Told Tales* (Columbus, Ohio, 1974), p. 63; Richard Drinnon, *Facing West: The Metaphysics of Indian Hating and Empire-Building* (Minneapolis, 1980), pp. 3–34; Neal Salisbury, *Manitou and Providence: Indians, Europeans and the Making of New England, 1500–1643* (New York, 1982), pp. 159–165.
2. James Axtell, *The European and the Indian* (New York, 1981), pp. 41–42.
3. Calvin Martin, *Keepers of the Game: Indian-Animal Relationships and the Fur Trade* (Berkeley, 1978), p. 62.
4. Frederick W. Turner, *Beyond Geography: The Western Spirit Against the Wilderness* (New York, 1980), pp. 273, 277.
5. Salisbury, *Manitou and Providence*, pp. 22–30; Henry F. Dobyns, *Native American Historical Demography: A Critical Bibliography* (Bloomington, 1976) pp. 10–21; Francis Jennings, *The Invasion of America* (Chapel Hill, 1975), pp. 15–31; Wilbur R. Jacobs, "The Tip of an Iceberg: Pre-Columbian Indian Demography," *William and Mary Quarterly*, XXXI (January 1974): 123–132.
6. Martin, *Keepers of the Game*, pp. 64, 65, 186. Compare Shepard Kiech, *Indians, Animals, and the Fur Trade: A Critique of Keepers of the Game* (Athens, Ga., 1981).
7. Anthony Wallace, *Death and the Rebirth of the Seneca* (New York, 1970), p. 75; Wilcomb Washburn, *The Indian in America* (New York, 1975), pp. 22–24, 111–112.
8. Robert F. Berkhofer, *The White Man's Indian* (New York, 1978), p. 75.
9. Quoted in Roy H. Pearce, *Savages in America* (Baltimore, 1965), p. 5.
10. Berkhofer, *White Man's Indian*, pp. 7–14.
11. Mona Etienne and Eleanor Leacock, eds., *Women and Colonization: Anthropological Perspectives* (New York, 1980), pp. 57–59.
12. Drinnon, *Facing West* (Minneapolis, 1980), p. 463.
13. D'Arcy McNickle, *They Came Here First* (New York, 1975), p. 278.
14. Hart Crane, *The Bridge* (New York, 1933), p. 26.

2
The Great Encounter: Native American and European

1. Columbus's journals, October 14, 1492, as quoted in Samuel Eliot Morison, *Admiral of the Ocean Sea: A Life of Christopher Columbus* (Boston, 1944), p. 305; Hans Koning, *Columbus: His Enterprise* (New York, 1976), pp. 52-54.
2. As quoted in Salvador de Madariaga, *Hernán Cortés: Conqueror of Mexico* (Coral Gables, Fla., 1942), p. 103.
3. Miguel Leon-Portilla, ed., *The Broken Spears: The Aztec Account of the Conquest of Mexico* (Boston, 1962), p. 6. Subsequent quotations are from pp. 23, 24, and 26.
4. William H. Prescott, *History of the Conquest of Mexico* (London, 1906), p. 141.
5. Leon-Portilla, *The Broken Spears*, p. 29.
6. William Brandon, *American Heritage Book of Indians* (New York, 1961), p. 87.
7. Charles Gibson, *The Aztecs Under Spanish Rule* (Stanford, 1964), pp. 5-6.
8. Lewis Hanke, *Bartolomé de Las Casas: An Interpretation of His Life and Writings* (The Hague, 1951), p. 2.
9. Ibid., p. 23.
10. Lesley Simpson, *The Encomienda in New Spain* (Berkeley, 1950), p. 203.
11. Clarence Haring, *The Spanish Empire in America* (New York, 1947), p. 186. Douglas Tunstell, in "The Emergence of Modern Mexico," *American Heritage* 20 (April 1969): 12, gives the figure as nine million.
12. Bartolomé de Las Casas, *Historia de las Indias*, ed. Augustín Millares Carlo, vol. 1 (Mexico City, 1951), p. 148.
13. Gibson, *The Aztecs Under Spanish Rule*, p. 81.
14. John F. Bannon, ed., *Bolton and the Spanish Borderlands* (Norman, Okla., 1964), p. 210.
15. Jean Francois de Lapérouse, *The First French Expedition to California: Lapérouse in 1786* (Los Angeles, 1959), p. 75; Carey McWilliams, *Southern California Country* (New York, 1946), p. 29; John R. Bartlett, *Personal Narrative*, vol. 2 (New York, 1854), pp. 93-94; Alfred L. Kroeber, quoted in Robert Heizer and Mary Anne Whipple, eds., *California Indians, a Source Book* (Berkeley, 1951), p. 76.
16. Tom Lea, *The King Ranch*, vol. 1 (Boston, 1957), p. 112.
17. Gibson, *The Aztecs Under Spanish Rule*, p. 280.
18. Bailey W. Diffie, *Latin-American Civilization: The Colonial Period* (Harrisburg, Pa., 1945), p. 117.
19. Eric Wolf, *Sons of the Shaking Earth* (Chicago, 1959), p. 161.
20. John Bartlett Brebner, *Explorers of North America, 1492-1806* (New York, 1955), p. 90.
21. Francis Parkman, *Pioneers of France in the New World* (Boston, 1902), p. 216.
22. Francis Parkman, *La Salle and the Discovery of the Great West* (London, 1885), p. 288.
23. Lallemant, quoted in John H. Kennedy, *Jesuit and Savage in New France* (New Haven, 1950), p. 88.
24. Bernard De Voto, *The Course of Empire* (Boston, 1952), p. 103.
25. Reuben G. Thwaites, ed., *The Jesuit Relations, and Allied Documents: Travels and Explorations of the Jesuit Missionaries in New France, 1610-1791*, vol. 22 (Cleveland, 1896-1901), pp. 241-43.
26. Salvador de Madariaga, *Englishmen, Frenchmen, Spaniards: An Essay in Comparative Psychology* (London, 1928), p. 3.
27. Edwin Scott Gaustad, *A Religious History of America* (New York, 1966), p. 28.
28. Henry Steele Commager, ed., *Documents of American History* (New York, 1948), pp. 1, 7. William Brandon, *American Heritage Book of Indians* (New York, 1961), p. 168.
29. Edmund S. Morgan, *Roger Williams: The Church and the State* (New York, 1967), p. 122.
30. Alden T. Vaughan, *New England Frontier: Puritans and Indians, 1620-1675* (Boston, 1965), p. 185.

31. Wilcomb E. Washburn, *The Governor and the Rebel: A History of Bacon's Rebellion in Virginia* (Chapel Hill, 1957), p. 76.
32. Ibid., p. 85.
33. Charles Woodmason, *The Carolina Backcountry on the Eve of the Revolution* (Chapel Hill, 1953), p. 43.
34. Richard Maxwell Brown, *South Carolina Regulators* (Cambridge, Mass., 1963), pp. 34-35.
35. Ibid., p. 135.
36. David Hawke, *In The Midst of Revolution* (Philadelphia, 1961), p. 67-68.
37. Theodore Roosevelt, *Winning of the West* (New York, 1962), p. 84.

3
The Land and Its Markers

1. Benjamin H. Hibbard, *A History of the Public Land Policies* (New York, 1924), p. 39.
2. James Woodress, *A Yankee's Odyssey: The Life of Joel Barlow* (New York, 1958), p. 103.
3. Joel Barlow, *The Vision of Columbus* (Paris, 1793), p. 30.
4. Ibid.
5. Harriet Louisa Arnow, *Seed Time on the Cumberland* (New York, 1960), p. 169.
6. Bernard De Voto, *The Journals of Lewis and Clark* (Boston, 1953), p. xxiv; Henry Adams' *History of the United States*, book 2 (New York, 1930), p. 49; Vine Deloria, Jr., *Behind the Trail of Broken Treaties* (New York, 1974), pp. 98-106.
7. James D. Richardson, ed., *A Compilation of the Messages and Papers of Presidents, 1789-1897*, vol. 1 (New York, 1901-07), p. 323.
8. Francis Wrigley Hirst, *The Life and Letters of Thomas Jefferson* (New York, 1926), p. 390.
9. E. Wilson Lyon, *Louisiana in French Diplomacy* (Norman, Okla., 1934), pp. 225-26.
10. De Voto, *The Journals of Lewis and Clark*, p. iii.
11. Reuben G. Thwaites, ed., *Early Western Travels* (Cleveland, 1904), XVII, 148.
12. John Charles Frémont, *Narratives of Exploration and Adventure*, ed. Allan Nevins (New York, 1956), pp. 192-93.

4
The Fur Trade and Freedom

1. Bernard De Voto, *The Course of Empire* (Boston, 1952), p. 527.
2. Kenneth Porter, *John Jacob Astor, Businessman*, vol. 2 (Cambridge, Mass., 1931), p. 939.
3. Porter, *John Jacob Astor, Businessman*, vol. 1, p. 235.
4. Hiram M. Chittenden, *The American Fur Trade of the Far West*, vol. 1 (Stanford, 1954), p. 263.
5. Dale Lowell Morgan, *Jedediah Smith and His Maps of the American West* (San Francisco, 1954), p. 7.
6. Ibid., pp. 310, 312.
7. Don Berry, *A Majority of Scandals* (New York, 1961).
8. Walter Blair and Franklin J. Meine, *Half Horse, Half Alligator: The Growth of the Legend of Mike Fink* (Chicago, 1956), p. 52.
9. William Brandon, "The Wild Freedom of the Mountain Man," *American Heritage* 6 (August 1955): 7.
10. William Goetzmann, "The Mountain Man as Jacksonian Man," *American Quarterly* XV (1963): 402-415.
11. De Voto, *The Course of Empire*, p. 103.
12. Sylvia Van Kirk, *Many Tender Ties: Women in Fur-Trade Society, 1670–1870* (Norman, Okla., 1983), pp. 4-8.
13. Lewis Saum, *The Fur Trader and the Indian* (Seattle, 1965), p. 51.
14. William Clark, "1830 Report on the Fur Trade," *Oregon Historical Quarterly* 48 (March 1947): 31.

5
The Settlement of Texas and Oregon

1. Stephen F. Austin to Fellow Citizens, August 6, 1823, from Austin, *Papers*, in American Historical Association, *Annual Report*, 1919 (Washington, D.C., 1924), vol. 2, part 1, p. 784.
2. T. R. Fehrenbach, *Lone Star: A History of Texas and the Texans* (New York, 1968), p. 247.
3. As quoted in Eugene C. Barker, *The Life of Stephen F. Austin: Founder of Texas, 1793-1836* (Austin, 1949), p. 93.
4. Mary A. Holley, *Texas: Observations, Historical, Geographical, and Descriptive* (Baltimore 1833; Reprint, N.Y., 1973), pp. 12, 128.
5. Fehrenbach, *Lone Star*, pp. 187, 287.
6. Barker, *The Life of Stephen F. Austin*, pp. 378-94.
7. Ibid., p. 394.
8. William Binkley, *The Texas Revolution* (Baton Rouge, 1952), p. 80.
9. Edwin Scott Gaustad, *A Religious History of America* (New York, 1966), p. 157.
10. Eliza Spalding Warren, ed., *Memoirs of the West: The Spaldings* (Portland, Ore., c. 1916), p. 54. For the subsequent discussion of conversions, see Alvin M. Josephy, Jr., *The Nez Percé Indians and the Opening of the Northwest* (New Haven, 1965), p. 183; and Deward Walker, *Conflict and Schism in Nez Percé Acculturation* (Pullman, Wash., 1968), pp. 43-44.
11. David Lavender, *Land of Giants: The Drive to the Pacific Northwest, 1750-1950* (New York, 1958), p. 248.

6
Two Wars and One Destiny

1. Lawrence Allin, "Log of Conquest," *Pacific Historical Review* 37 (May 1968): 147-49.
2. James D. Richardson, ed., *A Compilation of Messages and Papers of the Presidents, 1789-1897*, vol. 5 (New York, 1897), p. 2292.
3. Ralph Waldo Emerson, *Journals*, vol. 9 (Cambridge, Mass., 1971), pp. 430-31.
4. Josiah Royce, *California* (New York, 1948), p. 123.
5. Quoted in Stephen Oates, *To Purge This Land with Blood* (New York, 1970), p. 304.
6. Frederick Jackson Turner, *Significance of Sections in American History* (New York, 1950), p. 50.

7
Mining: The Restless Frontier

1. Peter Mode, ed., *Source Book and Bibliographical Guide to American Church History* (Menasha, Wis., 1921), p. 434.
2. Douglass North, *Economic Growth of the United States, 1790-1860* (Englewood Cliffs, N.J., 1961), p. 81; Ralph Roske, "World Impact of the California Gold Rush," *Arizona and the West* 5 (Autumn 1963): 187-232; Clark C. Spence, *British Investments and the American Mining Frontier, 1860-1901* (Ithaca, N.Y., 1958), pp. 9, 219.
3. Mary Austin, *Land of Little Rain* (New York, 1961), p. 44.
4. Robert Glass Cleland, *Cattle on a Thousand Hills* (San Marino, Calif., 1951).
5. John W. Caughey, *Gold Is the Cornerstone* (Berkeley, 1948), p. 210.
6. Rodman Paul, *Mining Frontiers of the Far West, 1848-1880* (New York, 1963), pp. 56-86.
7. Louisa Amelia Knapp Clappe, *The Shirley Letters from the California Mines, 1851-1852*, ed. Carl I. Wheat (New York, 1949), p. 121; J. S. Holliday, *The World Rushed In* (New York, 1981), p. 455. The two statistical references above are from Ralph Mann, *After the Gold Rush* (Stanford, Calif., 1982), pp. 17, 86.
8. Douglas Hill, *Opening of the Canadian West* (New York, 1967), pp. 110-111. For

material on blacks above, see Rudolph Lapp, *Blacks in Gold Rush California* (New Haven, 1977), pp. 12-16, 39, 52-55, 99-100. For that on women below, see Ann Ellis, *Life of an Ordinary Woman* (Boston, 1929), pp. x, 8, 11.

9. Francis Parkman, *Oregon Trail* (New York, 1946), p. 23.
10. As quoted in Dwight Clarke, *William Tecumseh Sherman: Gold Rush Banker* (San Francisco, 1969), p. 226.
11. Thomas Dimsdale, *The Vigilantes of Montana* (Norman, Okla., 1953), pp. 3, 15.

8
Cattle and the Cult of Masculinity

1. Robert R. Dykstra, *The Cattle Towns* (New York, 1968), p. 146.
2. Mari Sandoz, *The Buffalo Hunters: The Story of the Hide Men* (New York, 1954), p. 34.
3. Ernest S. Osgood, *The Day of the Cattleman* (Minneapolis, 1929), p. 193.
4. J. Frank Dobie, *The Longhorns* (Boston, 1941), p. 198.
5. Lewis Atherton, *Cattle Kings* (Bloomington, Ind., 1961), p. 161.
6. Philip Durham and Everett L. Jones, *The Negro Cowboys* (New York, 1965), pp. 44-45. See also Kenneth Porter, *The Negro on the American Frontier* (New York, 1971).
7. Edmond de Mandat-Grancey, *Cowboys and Colonels: Narrative of a Journey Across the Prairie and Over the Black Hills of Dakota*, trans. William Conn (Philadelphia, 1963), p. 279.
8. Quoted in Don Walker, *Clio's Cowboys: Studies in the Historiography of the Cattle Trade* (Lincoln, Nebr., 1981), pp. 131-133. For Lewis Atherton, above, see *Cattle Kings*, p. xi.
9. Joe B. Frantz and Julian E. Choate, Jr., *The American Cowboy: The Myth and the Reality* (Norman, Okla., 1955), p. 114; The Andy Adams reference in the following paragraph is from *Log of a Cowboy* (Lincoln, Nebr., 1964), p. 382. See also Clifford Westermeier, "The Modern Cowboy — An Image," in Robert Fervis, ed., *The American West: An Appraisal* (Santa Fe, N.M., 1963), p. 34.
10. Theodore Roosevelt, *Letters*, vol. 1, ed. E. E. Morison (Cambridge, Mass., 1951), pp. 74, 80.
11. Theodore Roosevelt, *Ranch Life and the Hunting Trail* (New York, 1902) p. 83.
12. Roosevelt, *Letters*, pp. 100, 390, 510.
13. Henry F. Pringle, *Theodore Roosevelt: A Biography* (New York, 1931), pp. 195-96.
14. G. Edward White, *The Eastern Establishment and the Western Experience* (New Haven, 1968), p. 83.
15. James R. McGovern, "David Graham Phillips and the Virility Impulse of Progressives," *New England Quarterly* 39 (1966): 334-55.

9
The Power of the Road

1. Bret Harte, "What Was It the Engines Said," *Poetical Works* (Boston, 1912) p. 304.
2. Mark Twain, *Roughing It* (Hartford, 1872), p. 59. The preceding quotes on the pony express are from ibid., pp. 70, 72.
3. As quoted in John L. Phillips, "Credit Mobilier," *American Heritage* XX (April, 1969): 109.
4. John F. Stover, *American Railroads* (Chicago, 1961), p. 70.
5. Remi Nadeau, *Fort Laramie and the Sioux Indians* (Englewood Cliffs, N.J., 1967), p. 250.
6. Robert Louis Stevenson, *Across the Plains* (London, 1918), pp. 32-33.
7. As quoted in David Lavender, *The Great Persuader* (New York, 1970), pp. 128-29.
8. As quoted in Stuart Daggett, *Chapters on the History of the Southern Pacific* (New York, 1922), p. 211.

9. Lavender, *The Great Persuader*, pp. 345, 360.
10. Henry David Thoreau, *Walden*, in *Writings* (Boston, 1906), pp. 102-103.
11. Nat Love, *The Life and Adventures of Nat Love* (New York, 1968), p. 156.
12. Lavender, *The Great Persuader*, p. 268.

10
Dugouts and Domesticity: Farming the Great Plains

1. John Faragher, "Constituents of Community: Sugar Creek, Ill, 1820-1850," Unpublished manuscript, 1982, pp. 8, 10. For quote below see Rudyard Kipling, *Writings*, vol. 28, (New York, 1899), pp. 25-26.
2. Walter Prescott Webb, *The Great Plains* (Boston, 1931), pp. 8-9.
3. "Horace Greeley, Advice to American Farmers," in James Parton, *Life of Horace Greeley* (Boston, 1869), pp. 595-96.
4. Paul W. Gates, "The Homestead Law in an Incongruous Land System," *American Historical Review* 41 (1936), 652-681. See also Gates, "The Homestead Act: Free Land Policy in Operation," in Howard Ottoson, ed., *Land Use Policy and Problems in the United States* (Lincoln, Neb., 1963), pp. 28-46. For the Iowa statistics above, see Robert P. Swierenga, *Pioneers and Profits: Land Speculation on the Iowa Frontier* (Ames, Iowa, 1968), p. xxvii. For a contrary view on tenancy: Donald Winters, *Farmers Without Farms* (Westport, Conn., 1978).
5. Mari Sandoz, *Old Jules* (Lincoln, Neb., 1962), p. 99.
6. Gilbert Fite, *The Farmers Frontier, 1865-1900* (New York, 1966), pp. 76-77.
7. _____ , *Cosmopolitan*, 7 (September 1889): 464-68; quoted in Ray Allen Billington, ed., *The Westward Movement in the United States* (Princeton, 1959), pp. 179-81.
8. William Appleman Williams, *The Roots of the Modern American Empire* (New York, 1969).
9. Sandoz, *Old Jules*, p. 113.
10. Hamlin Garland, *Son of the Middle Border* (New York, 1920), p. 402.
11. Ole Rölvaag, *Giants in the Earth* (New York, 1964), p. 188.
12. Donald Danker, ed., *Mollie: The Journal of Mollie Dorsey Sanford* (Lincoln, 1959), p. 15; Sandra Myers, *Western Women and the Frontier Experience, 1800-1915* (Albuquerque, N.M., 1982), p. 167.
13. Alan P. Grimes, *The Puritan Ethic and Woman Suffrage* (New York, 1967): Julie Jeffrey, *Frontier Women* (New York, 1979), p. 191.
14. Erik H. Erikson, *Childhood and Society*, 2d ed. (New York, 1963), pp. 288-98.
15. William Appleman Williams, *The Contours of American History* (Cleveland, 1961), p. 257.

11
Plunder and Preservation

1. Stewart, L. Udall, *The Quiet Crisis* (New York, 1963), p. 68.
2. William Vogt, *The Road to Survival* (New York, 1948).
3. Roderick Nash, *Wilderness and the American Mind* (New Haven, 1967), p. 108.
4. Ibid., p. 114.
5. Wallace Stegner, *Beyond the Hundredth Meridian* (Boston, 1954), p. 212.
6. Samuel P. Hays, *Conservation and the Gospel of Efficiency: The Progressive Conservation Movement, 1890-1920* (Cambridge, Mass., 1959), p. 2.
7. John Muir, *The Yosemite* (New York, 1962), p. 197.

12
The Ethnic Frontier

1. Walt Whitman, "Song of the Redwood Tree," *Complete Poetry and Prose*, vol. 1 (New York, 1948), p. 207.

2. Merle Curti, *The Making of an American Community* (Stanford, 1959), pp. 97-106.
3. Herbert Blalock, *Toward a Theory of Minority-Group Relations* (New York, 1967), p. 79.
4. Introduction to Nat Love, *The Live and Adventures of Nat Love* (New York, 1968), pp. 1-2.
5. *Harper's* 36 (February 1868): 305.
6. Mari Sandoz, *Old Jules* (Lincoln, Neb., 1962), p. 130.
7. Dee Brown, *Bury My Heart at Wounded Knee: An Indian History of the American West* (New York, 1970), p. 77.
8. Senate Report quoted in Brown, *Bury My Heart*, p. 85; Richard Drinnon, *Facing West* (Minneapolis), p. 199.
9. Brown, *Bury My Heart at Wounded Knee*, p. 343.
10. Report of Secretary of War, 1877, quoted in Ralph K. Andrist, *The Long Death: The Last Days of the Plains Indians* (New York, 1964), p. 315.
11. Philip Borden, "Found Cumbering the Soil," in Gary Nash and Richard Weiss, eds. *The Great Fear: Race in the Mind of America* (New York, 1970), p. 72.
12. Vine Deloria, *Custer Died for Your Sins* (New York, 1969).
13. Mari Sandoz, *Cheyenne Autumn* (New York, 1953), pp. 258-59.
14. Sandoz, *Old Jules*, p. 122.
15. Ibid., pp. 130-31.
16. William T. Hagan, *American Indians* (Chicago, 1961), pp. 123, 148; William Brandon, *American Heritage Book of Indians* (New York, 1966), p. 408; Brown, *Bury My Heart at Wounded Knee*, p. 446.
17. Kenneth W. Porter, *The Negro on the American Frontier* (New York, 1971), pp. 208-261; William L. Katz, *Eyewitness: The Negro in American History* (New York, 1967), pp. 71-73; Alvin M. Josephy, Jr., *The Patriot Chiefs: A Chronicle of American Indian Resistance* (New York, 1961), pp. 181-82, 184-85.
18. Quoted in Eugene H. Berwanger, *The Frontier Against Slavery* (Urbana, Ill., 1967), p. 3.
19. Ibid., p. 60. Peter H. Burnett, *An Old California Pioneer* (Oakland, 1946), p. 132.
20. Philip Durham and Everett Jones, *The Negro Cowboys* (New York, 1965), p. 44; Porter, *The Negro on the American Frontier*, p. 495.
21. Leon Litwack, "The Federal Government and the Free Negro," in Dwight Hoover, ed., *Understanding Negro History* (Chicago, 1968), p. 317.
22. V. Jacque Voegeli, *Free but Not Equal: The Midwest and the Negro During the Civil War* (Chicago, 1967), p. 173.
23. Everett Dick, *The Sod House Frontier* (Lincoln, Neb., 1954), pp. 196-97.
24. Mifflin Gibbs, *Shadow and Light* (New York, 1968), pp. 43, 46-50.
25. Angie Debo, *Prairie City: The Story of an American Community* (New York, 1944), p. 9.
26. Robert R. Dykstra, *The Cattle Towns* (New York, 1968), pp. 130-31.
27. Quoted in T. R. Fehrenbach, *Lone Star: A History of Texas and the Texans* (New York, 1968), p. 507.
28. Ibid., p. 521.
29. Alexander McLeod, *Pigtails and Gold Dust* (Caldwell, Idaho, 1947), p. 175; Gunther Barth, *A History of the Chinese in the United States, 1850-1870* (Cambridge, Mass., 1964), p. 67.
30. Rose Hum Lee, *The Chinese in the United States of America* (Hong Kong, 1960), pp. 188-91.
31. William Locklear, "The Celestials and the Angels," *Southern California Quarterly* 42 (September 1960): 239-56.
32. Stuart C. Miller, *The Unwelcome Immigrant: The American Image of the Chinese, 1785-1882* (Berkeley, 1969), p. 11.
33. Harry H. L. Kitano, *Japanese Americans: The Evolution of a Subculture* (Englewood Cliffs, N.J., 1969), pp. 15, 163.
34. Ibid., p. 3.
35. Judith Kramer, *The American Minority Community* (New York, 1970), p. 172.

13
Preachers and Teachers

1. Julia Lovejoy, "Letters, 1856-1864," *Kansas Historical Quarterly* 15 (1947): 400.
2. John A. Lomax and Alan Lomax, American Ballads and Folk Songs (New York, 1934), p. 564.
3. H. Richard Niebuhr, *The Kingdom of God in America* (Hamden, Conn., 1956), pp. 151, 179.
4. Will Herberg, *Protestant, Catholic, Jew* (New York, 1960), p. 99.
5. Stephen G. Taggart, *Mormonism's Negro Policy: Social and Historical Origins* (Salt Lake City, 1970).
6. Ann Eliza Young, *Wife Number Nineteen* (Hartford, Conn., 1876), p. 597.
7. Max Vorspan and Lloyd P. Gardner, *History of the Jews of Los Angeles* (San Marino, Calif., 1970), p. 6.
8. T. Scott Miyakawa, *Protestants and Pioneers: Individualism and Conformity on the American Frontier* (Chicago, 1964), p. 201.
9. Lovejoy, "Letters, 1856-1864," p. 319.
10. Merle Curti, *The Making of an American Community: A Case Study of Democracy in a Frontier County* (Stanford, 1959), p. 384.
11. Bernard Bailyn, *Education in the Forming of American Society* (Chapel Hill, 1960), p. 22.
12. Hamlin Garland, *Son of the Middle Border* (New York, 1920), p. 96.
13. Edward Eggleston, *The Hoosier Schoolmaster* (New York, 1887), p. 11.
14. Millard Fillmore Kennedy, *Schoolmasters of Yesterday: A Three-Generation Story* (New York, 1940), pp. 75-76.
15. Curti, *The Making of an American Community*, p. 389.
16. Garland, *Son of the Middle Border*, pp. 112-113.
17. Oscar Osburn Winther, "The Frontier Hypothesis and the Historian," *Social Education* 21 (1957): 295.
18. Donald. G. Tewksbury, *The Founding of American Colleges and Universities Before the Civil War* (New York, 1932), p. 2.
19. Ibid., pp. 31, 90.
20. John Mason Peck, *Memoir of John Mason Peck*, ed. Rufus Babcock (Carbondale, Ill., 1965), p. 151.
21. Frederick Rudolph, *The American College and University* (New York, 1962), p. 275.
22. Tewksbury, *The Founding of American Colleges and Universities*, pp. 183-207.
23. Rudolph, *The American College and University*, p. 252.
24. Ibid., pp. 234, 257.
25. Ibid., p. 314.
26. Mabel Newcomer, *A Century of Higher Education for American Women* (New York, 1959), p. 1.
27. Ibid., p. 19.
28. Richard Hofstadter, *Anti-Intellectualism in American Life* (New York, 1966), p. 308.
29. Rudolph, *The American College and University*, p. 60.

14
The Search for Community

1. Sinclair Lewis, *Main Street* (New York, 1920), pp. 26-27.
2. Zona Gale, *Friendship Village* (New York, 1923), p. 8.
3. Lewis Atherton, *Main Street on the Middle Border* (Bloomington, Ind., 1954), pp. xvi, 3.
4. Richard C. Wade, *The Urban Frontier: The Rise of Western Cities, 1790–1830* (Cambridge, Mass., 1959), pp. 1, 342.
5. Angie Debo, *Prairie City: The Story of an American Community* (New York, 1944), p. 27.

6. William Allen White, *Autobiography* (New York, 1946), p. 47.

7. Ibid., p. 313.

8. Debo, *Prairie City*, p. 29.

9. James Bryce, *The American Commonwealth*, vol. 2 (Chicago, 1891), pp. 703-04.

10. William Allen White, *Forty Years on Main Street*, comp. Russell H. Fitzgibbon (New York, 1937), p. 43.

11. T. Scott Miyakawa, *Protestants and Pioneers: Individualism and Conformity on the American Frontier* (Chicago, 1964), p. 44.

12. Frederick Russell Burnham, *Scouting on Two Continents* (Los Angeles, 1934), p. 10.

13. Miyakawa, *Protestants and Pioneers*, p. 229.

14. Robert R. Dykstra, *The Cattle Towns* (New York, 1968), pp. 108-09.

15. Ray Allen Billington, *America's Frontier Heritage* (New York, 1966), pp. 103-04.

16. Carl Bridenbaugh, *Cities in the Wilderness: The First Century of Urban Life in America* (New York, 1938), p. 478.

17. Merle Curti, *The Making of an American Community: A Case Study of Democracy in a Frontier County* (Stanford, 1959), p. 256.

18. Stephan Thernstrom, "Urbanization, Migration, and Social Mobility in Late Nineteenth Century America," *Towards a New Past: Dissenting Essays in American History*, ed. Barton J. Bernstein (New York, 1969), pp. 165 ff. For Don Doyle below, see *The Social Order of a Frontier Community* (Urbana, Ill., 1983), pp. 97-103.

19. Dykstra, *The Cattle Towns*, appendix A.

20. Thomas Wolfe, *You Can't Go Home Again* (New York, 1940), pp. 144-45.

21. Vachel Linsday, *Collected Poems* (New York, 1927).

22. Wade, *The Urban Frontier*, p. 2; Atherton, *Main Street on the Middle Border*, p. 32.

23. Thernstrom, "Urbanization," p. 159.

24. Sherwood Anderson, *Winesburg, Ohio: A Group of Tales of Ohio Small Town Life* (New York, 1919), pp. 197-212.

25. Ronald L. Davis, *A History of Opera in the American West* (Englewood Cliffs, N.J., 1965), pp. 1-14.

26. Leonard Arrington, *Great Basin Kingdom* (Cambridge, Mass., 1958), p. 337.

15
The Western Hero

1. Constance Rourke, *American Humor: A Study of the National Character* (New York, 1955), p. 64.

2. Don Berry, *A Majority of Scoundrels* (New York, 1961), p. 22.

3. Rourke, *American Humor*, pp. 52-53.

4. Owen Wister, *The Virginian*, ed. Philip Durham (Boston, 1968), pp. v-vii.

5. Ibid., p. 230.

6. Ibid., p. 14.

7. Ibid., p. 275.

8. Robert Warshow, *The Immediate Experience: Movies, Comics, Theater and Other Aspects of Popular Culture* (New York, 1962), p. 141.

9. Edwin Fussell, *Frontier: American Literature and the American West* (Princeton, 1964), p. 42.

10. James Fenimore Cooper, *The Prairie* (New York, 1963), p. 450.

11. Albert Johannsen, *The House of Beadle and Adams and Its Dime and Nickel Novels*, vol. 1 (Norman, Okla., 1950), p. 33.

12. Henry Nash Smith, *Virgin Land* (Cambridge, Mass., 1950), p. 91.

13. Ibid.

14. Philip Durham and Everett Jones, *The Negro Cowboys* (New York, 1965), p. 220.

15. Johannsen, *The House of Beadle and Adams*, vol. 1, p. 4.

16. The persistent popular appeal of the western has been demonstrated anew in television. The season of 1958-1959 provided a good example. Judged by Nielsen ratings of

listeners, eight of the top ten programs were westerns, including "Gunsmoke," "Wagon Train," "Have Gun, Will Travel," "Maverick," "Wyatt Earp," and "Zane Grey Theater." Fourteen new westerns were launched that one season alone.

17. Karl May, *Ich*, ed. E. A. Schnied, trans. Robert Schulmann (Dresden, 1938), p. 268. For Karl May, see also Ray Billington, *Land of Savagery, Land of Promise* (New York, 1981), pp. 53-56.

16
The Image of the West in Art

1. E. H. Gombrich, *Meditations on a Hobby Horse* (London, 1963), p. 11.
2. Robert Penn Warren, *Audubon: A Vision* (New York, 1969), p. 3.
3. Alexis de Tocqueville, *Democracy in America*, vol. 2 (New York, 1954), pp. 4-5.
4. Quoted in John Ewers, *Artists of the Old West* (New York, 1965), p. 26.
5. George Catlin, *Letters and Notes on the Manners, Customs and Conditions of the North American Indian*, vol. 1 (Minneapolis, 1965), p. 3.
6. Ibid., p. 2.
7. Catlin, *North American Indian*, vol. 2, p. 277.
8. Catlin, *North American Indian*, vol. 1, p. 10.
9. Catlin, *North American Indian*, vol. 2, p. 270.
10. Paul Kane, *Wanderings of an Artist* (Rutland, Vt., 1968), p. 53.
11. Ibid., p. 53.
12. Quoted in Ewers, *Artists of the Old West*, p. 137.
13. Quoted in G. Edward White, *The Eastern Establishment and the Western Experience: The West of Frederic Remington, Theodore Roosevelt, and Owen Wister* (New Haven, 1968), p. 109.
14. Harry T. Peters, *Currier and Ives: Printmakers to the American People* (New York, 1942), p. 2.
15. Daniel Bryan, *The Mountain Muse* (Harrisonburg, Pa., 1813), preface.

17
The Frontier Experience in Retrospect

1. Arthur K. Moore, *Frontier Mind: A Cultural Analysis of the Kentucky Frontiersman* (Lexington, 1957), p. viii.
2. Nathaniel Hawthorne, *Scarlet Letter* (Boston, 1888).
3. Quoted in Robert Taft, *Artists and Illustrators of the Old West* (New York, 1953), p. 14.
4. William Appleman Williams, *The Contours of American History* (Cleveland, 1961), p. 257.
5. Alexis de Toqueville, *Democracy in America*, vol. 1 (New York, 1954), p. 414.
6. Walt Whitman, *Complete Poetry and Prose*, vol. 1 (New York, 1948), p. 206. Emerson, *Works*, vol. 1 (Boston, 1903-1904), p. 370.
7. Frederick Jackson Turner, *The Frontier in American History* (New York, 1920), pp. 1, 37.
8. Ibid., pp. 244-47.
9. Hawthorne, *Scarlet Letter*, p. 239.
10. Mark Twain, *Life on the Mississippi* (New York, 1956), p. 71.
11. R. W. B. Lewis, *The American Adam: Innocence, Tragedy, and Tradition in the Nineteenth Century* (Chicago, 1955), p. 1.
12. David Riesman et al. *The Lonely Crowd: A Study of the Changing American Character* (New York, 1956), p. 3.

13. B. F. Skinner, *Beyond Freedom and Dignity* (New York, 1971).
14. Howard Mumford Jones, *O Strange New World: American Culture, the Formative Years* (New York, 1964), p. 352.
15. Stephen Vincent Benét, *Twenty-five Short Stories* (New York, 1943), p. 17.
16. Charles Dickens, *American Notes and Reprinted Pieces* (London, 1870), p. 78.
17. Ray Allen Billington, *America's Frontier Heritage* (New York, 1967), pp. 97-116.
18. William Wordsworth, "The Tables Turned," stanza 4.
19. Ralph Waldo Emerson, "Nature," *Works*, vol. 1 (Boston, 1883), pp. 14-16; Henry David Thoreau, *Walden*, in *Writings* (Boston, 1906), p. 350; James Fenimore Cooper, quoted in Moore, *Frontier Mind*, p. 210.
20. Jones, *O Strange New World*, p. 395.
21. John G. Neihardt, *Cycle of the West* (Lincoln, Neb., 1963), p. 65.
22. Quoted in William Brandon, *American Heritage Book of Indians* (New York, 1966), p. 157.
23. Horace Greeley, *Recollections of a Busy Life* (New York, 1868), p. 498.
24. Moore, *Frontier Mind*, p. 238.
25. Quoted in T. R. Fehrenbach, *Lone Star: A History of Texas and the Texans* (New York, 1968), p. 81.
26. Jones, *O Strange New World*, p. 352.
27. Walt W. Rostow, "The Nationalization of Take-Off," in William R. Polk, ed., *Developmental Revolution: North Africa, Middle East, Southeast Asia* (Washington, D.C., 1963). See also Douglass North, "International Capital Flows and the Development of the American West," *Journal of Economic History* 16 (1956): 493-505.
28. *Daily Missouri Democrat* (St. Louis), September 8, 1858; quoted in Clifford Westermeier, "The Cowboy — Sinner or Saint," *New Mexico Historical Review* 25 (April 1950): 107.
29. Willa Cather, *My Antonia* (Boston, 1946), p. 372.
30. Alexis de Tocqueville, *Democracy in America*, vol. 1 (New York, 1954), p. 279.
31. Richard Maxwell Brown, "Historical Patterns of Violence in America," in Hugh Graham and Ted Gurr, eds., *Violence in America: Historical and Comparative Perspectives* (New York, 1969), pp. 45-46.
32. Harold L. Nieburg, *Political Violence: The Behavioral Process* (New York, 1969), p. 8.
33. Eric Hobsbawm, *Primitive Rebels* (New York, 1963).
34. Ibid., p. 5.
35. Edith Abbott, "The Civil War and the Crime Wave of 1865-70," *Social Service Review* 1 (June, 1928): 224-27.
36. Philip D. Jordan, *Frontier Law and Order: Ten Essays* (Lincoln, Neb., 1970), preface.
37. Wayne Gard, *Frontier Justice* (Norman, Okla., 1949), pp. 57-58.
38. Jordan, *Frontier Law and Order*, p. 87; William M. Raine, *Famous Sheriffs and Western Outlaws* (Garden City, N.Y., 1929), p. 7; Frank Waters, *The Earp Brothers of Tombstone* (New York, 1960) pp. 154-172.
39. Richard E. Rubenstein, *Rebels in Eden: Mass Political Violence in the United States* (Boston, 1970), p. 25.
40. Joe B. Frantz, "The Frontier Tradition: An Invitation to Violence," in Graham and Gurr, *Violence in America*, p. 151.

18
The West in Our Time

1. Neil Morgan, *Westward Tilt: The American West Today* (New York, 1961), p. vii.
2. Paul Rink, *Building the Bank of America: A. P. Giannini* (Chicago, 1963), p. 182.
3. *Time*, XC (Sept. 1, 1967): 60.
4. Arrell Gibson, *The West in the Life of the Nation* (Lexington, Mass., 1976), p. 580.
5. The best biography is Donald Barlett and James Steele, *Empire: The Life, Legend and Madness of Howard Hughes* (New York, 1979).
6. *Statistical Abstract of the United States* (Washington, D.C., 1960), p. 13; ibid., (1982-83), p. 11; Morgan, *Westward Tilt*, p. 3.

7. Carey McWilliams, *Factories in the Field* (Boston, 1939), p. 48.
8. Melvyn Dubofsky, *We Shall Be All: A History of the Industrial Workers of the World* (Chicago, 1969), pp. 316, 445.
9. Warren Beck and David Williams, *California* (Garden City, N.Y., 1972), p. 462.
10. Stewart Udall, *Quiet Crisis* (New York, 1963), pp. 178, 190; quotation from Republican: *Business Week*, (April 3, 1965): 100.
11. Barbara Jordan and Shelby Hearon, *Barbara Jordan: a Self-Portrait* (Garden City, N.Y., 1979), p. 160.
12. Good for context of times is J. A. Parker, *Angela Davis: The Making of a Revolutionary* (New Rochelle, N.Y., 1973); see also Angela Davis *An Autobiography* (New York, 1974).
13. Vine Deloria, *Custer Died for Your Sins* (New York, 1969), pp. 1, 27, 279.
14. Vine Deloria, *God Is Red* (New York, 1973), p. 41.
15. Edwin Gaustad, *Dissent in American Religion* (Chicago, 1973), p. 129; Patrick Flores, "The Opportunity Hispanics Provide for the Church," *Origins*, X (Sept. 11, 1980): 201.
16. William Brown, *Imagemaker: Will Rogers and the American Dream* (Columbia, Mo., 1970), pp. 78, 224, 250-51.
17. Frank Lloyd Wright, *An Autobiography* (New York, 1977), pp. 163-64.
18. Helen Stauffer, *Mari Sandoz: Story Catcher of the Plains* (Lincoln, Nebr., 1982), pp. 46, 261.
19. Laurie Lisle, *Portrait of an Artist: A Biography of Georgia O'Keeffe* (New York, 1980), pp. 52, 89, 182; see also Arrell Gibson, *The Santa Fe and Taos Colonies* (Norman, Okla., 1983).
20. Lisle, *Portrait*, p. 181.

Bibliography

The following lists are highly selective, emphasizing both classic works and later interpretations, generally citing recent editions.

General Works

Bancroft, Hubert H. *Works*. 39 vols. San Francisco: The History Co., 1882–1890.

Billington, Ray A., and Ridge, Martin. *Westward Expansion*. 5th ed. New York: Macmillan, 1982.

Lamar, Howard, ed. *Reader's Encyclopedia of the American West*. New York: Crowell, 1977.

Pomeroy, Earl. *The Pacific Slope: A History of California, Oregon, Washington, Idaho, Utah, and Nevada*. New York: Knopf, 1965.

Thwaites, Reuben G., ed. *Early Western Travels, 1784–1846*. 32 vols. Reprint. New York: AMS Press, 1966.

Webb, Walter P. *The Great Frontier*. Boston: Houghton Mifflin, 1952.

1
Dancers and Shadows: A Reflection

Berkhofer, Robert F., Jr. *The White Man's Indian*. New York: Knopf, 1978.

Brandon, William. *American Heritage Book of Indians*. New York: Dell, 1961.

Crosby, Alfred W., Jr. *The Columbian Exchange: Biological and Cultural Consequences of 1492*. Westport, Conn.: Greenwood, 1972.

Dippie, Brian. *The Vanishing American*. Middletown, Conn.: Wesleyan University Press, 1982.

Drinnon, Richard. *Facing West: The Metaphysics of Indian Hating and Empire Building*. Minneapolis: University of Minneapolis Press, 1980.

Forbes, Jack D., ed. *The Indian in America's Past*. Englewood Cliffs, N.J.: Prentice-Hall, 1964.

Gibson, Arrell. *The American Indian*. Lexington, Mass.: D. C. Heath, 1980.

Jacobs, Wilbur, R. *Dispossessing the American Indian: Indians and Whites on the Colonial Frontier.* New York: Scribner's, 1972.

Josephy, Alvin M., Jr. *The Indian Heritage of America.* New York: Knopf, 1968.

McNickle, D'Arcy. *They Came Here First.* Rev. ed. New York: Octagon Books, 1975.

Martin, Calvin. *Keepers of the Game.* Berkeley: University of California Press, 1978.

Prucha, Francis Paul. *Indian Policy in the United States.* Lincoln: University of Nebraska Press, 1981.

Salisbury, Neal. *Manitou and Providence.* New York: Oxford, 1982.

Spicer, Edward H. *Cycles of Conquest.* Tucson: University of Arizona Press, 1962.

Stedman, Raymond. *Shadows of the Indian.* Norman: University of Oklahoma Press, 1982.

Wallace, Anthony F. C. *The Death and Rebirth of the Seneca.* New York: Knopf, 1970.

Washburn, Wilcomb. *The Indian in America.* New York: Harper & Row, 1975.

2
The Great Encounter: Native American and European

Axtell, James. *The European and the Indian: Essays in the Ethnohistory of Colonial North America.* New York: Oxford, 1981.

Bannon, John F. *The Spanish Borderlands Frontier, 1513-1821.* New York: Holt, Rinehart & Winston, 1970.

Brebner, John B. *The Explorers of North America, 1492-1806.* Garden City, N.Y.: Doubleday, 1955.

Brown, Richard M. *The South Carolina Regulators.* Cambridge, Mass.: Harvard University Press, 1963.

Cook, Warren. *Flood Tide of Empire.* New Haven, Conn.: Yale University Press, 1973.

Crane, Verner. *The Southern Frontier, 1670-1732.* Ann Arbor: University of Michigan Press, 1956.

Cronin, William. *Changes in the Land: Indians, Colonists, and the Ecology of New England.* New York: Hill & Wang, 1983.

DeVoto, Bernard. *The Course of Empire.* Boston: Houghton Mifflin, 1952.

Eccles, William J. *France in America.* New York: Harper & Row, 1972.

Gaustad, Edwin S. *A Religious History of America.* New York: Harper & Row, 1966.

Haring, Clarence. *The Spanish Empire in America.* New York: Harcourt, 1947.

Hawke, David. *In the Midst of a Revolution.* Philadelphia: University of Pennsylvania Press, 1961.

Horgan, Paul. *Conquistadors in North American History.* New York: Farrar, Straus & Giroux, 1963.

Horsman, Reginald. *The Frontier in the Formative Years, 1783-1815.* New York: Holt, Rinehart & Winston, 1970.

Jaenen, Cornelius, J. *Friend and Foe: Aspects of French-Amerindian Cultural Contact in the Sixteenth and Seventeenth Centuries.* New York: Columbia University Press, 1976.

Jennings, Francis. *The Invasion of America.* Chapel Hill: University of North Carolina Press, 1975.

Kennedy, John H. *Jesuit and Savage in New France*. New Haven, Conn.: Yale University Press, 1950.

Koning, Hans. *Columbus: His Enterprise*. New York: Monthly Review Press, 1976.

Leon-Portilla, Miguel, ed. *The Broken Spears: The Aztec Account of the Conquest of Mexico*. Boston: Beacon, 1962.

Morison, Samuel E. *The European Discovery of America: The Northern Voyages, A.D. 500-1600*. New York: Oxford, 1971.

Sosin, Jack M. *The Revolutionary Frontier, 1763-1783*. New York: Holt, Rinehart & Winston, 1967.

Turner, Frederick. *Beyond Geography: The Western Spirit Against the Wilderness*. New York: Viking, 1980.

Vaughan, Alden T. *New England Frontier: Puritans and Indians, 1620-1675*. Rev. ed. New York: Norton, 1980.

3
The Land and Its Markers

Arnow, Harriette Louisa. *Seedtime on the Cumberland*. New York: Macmillan, 1960.

Bakeless, John. *Daniel Boone*. Reprint. New York: Morrow, 1955.

_____. *Lewis and Clark, Partners in Discovery*. New York: Morrow, 1947.

Carstensen, Vernon, ed. *The Public Lands: Studies in the History of the Public Domain*. Madison: University of Wisconsin Press, 1963.

Deloria, Vine. *Behind the Trail of Broken Treaties*. New York: Delacorte, 1974.

DeVoto, Bernard. *The Journals of Lewis and Clark*. Boston: Houghton Mifflin, 1953.

Frémont, John C. *The Expeditions of John Charles Frémont*. Edited by Donald Jackson and Mary L. Spence. 2 vols. with supplements. Urbana: University of Illinois Press, 1970-73.

_____. *Narratives of Exploration and Adventure*. Edited by Allan Nevins. New York: Longmans, Green, 1956.

Goetzmann, William H. *Army Exploration in the American West, 1803-1863*. New Haven, Conn.: Yale University Press, 1959.

_____. *Exploration and Empire: The Explorer and Scientist in the Winning of the American West*. New York: Knopf, 1966.

Hibbard, Benjamin H. *A History of the Public Land Policies*. Reprint. Madison: University of Wisconsin Press, 1965.

Hollon, W. Eugene. *The Great American Desert: Then and Now*. New York: Oxford, 1966.

Nevins, Allan. *Frémont, Pathmarker of the West*. New York: Appleton-Century-Crofts, 1939.

Robbins, Roy M. *Our Landed Heritage: The Public Domain, 1776-1936*. Rev. ed. Lincoln: University of Nebraska Press, 1976.

Rohrbough, Malcolm J. *The Land Office Business: The Settlement and Administration of American Public Lands, 1789-1837*. New York: Oxford, 1968.

_____. *The Trans-Appalachian Frontier: People, Societies, and Institutions, 1775-1850*. New York: Oxford, 1978.

Wheat, Carl I. *Mapping the Trans-Mississippi West, 1540-1861*. 3 vols. San Francisco: Grabhorn, 1957-58.

4
The Fur Trade and Freedom

Berry, Don. *A Majority of Scoundrels: An Informal History of the Rocky Mountain Fur Company.* New York: Harper & Row, 1961.

DeVoto, Bernard. *Across the Wide Missouri.* Boston: Houghton Mifflin, 1947.

Hafen, LeRoy R., ed. *The Mountain Men and the Fur Trade of the Far West.* 10 vols. Glendale, Calif.: A. H. Clark, 1965-72.

Irving, Washington. *Astoria; Or Anecdotes of an Enterprise Beyond the Rocky Mountains.* Edgeley W. Todd, ed. Norman: University of Oklahoma Press, 1964.

Lavender, David. *The Fist in the Wilderness.* New York: Doubleday, 1964.

Morgan, Dale L. *Jedediah Smith and the Opening of the West.* Lincoln: University of Nebraska Press, 1965.

Oglesby, Richard E. *Manuel Lisa and the Opening of the Missouri Fur Trade.* Norman: University of Oklahoma Press, 1963.

O'Meara, Walter. *Daughters of the Country: The Women of the Fur Traders and Mountain Men.* New York: Harcourt, Brace and World, 1968.

Phillips, Paul. *Fur Trade.* Norman: University of Oklahoma Press, 1961.

Porter, Kenneth. *John Jacob Astor, Business Man.* 2 vols. Cambridge, Mass.: Harvard University Press, 1931.

Saum, Lewis. *The Fur Trader and the Indian.* Seattle: University of Washington Press, 1965.

Van Kirk, Sylvia. *Many Tender Ties: Women in Fur-Trade Society.* Norman: University of Oklahoma Press, 1983.

Wishart, David J. *The Fur Trade of the American West, 1807-1840: A Geographical Synthesis.* Lincoln: University of Nebraska Press, 1979.

5
The Settlement of Texas and Oregon

Barker, Eugene C. *The Life of Stephen F. Austin: Founder of Texas, 1793-1836.* Austin: Texas State Historical Association, 1949.

Binkley, William. *The Texas Revolution.* Baton Rouge: Louisiana State University Press, 1952.

Connor, Seymour V. *Texas: A History.* New York: Crowell, 1971.

DeVoto, Bernard. *The Year of Decision: 1846.* Boston: Little, Brown, 1942.

Faulk, Odie B. *Land of Many Frontiers: A History of the American Southwest.* New York: Oxford, 1968.

Fehrenbach, T. R. *Lone Star: A History of Texas and the Texans.* New York: Macmillan, 1968.

Gates, Charles M., and Johannsen, Dorothy O. *Empire of the Columbia: A History of the Pacific Northwest.* 2nd ed. New York: Harper & Row, 1967.

Hollon, W. Eugene. *The Southwest: Old and New.* New York: Knopf, 1961.

Lavender, David. *Land of Giants: The Drive to the Pacific Northwest, 1750-1950.* Garden City, N.Y.: Doubleday, 1958.

Pomeroy, Earl. *The Pacific Slope: A History.* New York: Knopf, 1965.

Simpson, Lesley B. *Many Mexicos.* Berkeley: University of California Press, 1952.

Unruh, John D. *The Plains Across: The Overland Emigrants and the Trans-Mississippi West.* Urbana: University of Illinois Press, 1979.

Webb, Walter P. *The Texas Rangers: A Century of Frontier Defense*. Boston: Houghton Mifflin, 1935.

Weber, David J. *The Mexican Frontier: 1821-1846*. Albuquerque: University of New Mexico Press, 1982.

6
Two Wars and One Destiny

Colton, Ray. *The Civil War in the Western Territories*. Norman: University of Oklahoma Press, 1959.

Connor, Seymour V., and Faulk, Odie B. *North America Divided: The Mexican War, 1846-1848*. New York: Oxford, 1971.

Graebner, Norman A. *Empire on the Pacific: A Study in American Continental Expansion*. New York: Ronald, 1955.

Henry, Robert S. *The Story of the Mexican War*. New York: Ungar, 1961.

Johannsen, Robert W. *Frontier Politics and Sectional Conflict: The Pacific Northwest on the Eve of the Civil War*. Seattle: University of Washington Press, 1955.

Lamar, Howard. *The Far Southwest, 1841-1912*. New Haven, Conn.: Yale University Press, 1966.

Marti, Werner. *Messenger of Destiny*. San Francisco: John Howell, 1960.

Merk, Frederick. *Manifest Destiny and Mission in American History*. Reprint. Westport, Conn.: Greenwood, 1983.

Monaghan, Jay. *Civil War on the Western Border*. Boston: Little, Brown, 1955.

Pletcher, David M. *The Diplomacy of Annexation: Texas, Oregon, and the Mexican War*. Columbia: University of Missouri Press, 1973.

Polk, James K. *Diary*. Edited by Allan Nevins, New York: Longmans, Green, 1952.

Royce, Josiah. *California, From Conquest in 1846 to the Second Vigilance Committee in San Francisco*. Reprint. Santa Barbara, Calif.: Peregrine, 1970.

Schmitt, Karl M. *Mexico and the United States, 1821-1923*. New York: Wiley, 1974.

Singletary, Otis. *The Mexican War*. Chicago: University of Chicago Press, 1960.

Smith, Justin H. *The War with Mexico*. 2 vols. New York: Macmillan, 1919.

Weinberg, Albert K. *Manifest Destiny: A Study of Nationalist Expansionism in American History*. Baltimore: Johns Hopkins, 1935.

7
Mining: The Restless Frontier

Caughey, John W. *Gold is the Cornerstone*. Berkeley: University of California Press, 1948.

Clappe, Louisa Amelia Knapp [Dame Shirley]. *The Shirley Letters from the California Mines, 1851-1852*. Edited by Carl I. Wheat. New York: Knopf, 1949.

Clemens, Samuel [Mark Twain]. *Roughing It*. Reprint. Berkeley: University of California Press, 1972.

De Quille, Dan. *The Big Bonanza*. New York: Knopf, 1947.

Greever, William S. *The Bonanza West: The Story of the Western Mining Rushes, 1848-1900*. Norman: University of Oklahoma Press, 1963.

Holliday, J. S. *The World Rushed In*. New York: Simon & Schuster, 1981.

Jackson, Donald D. *Gold Dust*. New York: Knopf, 1980.

Lapp, Rudolph M. *Blacks in Gold Rush California*. New Haven, Conn.: Yale University Press, 1977.

Lewis, Marvin, ed. *The Mining Frontier: Contemporary Accounts from the American West in the 19th Century*. Norman: University of Oklahoma Press, 1967.

Lingenfelter, Richard E. *The Hardrock Miners: A History of the Mining Labor Movement in the American West, 1863-1893*. Berkeley: University of California Press, 1974.

Mann, Ralph. *After the Gold Rush: Society in Grass Valley and Nevada City, California, 1849-1870*. Stanford, Calif.: Stanford University Press, 1982.

Paul, Rodman. *California Gold: The Beginning of Mining in the Far West*. Reprint. Lincoln: University of Nebraska Press, 1965.

———. *Mining Frontiers of the Far West, 1848-1880*. New York: Holt, Rinehart & Winston, 1963.

Royce, Sarah. *Frontier Lady*. Edited by Ralph H. Gabriel. New Haven, Conn.: Yale University Press, 1932.

Shinn, Charles. *Mining Camps: A Study in American Frontier Government*. Reprint. New York: Harper & Row, 1965.

Spence, Clark C. *British Investments and the American Mining Frontier, 1860-1901*. Ithaca, N.Y.: Cornell University Press, 1958.

Wyman, Mark. *Hard Rock Epic: Western Miners and the Industrial Revolution, 1860-1910*. Berkeley: University of California Press, 1979.

8
Cattle and the Cult of Masculinity

Adams, Andy. *Log of a Cowboy*. Reprint. Lincoln: University of Nebraska Press, 1964.

Atherton, Lewis. *Cattle Kings*. Bloomington: Indiana University Press, 1961.

Dary, David. *Cowboy Culture: A Saga of Five Centuries*. New York: Knopf, 1981.

Dobie, J. Frank. *The Longhorns*. Boston: Little, Brown, 1955.

Durham, Philip, and Jones, Everett L. *The Negro Cowboys*. New York: Dodd, Mead, 1965.

Dykstra, Robert. *The Cattle Towns*. New York: Atheneum, 1979.

Frantz, Joe B., and Choate, Julian E., Jr. *The American Cowboy: The Myth and the Reality*. Norman: University of Oklahoma Press, 1955.

Gressley, Gene M. *Bankers and Cattlemen*. New York: Knopf, 1966.

Hagedorn, Hermann. *Roosevelt in the Bad Lands*. Boston: Houghton Mifflin, 1921.

Kupper, Winifred. *The Golden Hoof: The Story of the Sheep of the Southwest*. New York: Knopf, 1945.

Osgood, Ernest S. *The Day of the Cattleman*. Reprint. Chicago: University of Chicago Press, 1954.

Savage, William W., Jr., ed. *Cowboy Life*. Norman: University of Oklahoma Press, 1975.

Siringo, Charles A. *A Texas Cowboy*. Reprint. Lincoln: University of Nebraska Press, 1966.

Smith, Helena Huntington. *The War on Powder River*. New York: McGraw-Hill, 1966.

Walker, Don D. *Clio's Cowboys: Studies in the Historiography of the Cattle Trade*. Lincoln: University of Nebraska Press, 1981.

White, G. Edward. *The Eastern Establishment and the Western Experience*. New Haven, Conn.: Yale University Press, 1968.

9
The Power of the Road

Barth, Gunther. *Bitter Strength: A History of the Chinese in the United States, 1850–1870*. Cambridge, Mass.: Harvard University Press, 1964.

Conkling, Roscoe and Margaret. *Butterfield Overland Mail, 1857–1869*. 3 vols. Glendale, Calif.: A. H. Clark, 1947.

Dodge, Grenville M. *How We Built the Union Pacific Railway*. Reprint. Denver, Colo.: Sage Books, 1965.

Gregg, Josiah. *Commerce of the Prairies*. Edited by Max L. Moorhead. Norman: University of Oklahoma Press, 1954.

Jackson, W. Turrentine. *Wagon Roads West: A Study of Federal Surveys and Construction in the Trans-Mississippi West, 1846–1869*. Reprint. New Haven, Conn.: Yale University Press, 1965.

Lass, William E. *From the Missouri to the Great Salt Lake: An Account of Overland Freighting*. Lincoln: University of Nebraska Press, 1972.

Lavender, David. *The Great Persuader*. Garden City, N.Y.: Doubleday, 1970.

Lewis, Oscar. *Big Four: The Story of Huntington, Stanford, Hopkins, and Crocker, and the Building of the Central Pacific*. New York: Knopf, 1938.

Quiett, Glenn C. *They Built the West: An Epic of Rails and Cities*. New York: Appleton-Century-Crofts, 1934.

Riegel, Robert E. *Story of the Western Railroads*. New York: Macmillan, 1926.

Winther, Oscar O. *The Transportation Frontier: Trans-Mississippi West, 1865–1890*. New York: Holt, Rinehart & Winston, 1964.

10
Dugouts and Domesticity: Farming the Great Plains

Bogue, Allan. *From Prairie to Corn Belt: Farming on the Illinois and Iowa Prairies*. Chicago: University of Chicago Press, 1963.

Brown, Dee. *The Gentle Tamers: Women in the Old Wild West*. New York: Putnam, 1958.

Danker, Donald, ed. *Mollie: The Journal of Mollie Dorsey Sanford*. Lincoln: University of Nebraska Press, 1959.

Davis, James. *Frontier America*. Glendale, Calif.: A. H. Clark, 1977.

Degler, Carl. *At Odds: Women and Family in America from the Revolution to the Present*. New York: Oxford, 1980.

Dick, Everett. *The Sod-House Frontier*. Lincoln: University of Nebraska Press, 1954.

Faragher, John M. *Women and Men on the Overland Trail*. New Haven, Conn.: Yale University Press, 1979.

Fite, Gilbert, A. *The Farmer's Frontier, 1865–1900*. New York: Holt, Rinehart & Winston, 1966.

Garland, Hamlin. *A Daughter of the Middle Border*. Reprint. New York: Sagamore, 1957.

———. *Son of the Middle Border*. Reprint. Lincoln: University of Nebraska Press, 1979.

Gates, Paul W. *The Farmer's Age: Agriculture, 1815–1860*. New York: Holt, Rinehart & Winston, 1960.

———. *Fifty Million Acres: Conflicts over Kansas Land Policy, 1854–1890*. Ithaca: Cornell University Press, 1954.

Goodwyn, Lawrence. *The Populist Moment*. New York: Oxford, 1978.

Grimes, Alan P. *The Puritan Ethic and Woman Suffrage*. New York: Oxford, 1967.

Hayter, Earl W. *The Troubled Farmer, 1850–1900: Rural Adjustment to Industrialism*. De Kalb: Northern Illinois University Press, 1968.

Jeffrey, Julie Roy. *Frontier Women: The Trans-Mississippi West, 1840–1880*. New York: Hill & Wang, 1979.

Lamar, Howard. *Dakota Territory, 1861–1889: A Study of Frontier Politics*. New Haven, Conn.: Yale University Press, 1956.

Malin, James C. *The Grassland of North America*. Reprint. Gloucester, Mass.: P. Smith, 1967.

Marx, Leo. *The Machine in the Garden: Technology and the Pastoral Ideal in America*. New York: Oxford, 1964.

Myres, Sandra L. *Western Women and the Frontier Experience, 1800–1915*. Albuquerque: University of New Mexico Press, 1982.

Nordin, Dennis S. *Rich Harvest: A History of the Grange, 1867–1900*. Jackson: University Press of Mississippi, 1974.

Riley, Glenda. *Frontierswomen*. Ames: Iowa State University Press, 1981.

Sandoz, Mari. *Old Jules*. Lincoln: University of Nebraska Press, 1962.

Shannon, Fred A. *The Farmer's Last Frontier: Agriculture, 1860–1897*. New York: Farrar and Rinehart, 1945.

Stewart, Elinore Pruitt. *Letters of a Woman Homesteader*. Reprint. Lincoln: University of Nebraska Press, 1961.

Stratton, Joanna L. *Pioneer Women: Voices from the Kansas Frontier*. New York: Simon & Schuster, 1981.

Swierenga, Robert P. *Pioneers and Profits: Land Speculation on the Iowa Frontier*. Ames: Iowa State University Press, 1968.

Webb, Walter P. *The Great Plains*. Reprint. Lincoln: University of Nebraska Press, 1981.

Williams, William A. *The Roots of the Modern American Empire*. New York: Random House, 1969.

11
Plunder and Preservation

Bartlett, Richard A. *Great Surveys of the American West*. Norman: University of Oklahoma Press, 1962.

Dasmann, Raymond. *The Destruction of California*. New York: Macmillan, 1965.

Hays, Samuel P. *Conservation and the Gospel of Efficiency: The Progressive Conservation Movement, 1890–1920*. Cambridge, Mass.: Harvard University Press, 1959.

Hundley, Norris, Jr. *Water and the West: The Colorado River Compact and the Politics of Water in the American West*. Berkeley: University of California Press, 1975.

Marine, Gene. *America the Raped: The Engineering Mentality and the Devastation of a Continent*. New York: Simon & Schuster, 1969.

Muir, John. *Story of My Boyhood and Youth*. Reprint. Madison: University of Wisconsin Press, 1965.

———. *The Yosemite*. Reprint. Garden City, N.Y.: Doubleday, 1962.

Nash, Roderick. *Wilderness and the American Mind*. New Haven, Conn.: Yale University Press, 1967.

Petulla, Joseph M. *American Environmentalism*. College Station: Texas A & M University Press, 1980.

Sandoz, Mari. *The Buffalo Hunters: The Story of the Hide Men*. Reprint. Lincoln: University of Nebraska Press, 1978.

Stegner, Wallace. *Beyond the Hundredth Meridian*. Boston: Houghton Mifflin, 1954.

Tobey, Ronald. *Saving the Prairies*. Berkeley: University of California Press, 1981.

Wild, Peter. *Pioneer Conservationists of Western America*. Missoula, Mont.: Mountain, 1979.

Wolfe, Linnie. *Son of the Wilderness: A Life of John Muir*. Reprint. Madison: University of Wisconsin Press, 1978.

12
The Ethnic Frontier

Acuña, Rudolfo. *Occupied America: A History of Chicanos*. New York: Harper & Row, 1981.

Andrist, Ralph K. *The Long Death: The Last Days of the Plains Indians*. New York: Macmillan, 1964.

Athearn, Robert. *In Search of Canaan: Black Migration to Kansas, 1879-80*. Lawrence: Regents Press of Kansas, 1978.

Barth, Gunther. *Bitter Strength: A History of the Chinese in the United States, 1850-1870*. Cambridge, Mass.: Harvard University Press, 1964.

Bowden, Henry W. *American Indians and Christian Missions*. Chicago: University of Chicago Press, 1981.

Brown, Dee. *Bury My Heart at Wounded Knee: An Indian History of the American West*. New York: Holt, Rinehart & Winston, 1970.

Daniels, Roger. *The Politics of Prejudice: The Anti-Japanese Movement in California and the Struggle for Japanese Exclusion*. Berkeley: University of California Press, 1962.

Dinnerstein, Leonard, et al. *Natives and Strangers*. New York: Oxford, 1979.

Josephy, Alvin M., Jr. *The Patriot Chiefs: A Chronicle of American Indian Resistance*. New York: Viking, 1961.

Katz, William L. *The Black West*. Garden City, N.Y.: Doubleday, 1971.

Kitano, Harry H. L. *Japanese Americans: The Evolution of a Subculture*. Englewood Cliffs, N.J.: Prentice-Hall, 1969.

Lanternari, Vittorio. *Religions of the Oppressed*. New York: Knopf, 1963.

Leckie, William H. *The Buffalo Soldiers: A Narrative of the Negro Cavalry*. Norman: University of Oklahoma Press, 1967.

Luebke, Frederick. *Ethnicity on the Great Plains*. Lincoln: University of Nebraska Press, 1980.

McWilliams, Carey. *North from Mexico: The Spanish Speaking People of the United States*. New York: Greenwood, 1968.

———. *Prejudice: Japanese-Americans, Symbol of Racial Intolerance*. Hamden, Conn.: Anchor, 1971.

Meinig, Donald W. *The Southwest: Three Peoples in Geographical Change, 1600–1970.* New York: Oxford, 1971.

Miller, Stuart C. *The Unwelcome Immigrant: The American Image of the Chinese, 1785–1882.* Berkeley: University of California Press, 1969.

Nash, Gary, and Weiss, Richard, eds. *The Great Fear: Race in the Mind of America.* New York: Holt, Rinehart & Winston, 1970.

Painter, Nell. *Exodusters: Black Migration to Kansas After Reconstruction.* New York: Knopf, 1976.

Pitt, Leonard. *The Decline of the Californios.* Berkeley: University of California Press, 1960.

Porter, Kenneth W. *The Negro on the American Frontier.* New York: Arno, 1971.

Prucha, Francis P. *Broadax and Bayonet: The Role of the United States Army in the Development of the Northwest, 1815–1860.* Madison: State Historical Society of Wisconsin, 1953.

Sandoz, Mari. *Cheyenne Autumn.* New York: Hastings, 1953.

Utley, Robert M. *Frontiersmen in Blue: The United States Army and the Indian, 1848–1865.* New York: Macmillan, 1967.

————. *Frontier Regulars: The United States Army and the Indian, 1866–1891.* New York: Macmillan, 1974.

————. *The Last Days of the Sioux Nation.* New Haven, Conn.: Yale University Press, 1963.

Weber, David J. *Foreigners in their Native Land: Historical Roots of the Mexican Americans.* Albuquerque: University of New Mexico Press, 1973.

Yinger, John M. *A Minority Group in American Society.* New York: McGraw-Hill, 1965.

13
Preachers and Teachers

Anderson, Nels. *Desert Saints: The Mormon Frontier in Utah.* Chicago: University of Chicago Press, 1966.

Arrington, Leonard J., and Bitton, Davis. *The Mormon Experience.* New York: Knopf, 1979.

Berkhofer, Robert F., Jr. *Salvation and Savage: An Analysis of Protestant Missions and American Indian Response, 1787–1862.* Lexington: University of Kentucky Press, 1966.

Cremin, Lawrence A. *American Education, The National Experience, 1783–1876.* New York: Harper & Row, 1980.

Eggleston, Edward. *The Hoosier Schoolmaster.* Reprint. New York: Sagamore, 1957.

Ellis, John T. *American Catholicism.* Rev. ed. Chicago: University of Chicago Press, 1969.

Gaustad, Edwin S. *A Religious History of America.* New York: Harper & Row, 1966.

Glazer, Nathan. *American Judaism.* Chicago: University of Chicago Press, 1957.

Herberg, Will. *Protestant, Catholic, Jew.* Rev. ed. Garden City, N.Y.: Doubleday, 1960.

Johnson, Charles A. *The Frontier Camp Meeting: Religion's Harvest.* Dallas, Tex.: Southern Methodist University Press, 1955.

Miyakawa, T. Scott. *Protestants and Pioneers: Individualism and Conformity on the American Frontier.* Chicago: University of Chicago Press, 1964.

Mosier, Richard D. *Making the American Mind: Social and Moral Ideas in the McGuffey Readers.* New York: King's Crown, 1947.

Newcomer, Mabel. *A Century of Higher Education for American Women.* Reprint. Washington: Zenger, 1975.

Niebuhr, H. Richard. *The Kingdom of God in America.* New York: Harper & Row, 1959.

Perkinson, Henry J. *The Imperfect Panacea: American Faith in Education, 1865-1965.* New York: Random House, 1968.

Shannon, James P. *Catholic Colonization on the Western Frontier.* New Haven, Conn.: Yale University Press, 1957.

Sweet, William W. *Religion on the American Frontier.* 4 vols. Reprint. New York: Cooper Square, 1964.

Veysey, Laurence. *Emergence of the American University.* Chicago: University of Chicago Press, 1965.

Wright, Louis B. *Culture on the Moving Frontier.* Bloomington: Indiana University Press, 1955.

14
The Search for Community

Atherton, Lewis. *Main Street on the Middle Border.* Bloomington: Indiana University Press, 1954.

Barth, Gunther. *Instant Cities: Urbanization and the Rise of San Francisco and Denver.* New York: Oxford, 1975.

Bestor, Arthur. *Backwoods Utopia.* Philadelphia: University of Pennsylvania Press, 1970.

Bridenbaugh, Carl. *Cities in the Wilderness: The First Century of Urban Life in America.* Reprint. New York: Knopf, 1955.

Curti, Merle. *The Making of an American Community: A Case Study of Democracy in a Frontier County.* Stanford, Calif.: Stanford University Press, 1959.

Davis, Ronald L. *A History of Opera in the American West.* Englewood Cliffs, N.J.: Prentice-Hall, 1965.

Debo, Angie. *Prairie City: The Story of an American Community.* New York: Knopf, 1944.

Doyle, Don H. *The Social Order of a Frontier Community.* Urbana: University of Illinois Press, 1978.

Dykstra, Robert R. *The Cattle Towns.* New York: Knopf, 1968.

Hine, Robert V. *Community on the American Frontier: Separate But Not Alone.* Norman: University of Oklahoma Press, 1980.

Mellers, Wilfrid. *Music in a New Found Land: Theses and Developments in the History of American Music.* New York: Knopf, 1965.

Reps, John W. *Cities of the American West: A History of Frontier Urban Planning.* Princeton, N.J.: Princeton University Press, 1979.

Wade, Richard C. *The Urban Frontier: The Rise of the Western Cities, 1790-1830.* Cambridge, Mass.: Harvard University Press, 1959.

White, William. *Forty Years on Main Street.* Compiled by Russell H. Fitzgibbon. New York and Toronto: Farrar and Rinehart, 1937.

Wiebe, Robert H. *The Search for Order, 1877-1920.* New York: Hill & Wang, 1967.

15
The Western Hero

Billington, Ray A. *Land of Savagery, Land of Promise: The European Image of the American Frontier*. New York: Norton, 1981.

Botkin, B. A. *A Treasury of Western Folklore*. New York: Crown, 1951.

Cawelti, John G. *The Six-Gun Mystique*. Bowling Green, Ohio: Bowling Green University Popular Press, 1971.

Etulain, Richard, ed. *The American Literary West*. Manhattan, Kans.: Sunflower, 1980.

Fussell, Edwin. *Frontier: American Literature and the American West*. Princeton, N.J.: Princeton University Press, 1964.

Greenway, John. *Folklore of the Great West*. Palo Alto, Calif.: American West, 1969.

Johannsen, Albert. *The House of Beadle and Adams and Its Dime and Nickel Novels*. 2 vols. Norman: University of Oklahoma Press, 1950.

Kitses, Demetrius. *Horizons West: Anthony Mann, Bud Boetticher, Sam Peckinpah; Studies of Authorship Within the Western*. Bloomington: Indiana University Press, 1969.

Monaghan, Jay. *The Great Rascal: The Life and Adventures of Ned Buntline*. Boston: Little, Brown, 1951.

Rosa, Joseph G. *The Gunfighter: Man or Myth?* Norman: University of Oklahoma Press, 1969.

Savage, William W. *The Cowboy Hero: His Image in American History and Culture*. Norman: University of Oklahoma Press, 1979.

Shackford, James A. *David Crockett: The Man and the Legend*. Chapel Hill: University of North Carolina Press, 1956.

Smith, Henry N. *Virgin Land*. Cambridge, Mass.: Harvard University Press, 1950.

Steckmesser, Kent. *The Western Hero in History and Legend*. Norman: University of Oklahoma Press, 1965.

Wister, Owen. *The Virginian*. New York: Macmillan, 1902.

16
The Image of the West in Art

Bloch, E. Maurice. *George Caleb Bingham: The Evolution of an Artist*. Berkeley: University of California Press, 1967.

Catlin, George. *Letters and Notes on the Manners, Customs and Conditions of the North American Indian*. 2 vols. Minneapolis, Minn.: Ross & Haines, 1965.

Ewers, John. *Artists of the Old West*. Garden City, N.Y.: Doubleday, 1965.

Haberly, Loyd. *Pursuit of the Horizon: A Life of George Catlin, Painter and Recorder of the American Indians*. New York: Macmillan, 1948.

Harris, Neil. *The Artist in American Society: The Formative Years, 1790–1860*. New York: Braziller, 1966.

Hassrick, Peter, and Trenton, Patricia. *Rocky Mountains: A Vision for Artists in the Nineteenth Century*. Norman: University of Oklahoma Press, 1983.

Hine, Robert V. *Bartlett's West: Drawing the Mexican Boundary*. New Haven, Conn.: Yale University Press, 1968.

Kane, Paul. *Paul Kane's Frontier*. Edited by Russell Harper. Austin: University of Texas Press, 1971.

McCracken, Harold. *Frederic Remington: Artist of the Old West*. Philadelphia: Lippincott, 1947.

Peters, Harry T. *Currier and Ives: Printmakers to the American People.* Reprint. New York: Arno, 1976.

Shaw, Renata V., comp. *A Century of Photographs, 1846-1946.* Washington, D.C.: Library of Congress, 1980.

Taft, Robert. *Artists and Illustrators of the Old West, 1850-1900.* New York: Scribners, 1953.

Wilkins, Thurman. *Thomas Moran: Artist of the Mountains.* Norman: University of Oklahoma Press, 1966.

17
The Frontier Experience in Retrospect

Allen, Harry C. *Bush and Backwoods: A Comparison of the Frontier in Australia and the United States.* East Lansing: Michigan State University Press, 1959.

Bancroft, Hubert H. *Popular Tribunals.* 2 vols. San Francisco: The History Co., 1887.

Bienen, Henry. *Violence and Social Change.* Chicago: University of Chicago Press, 1968.

Billington, Ray A. *America's Frontier Heritage.* New York: Holt, Rinehart & Winston, 1967.

_____. *Frederick Jackson Turner.* New York: Oxford, 1973.

Brown, Richard M. *Strain of Violence: Historical Studies of American Violence and Vigilantism.* New York: Oxford, 1975.

Caughey, John W. *Their Majesties the Mob.* Chicago: University of Chicago Press, 1960.

Ekirch, Arthur A. *Man and Nature in America.* New York: Columbia University Press, 1963.

Gard, Wayne. *Frontier Justice.* Norman: University of Oklahoma Press, 1949.

Graham, Hugh D., and Gurr, Ted R., eds. *Violence in America: Historical and Comparative Perspectives. A Report Submitted to the National Commission on the Causes and Prevention of Violence.* New York: Bantam, 1969.

Hill, Douglas A. *The Opening of the Canadian West.* New York: John Day, 1967.

Hobsbawm, Eric. *Primitive Rebels.* Reprint. New York: Norton, 1965.

Hofstadter, Richard. *The Progressive Historians.* New York: Knopf, 1968.

Hollon, W. Eugene. *Frontier Violence: Another Look.* New York: Oxford, 1974.

Jordan, Philip D. *Frontier Law and Order.* Lincoln: University of Nebraska Press, 1970.

Lamar, Howard, and Thompson, Leonard, eds. *The Frontier in History: North America and Southern Africa Compared.* New Haven, Conn.: Yale University Press, 1981.

Lewis, R. W. B. *The American Adam: Innocence, Tragedy, and Tradition in the Nineteenth Century.* Chicago: University of Chicago Press, 1955.

McDermott, John F., ed. *Frontier Re-examined.* Urbana: University of Illinois Press, 1967.

Moore, Arthur K. *The Frontier Mind: A Cultural Analysis of the Kentucky Frontiersman.* Lexington: University of Kentucky Press, 1957.

Pomeroy, Earl. "The Changing West." In *The Reconstruction of American History,* edited by John Higham. New York: Harper & Row, 1962.

Potter, David M. *People of Plenty.* Chicago: University of Chicago Press, 1954.

Prassell, Frank R. *The Western Peace Officer.* Norman: University of Oklahoma Press, 1972.

Sloane, Irving J. *Our Violent Past: An American Chronicle.* New York: Random House, 1970.

Slotkin, Richard. *Regeneration Through Violence.* Middletown, Conn.: Wesleyan University Press, 1973.

Turner, Frederick J. *The Frontier in American History.* Reprint. New York: Holt, Rinehart & Winston, 1962.

Webb, Walter P. *The Great Frontier.* Austin: University of Texas Press, 1951.

Wyman, Walker, and Kroeber, Clifton. *The Frontier in Perspective.* Madison: University of Wisconsin Press, 1957.

18
The West in Our Time

Garnsey, Morris E. *America's New Frontier: The Mountain West.* New York: Knopf, 1950.

Haystead, Ladd. *If the Prospect Pleases: The West the Guidebooks Never Mention.* Norman: University of Oklahoma Press, 1946.

Lamar, Howard R. *The Far Southwest, 1846–1912.* New Haven, Conn.: Yale University Press, 1966.

McWilliams, Carey. *Factories in the Field.* Santa Barbara, Calif.: Peregrine, 1971.

———. *Ill Fares the Land.* Reprint. New York: Arno, 1976.

Morgan, Neil. *Westward Tilt: The American West Today.* New York: Random House, 1963.

Nash, Gerald D. *The American West in the Twentieth Century.* Reprint. Albuquerque: University of New Mexico, 1977.

Pomeroy, Earl S. *The Pacific Slope.* New York: Knopf, 1965.

Toole, K. Ross. *Twentieth-Century Montana.* Norman: University of Oklahoma Press, 1972.

Webb, Walter P. *Divided We Stand: The Crisis of a Frontierless Democracy.* Rev. ed. Austin, Tex.: Acorn, 1944.

Wiley, Peter, and Gottlieb, Robert. *Empires in the Sun: The Rise of the New American West.* New York: Putnam, 1982.

Library of Congress. 68 — The InterNorth Art Foundation, Joslyn Art Museum, Omaha, Nebraska. 71 — The InterNorth Art Foundation, Joslyn Art Museum, Omaha, Nebraska. 73 — Reproduced from the collections of the Library of Congress. 76 — The InterNorth Art Foundation, Joslyn Art Museum, Omaha, Nebraska. 78 — The InterNorth Art Foundation, Joslyn Art Museum, Omaha, Nebraska. 80 — California Museum of Photography, University of California, Riverside. 86 — Bill Malone, Austin, Texas. 88 — Reproduced from the collections of the Library of Congress. 92 — Barker Texas History Center, University of Texas at Austin. 95 — Reproduced from the collections of the Library of Congress. 99 — Reproduced from the collections of the Library of Congress. 100 — Historical Pictures Service, Chicago. 106 — The San Jacinto Museum of History Association, Houston, Texas. 107 — Reproduced from the collections of the Library of Congress. 108 — Historical Pictures Service, Chicago. 110 — Reproduced from the collections of the Library of Congress. 112 — Reproduced from the collections of the Library of Congress. 120 — The Bancroft Library, Berkeley, CA. 123 — San Diego Historical Society, Ticor Collection. 126 — The Denver Public Library, Western History Department. 128 — Courtesy of The New-York Historical Society. 129 — Reproduced from the collections of the Library of Congress. 132 — Nevada Historical Society. 134 — Reproduced from the collections of the Library of Congress. 136 — Montana Historical Society, Helena. 140 — California Museum of Photography, University of California, Riverside. 143 — Whitney Gallery of Western Art, Cody, Wyoming. 144 — Philadelphia Museum of Art. Given by Mrs. Thomas Eakins and Miss Mary A. Williams. 146 — Western History Collections, University of Oklahoma Library. 147 — Western History Collections, University of Oklahoma Library. 151 — Theodore Roosevelt Collection, Harvard College Library. 156 — Reproduced from the collections of the Library of Congress. 160 — California Museum of Photography, University of California, Riverside. 163 — Nebraska State Historical Society, Lincoln. 164 — Union Pacific Railroad Museum Collection. 165 — Reproduced from the collections of the Library of Congress. 166 — Reproduced from the collections of the Library of Congress. 174 — Sharlot Hall Historical Society. 180 — Historical Pictures Service, Chicago. 181 — Reproduced from the collections of the Library of Congress. 182 — Reproduced from the collections of the Library of Congress. 185 — Reproduced from the collections of the Library of Congress. 187 — Kansas State Historical Society, Topeka. 192 — Reproduced from the collections of the Library of Congress. 195 — Historical Pictures Service, Chicago. 197 — Montana Historical Society. 198 — Historical Pictures Service, Chicago. 199 — California State Library. 204 — California Museum of Photography, University of California, Riverside. 210 — Smithsonian Institution Photo No. 991-A. 211 — Smithsonian Institution Photo No. 3678. 214 — Reproduced from the collections of the Library of Congress. 216 — Reproduced from the collections of the Library of Congress. 217 — Historical Pictures Service, Chicago. 223 — Century Magazine XXXVII (April, 1889). 225 — Historical Pictures Service, Chicago. 226 — The Denver Public Library, Western History Department. 227 — The Denver Public Library, Western History Department. 229 — Thomas Gilcrease Institute of American History and Art, Tulsa, Oklahoma. 230 — Historical Pictures Service, Chicago. 233 — California State Library. 234 — Historical Pictures Service, Chicago. 236 — The Denver Public Library, Western History Department. 240 — Reproduced from the collections of the Library of Congress. 241 — Reproduced from the collections of the Library of Congress. 248 — Reproduced from the collections of the Library of Congress. 249 — From Samuel Bowles, *Our New West* (Hartford, Conn.: Hartford Publishing Co., 1869), p. 61. 251 — From *Wilderness Kingdom* by Nicolas Point, S.J. © 1967 by Loyola University Press, Chicago. Granted by permission of Holt, Rinehart and Winston. 252 — From *Wilderness Kingdom* by Nicolas Point, S.J. © 1967 by Loyola University Press, Chicago. Granted by permission of Holt, Rinehart and Winston. 255 — No. 48-RST-7B-13 in National Archives Building. 257 — Reproduced from the collections of the Library of

Congress. 258 — The Butler Institute of American Art. 260 — Courtesy of the Illinois State Historical Library. 262 — Michigan State University Archives and Historical Collections. 263 — The Bancroft Library, Berkeley, CA. 269 — Reproduced from the collections of the Library of Congress. 270 — From Édouard Laveleye, "Excursion aux Nouvelles Découvertes Minières du Colorado" *Le Tour du Monde*, 1881. Drawing by A. Sirouy, p. 429. 277 — The Denver Public Library, Western History Department. 278 — Reproduced from the collections of the Library of Congress. 279 — Washington State Historical Society, Tacoma. 281 — Reproduced from the collections of the Library of Congress. 289 — Historical Pictures Service, Chicago. 291 — Historical Pictures Service, Chicago. 292 — California Museum of Photography, University of California, Riverside. 293 — Historical Pictures Service, Chicago. 294 — Courtesy Amon Carter Museum, Fort Worth, Texas. 297 — Culver Pictures. 304 — Rare Books and Manuscripts Division. The New York Public Library. Astor, Lenox, and Tilden Foundations. 307 — Wadsworth Atheneum, Hartford. Bequest of Alfred Smith. 309 — Courtesy Amon Carter Museum, Fort Worth, Texas. 311 — Wadsworth Atheneum, Hartford. The Elizabeth Hart Jarvis Colt Collection. 313 — Reproduced from the collections of the Library of Congress. 314 — Courtesy Amon Carter Museum, Fort Worth, Texas. 318 — Reproduced from the collections of the Library of Congress. 319 — Mrs. Ruth Koerner Oliver. 325 — California Museum of Photography, University of California, Riverside. 328 — Photo courtesy Remington Art Museum, Ogdensburg, New York. 330 — The Taft Museum, Cincinnati, Ohio. 335 — Arizona Historical Society, Tucson. 337 — Historical Pictures Service, Chicago. 339 — Reproduced from the collections of the Library of Congress. 343 — Kaiser Steel Corporation, Fontana, California. 349 — Riverside Press-Enterprise, California. 352 — Courtesy The White House, Washington, D.C. Photo by Bill Fitz-patrick. 354 — Photo Houston Chronicle. 359 — Department of Special Collections, University Research Library, UCLA. 360 — California Museum of Photography, University of California, Riverside. 363 — Courtesy Amon Carter Museum, Fort Worth, Texas.

Index